THE POETICAL WORKS

OF

ROBERT BROWNING

General Editor: MICHAEL MEREDITH

THE OXFORD ENGLISH TEXTS
EDITION OF THE POETICAL WORKS
OF ROBERT BROWNING

THE POETICAL WORKS
OF
ROBERT BROWNING

Volume VII

THE RING AND THE BOOK
Books I–IV

EDITED BY

STEFAN HAWLIN

AND

T. A. J. BURNETT

CLARENDON PRESS · OXFORD

1998

Oxford University Press, Great Clarendon Street, Oxford OX2 6DP
Oxford New York
Athens Auckland Bangkok Bogota Bombay
Buenos Aires Calcutta Cape Town Dar es Salaam
Delhi Florence Hong Kong Istanbul Karachi
Kuala Lumpur Madras Madrid Melbourne
Mexico City Nairobi Paris Singapore
Taipei Tokyo Toronto Warsaw
and associated companies in
Berlin Ibadan

Oxford is a registered trade mark of Oxford University Press

Published in the United States by
Oxford University Press Inc., New York

British Library Cataloguing in Publication Data
Data available

Library of Congress Cataloging in Publication Data
Data available

ISBN 0-19-812356-6

1 3 5 7 9 10 8 6 4 2

Typeset by Pure Tech India Ltd, Pondicherry
Printed in Great Britain
on acid-free paper by
Biddles Ltd,
Guildford and King's Lynn

PREFACE AND
ACKNOWLEDGEMENTS

In this volume Tim Burnett has been responsible for the preparation of the text and the textual part of the General Introduction, Stefan Hawlin for the literary part of the Introduction, the introductions to the individual Books, and the commentary.

Our work is founded on the assistance given by three people in particular. Ian Jack, the retiring General Editor, asked us to edit *The Ring and the Book*, and gave us sound advice at starting. We have learnt a great deal from the example of his scholarship in the earlier volumes of the edition, and he has also commented in detail on early drafts. Philip Kelley, the greatest authority on the Brownings' lives and letters, has been thanked in most scholarly works on the Brownings over the past decade, and this volume is no exception. We thank him for the time he has given us, his generosity in sharing his knowledge, and for the lines of inquiry he has suggested. Michael Meredith, the new General Editor, has supervised closely the completion of our work, and made many improvements. Browning scholarship is for ever in his debt for being the first to disentangle the almost comically disaster-prone publishing history of *The Ring and the Book*.

We thank the staff at the libraries where we have done most of our research, the British Library, the Bodleian Library, and the English Faculty Library, Oxford. At other libraries, individuals who have particularly helped us are Dr Penelope Bulloch and Alan Tadiello of Balliol College Library; Robert E. Parks, Curator of Autograph Manuscripts, the Pierpont Morgan Library; Vanessa Hayward, Reference Team Librarian, Brighton Public Library; Rita S. Humphrey, Curator of Manuscripts at the Armstrong Browning Library; and Dr Mark N. Brown, Curator of Manuscripts at the John Hay Library, Brown University. We are indebted to other libraries with holdings of Browning material either for their kindness during our research visits, or for sending

us copies of documents in their care. We would like to thank the staff at the following institutions: the Beinecke Rare Book and Manuscript Library, Yale University; the Library of the Fitzwilliam Museum, Cambridge; the Northamptonshire Records Office, Northampton.

Many friends and colleagues have contributed to our work in extensive ways, and we would like to thank them all. Particular mention should be made of Dr Marcella McCarthy for substantial help with the annotation; Dr Judy Rudoe, Geoffrey C. Munn, and Dr Mairi Calcraft-Rennie for help with 'the Ring'; Emma Payne for help with the early drafts of the annotation; Massimiliano Demata for help with Italian; and Scott Lewis, co-editor of *The Brownings' Correspondence*, for help with the letters.

The literary editor wishes to thank his own institution, the University of Buckingham, for its generous support, particularly for a grant towards research expenses, and the funding of additional research leave, during which this volume was completed.

Finally, we should like to thank Dr Leofranc Holford-Strevens, our editor at the Press, whose scrupulous scholarship has added many improvements to our text.

S. H., T. A. J. B.

2 October 1996

CONTENTS

INTRODUCTION

GENERAL

1. *The Old Yellow Book*

In Book I of *The Ring and the Book* Browning twice refers to the day of the poem's inception as 'that memorable day' (i. 91, 459). He was in the flea market of the Piazza San Lorenzo in Florence on a glaring June day in 1860—the Piazza was 'crammed with booths, / Buzzing and blaze' (i. 43–44)—when, from a stall selling picture-frames, chalk drawings, clay busts, tapestries, and etchings, he picked out an old book, attracted by the spine: 'Romana Homicid. an Maritus possit occidere Vxorem Adulteram' ('A Roman case of Homicides about whether a Husband may kill an Adulterous Wife'). He bought it for a small sum, and opening it, discovered its fuller title, in Italian: 'An exposition of the whole criminal case against Guido Franceschini, nobleman of Arezzo, and his hired assassins, who were executed in Rome 22 February 1698, the first by beheading, the other four by hanging'; then in Latin: 'A Roman case of homicides: it is disputed if and when a husband may kill an adulterous wife without incurring the regular death penalty.' The book consisted of a unique set of seventeenth-century legal pamphlets, mainly the pleas of the defence and prosecution law-yers, printed in Latin with some Italian intermixed. The grotesque-ness of the murder it revealed was so suited to his imagination that Browning affirmed that the guiding divine Hand had 'pushed' him in the direction of the stall (i. 40). He calls the volume 'the old yellow Book' in the poem, the name used for it ever since.[1] After

---

[1] Appendix A is a full bibliographical description of the Old Yellow Book, hereafter OYB. We infer the year of purchase as 1860 from two pieces of evidence, discussed later: (1) W. C. Cartwright's statement that Browning told him about OYB in the winter of 1860–1, and (2) Browning's letter to Julia Wedgwood of 21 Jan. 1869 which implies that it was bought during EBB's lifetime, though not in June 1861, the month of her death. Cartwright knew Browning well, and his testimony is likely to be trustworthy.

his purchase, he tells us that he walked back across the city, reading the book as he went, treading carefully round the straw and iron-work laid out for sale on the pavements. When he reached Casa Guidi, his absorption continued. Finally, he placed the book on the agate mantelpiece in the drawing-room, under the baroque mirror, and stepped out onto the terrace. Now that the heat of day had passed, the tiles had been sprinkled with water and the window shutters opened. Here, pacing up and down, watching a firefly among the lily-like flowers of the datura, he fused his 'live soul' and the 'inert stuff' of the Old Yellow Book, and daydreamed the murder in a reverie that lasted till long after dark (1. 469–526).

Book I enacts for the reader the workings of Browning's imag-ination on his historical sources. Pen Browning, the poet's son, believed that the account was 'without doubt true in every detail',[1] but he is not always a reliable authority, and there is now no way of recovering how much of it is literally accurate and how much elaboration. It implies that Browning's conception of the story was established straight away. Whether or not this is true, there is no evidence to suggest that he was immediately concerned to develop it into a poem. In the period 1860–1 neither Browning's letters nor those of EBB mention either the Old Yellow Book or any plans for writing derived from it, and EBB seems to have been uninterested in the murder-case. Later, in 1869, when Julia Wedgwood com-plained about the grotesque evil in the story, Browning was reminded of this: 'my wife would have subscribed to every one of your bad opinions of the book; she never took the least interest in the story, so much as to wish to inspect the papers.'[2] His circle, however, knew of his own interest both in his last year in Italy and in the early years of his widowerhood in London. Serious work on the poem was four years in the future, and meanwhile his sense of its narrative was developed and refined by recounting the murder-case to friends.

In the two years following his purchase of the Old Yellow Book Browning offered it to four different people for their own use (there may have been others of whom we are unaware). In July

[1] Pen Browning to Charles W. Hodell, 6 Jan. 1904: Hodell, 337.
[2] To Julia Wedgwood, 21 Jan. 1869: *Wedgwood*, 168.

1860, as in the previous year, the Brownings travelled to Siena to stay at the Villa Alberti, two miles outside the town, where they enjoyed the landscape and the quiet, but where EBB's life was overshadowed by the illness of her sister Henrietta and her own failing health. They returned to Florence on 11 October, and towards the end of the month Anthony Trollope came to see them twice at Casa Guidi. It is likely it was on one of these occasions that Browning discussed the Old Yellow Book with Trollope and offered it to him as material for a novel. About 19 November the Brownings travelled to Rome, staying six months until the end of May 1861. Browning wrote nothing this winter, instead spending between two and six hours a day learning clay modelling at the studio of his friend, the American sculptor William Wetmore Story. EBB's letters report his literary inactivity. She wrote to Isa Blagden: 'Since taking to clay, he has quite forgotten how to read—To my knowledge he has read one book this winter [probably Trollope's *Framley Parsonage*], and had to be jogged at the elbow to get done with it.'[1] To Sarianna Browning, on 11 May, she quotes his conversation: 'He says "all his happiness lies in clay now" . . . It's the mixture of physical and intellectual effort which makes the attraction.'[2] It may be that this work was a distraction from EBB's weakening health. Browning did, however, discuss the Old Yellow Book with his good friend William Cornwallis Cartwright, of Aynho, Northamptonshire, in Rome at this time living with his family. Cartwright was interested in contemporary Italian politics and also in Italian church history. Over thirty years later he could still remember the poet's 'very distinct suggestion': 'Browning at *that time* had so little in his mind writing his poem that he actually suggested to me to write an account of this curious story. He did this seriously & went so far as to say he would give me the Book'.[3]

[1] [May 1861]: Fitzwilliam Museum, Cambridge.
[2] *Letters of EBB*, ii. 443.
[3] W. C. Cartwright to W. Hall Griffin, 20 May [1900]: Griffin Collections, vii. 280–3. See also Griffin and Minchin, 234, 236 n. 1. Cartwright's interest in ecclesiastical history led to his book *On the Constitution of Papal Conclaves* (1868).

In early June 1861 the Brownings journeyed back from Rome to Florence, where, on 29 June, after a relatively brief final illness, EBB died. The period of grief and upheaval that followed was not a time when Browning thought much about his own poetry. In August and September he went on holiday with Pen, his father, and his sister to Saint-Énogat, near Dinard, on the Brittany coast, and in early October he settled in London. He saw few friends at this time. An exceptional visit was to Tennyson on 20 November at the Temple,[1] and this is the most likely occasion for the offer of the Old Yellow Book which Browning made to the Laureate to see what he might make of it, and which Tennyson recalled much later to Allingham.[2] He also lent it to Charlotte Ogle, author of *A Lost Love* (1855), a minor novelist whom he and Elizabeth had met in Italy, seemingly with the idea that she might use it for a novel. Miss Ogle recalled: 'I had the book for two years, but it was all in Latin & I could make nothing of it.'[3] We know neither the beginning nor the end of this period of loan, though the chronology of events suggests that two years is an exaggeration. The impression is that Browning's concentration was elsewhere. As he settled himself and Pen back in London, he was preparing EBB's *Last Poems* for the press, and gradually steeling himself to re-enter London society. In May 1862, he organized his move to what would become his long-term London address, 19 Warwick Crescent, Upper Westbourne Terrace.

2. *Plans for Writing, 1862–4*

Some time in 1862 Mrs Eric Baker (née Crossman), someone who had been in the Brownings' circle in Florence, told Browning that she possessed another account of the Franceschini murder in the form of an Italian manuscript tract, and this information seems to have acted as a stimulus to him to confirm more definite plans for the Old Yellow Book. After separation from her husband, Mrs

---

[1] *The Letters of Alfred Lord Tennyson*, ed. Cecil Y. Lang and Edgar F. Shannon, Jr. (3 vols., Oxford, 1982–90), ii (1987), 286.
[2] Allingham, 326.
[3] Recorded in Owen Seaman to W. Hall Griffin, 6 July 1898: Griffin Collections, vi. 88^r.

Baker had lived with her sister and mother in the Villa Colombaia at Bellosguardo. In 1855, when Daniel Dunglas Home, the famous medium, came into the anglophone circles in Florence, she became a devotee of spiritualism, which suggests that Browning, with his antipathy for this fashion, would not greatly have admired her. When exactly she acquired this account of the Franceschini murder is unknown, but she informed Browning of it either because she knew directly of his interest, or because she had been told of it by friends. She seems first to have shown it to Anthony Trollope's brother Thomas Adolphus, the historian, novelist, and long-time resident in Florence, supposing it might be useful for his historical research. It may have been Trollope who told her of the poet's interest.

The manuscript 'Morte dell'Uxoricida Guido Franceschini Decapitato' ('The Execution by Beheading of the Wife-Killer Guido Franceschini'), since known as the Secondary Source,[1] was of a type popular in the seventeenth and eighteenth centuries, with a resumé of the circumstances of the murder in restrained but explicit detail, and an account of how the criminal was brought to trial and executed. The Franceschini case attracted this kind of popular treatment because of its sensational nature. In the summer of 1862 Mrs Baker stayed for a few days in Bayswater, London, probably concerned with the publication of her pamphlet *Fraud, Fancy, Fact: Which Is It? An Enquiry into the Mystery of Spiritualism* (1862), a defence of Daniel Home. Browning was unable to call on her. Subsequently on holiday in Pornic, on the French Atlantic

---

[1] The Secondary Source is given in full, with translation, in Appendix B. Another fuller, though similar, manuscript account of the murder and trial was discovered in the Biblioteca Casanatense in Rome in 1900, MS 2037, fos. 179^r–201^r. A few critics have conjectured that Browning might have known it, notably Thurman Hood in *Letters*, 351, and Kay Austen: 'The Royal Casanatense Document: A Third Source for Browning's *The Ring and the Book*', SBC 4:2 (1976), 26–44. There is, however, no really convincing evidence. Browning did not tell John Simeon, Mrs Orr, or anyone else about a 'third source', though he alerted them to the Secondary Source. There is no material in the poem that can be shown only to derive from it, and there are vivid details which, had Browning known them, he would probably have used: Guido, for example, on his way to execution, praying the *Miserere* before the church of Agonizzanti, and, on the scaffold, clutching a crucifix to his chest at the moment his head was struck off. A translation of the Casanatense document is given in Griffin and Minchin, Hodell, and Everyman.

coast, he wrote to Isa Blagden in Florence on 19 September regretting this, and asking Isa to check with Thomas Trollope the nature of the manuscript: 'Can you ask him if there was no mistake in her [Mrs Baker's] statement, if the account really related to *my* Count Francesco Guidi of Arezzo? Because, in that case, with her leave (which I shall beg your kindness to ask) I should greatly like to see it.'[1] There is a hint of the proprietary here, and also an interesting mistake about the name: 'Count Francesco Guidi' for Count Guido Franceschini. In part, this may simply indicate that Browning was writing from memory, not having the Old Yellow Book with him; probably it was still in the possession of Charlotte Ogle. It may also, however, be an unconscious slip pointing towards one of his imaginative sources. A number of critics have noted similarities between Shelley's play *The Cenci* and *The Ring and the Book*: both are based on original historical records fortuitously discovered, both deal with a wicked Italian aristocrat whose victim is an innocent and beautiful girl.[2] In these circumstances 'Count Francesco Guidi' may be a reminiscence of Count Francesco Cenci, one which suggests that Browning's conception of Guido as a monster of evil was already established.

When the Italian manuscript was sent to him, Browning discovered a number of facts not available in the Old Yellow Book, confirming what he knew about the murder-case but also giving him a different perspective, particularly furnishing details about the executions. On 18 October 1862, shortly after returning from holiday, he wrote to Isa Blagden:

Thank you most truly for attending to my request so promptly, in the matter of the Account of the Murder &c which I found on my return— pray thank Mrs Baker for her kindness, & say it will be particularly useful to me: it would be of little use to anybody without my documents, nor is it correct in several respects, but it contains a few notices of the execution &c. subsequent to my account that I can turn to good: I am going to make a regular poem of it. I hope to print a new book of "Men & Women" (or under some such name) in April or May—& next year, *this* which shall be a strong thing, if I can manage it.[3]

---

[1] *Dearest Isa*, 124.
[2] e.g. Miller, 231–3; Jack, 275–6.   [3] *Dearest Isa*, 128.

This letter is concerned to establish the story as his property. On 19 November 1862 he confirmed his plans: 'Early in Spring, I print new poems, a number: then, a new edition of all my old things, corrected: then begin on my murder-case.'[1] Some time now he wrote to Charlotte Ogle for the return of the Old Yellow Book: 'Mr Browning sent for it saying that if no one would write the tale he must.'[2] These words are echoed in William Allingham's record of a later conversation: 'He has told the story over and over again to various friends; offered it to A. Trollope to turn into a novel, but T. couldn't manage it; then R.B. thought, "why not take it myself?"'[3]

Browning's intention was to publish *Dramatis Personæ* in the spring of 1863, then a collected *Poetical Works*, and then to set to work on his new poem. In fact, this plan was thwarted by his publisher. Chapman postponed publication of *Dramatis Personæ* so as not to impede the sales of the 1863 *Poetical Works*; it was not published until May 1864, and only at this time do the extant letters comment further on the murder-case. On 11 March 1864 Browning wrote to James Fields, his American publisher, telling him that he hoped to publish again 'soon' after *Dramatis Personæ*, 'for I am inclined to work, and have done somewhat. . . . the next poem will be a long affair—the choice thing, perhaps.'[4] Still prior to publication, on 11 May, he described the poems of *Dramatis Personæ* as 'the last things of the sort I shall do, for some time at least—my next venture being in another direction.'[5] By his own recollection he began serious work on *The Ring and the Book* six months later, so these allusions are probably not indications of very substantial writing. There had indeed been a false start at some stage: later Browning told Allingham, 'I began it in rhymed couplets, like *Laurence Bloomfield*, but thought by and by I might as well have my fling, and so turned to blank verse.'[6] The idea of rhymed couplets

---

[1] Ibid. 134.

[2] Recorded in Owen Seaman to W. H. Griffin, 6 July 1898: Griffin Collections, vi. 88[v].

[3] Allingham, 180.

[4] RB to J. T. Fields: Huntington Library, San Marino, Calif.

[5] RB to George Venables: National Library of Wales, Aberystwyth.

[6] Allingham, 181. *Laurence Bloomfield* (1864) was a successful poem by Allingham in rhymed couplets.

had been abandoned by 7 July, when Allingham, having lunch with the poet, records conversation about his 'new poem in blank verse'.[1]

In 1864 Browning's summer holiday was more adventurous than those of the previous two years in Pornic. With his father, his sister, and Pen, he travelled to the warmer, south-west corner of France, and about 13 August settled for a month at the village spa of Cambo-les-Bains, 15 miles south of Biarritz, on the edge of the Pyrenees. On at least two occasions he walked up from Cambo-les-Bains to the Pas de Roland, a mountain pass supposedly cut in the rock by Roland's sword, and on one of these, in this impressive setting, a defining moment in the conception of the poem took place. Four years later William Rossetti records his description: 'Was staying at Bayonne, and walked out to a mountain-gorge traditionally said to have been cut or kicked out by Roland, and there laid out the full plan of his twelve cantos, accurately carried out in the execution.'[2] The references in the letters point eagerly to future work. On 19 September 1864, at Biarritz, he wrote to Isa Blagden that his Roman murder-story, 'my new poem that is about to be . . . is pretty well in my head'.[3] On 3 October, near the end of his holiday, he told Julia Wedgwood: 'I have got the whole of that poem, you enquire about, well in my head, shall write the Twelve books of it in six months, and then take breath again.'[4] On 11 October he returned to Warwick Crescent and set to work.

3. *Browning's Research*

The plan that the poem would be completed in six months is a testament to Browning's energy at this point, and evidence that—though he had conceived it ambitiously in twelve books—he had only a limited sense of its scale, and was unaware how long it would eventually turn out to be. On 19 October he wrote to Isa Blagden repeating his intention: 'I hope to have a long poem ready by the summer, my Italian murder thing.'[5] He had a clear idea of the

[1] Allingham, 104.   [2] *Rossetti Papers*, 302.   [3] *Dearest Isa*, 193.
[4] *Wedgwood*, 95.   [5] *Dearest Isa*, 196.

narrative, and of the form, the different monologues, but as he approached the writing he discovered that he wanted more information about the 1690s and the background to his sources. Before beginning work he had read the Old Yellow Book 'fully eight times over'.[1] Now, however, he began a series of detailed inquiries.

Much later, during the poem's publication, he said to Allingham: 'a builder will tell you sometimes of a house, "there's twice as much work underground as above," and so it is with my poem'.[2] Over twenty years later, when F. J. Furnivall was asking for permission to publish the Old Yellow Book, he was wary at first, and then made a detailed statement:

Before setting to work on the Poem, I examined the "Book" thoroughly; and the result [i.e. the poem] is all that I wish my readers to be acquainted with: it is simply impossible that anybody else—for many a year to come, at least—will devote himself to such a business as a complete study of all the crabbed latin documents which themselves demand a previous series of studies: it would simply prove to be what I say—an useless uprooting of my tree—to the ruin of its branch as well as root.[3]

As he began work he was considering the possibilities of the scene where the Comparini's bodies are laid out in the Church of San Lorenzo in Lucina; the crowd is shocked to see the mutilated corpses of two septuagenarians. On 17 October he wrote to Frederic Leighton in Rome, asking him to visit the church and 'look attentively at it—so as to describe it to me on your return. . . . It will be of great use to me. I don't care about the *outside*.'[4] The details Leighton supplied him with are those now found at the beginning of Book II and elsewhere.

At some time now, or perhaps earlier, he drew up two chronologies of the story, beginning with the births of Innocent XII, Pietro, Violante, and Pompilia, continuing with dates in the 1690s—the marriage, the legal affidavits, the flight, the murder, the trial—and ending with the dates of the executions, and the death of Innocent XII.[5] The second of these chronologies is an amended version of the first. In making them he sought out

---

[1] *Life*, 270.   [2] Allingham, 195.   [3] 29 Jan. 1884: *Trumpeter*, 90–1.
[4] *Life*, 273.   [5] See Appendix C for all details here.

Augustus De Morgan's *Book of Almanacs* (1851), the best contemporary almanac, in order to calculate specific days and a lunar phase.[1] He wrote out a calendar for January and February 1698, and used the *Almanacs* to establish or confirm the days of the week for significant events: that 2 January, the day of the murders, was a Thursday; that 6 January, the day of Pompilia's death, was Epiphany and a Monday; that 18 February, the day of Guido's sentence, was a Tuesday; and that 22 February, the day of the executions, was a Saturday. He also established the date of Ash Wednesday as 12 February, so as to know that the executions took place well after the end of Carnival. Just below this he used the *Almanacs* again to determine the moon's phase on the night which he believed was that of Caponsacchi and Pompilia's flight: he wanted to know exactly how to imagine the lighting of the scene.[2]

He also made investigations into the operation of the seventeenth-century Roman courts, the law underlying the murder-case, and the use of torture in the legal system. These may not have been particularly deep, since one later authority complains of his lack of understanding of the work done by the defence and prosecution lawyers.[3] In December 1864, through Matthew Arnold,[4] he arranged an introduction for himself to Sir George Bowyer, a prominent Catholic lawyer, the author of works on general jurisprudence, on the laws of the Italian cities, and, in particular, 'On the Uses of the Roman Law and its Relation to the Common Law'.

Browning's meeting with Bowyer at his chambers in the Middle Temple was a failure from the poet's point of view. Allingham later records a conversation in which Browning described Shelley as 'not in his right senses—in the moon', and went on to remark:

Another man who lives in the moon is Sir George Bowyer. I called on him to ask some questions about *Romana Homicidiorum Lex* for my book,

[1] RB to [Augustus De Morgan], 26 Mar. 1866: Johns Hopkins University, Baltimore, Md.

[2] See RB to Leonard Henry Courtney, 14 May 1881: TLS, 25 Feb. 1909, 72.

[3] Gest, 44–50.

[4] Matthew Arnold to RB, 19 Dec. 1864: 'Some Letters from Matthew Arnold to Robert Browning', ed. John Drinkwater, *Cornhill Magazine*, NS 55 (Dec. 1923), 657–8.

but as to intelligible answers—you might as well ask a butterfly to fly straight across this room! He referred me to an Italian friend of his, who was ten times worse than himself.[1]

However, Browning read Bowyer's *A Dissertation on the Statutes of the Cities of Italy, and a Translation of the Pleading of Prospero Farinacio in Defence of Beatrice Cenci* (1838),[2] and it would seem likely that Prospero Farinacio or Farinacci (1544–1616), the leading lawyer of his day—whose works are cited over a hundred times in the Old Yellow Book—would have been part of the unsatisfactory discussion. Farinacci covered the entire field of the law, including the jurisprudence of torture. Later, perhaps at Bowyer's suggestion, Browning did more research in the British Museum,[3] in particular reading in Farinacci's *Variæ Quæstiones*, where he found details about the torture of the Cord which he used directly in the poem. In a letter of 1867 he writes: 'Farinacci in the aforesaid *Quæstiones*, when on the subject of Tortures, declares the *Tormentum Vigiliarum* (or *Corda*) to have been the severest of all—lasting from 7 to 10 hours—so that out of 100 cases he had never known more than 4 "martyrs", nor less than 96 "confessors." '[4]

Browning also discussed his work with W. C. Cartwright, the friend whom he had told about the Old Yellow Book in the winter of 1860–1. In these years Cartwright divided his time between England and Italy. In October 1864, quite by chance, he came across another narrative of the murder-case in the library of the Hon. Keppel Craven in Naples, and duly made a note of it to tell Browning. The event is recorded in his journal:

Oct 27th [1864] This is my last day at Naples. I breakfasted with [Augustus] Craven who afterwards ransacked his father's books & library. There are many valuable things amongst them. [He lists the papers of Sir William Gell, some manuscripts of Frederick the Great's sister, and some letters of Queen Caroline; he goes on:] Then there is a volume of

---

[1] Allingham, 194–5.
[2] RB to John Simeon, 23 Apr. 1867: ABL; RB to H. Buxton Forman, 25 Oct. 1876: *Letters*, 177.
[3] *Letters*, 177.
[4] RB to John Simeon, 23 Apr. 1867: ABL. This information appears in the poem at VIII. 327–44.

highly curious M.S.S. tracts of great scandals & trials & executions which happened at various times in Rome amongst which I found a narrative of the murder of his wife by Count Franchescini some M.S.S. tracts in reference to which were found by Browning who is engaged on a poem on the subject. N.B. to communicate this to him.[1]

The following May Cartwright travelled back from Rome to London, arriving on the evening of the 17th. He either wrote to Browning shortly before his arrival, or perhaps saw or wrote to him immediately, and Browning responded with a letter on 18 May asking him to check with Augustus Craven if the 'M.S. notice' was not simply another copy of Mrs Baker's pamphlet.[2] Whatever the nature of the document, it was probably never sent: a letter two years later to Cartwright indicates that Browning had still not received it,[3] and subsequently there is no word about it.[4]

Probably shortly after this, Browning sent a fuller letter of inquiry to Cartwright, his longest known letter of investigation, and one which suggests the particular trust of their friendship. The opening paragraph indicates that its occasion was another discussion of the work in progress: 'Dear Cartwright—this is the *memorandum* you so kindly choose to trouble yourself with: I have great guesses about most of the matters therein, but want their corroboration: of course, you will take care that nobody begins to book-make or article-make about this till I have done with it. RB.' There follows a historical outline of the murder and the main protagonists, the names of the advocates for the prosecution and defence, and then a wide-ranging series of questions:

I should be glad of any scrap of information respecting the principals above mentioned—with whom may be classed the Abate Paolo Franceschini, younger brother of Guido, and for many years resident in Rome: also,—respecting the Court of the *Gubernator in Criminalibus*—

---

[1] The journal of W. C. Cartwright, Aug. 1864–Aug. 1865, Cartwright (Aynho) Papers, Box 6: Northamptonshire Record Office, Northampton.

[2] RB to W. C. Cartwright, 18 May 1865: *Letters*, 85.

[3] See below: RB to W. C. Cartwright, 17 May 1867.

[4] The conjecture that this narrative was the Casanatense document, and therefore a 'third' source for the poem, was made before the discovery of Cartwright's journal which places the document in Craven's library: see our earlier note on the Secondary Source.

of how many Judges it was composed—what were the forms of a trial before it—how the examinations were taken—if the pleadings were oral—if the defendant could speak *in propriâ personâ*—if witnesses were examined by the Court, or privately by deposition: and if there were in all cases a final appeal from the judgment of this Court to the Pope, or only, as in this Case, when the privilege of a clerical person was infringed on— Guido having taken the minor orders, or declared so. (qy: how many could he have taken without preventing himself from marriage? How much of a priest must an Abate be? Could he marry a couple?)

Any particulars of the private life and character of Innocent XII: and of the Jubilee he instituted in 1694.

Any particulars of whatever incident, public or private, may have happened in Rome in 1697-8,—before and just after the murder; any stranger of distinction there, crime committed, accident &c.

The execution of Guido and his four associates took place in the Piazza del Popolo: he was beheaded, the others hanged—*con una manaja e due gran forche:*—any details of the usual procedure.

The *contemporary* plans of the *Città di Roma,—e dei Contorni, per le Ville,*—of Arezzo,—*con i suoi Contorni,*—a post-map of the route from Arezzo to Rome by Chiusi and Castel Vecchio—(with any particulars of this last place otherwise called simply *l'Osteria*, which used to be *one post from Roma*)—and an almanack or calendar of the Saints' Days and festivals at Rome for 1697: all or any of these would be most valuable—

It may be useful to mention while making enquiry, that the action of the Church in the whole matter was wholly laudable, and that it opposed the prejudices and passions of the time, for once, with success.[1]

The last paragraph of the letter is closely echoed in the poem at I. 433-8, which suggests that Browning's report there of his enquiries in Rome is likely to be substantively true, and that, as a Protestant and supporter of Italian nationalism, he had met with some suspicion in the winter of 1860-1 in asking about such a long-forgotten

[1] RB to W. C. Cartwright, [n.d.]: Berg Collection of English and American Literature, The New York Public Library, Astor, Lenox and Tilden Foundations. We date this letter as *c.* June 1865 based on: (1) its watermark of 1864; (2) the early stage of investigation it implies; (3) its possible relation to RB to W. C. Cartwright, 18 May 1865: *Letters,* 85; and (4) Cartwright's movements as given in his journal (see p. xx, n. 1). Cartwright arrived in London from Rome on 17 May 1865. We conjecture that Browning wrote the letter some time before Cartwright's return to Rome on 26 July. We are grateful to the Berg Collection of the New York Public Library for the use of this material.

legal case. The Romans he consulted had assumed he was digging around for some anti-Catholic or anti-Papal propaganda.[1]

4. *Major Phase of Writing, 1864–6*

The greater part of *The Ring and the Book* was written between October 1864 and May 1866. Later Browning described his working methods to William Rossetti, saying that he wrote not by 'the inspiring impulse', but by application and to 'a regular systematic plan', consciously sitting down to a work period of three hours each day.[2] He told his friend Thomas Woolner, the sculptor, that he wrote 'straight down [the page]', without looking back.[3] Under these conditions the poem grew in ways he had not expected, and his reports to friends of the number of books and lines he had written suggest that by May 1866 he was at least drafting Book X. If, as seems likely, he took a break from writing in the summer months, progress was at the rate of about 900 lines a month. Sometimes he sounds elated, at other times depressed. 'I throw down my pen after hours and hours of writing, sick of the sight of paper and ink', he tells Cartwright in February 1865.[4] To Julia Wedgwood, in March, he says he is working 'unintermittingly';[5] and on 18 March, to Isa Blagden: 'I am about a long poem to be something remarkable—work at it hard.'[6] By the end of June 1865, he was beginning to look back over this first period of work. On 30 June he wrote to George Howard:

As for the poem you enquire about—I can report that I am ending the seventh Book or Division—some eight thousand lines—and that I see the remaining five parts as though they were ended also: but I shall do things deliberately, and may hardly be ready before next year's end [1866]: if you cry out at 15,000 lines—remember that I have never been charged with "taking my ease in my Inn," or spinning out my work before: this admits of such treatment, and accordingly shall get it and welcome.[7]

---

[1] See 1. 422 n.   [2] *Rossetti Papers*, 302.
[3] *The Letters of Alfred Lord Tennyson*, ii. 415 n.
[4] RB to W. C. Cartwright, 24 Feb. 1865: *Checklist*, 122.
[5] *Wedgwood*, 136.   [6] *Dearest Isa*, 212.
[7] RB to George James Howard, later 9th Earl of Carlisle, 30 June 1865: Castle Howard, Yorkshire.

On 8 July 1865 he reported to Edith Story that it is both the end of the season and of *my* working season': 'I have written *8400* lines of my new poem since the autumn [1864]'.[1] This is his tally of lines prior to going on holiday. He is over half way through his original twelve-book plan—at the end of Pompilia's Book—in a draft version that was clearly different from the poem as we now have it. (Here the first seven books comprise 8,400 lines, whereas in the first edition they take up over 12,000.) In July he described the story to the Benzons, saying that he intended to publish it in two volumes, a detail that confirms his sense of its dimensions at this time.[2]

At Pornic, with his sister, father, and Pen, he swam and enjoyed the bracing climate through August and September, returning to London and work at the beginning of October. The poem now grew to a very substantial size. He later told William Rossetti that he wrote it 'all consecutively—not some of the later parts before the earlier',[3] a statement which, with the evidence below, confirms the view that this second phase of work took him up to the Pope's Book. On 19 May 1866 he reports to Isa Blagden:

My poem is nearly done—won't be out for a year or perhaps more. Suppose I am ruined by the loss of my Italian Rents,—how then? I shall go about and sell my books to the best bidder, and I want something, decidedly, for this performance: 16,000 lines, or over,—done in less than two years, Isa!—I having done other work besides,—and giving the precious *earlier* hours of the morning to it, moreover, which take the strength out of one.[4]

This account of progress suggests the impetus in the writing that has taken place since October 1864. When he describes the poem as 'nearly done', he does not imply that it is anywhere near ready for the press: submission to his publisher was still two years in the future. Rather he is telling Isa that, in draft form at least, the majority of the twelve-book plan is accomplished.

---

[1] *Letters*, 85.
[2] *The Birth of Rowland: An Exchange of Letters in 1865 between Robert Lytton and his Wife*, ed. Lady Emily Lutyens (1956), 99.
[3] *Rossetti Papers*, 302.   [4] *Dearest Isa*, 239.

5. *Further Researches*

In the second year of writing (1865–6) Browning continued his inquiries into historical detail and background. In March 1866 he consulted Antony Panizzi, the Italian patriot and political refugee, who since 1856 had been principal librarian at the British Museum. Panizzi had helped to establish the British Museum collection, now the British Library, on a sound footing, and he was also responsible for the conception of the great circular Reading Room. Browning told him about his work, and on 19 March 1866 wrote a letter giving details of the murder-case and the historical sources, and then setting out a series of queries:

I would gladly be put in the way of getting, through any memoirs or letters of the time, at the *gossip* of Rome during the reign of Innocent XII—or between 1690 and 1700:—any particulars of the Pope's private life, the persons, resident or foreign, remarkable at Rome: the Jubilee of 1694 or 5: anything illustrative of the social life there, in short.

I wish also for any notices of the like kind respecting Arezzo from 1650 to 1700: but more especially, an exact account of the city, a plan of its streets and neighbourhood, the genealogy of its chief families; any old prints of costumes &c.

Of course I have passed through Arezzo many times: but I want to know accurately certain minute points which I can only suspect.[1]

Panizzi replied: 'I cannot give a good report of my searches after the Franceschini murder.'[2] Nevertheless, he asked Mr Bond of the Manuscript Department to draw up a list of works that might be relevant to these queries, and sent the list to Browning. He also collected together some histories of Arezzo in his study and invited the poet to come and consult them, bringing with him his source-book. This meeting took place on 22 March, when Browning was issued with a six-month reader's ticket. He renewed this ticket the following October.[3]

The letter to Panizzi clearly suggests that Browning was research-ing Book X, 'The Pope', trying to gather information about

---

[1] MS: ABL.   [2] 21 Mar. 1866: Harvard University, Cambridge, Mass.
[3] The ticket, dated 22 Mar. 1866, is at Harvard University; the indication of renewal is written on the back.

Innocent XII (1615–1700). He also wants to know more about the historical Arezzo, one of the most important locations of the poem, and in particular 'certain minute points which I can only suspect'—perhaps the route taken by Pompilia as she fled from Guido's house.

This same month Browning sought out details concerning dates in 1697–8—probably the position of Catholic feasts and saints' days—from Augustus De Morgan, Professor of Mathematics at University College, London, to whom he sent a series of questions. When De Morgan replied by directing him to his *Book of Almanacs*, Browning told him that he had already made 'great use' of it, and asked De Morgan whether he possessed a seventeenth-century Roman almanac; also: 'I shall easily get the information I want from a Breviary, as M. Libri suggests: may I beg you to thank that gentleman for his obliging reference?'[1]

In this period his father in Paris became another source of information. In 1861 or 1862, in the Paris libraries, Robert Browning sen. had begun to research the history of Marozia (AD 892–937), a Roman noblewoman famous for her profligacy and for her family's influence on the papacy. He described his researches as his 'amusement', but by late 1865 he had filled over forty notebooks with his discoveries, and—because of the connections of Marozia's family with the papacy—become an expert in the conflict-filled lives of the popes in the late eighth and early ninth centuries. His notebooks contain a mass of information: extracts from biographical dictionaries, chronicles, and ecclesiastical histories; elaborately drawn genealogies; great lists of dates; indexes; cross-references; queries; attempts at drafts of sustained historical narrative.[2] By the end of 1865 Browning sen. was eager to pass this material on, either to his son or to one of his son's 'numerous literary acquaintances', so that an 'entertaining' as well as 'useful' biography might be made.[3] The old man's letters are importunate: 'I feel ashamed at

[1] RB to [Augustus De Morgan], 26 Mar. 1866: Johns Hopkins University.
[2] The six manuscript volumes of RB sen.'s researches are in the Bloomfield Collection of the East Sussex County Libraries, Brighton Public Library, Brighton. They are listed as J90 in Kelley and Coley.
[3] Three undated letters about his research from RB sen. to RB are MSS Cambridge: Fitzwilliam Museum, 'EBB Letters', nos. 229–31. The quotations are from nos. 231 and 230.

continuing to trouble you about Marozia; & the only apology I can offer, is that she was a plague to every body.'[1] Trying to demonstrate the historical importance of the material, he drew up a list of 'many interesting narratives connected with the History of Marozia', beginning with 'The remarkable trial of the dead body of *Formosus*'.[2] As background to Marozia's story, he knew all about the cadaver synod of 897, when the corpse of Pope Formosus was brought into open court and abused and sentenced to 'death' by his successor, Stephen VI, resulting in a controversy that ran through several pontificates. Browning knew the frailty of his father's health and wanted to show an interest; perhaps he already sensed how the cadaver synod might have a bearing on his imaginative engagement with Innocent XII. In his letters he makes an anecdote of the matter, referring at different dates to what was probably one occasion.[3] On 19 May 1866 he tells Isa Blagden that his father's mind is still alert, 'and the other day when I wanted some information about a point of mediaeval history, he wrote a regular bookful of notes and extracts thereabout.'[4] In the following year, reviewing what he now knew were the final months of his father's life, he gave another account to Seymour Kirkup:

The intellect [of my father], always very extraordinarily active, was quite unaffected: he continued his studies to the very last—and, on my requesting him to investigate the history of one of the Popes—(I did it to interest him, mainly) he sent me, a few weeks before the end, a regular book of researches, and a narrative of his own, exhausting the subject.[5]

The material on Pope Formosus from his father's notebooks was drawn into the opening of Book X of the poem, either now in 1866, or in 1867.[6]

---

[1] 'EBB Letters', no. 229.   [2] Ibid.

[3] We conjecture this from the informal phrasing in the letters cited here, and also in RB to Louisa Browning, 26 Feb. 1866: University of Iowa, and RB to Edward T. B. Twisleton, 29 June [1866]: Harvard University.

[4] *Dearest Isa*, 238.

[5] RB to Seymour Kirkup, 19 Feb. 1867: *Letters*, 105–6.

[6] See Stefan Hawlin, 'A New Source for *The Ring and the Book*, Book X', BSN 23 (1996), 27–34.

6. *Finishing, 1867–8*

The death of Robert Browning sen. on 14 June 1866 marked a natural break in the poem's composition. Browning had visited him in April in Paris. In May, four weeks before his death, he reported to Isa Blagden that the poem was 16,000 lines long, but almost a year later, in April 1867, he still refers to it at this length. Though on 19 October 1866 he told Isa Blagden 'I have my poem to mend and end',[1] there is no evidence of consistent work until the next year. In June 1866 his sister, Sarianna—who had looked after their father for so long in Paris—came to live with him in Warwick Crescent. From August to October she, Browning, and Pen went on holiday to Le Croisic near the mouth of the Loire. In October and November Browning entertained Joseph Milsand in London. His statement that he has to 'mend and end' the poem is probably accurate: he has to finish the 16,000-line work and redraft and shape it for the press. But this was a major undertaking: parts of it were still fluid in his mind or yet to be imagined.

At the beginning of 1867 Browning was still seeking out more historical details. On 28 January 1867 he writes to George Barrett: 'should you happen to come across any old postal map of the road between Arezzo and Rome, via Perugia,—containing the names of *all* the little villages by the way,—of the year 1700, a little earlier or later,—I should be glad to have such a thing'.[2] On 17 May he presses Cartwright about Augustus Craven's 'paper' on the murder-case, which he has still not received, and asks two further questions: 'What is Cardinal Franceschini,—of Tuscan extraction, or anyhow of the Arezzo family,—if so, what are his *arms*? Ask any instructed person, why a mother in want of a name for her child would be led to call him "Gaetano"—what virtues are there in that saint's patronage?'[3]

Clear evidence of a resumption of work and a resolve to finish and publish the poem comes in April 1867. On 23 April he tells Isa Blagden that the poem is 16,000 lines in length and that 'Book-sellers are making me pretty offers for it. . . . I ask £200 for the sheets

---

[1] *Dearest Isa*, 249.   [2] Landis, 288.
[3] RB to W. C. Cartwright, 17 May 1867: ABL.

to America and shall get it.'[1] In May he reports the poem at 18,000 lines, and in July it is 'somewhat exceeding 20,000'.[2] He has something approaching a complete draft and is determined to take it on holiday and 'get it ready, I hope, to go to press next Oct. or November [1867].'[3] Terms with the firm Ticknor & Fields were settled for publication in America, and on 19 July, prior to going on holiday, he wrote a note for their guidance:

The poem is *new* in subject, treatment and form. It is in Twelve Parts, averaging, say, 1600 lines each. The whole somewhat exceeding 20,000. (It is the shortest poem, for the stuff in it, I ever wrote.) This will be printed here in two volumes of six parts each. The name is that of the collection of law-papers on which, or out of which, rather, the poem is developed. I hope to be able to begin to print in October.[4]

Here, and in other letters, he is anticipating going to press towards the end of 1867. Word of the massive work was beginning to pass around London literary circles. Later in the year George Eliot wrote to John Blackwood: 'Imagine—Browning has a poem by him which has reached 20,000 lines. Who will read it all in these busy days?'[5] It is notable, at this stage, that there is still no clear idea of a title. The note to the American publisher is not specific, but it would seem to suggest that the working title is either 'A Roman Murder Case' or 'A Roman Murder Story'.

About 27 July 1867 Browning left London for his customary two-month holiday, again at Le Croisic. His sister and Pen accompanied him, and he took his manuscript, aiming to complete three-quarters of a final draft. The quiet of the town was relaxing, and he swam daily in the sea, but progress was not as fast as he had hoped. When he returned to London in October he began getting up at 5 a.m. in order to complete it. 'I am finishing the exceedingly lengthy business,' he wrote to Edward Dowden on 16 October,

---

[1] *Dearest Isa*, 263.

[2] RB to Julia Wedgwood, 17 May 1867: *Wedgwood*, 140; RB to Messrs Ticknor & Fields, 19 July 1867: *Letters*, 114.

[3] RB to Isa Blagden, 19 July 1867: *Dearest Isa*, 274.

[4] *Letters*, 114.

[5] 9 Nov. 1867: *The George Eliot Letters*, ed. Gordon S. Haight (9 vols., New Haven and London, 1954–78), iv (1956), 396–7.

'and hope to be rid of it in a few months more.'[1] However, he changed his publisher from Chapman & Hall to Smith, Elder & Co., and increased his work-load by making an agreement with George Smith for a new edition of his works. This involved him in the rearrangement of his poems and then in the proof-reading of the six-volume *Poetical Works*, published one volume a month between March and August 1868. At this time much of his work on 'A Roman Murder Case' was probably revision. In January 1868 he says: 'I like to keep turning and touching it'. In February he shows Allingham the manuscript 'in bird's-eye view'. Finally, in May 1868 he says that the poem is 'as good as done'.[2]

Though he had dined out a great deal during the main period of composition, and often told friends the story of the poem, he let no one read the manuscript. He was now emerging from a period of creative loneliness, conscious that the new poem was unusual in subject and form, and anxious about its reception. Later, he told George Smith how difficult he found it to '*see*' his lines in his own handwriting.[3] Some time in the spring of 1868 he gave Joseph Milsand the first two books to read, an indication of his friendship for Milsand and his trust in his critical judgement. In May, as he finished the manuscript, he was thinking about the form of publication, seemingly considering the possibility of serialization in the manner of the Victorian novel. Perhaps this would have been his second choice if his new publisher had balked at its size.

7. *Publication and Completion, 1868–9*

On 26 May 1868 Allingham records a conversation in which Browning said:

I'm puzzled about how to publish it. I want people not to turn to the end, but to read through in proper order. Magazine, you'll say: but no, I don't like the notion of being sandwiched between Politics and Deer-Stalking, say. I think of bringing it out in four monthly volumes, giving people

[1] *Letters*, 123.
[2] RB to Bayard Taylor, 25 Jan. 1868: R. H. Taylor Collection, Princeton University, New Jersey; Allingham, 173; RB to T. F. Kelsall, 15 May 1868: *The Browning Box*, ed. H. W. Donner (London, 1935), 101–2.
[3] RB to George Smith, 8 July 1868: John Murray, London.

time to read and digest it, part by part, but not to forget what has gone
before.[1]

The second idea here is for four volumes each containing three
books of the poem. At some point before 3 June he sent the
manuscript of Books I–VI to George Smith. On 11 June he was
distracted from any anxiety he might have felt about Smith's
reaction by the death of Arabel Barrett, his favourite sister-in-
law. In early July, Smith praised the poem to him, and said that it
was potentially 'popular'.[2] Moreover, Smith accepted the idea of
publication in four volumes. When he wrote to his American
publisher, Browning (knowing that he had previously agreed to
two-volume publication) chose to imply that the idea was Smith's:

it is considered by Mr Smith, who modestly chooses to represent the
"public", that the mere interest of the story is enough not only to live
through the intervals, but even gain by them: and that by giving time to
digest one portion, we assist the appetite for another: I don't know, but
hope it may be so.[3]

This decision had repercussions for the poem's reception: the
public was to be alerted to its length without being able to complete it; the judgements of critics would have to be suspended in
some sense. The unusual procedure was itself a form of publicity.
On 11 July Browning called on Smith at his Pall Mall office to
finalize their publishing agreement, and the manuscript of Books
I–VI was sent to the printer.

The composition of the poem was not finished at this stage. The
first six books were in a version that the printer could work on—
though they were still capable 'of plenty improvement of the
minuter kind'[4]—but Browning had not completed the manuscript
of the last six books. An indication of this comes in a letter to Smith
on 8 July: 'Don't concern yourself about the thinness of Vol. III: it
will be increased to the size of the other two,—I made a note that I
should increase parts 8 & 9 in the list of parts, I gave you.'[5] This

[1] Allingham, 181.
[2] RB to George Smith, [7 July 1868]: John Murray, London.
[3] RB to J. T. Fields, 12 July 1868: ABL.
[4] RB to George Smith, 8 July 1868: John Murray, London.   [5] Ibid.

seems to indicate that the monologues of the lawyers, Books VIII and IX, were too short, and that they were going to be reworked or extended.

At the end of July he went on holiday, and Smith sent after him the proofs of Books I–III, which reached him at Paris on 30 July. Acknowledging their arrival, Browning wrote:

I have been thinking over the "name" of the Poem, as you desired,—but do not, nor apparently shall, come to anything better than "The Franceschini;" *that* includes everybody in the piece, inasmuch as every one is for either Franceschini or his wife, a Franceschini also. I think "the Book & the Ring" is too pretty-fairy-story-like. Suppose you say "*The Franceschini*" therefore. Good luck to it![1]

The poem, in other words, had begun to go to press without a definite title, and the title we have was not a shaping influence on Book I. It is not known whether it was Smith or Browning who reversed this suggestion, making 'The Book and the Ring' into 'The Ring and the Book'.

After he had followed a roundabout route from Paris into the westernmost part of Brittany, Browning settled at the fishing village of Audierne, and there, the journey having cleared his brain 'of no end of cobwebs', about 14 August he set to work 'tooth & nail' on the proofs of Books I–III.[2] By 27 August he had finished, making 'so few, or indeed no one change of importance' but 'many little improvements in dotting i,s & crossing t,s'.[3] The second batch of proofs, Books IV–VI, reached him on 29 August, and he worked on them in the following month. At this time, he was annoyed by a letter from the American publishers, who, in the face of the plan for four volumes, wanted either to offer a reduced price or to rescind their agreement. He wrote furiously to them on 2 September,[4] but the quarrel seems to have been smoothed over by October, by which time it had been agreed that, for the original price of £200, Fields, Osgood, & Co. (the new name of Ticknor & Fields) could still publish the poem in two volumes rather than four.

[1] RB to George Smith, 30 July 1868: British Library, London.
[2] RB to George Smith, [13 Aug.] and 27 Aug. 1868: John Murray, London.
[3] RB to George Smith, 27 Aug. 1868: John Murray, London.
[4] *Letters*, 127.

About 8 October, Browning returned to London, bringing the corrected proofs of Books IV–VI. On 30 October he sent the revised sheets of the first six books to the American publisher, indicating an important difference between Books I–III and Books IV–VI concerning the extent of revision: 'I have *hardly* a minute to say that here are the corrected revises: the changes in the first three books are unimportant, but the remaining three are *much* affected by revision.'[1] Prior to publication he sent a copy of the proofs of Books I–VI to Julia Wedgwood on 5 November, initiating an important correspondence about the poem.[2] As a kind of formal launch he gave a reading of Book I at James Knowles's house at Clapham on the evening of 20 November. Tennyson, who was present, wrote to his wife: 'Browning read his Preface to us last night, full of strange vigour and remarkable in many ways; doubtful whether it can ever be popular.'[3] The first volume, containing Books I–III, was published on 21 November.

At some time now he was doing the new writing and revision required in the latter half of the poem, which perhaps accounts for his remark on 27 November that he is 'far from well, and oppressed by work.'[4] On 1 December he signed complimentary copies of volume I for Matthew Arnold, Benjamin Jowett, Dante Gabriel Rossetti, W. C. Cartwright, John Trivett Nettleship, and Lady Colvile. Through December he received letters of praise from D. G. Rossetti, Jowett, John Simeon, and others, and by the end of the month he had seen the beginning of positive appraisal in the reviews. The second volume (Books IV–VI) was published on 26 December, and on 1 January 1869 he wrote to George Smith: 'with the slips, I send in the 9th, or last part of the III[d] Volume, and the 10th & 11th or all but last parts of the IV: I shall be very glad to get these in type, and you shall have the last of the last in due time.'[5] He was only now, in other words, submitting corrected proofs for Books VII and

[1] RB to J. T. Fields, 30 Oct. 1868: *New Letters*, 183–4.
[2] *Wedgwood*, 148–96. Smith, Elder & Co. always sent Browning three copies of proofs.
[3] Hallam Lord Tennyson, *Alfred Lord Tennyson: A Memoir By His Son* (2 vols., 1897), ii. 59.
[4] To W. G. Kingsland: *Letters*, 128.
[5] MS: British Library, London.

VIII, and manuscript for Books IX to XI. Book XII was still not finalized.

The fact that he was completing the work as the first two volumes were published is attested in other ways. In July, Seymour Kirkup had gone to Arezzo and had sketched the Franceschini coat of arms from a manuscript record of leading Aretine families preserved by the Albergotti family.[1] This sketch, which Browning pasted onto the inside front cover of the Old Yellow Book, provided details which he worked into the end of Book XI and into Book XII. On 19 November, writing to Julia Wedgwood—who at this stage had seen Books I–VI—he outlined some of the contents of the remaining books, ending with the statement: 'the Augustinian preaches a sermon, and the Priest has a final word to add in his old age. "I can no more"—as dying operatic heroes sing.'[2] This projected speech, where Caponsacchi muses on his youthful encounter with Pompilia, was evidently either unwritten or excluded from Book XII. Since he did not submit manuscript for Book XII till after the new year, the words 'British Public, who may like me yet' (XII. 831)—the witty recollection of 'British Public, ye who like me not' (I. 410, 1379)—are presumably a response to the first reviews, particularly to the review in December's *Athenæum*.[3]

The third volume, containing Books VII–IX, came out on 30 January 1869, and the fourth volume, containing X–XII, on 27 February.

8. *Critical Reception*

'The newspaper critics have I see got it into their heads that it looks intellectual to admire or rather to praise Browning', John Blackwood wrote to George Eliot on 29 December 1868, confessing that he himself was still 'a heretic as to Browning'.[4] The critical reception of the poem was mixed, unfavourable judgements and old prejudices

---

[1] Reproduced near the beginning of Hodell, n.p.

[2] *Wedgwood*, 161.

[3] RB had seen this review by 27 Dec. 1868, when Allingham reports his comment 'The *Athenæum* notice is good': Allingham, 195.

[4] *The George Eliot Letters*, ed. Haight, iv. 497.

mixing with a general mood of reappraisal. Griffin and Minchin's statement that 'the weightier reviews . . . were practically unanimous in their approval', and Mrs Orr's that the poem marks 'the full recognition of his genius', are both too simple, since they obscure the division of opinion on many points concerned with style, form, and subject-matter.[1] There were a number of causes for the mood of revaluation. Browning was no longer a poet resident abroad, but had been in London and in London society since 1861. He was the widower of Elizabeth Barrett Browning, a much-admired poet. He had been elected an Honorary Fellow of Balliol College in 1867. The long-established body of his work—he had been publishing for thirty-five years—had been consolidated again in the six-volume *Poetical Works* of 1868. Now fresh judgements seemed required in the face of the obvious *tour de force* of his new work.

In the unfavourable criticism there are some common themes concerned with style and subject-matter. Generally, such criticism wants a less colloquial, more elevated style, and a more idealized, less realistic treatment and subject-matter. 'It is a primary canon of criticism', said the *British Quarterly Review*, 'that a great poem can be based only upon a great human action: the classic works of all languages have this common characteristic, that always the action is noble, the actors are noble. . . . Guido's murder is no worthier theme for a great poem than the crime of Tawell the Quaker, or of Palmer the betting-man.'[2] 'If realism be truth,' declared *The Times*, 'then ugliness is art and the photographer is the master; but we ourselves prefer what we shall venture to call by distinction the Beauty of Reality.'[3] In keeping with these perspectives, there were complaints about 'carefully eccentric English', 'oddly interpolated ejaculations', a use of parenthesis 'so long, striking, and interesting in itself as to break the current of the story in which it is imbedded, and give a grotesque effect to the whole'.[4] The *Westminster Review* worried about the use of 'ring-thing' (1. 17) which 'has a perilous

[1] Griffin and Minchin, 240; *Life*, 268; B. R. McElderry, 'Victorian Evaluation of *The Ring and the Book*', *Research Studies of the State College of Washington* 7 (June 1939), 75–89.

[2] *British Quarterly Review*, 49 (Mar. 1869), 456.

[3] 11 June 1869, p. 4.   [4] *The Spectator*, 12 Dec. 1868, xli. 1464–6.

resemblance to the vulgar "thingumbob" '.[1] The *Cornhill Magazine* noted the line 'A-smoke i' the sunshine, Rome lies gold and glad' (I. 907): 'What would be thought of the prose which set forth that a city lay gold and glad?'[2] The reviewer in *The Times* made a guardedly favourable judgement only after censuring Browning for verbosity, abruptness, 'jolting violence' of rhythm, and 'abortive creations' of vocabulary.[3]

In many of the reviews, however, there was a real appreciation of the breadth, intensity, and originality of the work, the moving nature of its story, and the quality of the characterization—Pompilia, in particular, was much admired. Some important reviews made very strong statements indeed. Initially commenting on the first volume in the *Athenæum*, R. W. Buchanan expressed limited praise—the work was 'perfectly successful, within the limitations of Mr Browning's genius';[4] but in his review of the completed work, also in the *Athenæum*, he described it as 'the supremest poetical achievement of our time', containing 'a wealth of nature and a perfection of spiritual insight which we have been accustomed to find in the pages of Shakespeare, and in those pages only.'[5] John Morley, the editor of the *Fortnightly Review*, attacked the sentimental criteria which might limit appreciation, and contrasted Browning with Tennyson. While Tennyson was writing 'tracts in polished verse of blameless Arthurs and prodigious Enochs', Browning's work was strenuously realistic, moral, and intellectual: 'It is this resolute feeling after and grip of fact which is at the root of his distinguishing fruitfulness of thought, and it is exuberance of thought, spontaneous, well-marked, and sapid, that keeps him out of poetical preaching, on the one hand, and mere making of music, on the other.'[6] Walter Bagehot, in *Tinsley's Magazine*, praised 'this powerful and elaborate work of art, written by one of the few strong men of our time.'[7]

Apart from the reviews, Browning received private letters of praise. John Forster said of 'Pompilia': 'You have written nothing

---

[1] Vol. 91 NS 35 (Jan. 1869), 298–300 at 300.
[2] Vol. 19 (Feb. 1869), 249–56 at 255.
[3] 11 June 1869, p. 4.   [4] 26 Dec. 1868, p. 876.
[5] 20 Mar. 1869, pp. 399–400.   [6] NS 5 (Mar. 1869), 336, 341–2.
[7] Vol. 3 (Jan. 1869), 665–74 at 674.

more—well, I will say, *so* beautiful: so profoundly affecting; higher in its order of poetry, or reaching down to such depths of wisdom and humanity.'[1] Dante Gabriel Rossetti, who expressed reservations to Allingham about the first volume,[2] went on to write a remarkable series of letters to Browning, one for each volume. The last of these (13 March 1868) is the most interesting:

I feel as if we were in communication now even before I put pen to paper: for is not your completed thought now filling me?—in how many ways, at what strange junctures; to recur to me for ever? Such function I have long acknowledged as yours; but now most strongly, by this confirmed and controlling impression of your greatness at a time when judgment should be mature in me.

How you have summed up the whole drama of your book in that supreme master-stroke at the end of the second "Guido"!—where the wretch, in his one terror-stricken flash of truth, winds up his shriek to the Saving Powers with the name of his wife. This leaves her crowned of unrighteousness itself. When you wrote that line, you must have felt that you owed your Muse a votive wreath; as the world, reading it, awards one to you.

The serene splendour of the Pope's section comes most nobly between the fluctuating contest of the actors and audience, and the final consummation. In itself I suppose it must be admitted as the grandest piece of sustained work in the whole cycle of your writings. The passage from the Friar's Sermon worthily "repeats the colour" in the winding-up.

And highest of all is the fact that it is to the inmost centre of the emotion that the mind reverts on closing the book; and finds itself still gazing with Caponsacchi on the "lady, tall, pale, beautiful, strange & sad," and still thrilling to those all-expressive words of his,—

> "You see, we are
> So very pitiable, she and I,
> Who had conceivably been other-wise."

I quote from memory, and perhaps not quite correctly, as Vol. 2 is still among the borrowers.

For this great work of yours now let me thank you, as for a fulness which I have lived to see.[3]

---

[1] 4 Feb. 1869: Berg Collection, New York Public Library.
[2] *Rossetti Letters*, ii. 679–80.
[3] MS: Princeton University; published in Rosalie Grylls, 'Rossetti and Browning', *Princeton University Library Chronicle*, 33 (Spring 1972), 247–8.

Swinburne and Henry James were two other writers much affected by the work. In his diary for 12 January 1869 William Rossetti noted that Swinburne, who had called on him to discuss Shelley, was 'excessively enthusiastic about Browning's new poem'.[1] Swinburne wrote to Lord Houghton:

What a wonderful work this is of Browning's. I tore through the first volume in a day of careful study, with a sense of absolute possession. I have not felt so strongly that delightful sense of being mastered—dominated— by another man's imaginative work since I was a small boy. I always except, of course, Victor Hugo's, which has the same force and insight and variety of imagination together with that exquisite bloom and flavour of the highest poetry which Browning's has not: though it has perhaps a more wonderful subtlety at once and breadth of humorous invention and perception.[2]

Henry James read the poem in 1870 when he was 26: the development of his first impression was the basis for one of the finest pieces of his late criticism, 'The Novel in *The Ring and the Book*' (1912).[3] Here he rewrites the poem into a prose fiction, fashioning its 'gothic' excess into an imagined Jamesian novel. At times he seems to find it wanting in terms of 'achieved form', but the celebration of the poem's breadth and intensity calls into question the underlying Jamesian criteria. He praises its 'proportioned monstrous magnificence', 'its tremendous push', the 'intellectual splendour' of the characters' thought, and the poet's 'complexity of suggestion'.[4] The quantity of Italian atmosphere 'is like nothing else in English poetry . . . a perfect cloud of gold-dust'.[5] This subtle lecture remains one of the best assessments of the poem, and an

---

[1] *Rossetti Papers*, 379–80.

[2] *The Letters of Algernon Charles Swinburne*, ed. Edmund Gosse and T. J. Wise (2 vols., London, 1918), i. 77–8; this letter is omitted from the standard edition of Swinburne's letters by Cecil Lang.

[3] This was originally given as an address to the Royal Society of Literature on 7 May 1912 and published in *Transactions of the Royal Society of Literature*, 31 (1912), 269–98. It was subsequently published in the *Quarterly Review*, 217 (July 1912), 68–87, and in his *Notes on Novelists* (1914), in both cases in a slightly revised form: see Susan M. Griffin, 'James's Revisions of "The Novel in *The Ring and the Book*"', MP 85 (1987), 57–64.

[4] James, 309, 312, 314, 321.   [5] Ibid. 318.

important witness to the larger relationship between James and Browning.[1]

All this was a long way in the future. On 4 March 1869, with his poem now completely before the public, Browning was invited to take tea with the Queen, along with Carlyle, George Grote, and Sir Charles Lyell. The *Court Circular* described Browning and Carlyle as 'two of the most distinguished writers of the age ... who, so far as intellect is concerned, stand head and shoulders above their contemporaries.'[2] Browning noted the effect of the meeting on his reputation in a letter to Julia Wedgwood on 8 March: 'Yes, the British Public like, and more than like me, this week ... I am in a way to rise.'[3] A more ironic remark, perhaps registering the complexity of response in the Reviews, is recorded in the diary of Sir Frederick Pollock. On 3 April he wrote:

In the afternoon talked with Browning at the Athenæum about *The Ring and the Book*. He said that he had at last secured the ear of the public, but that he had done it by vigorously assaulting it, and by telling his story four times over. He added that he had perhaps after all failed in making himself intelligible, and said it was like bawling into a deaf man's trumpet, and then being asked not to speak so loud, but more distinctly.[4]

TEXT

1. *Textual History*

The textual history of *The Ring and the Book* spans twenty-one years, from July 1868, when Browning submitted his manuscript of the first six books to the printer, to December 1889, when his final corrections to the *Poetical Works* of 1888–9 were incorporated in a revised text. There were six distinct stages:

---

[1] The fullest treatment is Ross Posnock, *Henry James and the Problem of Robert Browning* (Athens, Ga., 1985). For important articles on the relationship see *The Art of Criticism: Henry James on the Theory and the Practice of Fiction*, ed. William Veeder and Susan M. Griffin (Chicago and London, 1986), 482.

[2] *Court Circular*, 13 Mar. 1869.

[3] *Wedgwood*, 195–6.

[4] Sir Frederick Pollock, *Personal Remembrances* (2 vols., 1887), ii. 202.

(i) *The Printer's Copy Manuscript 1868–9*

In the absence of any drafts, if we except two chronologies of events drawn up by Browning to guide him in the composition of the poem,[1] the earliest surviving witness is the autograph printer's copy manuscript as sent to the printers for the first edition.[2] The poem is written in a dark brown ink on one side only (with the exception of vol. 1, fo. 172, where Browning has written the last eight lines of Book III on the verso) of 745 leaves of unwatermarked cream laid paper, ruled on both sides in blue. The manuscript has been bound up in two volumes, the first containing 383 leaves, the second 362. Throughout the manuscript, compositors' names, and slip numbers, not to speak of numerous inky thumb- and fingerprints, provide plentiful evidence of the process of setting the poem up in print. A table of compositors and their stints forms Appendix F.

The manuscript has been revised throughout, the evidence of pen and ink suggesting that this was carried out both *currente calamo* and retrospectively. The revisions consist of deletions, substitutions, and additions of individual words, of phrases, and on occasion of whole lines. The pattern of revision, however, varies between the earlier and the later part of the poem. In the first five books, apart from a few passages where Browning has had something of a struggle with a group of lines, the manuscript is quite lightly revised. Revisions to punctuation are rare. In Book III, for example, the average page of manuscript would reveal fifteen lines containing no variants whatever from the edition of 1888–9, and no revisions, as opposed to eleven lines containing either a variant,

---

[1] See Appendix C.   [2] British Library Additional MSS 43485–6.

a revision, or both. Collation of this part of the manuscript with the first edition, and, indeed, with the page proofs for that edition as corrected by Browning, suggests that heavy revision must have taken place at the galley proof (or what Browning refers to as 'slip') stage. A more detailed discussion of these points as evidenced in the first third of the poem will be found in the editorial note to Books I–IV.

(ii) *The Yale Proofs*

The proofs for the first edition, preserved in the Beinecke Library at Yale,[1] consist of corrected page proofs of Books I–VI (with the exception of quires H and I, that is to say, II. 415–1032, which are from the second edition, and carry no corrections), and corrected galley proofs of Books VII–XI, together with corrected but deleted page proofs of Book XI, pp. 193–5, and uncorrected page proofs of Book XII. The corrected galley proofs, at first sight surprisingly, in view of the evidence from Books I–IV, while more heavily revised than the page proofs, are not strikingly so. In this part of the poem, however, the manuscript is much more heavily revised, especially so in the case of Books VII–IX. Once Browning had finished revising his text, it remained remarkably stable. The final text found in the manuscript for those books varies very little from that found in the first edition.

The revisions made between the manuscript and the first edition of 1868 were, therefore, much heavier in the first half of the poem than in the second. In general, however, there is a move towards greater metrical regularity, of which the consistent changes from 'of' and 'on' to 'o'' and 'in' to 'i'', for instance, are part. The evidence of the proofs for the first edition demonstrates that it is Browning who made these changes, and that they are not the result of house-styling, though initial quotation marks for each line of long passages, and the substitution of 'colour' for 'color' and 'honour' for 'honor', probably are. There is also a move to heavier and more specific punctuation which may in part be due to house-styling, but appears more likely to be a deliberate tightening-up of

---

[1] Yale MS 1p / B821 / 868a.

the scansion. In the course of correcting page proofs for Book II, for instance, Browning made fifty-one corrections and revisions, of which three were corrections of typographical errors, thirty-eight were revisions of accidentals, and ten were revisions of substantives. Again, a more detailed discussion of the revisions as evidenced in the first third of the poem will be found in the editorial note to Books I–IV.

(iii) *The First Edition 1868–9*

On 17 November 1868, 3,000 copies of the first volume of *The Ring and the Book* were printed, 1,500 of which were immediately bound. The same number of vol. II were printed on 17 December, but they were bound in two batches, 800 immediately, and 1,311 early in the New Year; 2,000 copies of vol. III were printed in January 1869, and almost the complete printing was bound immediately. On 23 February, 2,000 sheets of vol. IV were printed, plus a surplus of 33 to be used as gifts to reviewers and friends.

(iv) *The Second Edition 1872*

By early 1872 the problems inherent in publishing such a long poem became apparent. On the one hand stocks of vols. III and IV were becoming low, and a second edition was called for. On the other hand, there were approximately 950 sets of sheets of vols. I and II left unbound. George Smith accordingly suggested to Browning that he should correct vols. III and IV only, and wait until stocks of vols. I and II were almost exhausted before correcting them. Browning corrected vols. III and IV early in 1872; 2,000 copies of vol. III were printed on 9 February, of which 220 were immediately bound. On 8 March, 2,000 copies of vol. IV were printed, 219 of which were bound.

The supposed 'second edition' of *The Ring and the Book*, published in 1872, was in fact a hybrid: vols. I and II consisted of sheets of the first edition preceded by a cancel title-page; vols. III and IV really were a new edition, corrected and reset. The four volumes were all bound in chocolate cloth to match the *Poetical Works*, with roman numbering on the spine. The situation is further complicated by the fact that some copies of vol. I were issued without the

cancel title, which can give the false impression that there was once a complete first edition of the poem in a brown binding.

(v) *The Second Edition 1882–3*

By the end of 1881 seventy-nine sets of sheets of vol. 1 of the first edition remained, and by the end of 1882 one hundred and ten of volume 11. In March and April of 1882, therefore, Browning at last had an opportunity to correct vol. 1. In June 1882 Smith printed 1,250 copies of a text which had been corrected, but which still retained an 1872 title-page. Browning corrected vol. 11 in March 1883, of which Smith printed 1,000 copies in the summer of 1883. The true second edition of *The Ring and the Book* consists therefore of vol. 1 printed in 1882, vol. 11 in 1883, and vols. 111 and 1V in 1872, all prefaced by an 1872 title-page, a combination which is rare. Luckily, the corrected vols. 1 and 11 of 1882 and 1883 may readily be identified as their title-pages lack the words 'M.A., Honorary Fellow of Balliol College, Oxford' after Browning's name.[1]

As might, perhaps, have been expected, the revisions made by Browning for the second edition differ as between those made in 1872 for vols. 111 and 1V, and those made in 1882 and 1883 for vols. 1 and 11. In 1872 his concerns were closer to those observed in his revision of the manuscript, and especially of the proofs, for the first edition. He was concerned with the sense of the poem, and with regularizing the scansion. This involved, among other things, the addition of extra lines, and careful attention to the accidentals. In 1882 and 1883 the text is more lightly revised, and the revisions, while still concerned with scansion, are more concerned with substantives. The elapse of so much time gave Browning a different approach to his work.

In March 1883 Browning wrote to Smith that he would like to correct all twelve books of *The Ring and the Book* while he prepared the three books of vol. 11 for the second edition:

[1] Meredith notes that typographically also the second edition is a hybrid. Volumes 111 and 1V were printed by Smith, Elder, and vols. 1 and 11 by Spottiswoode. Spottiswoode followed the Smith, Elder house style but there are a number of variants particularly in the preliminaries. See Michael Meredith, 'A Botched Job: Publication of *The Ring and the Book*', SBC 15 (1988), 41–50, from which all publishing and sales figures are taken.

Among the pleasant things told me by my Sister, arising out of the visit I had not the pleasure of being present at, was this about the 2^{d} Volume. I should much like to correct what little there may be to correct in it, but can hardly do so independently of the other volumes—which I have long wanted to put in thorough order, once for all. Now, if you would kindly supply me with all of these in sheets I would do the thing effectually and consign it to you for use as need may require in days to come, if such days are ordained us.[1]

Smith duly complied with Browning's request, and sent him sheets from the first edition of vol. II and from the second edition of the other three volumes. As we have seen, Browning returned vol. II, which became the true second edition, printed three months later. He retained the other sheets, and knowing that there was no immediate prospect of reprinting vols. I, III, and IV, worked on them in a relaxed, even casual, fashion.

(vi) *Yale Sheets 1883–188?*

The corrected sheets of volumes I, III, and IV, preserved in the Beinecke Library at Yale,[2] are so interesting and significant that we have devoted an appendix, Appendix E, to a comparison of the revisions found in them with those found in the *Poetical Works* of 1888–9, together with a table and a discussion of the results. This treatment is made necessary by the unfortunate fact that Browning mislaid the sheets, and had either forgotten about them, or had no access to them, when he came to revise the text of the poem in May 1888 for the *Poetical Works* of 1888–9. He therefore revised the poem over again, not necessarily with the same results.

(vii) *Poetical Works 1888–9*

In May 1888 George Smith sent Browning a fresh set of sheets of the second edition of *The Ring and the Book* to correct for the projected *Poetical Works*. On 8 May Browning confessed:

By what seems like an hallucination, I have corrected *my own copy* of the Ring and the Book,—and put it back on the shelf! When the sheets of

---

[1] RB to George Smith, 7 Mar. 1883: John Murray.
[2] Yale MS 1p / B821 / 868c.

the four volumes were sent with the others, I forgot what I had done,—supposed that I had sent the books with those preceding,—and that the Printers had made a mistake in giving me work to do I had already done. As it is—I need only copy the corrections already made,—so that you will receive the sheets in a very few days.[1]

As far as we know, this is what Browning did, but unfortunately what appears to have been his own copy of *The Ring and the Book*, purchased by Sotheran at Sotheby's in the sale of 5 May 1913 (lot 458), is lost.

The proofs of *The Ring and the Book* were sent to Browning in Venice in September 1888, and he finished correcting them on 3 December. Although Browning praised the 'scrupulous accuracy of the Printers' in setting up the 1888–9 edition, he noticed a number of errors in the course of publication. Consisting of sixteen volumes in all, the edition was issued at the rate of one volume a month between April 1888 and July 1889, the three volumes containing *The Ring and the Book* (viii, ix, and x) being published on 19 November 1888, 10 December 1888, and 18 January 1889 respectively. From 10 April to 5 June 1889 Browning sent corrections for the volumes already published. The printer used up uncorrected sheets before resetting the type; thus as Philip Kelley and W. S. Peterson explain, errors are corrected in some copies and not in others.[2] 'Some of these corrected volumes—identical in appearance to those of the first "printing"—were issued during 1889 as part of the 1888–9 edition, so that thereafter any given set of the edition might contain one or more corrected volumes.'

(viii) *Poetical Works 1889*

Before his death in December 1889 Browning provided additional lists of corrections for the first ten volumes: one set written as revisions in the copy of the 1888–9 edition formerly owned by James Dykes Campbell, Honorary Secretary of the London Browning Society, now in the British Library, and another for

[1] RB to George Smith, 8 May 1888: John Murray.
[2] P. Kelley and W. S. Peterson, 'Browning's Final Revisions', in BIS 1 (1973), 87–118. See also A. C. Dooley, 'Browning's *Poetical Works* of 1888–1889', SBC 7:1 (Spring 1979), 43 ff.

vols. iv–x in the form of a list now in Brown University Library. Most, but not all, of these corrections were incorporated in the corrected reprint published after Browning's death, of which all the volumes were dated 1889.

2. *Primary materials consulted for the edition*

(*a*) Manuscript: British Library Additional MSS 43485, 43486. Printer's copy: the *autograph* manuscript as sent to the printers for the first edition. MS 43485 (v+383 fos.) contains Books I–VI, 43486 (362 fos.) Books VII–XII. At the beginning of 43485 (fos. i–v) are four letters from Browning to George Smith, dated 30 July 1868, 1 January, 11 February 1869, and 8 September 1875. The first three relate to *The Ring and the Book*, the last to *The Inn Album*. The manuscript was presented by Browning to Mrs George Smith in 1869. Quarto; bound in green morocco, gilt-tooled. *MS*

(*b*) Proof for first edition: Yale MS 1p / B821 / 868a. Corrected page proofs of Books I–VI (with the exception of quires H and I, ll. 415–1032, which are from the second edition, and carry no corrections), and corrected galley proofs of Books VII–XI, together with corrected but deleted page proofs of Book XI, pp. 193–5, and uncorrected page proofs of Book XII. *Yale 1*

(*c*) First edition: four volumes, 21 November 1868–27 February 1869. Smith, Elder & Co. *1868*

(*d*) Second edition: four volumes, 1872, true second edition of vols. III and IV only; [June 1882], but with 1872 title-page, true second edition of vol. I; [Summer 1883], but with 1872 title-page, true second edition of vol. II. Smith, Elder & Co. *1872*

(*e*) Revised sheets from the second edition, vols. I, III, and IV. Summer 1883–188? Browning mislaid the sheets and the revisions never appeared in print: Yale MS 1p / B821 / 868c. *Yale 2*

(*f*) *The Poetical Works*, 16 volumes, 1888–9. Smith, Elder & Co. Issued monthly from April 1888 to July 1889. Volumes viii, ix, and x contain *The Ring and the Book*. *1888*

(*g*) *The Poetical Works*, 16 volumes, 1888–9. Smith, Elder & Co. Issued monthly from April 1888 to July 1889. Volumes viii, ix,

and x contain *The Ring and the Book*. A large-paper copy
formerly belonging to James Dykes Campbell and containing
revisions by RB. British Library C. 116. d. 1. *DC*

(*h*) List of revisions in RB's hand to vols. iv–x of *The Poetical
Works*, 1888–9, preserved at Brown University. *Br U*

(*i*) *The Poetical Works*, 16 volumes, 1889. Smith, Elder & Co. A
corrected reprint of the 1888–9 edition. All volumes dated
1889; issued between 9 May 1889 and 5 March 1890. *1889*

3. *Editorial procedures*

(*i*) *Copy Text*

The copy text for this edition is the last edition to be read in proof
by Browning, that of 1888–9. The reprint of 1889 is not a satisfactory basis for an authoritative edition. It was not read in proof by
Browning, it does not incorporate all the corrections he provided,
its end-of-line punctuation is unreliable, and it contains some
glaring misprints not present in the volumes published in 1888–
July 1889. Line-numbering follows that of the copy text; note that
it relates to lines of type, not of verse, so that the very first
pentameter of the poem is 1. 1–2.

(*ii*) *Variants*

All variants, accidental as well as substantive, have been recorded.
Browning made an idiosyncratic and creative use of punctuation,
and the evidence of the surviving galley proofs and page proofs
shows that he paid meticulous attention to it. The same evidence
makes clear that many changes such as 'of' and 'on' to 'o'' and 'in'
to 'i'' were deliberately made by Browning, and were not the
result of house-styling. By recording all variants, we hope that our
critical text will also serve as a genetic text, providing the evidence
of the creative process.

(*iii*) *Emendations to the copy text*

We have been conservative in making alterations to the copy text,
reserving them for obvious inadvertence or slips of the pen on

Browning's part, and for typographical errors on the part of his printers which he did not pick up himself. Both cases are rare. Where the witness of the manuscript and the first and second editions agrees against the copy text, we have taken a hard look at the reading in question, but, given Browning's meticulous attention to his text, if the reading, even while odd or awkward, could nevertheless conceivably be the result of a deliberate choice by Browning we have let it stand, however tempting it might be to choose one more satisfying. Emendations to the copy text are listed in the Editorial Note to Books I–IV.

(iv) *Apparatus*

At the foot of the page we list readings from the printer's copy manuscript, the corrected and revised proofs, the editions of 1868, 1872 and 1889, and the Dykes Campbell and Brown University lists of revisions. The words before and after substantive variants are not given where the identity of the variant word or phrase is obvious, but in any case of possible ambiguity either or both are supplied to aid identification. Where the variant begins or ends a line, the preceding or following word is not normally given. No punctuation has been added by the editors; if a word which comes at the end of a line is followed or not followed by punctuation, then this exactly reflects the situation in the particular witness. If a variant adds or omits a punctuation mark within a line, then the preceding and following words are given. Abbreviations and signs are listed on pp. lv–lvi.

In order to improve the reader's understanding of the growth of the text we have simplified the practice of earlier volumes. Additions within the body of the text are rendered thus: ^decent^. Revisions, including deletions, are shown with one pointed bracket, thus: monies,—>moneys,—, or: And idealize>Idealize. Text in the manuscript which is illegible is rendered by empty square brackets, the distance between the brackets representing the length of the illegible portion of text; dubious readings are contained within square brackets and preceded by a question mark. Editorial comment is contained within ogee brackets, as: {new paragraph— paragraphing obscured in *1889* by 70 being at the head of the page}.

The first lines of each page of the manuscript are recorded, together with casting-off marks, signatures, and any other evidence relating to the setting-up of the first edition. Compositors' names are set out in a table in Appendix F.

The primary sources provide evidence of the growth of Browning's text, as follows:

1. *The Printer's copy manuscript.* The first four books of the poem are lightly revised in manuscript. In the course of the first five pages of Book III (vol. 1, fos. 111–15), for instance, there are no revisions to accidentals, and thirteen revisions to substantives. Of the latter, about half are designed to improve the scansion or rhythm of a line, the others to tighten up the sense. For instance, in l. 5 little Pompilia is no longer to be frightened 'with a bruise' but 'at a bruise'—a more remote threat, implying even greater delicacy on her part. In l. 19, the friar takes confession no longer from the conventional 'her lips', but from the more unusual 'her lip'. In ll. 36 and 37, the leaden-footed and somewhat unspecific 'Rome has flocked these two last days, never doubt, / To the place where thus she waits her death, to hear' becomes 'Rome has besieged, these two days, never doubt, / Saint Anna's where she waits her death, to hear'. In l. 90 the change from 'For Christ's particular sake: so I say' to 'For Christ's particular love's sake: so I say' greatly improves the rhythm, while the addition of l. 109, changing 'Why was she made to learn / What Guido Franceschini's heart could hold?' to 'Why was she made to learn / Not you, not I, not even Molinos' self, / What Guido Franceschini's heart could hold?' has the effect of underlining 'she'.

Examination of the manuscript of Book IV, a book which we know from Browning himself to have been heavily revised before publication, confirms the picture of light revision at the printer's copy stage. Folios 191–8 contain no revisions to accidentals, and but six revisions to substantives. Of these, none is of any great significance except for the addition of l. 660, making the reference

to the Comparini more specific, and the creation of ll. 716 and 717 out of a single line, providing a more concrete image, and at the same time improving the rhythm of the lines.

2. *The First Edition.* The revisions made to the text at proof stage reveal a striking difference as between the first three books of the poem and the fourth. In the case of Book III, for instance, the text is, on the whole, very stable. Line follows line where the text found in the manuscript is identical with that found in the first edition. In the course of four sample pages of the manuscript there is only one substantive variant plus the addition of a whole line, and twenty-six variants in the accidentals. In the case of Book IV, on the other hand, four sample pages of the manuscript reveal thirty-six accidental variants, and sixty-seven substantive variants, including eight whole lines, together with the addition of three lines and the deletion of two lines. The principal object of the revisions was to achieve metrical regularity. For example, in the manuscript l. 620 has no less than fifteen syllables, and many other lines have twelve or fourteen. In many cases two lines are made into three. Browning must have been in a hurry, and have written with little regard for scansion—indeed, one is entitled to wonder whether at this point he ever repeated his verse to himself aloud, or whether he only committed it silently to paper.

Emendations to the text

Accidentals

Book I: 53, 323, 816, 1058, 1148, 1174, 1190, 1306. Book II: 88, 541, 633, 1153, 1345, 1373, 1374. Book III: 317, 1077, 1368. Book IV: 268, 363, 379, 516, 676, 906, 1131, 1383, 1423, 1427, 1428, 1536.

Substantives

Book I: 1366. Book II: 252, 844. Book III: 238. Book IV: 289, 577.

Restored paragraphs

Book I: 31, 241, 1162. Book II: 344, 1537. Book III: 469, 839, 1376, 1464. Book IV: 70, 424, 903.

Accidentals

The great majority of the emendations which we have made to accidentals result from revisions made by Browning in either or both of the Dykes Campbell copy of *The Poetical Works*, 1888–9, and the list of revisions in RB's hand to vols. iv–x of *The Poetical Works*, 1888–9, preserved at Brown University, and adopted in *The Poetical Works*, 1889, or from supplying missing characters caused by broken sorts found in the printing of those two editions. The remainder, with one exception, result from editorial correction of inaccurate typesetting in the editions of 1888–9 and 1889. Of these only two are of significance, II.1153, where the line must end with a comma for the passage to make sense syntactically, and IV. 1536 (the exception) where Browning has been confused by the rule that punctuation should go within quotation marks, and has placed the question mark within them, although in fact it belongs with 'Shall I comfort you, explaining' and not with the text within the quotation marks.

Substantives

We have only made six emendations to substantives. To deal with the simple cases first, IV. 577, results from a deliberate change made by RB in both the Dykes Campbell copy and the Brown University list, while II. 844, is a case of inaccurate typesetting in *1888* corrected by RB in both the Dykes Campbell copy and the Brown University list. In III. 238, the editors correct inaccurate typesetting which led to an obviously ungrammatical verb in *1888* and *1889*. That leaves three cases where the text found in *1888* and *1889* can be improved by critical examination of the witnesses. In two of the cases, II. 252, and IV. 289, all the printed witnesses agree against the manuscript, but we are convinced that the latter, the latest text over which RB had immediate physical control, has the correct readings. In II. 252, RB has clearly written 'Lend', but the letter-form deceived the compositor, who set up 'Send', a reading not wrong enough to be picked up in any of the subsequent editions. In IV. 289, the manuscript reads 'Paradise wall', but in the first and all subsequent editions 'wall' has dropped out, leaving a reading which, while it does not make sense, was not egregiously

nonsensical enough to be noticed. In the third case, I. 1366, the manuscript and the first edition agree against all subsequent editions in reading 'now shrouds, now shows', a reading which reflects the sense of the whole passage, with its emphasis on variance and changeability—a sense lost in the reading found in *1872, 1888,* and *1889*: 'now shrouds, nor shows'.

REFERENCES AND ABBREVIATIONS

Note: the place of publication is given if it is not London or Oxford.

ABL   The Armstrong Browning Library, Baylor University, Waco, Texas.

Allingham   *William Allingham: A Diary*, ed. Helen Allingham and Dollie Radford (1907).

Altick   Richard D. Altick (ed.), *The Ring and the Book* (Harmondsworth, 1971).

Aurora Leigh   *Aurora Leigh*, ed. Margaret Reynolds (University of Ohio, Athens, 1992).

Biographie universelle   *Biographie universelle, ancienne et moderne*, 52 vols. (Paris, 1811–28).

BIS   *Browning Institute Studies*, annual volumes, 1973–90.

BN   *The Browning Newsletter* (Armstrong Browning Library, Waco, Tex.)

Buckler   William E. Buckler, *Poetry and Truth in Robert Browning's The Ring and the Book* (New York and London, 1985).

BSN   *Browning Society Notes* (Browning Society of London).

Carlyle: *Works* (Centenary ed., 30 vols., 1896–9).

Checklist   *The Brownings' Correspondence: A Checklist*, compiled by Philip Kelley and Ronald Hudson, The Browning Institute and Wedgestone Press (Winfield, Kan., 1978; supplements in later vols. of BIS).

Cook   A. K. Cook, *A Commentary Upon Browning's 'The Ring and the Book'* (1920).

Correspondence   *The Brownings' Correspondence*, ed. Philip Kelley and Ronald Hudson (to vol. viii), ed. Philip Kelley and Scott Lewis (Wedgestone Press, Winfield, Kan., 1984–   ).

Curious Annals   Beatrice Corrigan (ed.), *Curious Annals: New Documents Relating to Browning's Roman Murder Story* (University of Toronto Press, Toronto, 1956).

Dearest Isa: Robert Browning's Letters to Isabella Blagden, ed. Edward C. McAleer (Austin, Tex. and Edinburgh, 1951).

EBB   Elizabeth Barrett Browning

Everyman   *The Old Yellow Book: Source of Robert Browning's The Ring and the Book*, translated and edited by Charles W. Hodell (Everyman Library series, 1911).

Gest   John Marshall Gest, *The Old Yellow Book, Source of Browning's The Ring and the Book: A New Translation with Explanatory Notes and Critical Chapters upon the Poem and Its Source* (University of Pennsylvania, Philadelphia, 1927).

Griffin and Minchin   *The Life of Robert Browning*, by William Hall Griffin, completed and edited by Harry Christopher Minchin, 3rd ed., revised and enlarged (1938; 1st ed., 1910).

Griffin Collections   William Hall Griffin, biographer of Robert Browning, 'Collections for his *Life* of Robert Browning', 7 vols., British Library, Additional MSS 45558–45564.

Hawthorne   Nathaniel Hawthorne, *The French and Italian Notebooks*, ed. Thomas Woodson (Ohio State University, Columbus, 1980), vol. xiv of the *Centenary Edition of the works of Nathaniel Hawthorne*, 23 vols. (1964–).

Hodell   Charles W. Hodell, *The Old Yellow Book, Source of Browning's The Ring and the Book, in Complete Photo-Reproduction, with Translation, Essay, and Notes*, 2nd ed. (Carnegie Institution of Washington, 1916; 1st ed., 1908).

Hudson   *Browning to his American Friends*, ed. Gertrude Reese Hudson (1965).

It.   Italian.

Jack   Ian Jack, *Browning's Major Poetry* (1973).

James   Henry James, 'The Novel in "The Ring and the Book"', in *Notes on Novelists* (1914).

Johnson   Samuel Johnson, *A Dictionary of the English Language*, Times Books facsimile of the 1755 text (1979).

Kelley and Coley   *The Browning Collections: A Reconstruction with Other Memorabilia*, compiled by Philip Kelley and Betty A. Coley, Armstrong Browning Library, Baylor University, Texas (1984).

L.   Latin.

Landis   *Letters of the Brownings to George Barrett*, ed. Paul Landis and R. E. Freeman (Urbana, Ill., 1958).

Learned Lady   *Learned Lady: Letters from Robert Browning to Mrs Thomas FitzGerald*, ed. Edward C. McAleer (Cambridge, Mass., 1966).

Letters   *Letters of Robert Browning Collected by Thomas J. Wise*, ed. Thurman L. Hood (1933).

Letters of EBB   *The Letters of Elizabeth Barrett Browning*, ed. Frederic G. Kenyon, 2 vols. (1898).

Life   *Life and Letters of Robert Browning*, by Mrs Sutherland Orr, new ed. rev. by Frederic G. Kenyon (1908; 1st ed. 1891).

Miller   Betty Miller, *Robert Browning: A Portrait* (1952).

MLR   *Modern Language Review.*

MP   *Modern Philology.*

New Letters   New Letters of Robert Browning, ed. William Clyde DeVane and Kenneth Leslie Knickerbocker (1951).

ODEP   *Oxford Dictionary of English Proverbs*, 3rd ed., ed. F. P. Wilson (1970).

OED²   *Oxford English Dictionary*, 2nd ed., ed. J. A. Simpson and E. S. C. Weiner, 20 vols. (1989).

Ogilvy   *Elizabeth Barrett Browning's Letters to Mrs. David Ogilvy 1849–1861*, ed. Peter N. Heydon and Philip Kelley (1974).

OYB   Old Yellow Book. In references in the style 'OYB lxxi (78)' the roman numeral refers to Hodell's complete facsimile and translation (see Hodell), and the arabic numeral to the more widely available Everyman reprint of Hodell's translation (see Everyman). Quotations have been freshly translated, and do not necessarily correspond exactly with Hodell's translation.

Pettigrew and Collins   *Robert Browning: The Poems*, ed. John Pettigrew, supplemented and completed by Thomas J. Collins, 2 vols. (Penguin English Poets, Harmondsworth; Yale University Press, New Haven, 1981).

PK   References in the style 'PK 53:24' are to letters listed in *Checklist*.

R&B   *The Ring and the Book.*

RB   Robert Browning.

Roba di Roma   William Wetmore Story, *Roba di Roma*, 2 vols. (1863). Browning helped to edit this work: see *Story*, ii. 143–6.

Rossetti Letters   Letters of Dante Gabriel Rossetti, ed. Oswald Doughty and John Robert Wahl, 4 vols. (1965–7).

Rossetti Papers   Rossetti Papers, 1862 to 1870, compiled by William Michael Rossetti (1903).

SBC   *Studies in Browning and his Circle* (Armstrong Browning Library, Waco, Tex.)

SS   Secondary Source: Browning's secondary source for the poem, the Italian manuscript 'Morte dell'Uxoricida Guido Franceschini Decapitato'. References in the style 'SS 12' are to the paragraph numbers in our reprint and translation: Appendix B.

Story   Henry James, *William Wetmore Story and his Friends*, 2 vols. (1903).

Sullivan   Mary Rose Sullivan, *Browning's Voices in The Ring and the Book* (University of Toronto Press, Toronto, 1969).

Thomas   Charles Flint Thomas, *Art and Architecture in the Poetry of Robert Browning* (Troy, NY, 1991).

Tilley   M. P. Tilley, *A Dictionary of the Proverbs in England in the Sixteenth and Seventeenth Centuries* (Ann Arbor, Mich., 1950).

TLS   *Times Literary Supplement.*

Treves   Frederick Treves, *The Country of 'The Ring and the Book'* (1913).

Trumpeter   *Browning's Trumpeter: The Correspondence of Robert Browning and Frederick J. Furnivall 1872–1889*, ed. William S. Peterson (Washington, DC, 1979).

Wedgwood   *Robert Browning and Julia Wedgwood*, ed. Richard Curle (1937).

Note: references to Shakespeare are to *The Riverside Shakespeare*, ed. G. Blakemore Evans, *et al.* (Houghton Mifflin Company, Boston, 1974).

Abbreviations and signs used in the text and textual notes

★	An emendation by the editors.
....	Omission by the editors.
{ }	Comment by the editors.
>	Substitution by RB of the word or passage preceding the symbol with the word or passage following the symbol (e.g. this>that means that RB has substituted 'that' for 'this' in the MS, proof, or printed work).
^ ^	Additions within the body of the text (e.g. ^decent^ means that RB inserted 'decent' between 'as' and 'wrappage' after he had written 'as wrappage' in order to make the text read 'as decent wrappage').
⟨ ⟩	Deletion in manuscript.
[ ]	Text which is illegible in the MS. The distance between the brackets represents the length of the illegible portion of text; dubious readings are contained within square brackets and preceded by a question mark.
|	Division between lines.
[—]	In the main text, a paragraph-break obscured by the pagination.
BrU	List of revisions in RB's hand to vols. iv–x of *Poetical Works*, 1888–9, preserved at Brown University Library, Providence, RI.
DC	Copy of *Poetical Works*, 1888–9, formerly belonging to James Dykes Campbell, and containing revisions by RB, preserved in the British Library.
MS	The *autograph* printer's copy MS for *The Ring and the Book*, 1868–9, preserved in the British Library.

Yale 1   Proofs for *The Ring and the Book*, 1868–9. Corrected page proofs of Books I–VI (with the exception of quires H and I of Book II, lines 415–1032, which are from the second edition, and carry no corrections), and corrected galley proofs of Books VII–XI, together with corrected but deleted page proofs of Book XI, pp. 193–5, and uncorrected page proofs of Book XII. Preserved in the Beinecke Library, Yale University, as 1p / B821 / 868a.

1868   *The Ring and the Book*, 1868–9.

1872   *The Ring and the Book*, 1872, [1882], [1883].

Yale 2   Sheets from the Second Edition, vols. I, III, and IV, revised by RB but mislaid so that the revisions never appeared in print. Preserved in the Beinecke Library, Yale University, as 1p / B821 / 868c.

1888   *The Poetical Works of Robert Browning*, 16 vols., 1888–9.

1889   *The Poetical Works of Robert Browning*, second impression, 16 vols., 1889.

THE RING AND THE BOOK

Books I–IV

INTRODUCTION TO BOOK I
THE RING AND THE BOOK

BOOK I of *The Ring and the Book* is one of the most brilliant parts of the Browning canon, zestful and enthusiastic, with Byronic élan. It has a fast, breathless movement, as though it were important to get the reader quickly into the substance of the work. In November 1868 Tennyson heard Browning perform it, and, commenting on its 'strange vigour', described it as a 'Preface', which may be what Browning had called it.[1] Certainly, it is self-consciously an introduction, and it is easy to see how Browning, aware of the challenge in subject and form of the new poem, and conscious of his own relative unpopularity, was drawn to make this first Book a clear explanation of the work that follows.

The Book as a whole is also a disquisition on the imagination: it describes vividly how the poet bought his source-book, the Old Yellow Book, from a stall in the flea market in Piazza San Lorenzo, how he carried it back with him to Casa Guidi, and how his imagination worked upon it. The overarching 'Ring' metaphor, beginning in the opening lines, and continuing through the Book, is the central image for conveying this process: the poet is the master jeweller—by implication as brilliant as Castellani, the great contemporary firm—making his poem (his 'Ring') out of the historical documents (the raw 'ore') by the workings of artistic consciousness. The metaphor is reinforced by other images: the poet is a 'resuscitator' of dead voices (719), a 'mimic' creator after the manner of God (740), a prophet-like being, like Elisha in the Second Book of Kings, laying his vital being on the corpse of the historical past till 'flesh waxed warm' (768).

Hopkins felt that the description of the street-market in Florence where Browning purchased his source-book (38–100) was 'a pointless photograph of still life, such as I remember in Balzac, minute upholstery description; only that in Balzac ... all tells and is given with a reserve and simplicity of style which Browning has not got.'[2] In fact, the evocation of the quiddity of the contemporary scene—the details of 'picture-frames / White through the worn gilt, mirror-sconces chipped, / Bronze

---

[1] See Introduction, p. XXXII.

[2] Hopkins to R. W. Dixon, 12 Oct. 1881: *The Correspondence of Gerard Manley Hopkins and Richard Watson Dixon*, ed. Claude Colleer Abbott (1935), 74.

angel-heads once knobs attached to chests' (53–5)—like the description of
Casa Guidi later (469–96), is a way of drawing the reader, via the physi-
cality of the immediate present, into the once equally real historical past.
An air of reminiscence attaches itself to the process: Browning, now a
widower settled in London, with a great longing for Italian scenes, is
recalling happy places and settings in Florence from a time when EBB was
still alive.[3] There is also an attitude of enthusiasm and intensity: Mary
Rose Sullivan points out that in the opening 520 lines the most prominent
speech pattern is the first-person pronoun in conjunction with a strong,
brief verb—'I found ... I picked ... I leaned ... I read'—emphasizing
the 'productive quality' of the process by which the poet found his
source-book and mastered its contents.[4] This is part of a bantering rhetorical intimacy, often ironic and teasing, which the poet-speaker sets up
with the slightly disdaining 'British Public' (410), his imagined audience,
the 'London folk' (422) who still find his work difficult or unworthy of
attention. Whatever Browning's actual feelings about being 'the most
unpopular poet that ever was',[5] his direct address to the audience about
his unpopularity is robustly witty in a way that is characteristic of the Book
as a whole (410–21, 1379–89). At one point, having suggested the fascina-
tions of the murder-case, he has a game with his readers of pretending that
the case is not historically obscure, and that they, therefore, do not need
his intervention concerning it (364–409). This passage is typical of some of
the Book's tones: wry, playful, and ironic.

In this Book, Browning gives three different versions of the story,
which lead his audience back into the world of late-seventeenth-century
Rome, or—in his splendid metaphor—take us 'from the level of to-day /
Up to the summit of so long ago' (1331–2). The first telling (141–363) is
breezy and impressionistic: it concentrates on the trial of Count Guido
Franceschini for murder in January and February 1698, the surviving legal
documents, their confusions and farcical use of legal precedent, the trial's
verdict and its ratification by the Pope. The second telling (469–678) is a
description of how the poet fuses his 'live soul' and the 'inert stuff' of the
old legal documents: vivid, emotional, and metaphysical—it emphasizes
the battle of good and evil implicit in the story—it takes the audience
back to the events of 1694, the history that led up to the murders and the
trial. The third, shortest telling (780–823) is factual and restrained, and
serves to introduce the descriptions of the speakers of the ten monologues
of Books II to XI.

---

[3] See I. 43, 473 nn.   [4] Sullivan, 11.   [5] See I. 410 n.

These descriptions (838–1329) include important matters of characterization and setting. They owe a debt to *The Canterbury Tales*, at one point
by direct allusion (1203–4), and more generally in their wryly witty
observations of the voice, appearance, and manner of the different speakers. The portraits anticipate the intertwining of comedy and tragedy that
is a larger feature of the poem. There is the young-old lawyer Bottini,
practising his defence of Pompilia alone in his room, straining his voice
like Chaucer's Chauntecleer, with eyes shut and standing on tiptoe
(1162–1219); and the other lawyer, Arcangeli, with his cheek and jowl
'all in laps with fat' (1132) and his love of food, reminding us, perhaps, of
the Franklin. Against this, there is the pathos of Pompilia's deathbed,
where her various audience is drawn together, by empathy, into a kind of
crucifix that supports her during her dying moments (1076–1104); and
then the octogenarian Pope Innocent XII, making a difficult judgement
on the murder-case in the 'droop' of a cold February evening (1220–71).

The Book ends with the famous invocation to 'Lyric Love' (1391–
1416), the Muse who is also Elizabeth Barrett Browning. As Appendix D
makes clear, the opening of the Book also contains implicit memories
focused on EBB, and these, and the vivid reminiscences of Florence, may
alert us to a slightly buried aspect of things: that the sheer imaginative
effort of writing the poem during his widowerhood in the 1860s was a
way through grief for a poet who had loved deeply.

THE RING AND THE BOOK.
1868–9.

I.

THE RING AND THE BOOK.

Do you see this Ring?
         'T is Rome-work, made to match
(By Castellani's imitative craft)
Etrurian circlets found, some happy morn,
After a dropping April; found alive   5
Spark-like 'mid unearthed slope-side figtree-roots
That roof old tombs at Chiusi: soft, you see,

---

1 MS {fol. 1 numbered (1. by RB. In the top left-hand corner is written in pencil 'Proofs July [13]/1868'.}

   1 *this Ring*: Browning describes a gold ring made in Rome by the Castellani firm, in a style imitating ancient Etruscan rings. Probably he has in mind a distinct Etruscan style, weighty, with a large, domed boss (or bezel), and with a thick band. Scholarship has wanted to associate the image with one particular ring, but the evidence suggests that this is not the case: the image may have been influenced by rings Browning owned, but it was probably also influenced by a general familiarity with ancient Etruscan jewellery and with Castellani imitations. Primarily, of course, the manufacture of the ring is a 'figure' for the poet's art: see ll. 31, 32 n. For a fuller discussion see Appendix D.

   3 *Castellani's imitative craft*: the brilliant family firm of jewellers, Castellani, was reaching the height of its fame in the 1860s, and was well known for its reproductions of ancient Etruscan jewellery, and also for its commitment to liberal politics and the Risorgimento. Its shop at 88 Via Poli, Rome, was an established tourist attraction; for the Brownings' visit there see Appendix D. There are important entries on the Castellani in *Dizionario biografico degli italiani* (Rome, 1960–), xxi. 590–605; the fullest study is Geoffrey C. Munn, *Castellani and Giuliano* (1984).

   4 *Etrurian circlets*: Etruscan rings.

   5 *dropping*: rainy.

   7 *Chiusi*: this small town, on the road between Orvieto and Siena, is one of the great sites of the ancient Etruscan civilization, being surrounded by over 400 Etruscan tombs. In the nineteenth century much jewellery had been unearthed there. The Brownings stayed at Chiusi on 6–7 June 1860 as they travelled from Rome to Florence, and Browning visited some of the tombs early on 7 June: Hudson, 58; *Letters of EBB*, ii. 394.

Yet crisp as jewel-cutting. There's one trick,
(Craftsmen instruct me) one approved device
And but one, fits such slivers of pure gold   10
As this was,—such mere oozings from the mine,
Virgin as oval tawny pendent tear
At beehive-edge when ripened combs o'erflow,—
To bear the file's tooth and the hammer's tap:
Since hammer needs must widen out the round,   15
And file emboss it fine with lily-flowers,
Ere the stuff grow a ring-thing right to wear.
That trick is, the artificer melts up wax
With honey, so to speak; he mingles gold
With gold's alloy, and, duly tempering both,   20
Effects a manageable mass, then works:
But his work ended, once the thing a ring,
Oh, there's repristination! Just a spirt
O' the proper fiery acid o'er its face,
And forth the alloy unfastened flies in fume;   25
While, self-sufficient now, the shape remains,
The rondure brave, the lilied loveliness,
Gold as it was, is, shall be evermore:
Prime nature with an added artistry—
No carat lost, and you have gained a ring.   30

What of it? 'T is a figure, a symbol, say;

---

12 *MS* tears>tear   14 *MS* tap;   20 *MS* {first comma added later}
21 *MS 1868* works.   *1872* works,   *Yale 2* works,>works.   22 *Yale 2* But>
But,   24 *MS* Of   28 *MS* {beginning of fo. 2}   *MS* evermore—
30 *MS* Ring   ⋆31 *MS* {New paragraph (already written thus) indicated by
'N.P.' in left-hand margin. In *1868* and *1872* l. 31 is at the head of p. 3, thus obscuring
the paragraphing. In *1888* and *1889* there is no new paragraph}   *MS* say,

8–30 *There's one trick . . . a ring*: Mairi Calcraft-Rennie suggests that the process of
manufacture is accurately described: 'Wordcraft and the Goldsmiths: Browning and
the Castellani', BSN 23 (1996), 54–66.

23 *repristination*: restoration (to purity, to original state); cf. ll. 685–6. An unusual
word, but compare the use of 'pristine' in, for example, *Sordello*, v. 45, and *Paracelsus*,
iii. 337.

27 *rondure brave*: splendid circle; cf. 'the round' of l. 15.

A thing's sign: now for the thing signified.

Do you see this square old yellow Book, I toss
I' the air, and catch again, and twirl about
By the crumpled vellum covers,—pure crude fact   35
Secreted from man's life when hearts beat hard,
And brains, high-blooded, ticked two centuries since?
Examine it yourselves! I found this book,
Gave a *lira* for it, eightpence English just,
(Mark the predestination!) when a Hand,   40
Always above my shoulder, pushed me once,
One day still fierce 'mid many a day struck calm,
Across a Square in Florence, crammed with booths,

---

33 *MS* {New paragraph (already written thus) indicated by 'N.P.' in left-hand margin}   34 *MS* In>I'   36 *MS* hard   38 *MS* yourselves.   42 *MS* On a>One   43 *MS* Florence

32 *thing signified*: i.e. the image's meaning. The metaphor of the manufacture of the ring is a way of describing the transforming power of Browning's art on his source, the *Old Yellow Book*, hereafter OYB. Gold ore (the 'pure crude fact' of OYB) is mixed with alloy (imagination) and shaped with file and hammer (the poet's art) into a ring (*The Ring and the Book* itself): see ll. 141–6, 364–6, 458–75, 679–706, 1386–9.

33 *old yellow Book*: a unique collection of late seventeenth-century legal pamphlets, in Latin and Italian, bound together in vellum. It is a neat, well-made volume of about 250 pages, probably bound by the Florentine lawyer Francesco Cencini as part of his legal library: see ll. 689–90, 694 nn. Throughout the rest of his life Browning often showed it to friends, and seems usually to have handled it with considerable care, rather than, as here, throwing it in the air: Hodell, 237 n. Some time after Browning's death in 1889, Pen Browning went to stay with Benjamin Jowett and presented OYB to Balliol College, as Browning had intended, where it remains today. Philip Kelley suggests to us that in George Mignaty's oil painting of the drawing-room of Casa Guidi (July 1861) the OYB is just visible as the white volume on the right-hand bookcase. In one of Pen Browning's portraits of his father (1885), which Pen presented to Balliol College, Browning holds OYB proudly on his lap: see also Introduction and Appendix A.

37 *high-blooded*: i.e. of high race, aristocratic.

40 *Hand*: Hand of God (pushing Browning towards OYB). Browning's sense of providence also appears in the quotation he wrote in the front of OYB, from Pindar, *Olympian Odes*, I. 111–12: ἐμοὶ μὲν ὦν Μοῖσα καρτερώτατον βέλος ἀλκᾷ τρέφει: 'The Muse is nourishing for me a spear marvellously valiant and strong'. The *Olympian Odes* are also alluded to at l. 490.

42 *One day*: in June 1860.

43 *Square in Florence*: Piazza San Lorenzo. Browning's Italian guidebook notes that 'by ancient custom it is used as a daily flea market (*mercato de'Rigattieri*)':

Buzzing and blaze, noontide and market-time,
Toward Baccio's marble,—ay, the basement-ledge   45
O' the pedestal where sits and menaces
John of the Black Bands with the upright spear,
'Twixt palace and church,—Riccardi where they lived,
His race, and San Lorenzo where they lie.
This book,—precisely on that palace-step   50

---

44 *MS* {? [ ]>Buzzing   *1868* market-time;   45 *MS* {dash added later}
46 *MS* Of his   47 *MS* {? comma added later}   48 *MS* {dash added
later}   50 *MS* {dash added later}

Federigo Fantozzi, *Nuova guida ovvero descrizione storico-artistico-critica della città e contorni di Firenze* (Florence, 1852), 467. For Browning's copy, see Kelley and Coley, A927. Though Browning left Florence in August 1861 after the death of EBB, and never returned, his love for the city was often in his mind during the early years of his widowerhood in London. Here the exactness of his description of Piazza San Lorenzo and the buying of OYB seems a deliberate act of reminiscence. Compare RB to Isa Blagden, 19 Sept. 1862: 'With respect to Florence, I cannot tell how I feel about it, so do I change in my feelings in the course of a quarter of an hour sometimes: particular incidents in the Florence way of life recur as if I could not bear a repetition of them—to find myself walking among the hills, or turnings by the villas, certain doorways, old walls, points of sight, on a solitary bright summer Sunday afternoon—there, I think that would fairly choke me at once: on the other hand, beginning from another point of association, I have such yearnings to be there!': *Dearest Isa*, 122.

45 *Baccio's marble*: the so-called *Base di San Lorenzo* (It.), a prominent feature of the Piazza San Lorenzo. It is a four-sided cenotaph approximately 16 ft. high, designed by Baccio Bandinelli (1488?–1560) to commemorate Giovanni delle Bande Nere—'John of the Black Bands', l. 47—(1498–1526), the fierce warrior of the Medici family who was the founder of the grand-ducal dynasty of the Medici; hence the Medici are called his 'race' at l. 49. Browning here refers to the bas-relief on the side of the monument which shows Giovanni receiving defeated prisoners and spoils of war. The next two lines (46–7) refer to the grand, seated statue of Giovanni, commander's baton in hand, on top of the cenotaph. Originally intended for this position by Bandinelli, the statue languished in the Palazzo Vecchio until 1850, when it was reunited with its base. Browning's amused attitude towards the statue, and his casual use of Bandinelli's Christian name, derive from his reading of Vasari, who wrote disparagingly of the sculptor in *Vite de' più eccellenti pittori, architetti, e scultori*.

45–6 *basement-ledge / O' the pedestal*: i.e. the lower part of the monument; 'base-ment' was perhaps suggested by *Base*: see previous note.

48–9 *'Twixt palace and church . . . lie*: the monument stands in Piazza San Lorenzo, between the Medici palace (subsequently the Riccardi palace) at the north-east corner, and the Medicis' church of San Lorenzo to the west, where all the principal members of the family, from Cosimo il Vecchio to Cosimo III, lie buried.

Which, meant for lounging knaves o' the Medici,
Now serves re-venders to display their ware,—
'Mongst odds and ends of ravage, picture-frames
White through the worn gilt, mirror-sconces chipped,
Bronze angel-heads once knobs attached to chests,   55
(Handled when ancient dames chose forth brocade)
Modern chalk drawings, studies from the nude,
Samples of stone, jet, breccia, porphyry
Polished and rough, sundry amazing busts
In baked earth, (broken, Providence be praised!)   60
A wreck of tapestry, proudly-purposed web
When reds and blues were indeed red and blue,
Now offered as a mat to save bare feet
(Since carpets constitute a cruel cost)
Treading the chill scagliola bedward: then   65
A pile of brown-etched prints, two *crazie* each,
Stopped by a conch a-top from fluttering forth
—Sowing the Square with works of one and the same
Master, the imaginative Sienese
Great in the scenic backgrounds—(name and fame   70
None of you know, nor does he fare the worse:)

---

51 *MS* of   53 *MS* {beginning of fo. 3}   *MS 1868 1872* 'Mongst   1889
Mongst {a broken sort. There is space for the missing apostrophe}   57 *MS*
chalk-drawings   58 *MS* porphyry,   60 *MS* {no   parentheses}
65 *MS* bedwards>bedward   67 *MS* forth,   68 *MS* {dash added later}
70 *MS* —name   71 *MS* worse:

51 *lounging knaves*: casually waiting servants. The Medici used the palace as their
business headquarters.

52 *re-venders*: perhaps suggested by It. *rivenditori*: sellers, retailers.

54 *mirror-sconces*: ornamental brackets for holding candles, backed with mirrors for
reflecting the light.

58 *breccia*: a kind of marble (as Browning uses it): cf. *Christmas-Eve*, 1292 n.

65 *scagliola*: imitation marble or stone flooring. Browning had it on his bedroom
floor in Casa Guidi.

66 *two crazie*: about $1\frac{1}{2}$ d. in the money of Browning's time. The *crazia* was a Tuscan
copper coin worth one-twelfth of a lira.

69 *imaginative Sienese*: the painter and engraver Luigi Ademollo (1764–1849),
referred to at l. 369. Here, anticipating his later allusion to the artist's obscurity,
Browning does not even name him.

From these . . . Oh, with a Lionard going cheap
If it should prove, as promised, that Joconde
Whereof a copy contents the Louvre!—these
I picked this book from. Five compeers in flank   75
Stood left and right of it as tempting more—
A dogseared Spicilegium, the fond tale
O' the Frail One of the Flower, by young Dumas,
Vulgarized Horace for the use of schools,
The Life, Death, Miracles of Saint Somebody,   80
Saint Somebody Else, his Miracles, Death and Life,—
With this, one glance at the lettered back of which,
And "Stall!" cried I: a *lira* made it mine.

Here it is, this I toss and take again;
Small-quarto size, part print part manuscript: 85
A book in shape but, really, pure crude fact
Secreted from man's life when hearts beat hard,
And brains, high-blooded, ticked two centuries since.
Give it me back! The thing's restorative

---

72 *MS* 'Mongst *MS 1868 1872* . . 74 *MS* Louvre . . 75 *MS* from:
five 77 *MS* famed>fond *MS* Tale 78 *MS* Of *MS* Flower by
80 *MS* {beginning of fo. 4} 81 *MS* else, *MS* Death, Life, 82 *MS*
And this, *MS* {comma at end added in pencil} 84 *MS* {New paragraph
indicated with line and 'N.P.' in left-hand margin} 85 *MS* manuscript, 87 *MS* hard 88 *1872* since *Yale 2* since>since. 89 *MS*
back, the>back! The

---

72 *Lionard*: a painting by Leonardo da Vinci (1452–1519).

73 *Joconde*: the French name for the famous painting known in English-speaking
countries as the Mona Lisa. Dubiously ascribed paintings and copies were the stock-in-
trade of some Florentine picture-dealers; Browning is teasing and ironic about the far-
fetched claim being made here.

77 *Spicilegium*: a collection or anthology, commonly of religious writings, from L.
spīcilegium, a gleaning.

78 *Frail One of the Flower*: La Dame aux Camélias (1848), the popular romantic novel,
or the play of the same name adapted from it (1852), both by Alexandre Dumas fils. In
April 1852 the Brownings saw Dumas's play in Paris and were both deeply moved:
'Even Robert, who gives himself out for *blasé* on dramatic matters, couldn't keep the
tears from rolling down his cheeks': *Letters of EBB*, ii. 66; see also Landis, 181. In his
translation 'Frail One', Browning may be thinking of Verdi's opera *La Traviata* (1853),
based on Dumas's work and hugely popular.

79 *Vulgarized*: i.e. with translation into Italian.

I' the touch and sight.   90

That memorable day,
(June was the month, Lorenzo named the Square)
I leaned a little and overlooked my prize
By the low railing round the fountain-source
Close to the statue, where a step descends: 95
While clinked the cans of copper, as stooped and rose
Thick-ankled girls who brimmed them, and made place
For marketmen glad to pitch basket down,
Dip a broad melon-leaf that holds the wet,
And whisk their faded fresh. And on I read   100
Presently, though my path grew perilous
Between the outspread straw-work, piles of plait
Soon to be flapping, each o'er two black eyes
And swathe of Tuscan hair, on festas fine:
Through fire-irons, tribes of tongs, shovels in sheaves, 105
Skeleton bedsteads, wardrobe-drawers agape,
Rows of tall slim brass lamps with dangling gear,—
And worse, cast clothes a-sweetening in the sun:
None of them took my eye from off my prize.
Still read I on, from written title-page   110
To written index, on, through street and street,

---

90 *MS* In   *MS* of it>and sight   91 *MS* {New paragraph (already written thus) indicated by 'N.P.' in left-hand margin}   95 *MS* descends,   96 *MS* copper as   97 *MS* Thick-ancled   *Yale 1* {'ancled' is underlined in pencil and '?' written in left-hand margin. This pencil correction is similar to those in *Yale 2*}   *MS* them and   102 *MS* straw work,   104 *MS* And a swathe   107 *MS* {beginning of fo. 5}   109 *MS* these>them   *MS* page.>prize.

100 *whisk their faded fresh*: i.e. the men who have come to the market freshen the look of their goods with water from the fountain.

102–3 *straw-work . . . flapping*: plaited straw, laid out on the pavements, soon to be made into the traditional form of Tuscan hats. This is another vivid visual memory. Others noticed the flapping motion: 'The broad-brimmed, high-crowned hat of Tuscan straw is the customary female-headdress,. . . of little use, one would suppose, as a shelter from the sun; the brim continually blowing upward from the face': Hawthorne, 271–2.

105 *fire-irons . . . sheaves*: 'Both here and in Rome, they have this odd custom of offering rusty iron implements for sale, spread out on the pavements': Hawthorne, 413.

108 *cast clothes*: second-hand clothes.

At the Strozzi, at the Pillar, at the Bridge;
Till, by the time I stood at home again
In Casa Guidi by Felice Church,
Under the doorway where the black begins 115
With the first stone-slab of the staircase cold,
I had mastered the contents, knew the whole truth
Gathered together, bound up in this book,
Print three-fifths, written supplement the rest.
"*Romana Homicidiorum*"—nay, 120
Better translate—"A Roman murder-case:
"Position of the entire criminal cause
"Of Guido Franceschini, nobleman,
"With certain Four the cutthroats in his pay,
"Tried, all five, and found guilty and put to death 125
"By heading or hanging as befitted ranks,
"At Rome on February Twenty Two,
"Since our salvation Sixteen Ninety Eight:
"Wherein it is disputed if, and when,
"Husbands may kill adulterous wives, yet 'scape 130
"The customary forfeit."

Word for word,
So ran the title-page: murder, or else
Legitimate punishment of the other crime,

---

112 *MS* Bridge,   114 *MS* Felice's>Felice   116 *MS* stone slab
119 *MS* rest,   120 *MS* no,>nay,   121 *MS* Murder Case   122–
31 *MS* {initial quotation marks added later}   125 *MS* Tried all five
130 *MS* wives yet   132 *MS* {New paragraph break indicated by 'N.P.' in right-
hand margin and line between 'forfeit." and 'Word'}   *MS* for word

    112 *Strozzi, at the Pillar, at the Bridge*: having lingered in Piazza San Lorenzo,
Browning walks south, past the Strozzi palace, and the Pillar of Justice (in Piazza
Santa Trinita), and over the Bridge of Santa Trinita, and so home to Casa Guidi—a
journey of less than a mile.
    115 *black begins*: the immediate entrance hall of Casa Guidi is indeed very dark; this
is another exact memory.
    119 *Print three-fifths*: actually only 13 of the 262 pages are handwritten.
    120 *Romana Homicidiorum*: 'a Roman [case] of Homicides' (L.).
    121–31 *"A Roman . . . forfeit*: a close translation of the handwritten title-page of OYB.
    122 *Position*: an exposition, a setting-forth, from OYB's *Posizione* (It.).

Accounted murder by mistake,—just that   135
And no more, in a Latin cramp enough
When the law had her eloquence to launch,
But interfilleted with Italian streaks
When testimony stooped to mother-tongue,—
That, was this old square yellow book about.   140

Now, as the ingot, ere the ring was forged,
Lay gold, (beseech you, hold that figure fast!)
So, in this book lay absolutely truth,
Fanciless fact, the documents indeed,
Primary lawyer-pleadings for, against,   145
The aforesaid Five; real summed-up circumstance
Adduced in proof of these on either side,
Put forth and printed, as the practice was,
At Rome, in the Apostolic Chamber's type,
And so submitted to the eye o' the Court   150
Presided over by His Reverence
Rome's Governor and Criminal Judge,—the trial
Itself, to all intents, being then as now
Here in the book and nowise out of it;
Seeing, there properly was no judgment-bar,   155
No bringing of accuser and accused,
And whoso judged both parties, face to face
Before some court, as we conceive of courts.
There was a Hall of Justice; that came last:

135 *MS* {beginning of fo. 6}   137 *MS* Law   138 *MS* interfilletted   *MS*
Italian>vulgar>Italian   141 *MS* {New paragraph (already written thus) indicated by 'N.P.' in left-hand margin}   142 *MS* gold (beseech   146 *MS*
Five,   149 *MS* {no commas}   150 *MS* of   152 *MS* Trial
155 *MS* Seeing there   *MS* Judgment-   *MS* seat,>bar,   157 *MS* face to
face,   158 *MS* courts[ ]>courts.   159 *MS* last,

136 *cramp*: 'difficult, knotty': Johnson.
138 *interfilleted*: OED² gives only this instance.
149 *Apostolic Chamber's type*: in OYB each pamphlet ends with 'ROMÆ, Typis
R. Cam. Apost. 1698': 'at Rome, in the type of the Reverend Apostolic Chamber,
1698'.
155 *no judgment-bar*: there were no courtroom scenes. Evidence was presented to
the court in written form, as given in OYB.

For Justice had a chamber by the hall   160
Where she took evidence first, summed up the same,
Then sent accuser and accused alike,
In person of the advocate of each,
To weigh its worth, thereby arrange, array
The battle. 'T was the so-styled Fisc began,   165
Pleaded (and since he only spoke in print
The printed voice of him lives now as then)
The public Prosecutor—"Murder's proved;
"With five . . . what we call qualities of bad,
"Worse, worst, and yet worse still, and still worse yet;   170
"Crest over crest crowning the cockatrice,
"That beggar hell's regalia to enrich
"Count Guido Franceschini: punish him!"
Thus was the paper put before the court
In the next stage, (no noisy work at all,)   175
To study at ease. In due time like reply
Came from the so-styled Patron of the Poor,
Official mouthpiece of the five accused
Too poor to fee a better,—Guido's luck

---

160 *1868* justice   *MS* closet>chamber   161 *MS* {beginning of fo.
7}   164 *MS* the evidence' worth, arrange   *1868 1872* that evidence' worth,
arrange   166 *MS* Pleaded—and   167 *MS* then—   168 *MS* Public
MS {All the quotation marks from here to 213 were added later}   169 *MS 1868*
1872 five . .   170 *MS* yet,   172 *MS* Hell's   174 *MS* Court
175 *MS* —no noisy work at all,—   178 *MS* Five

165 *Fisc*: public prosecutor, from OYB's *fisco*.
169 *qualities*: aggravating circumstances of the murder, from *qualitates* (L. characteristics, conditions), often used in OYB. Arcangeli outlines these at VIII. 1108–381. In
'bad, / Worse, worst' etc. there is a pun on comparative adjectives, which express
degrees of quality.
171–3 *Crest . . . Franceschini*: the imagery connecting 'crest', 'cockatrice', and 'regalia' is from heraldry. The ugly murder is like a cockatrice, a monster represented as a
two-legged dragon (or wyvern) with a cock's head and a barbed tongue, a device used
on coats of arms. A crest is the ornament originally worn by knights on their helmets,
and then represented above the coat of arms. Guido is a nobleman with, metaphori-
cally, the cockatrice (the murder) on his coat of arms, with heraldic crests piled above
it, making his arms ever more hellish, as though he had taken over all the emblems of
Hell (regalia). 'Crest' is also a pun on the comb of the cock (of the cockatrice),
suggesting an overblown cockatrice with multiple crests.

Or else his fellows',—which, I hardly know,—   180
An outbreak as of wonder at the world,
A fury-fit of outraged innocence,
A passion of betrayed simplicity:
"Punish Count Guido? For what crime, what hint
"O' the colour of a crime, inform us first!   185
"Reward him rather! Recognize, we say,
"In the deed done, a righteous judgment dealt!
"All conscience and all courage,—there's our Count
"Charactered in a word; and, what's more strange,
"He had companionship in privilege,   190
"Found four courageous conscientious friends:
"Absolve, applaud all five, as props of law,
"Sustainers of society!—perchance
"A trifle over-hasty with the hand
"To hold her tottering ark, had tumbled else;   195
"But that's a splendid fault whereat we wink,
"Wishing your cold correctness sparkled so!"
Thus paper second followed paper first,
Thus did the two join issue—nay, the four,
Each pleader having an adjunct. "True, he killed   200
"—So to speak—in a certain sort—his wife,

---

180 *MS 1868 1872* fellows', which   *Yale 2* fellows', which>fellows',—which
181 *MS* {line added later}   183 *Yale 2* simplicity:>simplicity.   184 *MS*
cause>hint   185 *MS* Of   187 *MS* dealt:>dealt!   188 *MS*
A....a>All....all   *MS* the man   189 *MS* {line added later}   190 *MS*
{beginning of fo. 8}   *MS* Who>He   *MS* privilege.>privilege,   191 *MS*
{line added later}   *MS Four more with courage and a conscience too:>* Found four
courageous conscientious friends—   *Yale 2* friends:> friends. 192 *MS* Absolve and
praise the Five, law's instruments,>Absolve, applaud all Five, as props of
law,   193 *MS* ;>!   *MS* ! perchance   194 *MS* over hasty 195 *MS*
prop>hold {this change suggests that B had got at least this far before he emended l.
192}   *MS* ark had

195 *her tottering ark*: law's tottering ark, i.e. Roman law, compared with the ark of
the holy covenant in which the tablets of the Mosaic Law were kept. Guido is like
Uzzah, who touched the holy ark to stop it from falling, and was killed by God: 2 Sam.
6: 6–7. The allusion contains an irony unintended by the speaker, for Uzzah acts
impiously. Cf. IV. 834.
   200 *adjunct*: assistant lawyer: Arcangeli has Spreti to help him, and Dr Bottini has
Gambi.

"But laudably, since thus it happed!" quoth one:
Whereat, more witness and the case postponed.
"Thus it happened not, since thus he did the deed,
"And proved himself thereby portentousest   205
"Of cutthroats and a prodigy of crime,
"As the woman that he slaughtered was a saint,
"Martyr and miracle!" quoth the other to match:
Again, more witness, and the case postponed.
"A miracle, ay—of lust and impudence;   210
"Hear my new reasons!" interposed the first:
"—Coupled with more of mine!" pursued his peer.
"Beside, the precedents, the authorities!"
From both at once a cry with an echo, that!
That was a firebrand at each fox's tail   215
Unleashed in a cornfield: soon spread flare enough,
As hurtled thither and there heaped themselves
From earth's four corners, all authority
And precedent for putting wives to death,
Or letting wives live, sinful as they seem.   220
How legislated, now, in this respect,
Solon and his Athenians? Quote the code

---

202 *MS* happed,   208 *MS* miracle,   209 *MS* witness and   210 *MS*
aye   211 *MS* !"—   212 *MS* !"—   214 *MS* A cry from both at
once>From both at once a cry   215 *MS* foxes   216 *MS* —>:
218 *MS* {beginning of fo. 9}   220 *MS* live sinful   221 *MS* legislated
they,>legislated, now,

205 *portentousest*: 'Browning uses the superlative inflection more freely than other
modern writers (except perhaps Carlyle), more freely even than Shakespeare': Cook, 10.
    213 *precedents*: the opposing lawyers in OYB cite extensively their legal precedents
from Roman law and the Italian jurists, these being given in abbreviated form in italic
type. Of the precedents and authorities in the following passage, all but Ælian (l. 232)
occurs in the first two pamphlets of OYB, and in roughly the order Browning refers to
them here.
    215 *firebrand . . . tail*: cf. Judg. 15: 4–5: in anger at his father-in-law, Samson captured
300 foxes, turned pairs of foxes tail to tail, tied a firebrand between each pair of tails,
and let them loose through the Philistines' cornfields. The legal precedents are like the
firebrands tied to the tails of the foxes (the pairs of lawyers). As the lawyers run hither
and thither with their pleadings, the precedents (like firebrands) ignite a great and
confusing fire of argument.
    222–3 *Solon . . . Rome*: these examples are given by the defence lawyer Arcangeli,
OYB x (12): '[The killing of adulterous wives] was sanctioned in the laws of the

Of Romulus and Rome! Justinian speak!
Nor modern Baldo, Bartolo be dumb!
The Roman voice was potent, plentiful;   225
Cornelia de Sicariis hurried to help
Pompeia de Parricidiis; Julia de
Something-or-other jostled *Lex* this-and-that;
King Solomon confirmed Apostle Paul:
That nice decision of Dolabella, eh?   230
That pregnant instance of Theodoric, oh!
Down to that choice example Ælian gives
(An instance I find much insisted on)

223 *MS* Justinian, speak!   228 *MS* Something or other jostled *Lex* this and that.

Athenians and of Solon (the wisest of legislators), and what is more, even in the rude age of Romulus, law 15, where we read: "A man and his relatives may kill as they wish a wife convicted of adultery".'

223 *Justinian*: emperor (AD 482–565) who ordered the great compendium of Roman law, the *Pandects* (533), and also the short guide, the *Institutes*. The laws mentioned in ll. 226–8 are in both works.

224 *Baldo, Bartolo*: fourteenth-century Italian legal authorities, often cited by the lawyers in OYB.

226–8 *Cornelia de Sicariis . . . Something-or-other*: three of the laws most often cited in the arguments of OYB, where the case hinges on justifications for murder in response to presumed adultery. *Lex Cornelia de sicariis* (Cornelius' [Sulla's] law on murderers) 'pursues murderers with an avenging sword'; *lex Pompeia de parricidiis* (Pompey's law on parricide) applied to the murder of relatives, or, as in this case, spouses; *lex Julia de adulteriis* (Julius' [Augustus'] law on adulterers) 'punishes with death those guilty of adultery': *Institutes of Justinian*, iv. 18.

229 *Solomon . . . Paul*: Browning is being sarcastic: the lawyers cite Old and New Testament texts in confused and unlikely ways.

230 *nice decision of Dolabella*: faced with a revenge murder, in which a wife had killed her husband and their son because her husband had killed a son from her first marriage, the Proconsul Dolabella passed the case to the Areopagus; it was in fact the Areopagus that made the nice decision 'that she and her accuser should come back in a hundred years' time'. The case is cited by Arcangeli in defence of Guido's 'just anger': OYB xxii (22).

231 *pregnant instance of Theodoric*: the lawyer Spreti cites Theodoric's words in Guido's defence: '"Bulls defend their cows with their horns, rams fight with their heads for their ewes, horses vindicate their mares with kicks and bites . . . . How then can a man endure to leave adultery unavenged?"': OYB xxviii (28–9).

232 *choice example Ælian gives*: in Aelian's *De Natura Animalium* (*c.* AD 200), xi. 15: 'An elephant punishes adultery'. The pro-Guido pamphleteer refers to this story in deadly earnest at OYB cxlv (149); Browning's reference here is ironically humorous, the culmination of the sense of the absurdity of the lawyers' citation of authorities conveyed in this passage. Aelian was well known to both Brownings and is referred to in the love correspondence; see also *Aurora Leigh*, i. 714 n.

Of the elephant who, brute-beast though he were,
Yet understood and punished on the spot   235
His master's naughty spouse and faithless friend;
A true tale which has edified each child,
Much more shall flourish favoured by our court!
Pages of proof this way, and that way proof,
And always—once again the case postponed.   240

Thus wrangled, brangled, jangled they a month,
—Only on paper, pleadings all in print,
Nor ever was, except i' the brains of men,
More noise by word of mouth than you hear now—
Till the court cut all short with "Judged, your cause.   245
"Receive our sentence! Praise God! We pronounce
"Count Guido devilish and damnable:
"His wife Pompilia in thought, word and deed,
"Was perfect pure, he murdered her for that:
"As for the Four who helped the One, all Five—   250
"Why, let employer and hirelings share alike
"In guilt and guilt's reward, the death their due!"

So was the trial at end, do you suppose?
"Guilty you find him, death you doom him to?
"Ay, were not Guido, more than needs, a priest,   255
"Priest and to spare!"—this was a shot reserved;
I learn this from epistles which begin

---

234 *MS* was,>were,   236 *MS* wife>spouse   *MS* friend—   238 *MS*
^shall^   *MS* Judge.—>court!   239 *MS* way and>way, and   *MS* proof—>
proof,   *241 *MS* {no new paragraph}   *1868 1872* {new paragraph. Paragraphing obscured in *1888* and *1889* by this line's being at the head of the page}   242 *MS*
{? dash added later}   243 *MS* in>i'   245 *MS* {beginning of fo.
10}   *MS* cause!   246–75 *MS* {quotation marks throughout added later}
246 *MS* sentence. Praise God.   252 *MS* Guilt and that>In guilt and
253 *MS* {New paragraph indicated by 'N.P.' in left-hand margin and line between
252 and 253}   *MS* Trial   255 *MS* Priest   256 *MS* reserved,   257 *MS*
the letters

---

241 *wrangled, brangled, jangled*: synonyms of 'argued': a learned flourish.
257 *epistles*: at OYB ccxxxv–ccxl (235–8): the three, handwritten letters are the
source for Arcangeli's last attempt to save Guido from execution by claiming 'Chier-
icato' (priestly status): that because Guido was partially a priest he could not be executed.

Here where the print ends,—see the pen and ink
Of the advocate, the ready at a pinch!—
"My client boasts the clerkly privilege,   260
"Has taken minor orders many enough,
"Shows still sufficient chrism upon his pate
"To neutralize a blood-stain: *presbyter*,
"*Primæ tonsuræ, subdiaconus*,
"*Sacerdos*, so he slips from underneath   265
"Your power, the temporal, slides inside the robe
"Of mother Church: to her we make appeal
"By the Pope, the Church's head!"

                                    A parlous plea,
Put in with noticeable effect, it seems;   270
"Since straight,"—resumes the zealous orator,
Making a friend acquainted with the facts,—
"Once the word 'clericality' let fall,
"Procedure stopped and freer breath was drawn
"By all considerate and responsible Rome."   275
Quality took the decent part, of course;
Held by the husband, who was noble too:
Or, for the matter of that, a churl would side

259 *MS* Advocate   *MS* ,>!   262 *MS* his curls   267 *MS* Mother
268 *MS* Churches Head!   *MS* {New paragraph break indicated with 'N.P.' in
right-hand margin}   269 *Yale 1* parlour>parlous   270 *MS* seems,
271 *MS* man of law   273 *MS* {line added later}   *MS* {beginning of fo. 11}
276 *MS* course,   277 *MS* ^the^   *MS* too,

262 *chrism*: holy oil, used in consecrating priests.

263–5 *presbyter . . . Sacerdos*: presbyter, new-tonsured, subdeacon, priest (L.): an inaccurate list of 'minor orders', but at this point Browning is inventing speech for Arcangeli and being impressionistic.

269 *parlous*: risky.

271 *zealous orator*: Arcangeli, continuing on ll. 254–68. In OYB it is in fact Carlo Ugolinucci's letter that gives the information here; Browning simply conflates this letter with Arcangeli's letter to his friend Cencini shortly before it: OYB ccxxxix (238).

276 *Quality*: people of rank, the upper classes. Cf. 'Up at a Villa—Down in the City (As distinguished by an Italian person of quality)'. Browning, a liberal, takes a sceptical view of the social structure he creates in the poem, seeing aristocracy or allegiance to aristocracy as warping people's ability to see the truth of the murder-case. The lines here ironize the Quality's viewpoint, particularly their anti-Semitism.

With too-refined susceptibility,
And honour which, tender in the extreme,   280
Stung to the quick, must roughly right itself
At all risks, not sit still and whine for law
As a Jew would, if you squeezed him to the wall,
Brisk-trotting through the Ghetto. Nay, it seems,
Even the Emperor's Envoy had his say   285
To say on the subject; might not see, unmoved,
Civility menaced throughout Christendom
By too harsh measure dealt her champion here.
Lastly, what made all safe, the Pope was kind,
From his youth up, reluctant to take life,   290
If mercy might be just and yet show grace;
Much more unlikely then, in extreme age,
To take a life the general sense bade spare.
'Twas plain that Guido would go scatheless yet.

But human promise, oh, how short of shine!   295
How topple down the piles of hope we rear!
How history proves . . . nay, read Herodotus!
Suddenly starting from a nap, as it were,
A dog-sleep with one shut, one open orb,

---

279 *MS* too refined   280 *MS* And>With   283 *MS* would if   *MS* wall   284 *MS* seems   286 *MS* subject, might not see unmoved 288 *MS* here: 289–93 {not found in *MS*}   295 *MS* {New paragraph indicated by 'N.P.' in left-hand margin and line between 294 and 295}   *MS* short of shine turns shade!>oh, how brief of shine!>oh, how short of shine! 296 {not found in *MS*}   297 *MS* but>nay,   299 *MS* dogs' sleep>dog-sleep   *MS* eye>orb

---

285 *Emperor's Envoy*: the arrogant Count Martinitz, ambassador of the Holy Roman Emperor Leopold I. His words are imagined at XII. 96–7.

287 *Civility*: the civilized ideal; here implicitly personified by the Quality (the upper classes), 'the nice and cultivated everywhere': XII. 278. Browning's use is ironic.

297 *Herodotus*: (*c*.484–425 BC), the Greek historian. In his *Histories* he shows the uncertainties of human life, particularly in the case of Xerxes, the Persian king, who was certain of victory over the Greeks, and then defeated. There is a ludicrous humour in seeing Guido's failure to avoid the death-sentence in the epic context of battles like Marathon and Salamis.

299 *dog-sleep*: a light or feigned sleep, 'in reference to the light sleeping of dogs, and the difficulty of telling whether, when their eyes are shut, they are asleep or not': OED[2]. The Pope is far from senile, as Guido supposes.

Cried the Pope's great self,—Innocent by name   300
And nature too, and eighty-six years old,
Antonio Pignatelli of Naples, Pope
Who had trod many lands, known many deeds,
Probed many hearts, beginning with his own,
And now was far in readiness for God,—   305
'T was he who first bade leave those souls in peace,
Those Jansenists, re-nicknamed Molinists,

300 *MS* {dash added later}   301 *MS* too and eighty six   302 *MS* one>
Pope   303 *MS* trod>seen>trod   *MS* known>rued>known   *MS* men>
deeds   304 *MS* hearts beginning   306 *1868 1872* 'Twas   *MS* peace
307 *MS* {beginning of fo. 12}   *MS* Molinists

300 *Innocent*: Antonio Pignatelli (1615–1700), who became Pope Innocent XII in 1691.

303 *trod many lands*: Pignatelli, from the south of Italy, had served the Church in Malta, northern Italy, Poland, and Vienna. Cf. *Odyssey* i. 3.

307 *Jansenists, re-nicknamed Molinists*: 're-nicknamed' is historically misleading, since Jansenism and Molinism were distinct movements, but Browning's point is that one heretical movement or sect replaces another as the focus of society's casual abuse, and that Pope Innocent XII, in his goodness, refused to participate in easy persecution of such sects.

Jansenism and Quietism (the historically more accurate term for Molinism) were seventeenth-century reforming movements within the Roman Catholic Church that it judged heretical. Cornelius Jansen (1585–1638) was a Dutch theologian who held quasi-Calvinistic views of divine grace and human depravity; his followers tended to think in terms of predestination, and lived austerely. The first flourishing of Jansenism was in the 1640s onwards. Miguel de Molinos (1627–96), the founder of the sect that Browning imagines as Molinists, arrived in Rome from Spain in 1663, and began teaching a form of mental prayer while at the same time deprecating a range of more normal Catholic practice: attendance at sacraments, charitable actions, vocal prayers, etc. He was arrested in 1685, his personal life censured, and his quietist teaching judged heretical. He died in prison in Rome in 1696, while Guido and the Comparini were battling each other in the law courts.

Browning makes Molinism a phenomenon in his story. 'Molinist' is used by most characters as a catchword of simple abuse, showing how they have accepted unthinkingly what is passed down from above. Jansenism and Molinism had little in common, and Browning's juxtaposition of them shows his Protestant-liberal thinking. Himself a Nonconformist in religion, he sees them as independent-minded sects at odds with the potentially stifling effects of Catholicism. In the poem Molinism is almost a synonym for Nonconformity being suppressed by a falsely authoritative Catholic Church. The Molinists have made a quasi-Protestant act of 'private judgement': through the poem we see the tyranny of Church and society trying to crush this. Here it is a mark of the Pope's integrity that he does not vilify Molinism. Cf. l. 315 n. See also William Coyle, 'Molinos: "The Subject of the Day" in *The Ring and the Book*', PMLA 67 (1952), 308–14.

('Gainst whom the cry went, like a frowsy tune,
Tickling men's ears—the sect for a quarter of an hour
I' the teeth of the world which, clown-like, loves to chew
Be it but a straw 'twixt work and whistling-while,   311
Taste some vituperation, bite away,
Whether at marjoram-sprig or garlic-clove,
Aught it may sport with, spoil, and then spit forth)
"Leave them alone," bade he, "those Molinists!   315
"Who may have other light than we perceive,
"Or why is it the whole world hates them thus?"
Also he peeled off that last scandal-rag
Of Nepotism; and so observed the poor
That men would merrily say, "Halt, deaf and blind,   320
"Who feed on fat things, leave the master's self
"To gather up the fragments of his feast,
"These be the nephews of Pope Innocent!—
"His own meal costs but five carlines a day,

308–14 MS {lines added later, 308 interlined, 309–14 in margin with note by B
"Insert underneath"}   308 MS fetid tune   310 MS In   MS clown
like 311 MS flower>straw   MS 1868 1872 twixt   MS whistling while—
315 MS {line not found}   316 MS perceive.   317 MS {line added
later}   MS so>thus   319 MS the Pope's Nephews:>Nepotism;   MS
loved>observed   320 MS say "Halt   321 MS on the>on   MS master
then>master's self   *323 1888 1889 'These {a misprint or broken sort}
324 MS Whose own meal costs us

308 frowsy: tawdry, old.
311 'twixt work and whistling-while: between work and play, i.e. at odd moments.
315 "Leave . . . Molinists: this is unhistorical. Browning seems to have transferred to
Molinism what he thought of as Innocent XII's tolerance towards Jansenism: 'Innocent XII forbade the Archbishop of Malines from troubling certain people about some
vague accusations of Jansenism and heresy, when those people had not been legally
convicted of fidelity to censured errors': Biographie universelle, xxi. 247.
319 Nepotism: Innocent XII's Bull of 1692 severely limited the power of the pope to
favour his relations with church positions. The original meaning of nepotism—from
the L. nepos (grandson, nephew)—was the practice, on the part of the Popes or other
ecclesiastics, of showing special favour to nephews or other relatives in conferring offices.
observed: paid attention to.
320 Halt: lame.
323 nephews of Pope Innocent: i.e. the poor and infirm (not his own relations) get
Innocent's care and money. In a joke against nepotism, Innocent referred to the poor
as his 'nephews'. The humour here is that the traditional picture of the poor and weak
picking up crumbs from the rich man's table is reversed.
324 carlines: a carlino was a Neapolitan silver coin of small value.

"Poor-priest's allowance, for he claims no more."   325
—He cried of a sudden, this great good old Pope,
When they appealed in last resort to him,
"I have mastered the whole matter: I nothing doubt.
"Though Guido stood forth priest from head to heel,
"Instead of, as alleged, a piece of one,—   330
"And further, were he, from the tonsured scalp
"To the sandaled sole of him, my son and Christ's,
"Instead of touching us by finger-tip
"As you assert, and pressing up so close
"Only to set a blood-smutch on our robe,—   335
"I and Christ would renounce all right in him.
"Am I not Pope, and presently to die,
"And busied how to render my account,
"And shall I wait a day ere I decide
"On doing or not doing justice here?   340
"Cut off his head to-morrow by this time,
"Hang up his four mates, two on either hand,
"And end one business more!"

                              So said, so done—
Rather so writ, for the old Pope bade this,   345
I find, with his particular chirograph,
His own no such infirm hand, Friday night;
And next day, February Twenty Two,
Since our salvation Sixteen Ninety Eight,
—Not at the proper head-and-hanging-place   350

326 *MS* same>great   *MS* Pope>Prince>Pope   328 *MS* and>: I   330 *MS*
one,   333 *MS* by the   335 *MS* robe,   343 *MS* {beginning of fo.
13}   344 *MS* {New paragraph break indicated by 'N.P.' in right-hand margin and
line between 343 and 344}   345 *MS* wrote this,   347 *MS* :>;   350 *MS*
{dash added later}   *MS* by>at

  335 *blood-smutch*: slight mark or stain of blood.
  346 *chirograph*: handwriting. The phrase here is a direct translation of 'con Chirografo particolare': OYB ccxxxv (235). From its etymology Browning seems to take
chirograph to mean 'handwriting', perhaps unaware that it is a specific name for one
kind of papal document: see OED² 1.d.
  350 *Not at the proper head-and-hanging-place*: i.e. not near Ponte Sant'Angelo; rather
the execution took place at the north end of the city, the Piazza del Popolo. The

On bridge-foot close by Castle Angelo,
Where custom somewhat staled the spectacle,
('Twas not so well i' the way of Rome, beside,
The noble Rome, the Rome of Guido's rank)
But at the city's newer gayer end,—   355
The cavalcading promenading place
Beside the gate and opposite the church
Under the Pincian gardens green with Spring,
'Neath the obelisk 'twixt the fountains in the Square,
Did Guido and his fellows find their fate,   360
All Rome for witness, and—my writer adds—
Remonstrant in its universal grief,
Since Guido had the suffrage of all Rome.

This is the bookful; thus far take the truth,
The untempered gold, the fact untampered with,   365
The mere ring-metal ere the ring be made!
And what has hitherto come of it? Who preserves
The memory of this Guido, and his wife

---

351 *MS* At>On   *MS* the Bridge-foot by   352 *MS* show—beside>spec-
tacle,   353 *MS* {bracket added later}   *MS* in   *MS* noble Rome>Rome,
beside)—>Rome, beside,   354 *MS* {line added later}   355 *MS* City's
MS {dash added later}   359 *MS* By the middle of the Square, Del Popolo,
>By the obelisk 'twixt the fountains in the Square,   360 *MS* meet their
death>find their fate,   362 *MS* Remonstrance>Remonstrant   363 *MS*
passed for a wronged man in>had the suffrage of all   364 *MS* {New paragraph
indicated with line and 'N.P.' in left-hand margin}   365 *MS* and>the
366 *MS* the ring be>a ring is>the ring be   *MS* made.   367 *MS* {New paragraph (already written thus) indicated by 'N.P.' in left-hand margin}   368 *MS*
Guido and

---

emphasis on the change of location is an addition to OYB. Browning makes the place
of execution a quasi-democratic gesture by the Pope against the corrupt aristocracy:
see XII. 106–9, 308–13.

355 *city's newer gayer end*: the Piazza del Popolo. The description in the next four
lines is anachronistic; Browning is really describing the piazza as it was in the 1850s.
The drive up to the Pincian Hill from the piazza, and the beautiful gardens on the hill,
were mainly developed in the 19th century. Only then could this end of the city aptly
be described as the 'cavalcading promenading place': see Treves, 148; and also Nathaniel Hawthorne, *The Marble Faun* (1860), ch. 12.

362 *Remonstrant*: protesting, reproachful; derived from OED² *remonstrate* v. 2.a.

363 *suffrage*: support.

Pompilia, more than Ademollo's name,
The etcher of those prints, two *crazie* each,   370
Saved by a stone from snowing broad the Square
With scenic backgrounds? Was this truth of force?
Able to take its own part as truth should,
Sufficient, self-sustaining? Why, if so—
Yonder's a fire, into it goes my book,   375
As who shall say me nay, and what the loss?
You know the tale already: I may ask,
Rather than think to tell you, more thereof,—
Ask you not merely who were he and she,
Husband and wife, what manner of mankind,   380
But how you hold concerning this and that
Other yet-unnamed actor in the piece.
The young frank handsome courtly Canon, now,
The priest, declared the lover of the wife,
He who, no question, did elope with her,   385
For certain bring the tragedy about,
Giuseppe Caponsacchi;—his strange course
I' the matter, was it right or wrong or both?
Then the old couple, slaughtered with the wife
By the husband as accomplices in crime,   390
Those Comparini, Pietro and his spouse,—
What say you to the right or wrong of that,
When, at a known name whispered through the door
Of a lone villa on a Christmas night,
It opened that the joyous hearts inside   395

---

369 *MS* Pompilia more   *MS* name>fame,>name,   370 *MS* That>The
MS prints two *crazie* each   371 *MS* {beginning of fo. 14}   *MS* white>broad
375 *MS* the>my   *MS* book   376 *MS* what's   *MS* your>the   377 *MS*
ask   378 *MS* ^to tell^   *MS* {dash added later}   379 *MS* this,>
you   382 *MS* actors   *MS* piece: 383 *MS* bright>frank 384 *MS*
priest declared   386 *MS* bring>brought>bring   387 *MS* {dash added
later}   388 *MS* In   *MS* —>,   389 *MS* couple slaughtered

369 *Ademollo's name*: referring back to ll. 68–71.
372 *Was this truth of force?*: Was this truth strong? compelling (beyond its own
historical time)? Cf. Heb. 9: 17: 'For a testament is of force after men are dead.'

Might welcome as it were an angel-guest
Come in Christ's name to knock and enter, sup
And satisfy the loving ones he saved;
And so did welcome devils and their death?
I have been silent on that circumstance   400
Although the couple passed for close of kin
To wife and husband, were by some accounts
Pompilia's very parents: you know best.
Also that infant the great joy was for,
That Gaetano, the wife's two-weeks' babe,   405
The husband's first-born child, his son and heir,
Whose birth and being turned his night to day—
Why must the father kill the mother thus
Because she bore his son and saved himself?

Well, British Public, ye who like me not,   410
(God love you!) and will have your proper laugh
At the dark question, laugh it! I laugh first.
Truth must prevail, the proverb vows; and truth

396 *MS* angel guest   *Yale 1* angel guest>angel-guest   398 *MS* {beginning
of fo. 15}   *MS* saved,   403 *MS* parents—   404 *MS* that the joy>the
great joy   *MS* for   405 *MS* two-weeks   407 *MS* being had turned
410 *MS* {New paragraph indicated with line and 'N.P.' in left-hand
margin}   411 *MS* usual laugh>laugh beside   412 *MS* do so>laugh it!
413 *MS* Here's Truth and prevalent, as the proverb runs:>Truth must prevail—the
proverb vows, and truth

396 *angel-guest*: cf. Heb. 13: 2: 'Be not forgetful to entertain strangers: for thereby
some have entertained angels unawares.'

409 *saved himself*: the meaning here is deliberately obscure, part of the poet's teasing
address to his audience. We only learn later that the birth of a son 'saved' Guido in the
sense that, regardless of the conflicting lawsuits over the dowry money, through his
heir he would capture the Comparini's wealth.

410 *British Public, ye who like me not*: Browning's work was still neglected at the
beginning of the 1860s; *Men and Women*, for example, had not gone into a second
edition. His reputation grew modestly from 1863 onwards with the publication of
Selections and *Poetical Works* in 1863, *Dramatis Personæ* in 1864, and *Poetical Works* and
Moxon's *Selection* in 1865, but reviews spoke of him as an 'unpopular' poet and were
sometimes hostile. In January 1867 Browning described himself wryly to Euphemia
Millais as 'the most unpopular poet that ever was': J. G. Millais, *The Life and Letters of
Sir John Everett Millais* (2 vols., 1899), i. 440. Here he is teasing and ironic about his
relative unpopularity, flaunting it in the face of his readers. See also C. C. Watkins,
'Browning's "Fame Within These Four Years"', MLR 53 (1958), 492–500.

—Here is it all i' the book at last, as first
There it was all i' the heads and hearts of Rome   415
Gentle and simple, never to fall nor fade
Nor be forgotten. Yet, a little while,
The passage of a century or so,
Decads thrice five, and here's time paid his tax,
Oblivion gone home with her harvesting,   420
And all left smooth again as scythe could shave.
Far from beginning with you London folk,
I took my book to Rome first, tried truth's power
On likely people. "Have you met such names?
"Is a tradition extant of such facts?   425
"Your law-courts stand, your records frown a-row:
"What if I rove and rummage?" "—Why, you'll waste
"Your pains and end as wise as you began!"
Everyone snickered: "names and facts thus old
"Are newer much than Europe news we find   430

414 *MS* {dash added later}   *MS* in   415 *MS* in   416 *MS* and> nor
417 *MS* And>Nor   *MS* forgotten: yet,   420 *MS* {line added later}   *MS*
off>home   421 *MS* And all smooth shaven as the scythe will play.>And all left
smooth again as scythe would shave.   422 *MS* folk   424 *MS* On the
likely   425–56 *MS* {quotation marks added later}   425 *MS* no tradition
426 *MS* a-row,   *MS* {beginning of fo. 16}   427 *MS* "Why,   428 *MS*
began,"   430 *MS* Europe's

415–16 *Rome / Gentle and simple*: upper- and lower-class Rome.

419–21 *time . . . shave*: Oblivion (the state of something being forgotten) personified
as a female reaper, pays Time (a masculine figure) a tithe of events (the harvest), before
carrying off all the rest of them: the field of history is cleared, as though the murder-
case had never happened at all. Cf. *Troilus and Cressida*, III. iii. 145–6.

422 *Far from beginning*: the following description of enquiries made in Rome presumably relates to the winter of 1860–1. An echo of ll. 433–8 below is in a letter from
Browning to W. C. Cartwright of *c.* June 1865, which suggests that, in casual enquiries,
Browning did meet opposition as a Protestant investigating a long-forgotten legal case:
see General Introduction, xxi. Mrs Orr, however, believed this passage indicated 'a
purely imaginative process', perhaps because she conceived his researches in more formal
terms: 'Had Browning really gone to Rome and "tried truth's power" in the manner
supposed—if he had even done it while spending his last winter there—we should have
had letters, fragments of conversation, a whole chapter of biography. Every friend of his
in London who was interested in his work would have heard of it; I could not have failed
to do so': Mrs Orr to W. H. Griffin, 25 Mar. 1897: Griffin Collections, vi. 62.

427 *rove*: search in a random way.

429 *snickered*: laughed in a half-suppressed or mischievous way. Cf. 'The Heretic's
Tragedy', 70.

"Down in to-day's *Diario*. Records, quotha?
"Why, the French burned them, what else do the French?
"The rap-and-rending nation! And it tells
"Against the Church, no doubt,—another gird
"At the Temporality, your Trial, of course?"   435
"—Quite otherwise this time," submitted I;
"Clean for the Church and dead against the world,
"The flesh and the devil, does it tell for once."
"—The rarer and the happier! All the same,
"Content you with your treasure of a book,   440
"And waive what's wanting! Take a friend's advice!
"It's not the custom of the country. Mend
"Your ways indeed and we may stretch a point:
"Go get you manned by Manning and new-manned
"By Newman and, mayhap, wise-manned to boot   445

431 *MS* In our>Down in   *MS Diario*: records,   434 *MS* {dash added later}
435 *MS* Temporalities>Temporality   436 *MS* {dash added later}   *MS* time"
submitted   437 *MS* world   439 *MS* {dash added later}   441 *MS*
wanting: take>wanting! Take   *MS* advice:>advice!   442 *MS* country:
mend   443 *MS* might>may   *MS* point.

431 *Diario*: *Diario Romano*, in Browning's time Rome's second, less good newspaper, after the *Giornale di Roma*.
quotha?: do you say?
432–3 *French ... nation*: the French occupied Rome from 1849 to 1870 (with a
break in 1867), supporting the Pope's temporal rule against his popular and national
enemies. The speakers' remark that the French have burned the legal records is most
likely casual exaggeration, but it is coloured by old Roman resentments: the looting by
the French in 1798 after Napoleon's victories in Italy, and more recent damage caused
during their siege of 1849.
433 *rap-and-rending*: looting, destroying (archaic); cf. *Fifine at the Fair*, 'Epilogue', 13.
434 *gird*: attack, gibe.
435 *Temporality*: the lands over which the Church exercised political ('temporal')
rule, with the Pope as head of state. These were drastically reduced in 1860 but still
comprised Rome and the Patrimony of St Peter. When this political rule ended
in 1870 Browning spoke of 'the extinguishment of this inveterate nuisance': *Dearest
Isa*, 348.
442–3 *Mend / Your ways*: i.e. become a convert to Catholicism.
444–6 *Manning ... Wiseman*: exuberant word-play on the names of the most famous
nineteenth-century English Catholic priests, Henry Manning, John Henry Newman,
and Nicholas Wiseman, all of whom became cardinals. Manning and Newman were
notable converts. Browning saw 'not a little' of Manning at Rome in the winter
of 1859–60. He heard Cardinal Wiseman lecture at the Royal Institution in January

"By Wiseman, and we'll see or else we won't!
"Thanks meantime for the story, long and strong,
"A pretty piece of narrative enough,
"Which scarce ought so to drop out, one would think,
"From the more curious annals of our kind.   450
"Do you tell the story, now, in off-hand style,
"Straight from the book? Or simply here and there,
"(The while you vault it through the loose and large)
"Hang to a hint? Or is there book at all,
"And don't you deal in poetry, make-believe,   455
"And the white lies it sounds like?"

                                   Yes and no!
From the book, yes; thence bit by bit I dug
The lingot truth, that memorable day,
Assayed and knew my piecemeal gain was gold,—   460
Yes; but from something else surpassing that,
Something of mine which, mixed up with the mass,
Made it bear hammer and be firm to file.
Fancy with fact is just one fact the more;
To-wit, that fancy has informed, transpierced,   465
Thridded and so thrown fast the facts else free,
As right through ring and ring runs the djereed

447 *MS* but>and   448 *MS* enough   449 *MS* thus have dropt>so to drop
452 *MS* there   453 *MS* {beginning of fo. 17}   *MS* "The.... large,
454 *MS* there a book at all   455 *MS* make-believe?>make-believe,
456 *MS* It sounds so—come be candid>It sounds so,—come, be candid>And the
white lies it sounds like?"   457 {New paragraph indicated with 'N.P.' in left-
hand margin}   459 *MS* entire>lingot   *MS* on that>that   460 *MS*
{comma added later}   466 *MS* fastened so>so thrown fast   467 *MS* fifty
rings>ring and ring

1863. Newman's name was kept in his mind by the controversy over the *Apologia Pro
Vita Sua* (1864): see *Wedgwood*, 89–90, 93.

453 *vault...large*: move swiftly and freely, from point to point, through the ram-
bling and long [book].

459 *lingot*: ingot (from the French): cf. *Aurora Leigh*, vii. 1124.

465–6 *informed, transpierced, / Thridded .. thrown fast*: pervaded, penetrated, threaded,
given form to; leading to the image of the djereed.

467 *djereed*: a wooden spear with which Arab horsemen would catch up wooden
rings at a gallop. The *MS* reading, 'As right through fifty rings...', shows the

And binds the loose, one bar without a break.
I fused my live soul and that inert stuff,
Before attempting smithcraft, on the night   470
After the day when,—truth thus grasped and gained,—
The book was shut and done with and laid by
On the cream-coloured massive agate, broad
'Neath the twin cherubs in the tarnished frame
O' the mirror, tall thence to the ceiling-top.   475
And from the reading, and that slab I leant
My elbow on, the while I read and read,
I turned, to free myself and find the world,
And stepped out on the narrow terrace, built
Over the street and opposite the church,   480
And paced its lozenge-brickwork sprinkled cool;
Because Felice-church-side stretched, a-glow
Through each square window fringed for festival,
Whence came the clear voice of the cloistered ones
Chanting a chant made for midsummer nights—   485
I know not what particular praise of God,

---

469 *MS* w>and   *MS* stuff   475 *MS* Of   476 *MS* and>from   479 *MS*
terrace built   480 *MS* church   481 *MS* {beginning of fo. 18}   *MS*
lozenge brickwork   *MS* cool,   482 *MS* {comma added later}

---

excitement of the image. Fancy (imagination) pierces through all the loose and random
facts of the story—like the spear through the rings—and so gives them form.

473 *massive agate*: the fireplace, still in place today. After EBB's death in June 1861,
Browning tried to have the rooms at Casa Guidi photographed as a momento, and
when this proved unsuccessful he commissioned George Mignaty, the Greek artist—
one of his circle in Florence—to do a detailed oil painting of the drawing-room (July
1861). This passage seems partly in the same spirit of reminiscence, a detailed recollection of the drawing-room and the balcony, one of the happiest spaces of Browning's
life. The painting, now at Mills College, Oakland, Calif., has been variously reproduced.

475 *mirror*: this large, gilded, baroque mirror, immediately above the fireplace, was
one of the most expensive pieces that the Brownings bought for Casa Guidi.

479 *narrow terrace*: 'There's the plan of the apartment! The eight windows which are
very large, opening from ceiling to floor, open on a sort of balcony-terrace .. not quite
a terrace, yet no ordinary balcony neither .. which is built out from the house, giving it
an antique & picturesque appearance to the exterior. [. . .] Opposite is the grey wall of a
church, San Felice, and we walk on the balcony listening to the organ & choir': EBB
to Arabel Moulton-Barrett, 26 July 1847: Berg Collection, New York Public Library.

It always came and went with June. Beneath
I' the street, quick shown by openings of the sky
When flame fell silently from cloud to cloud,
Richer than that gold snow Jove rained on Rhodes,   490
The townsmen walked by twos and threes, and talked,
Drinking the blackness in default of air—
A busy human sense beneath my feet:
While in and out the terrace-plants, and round
One branch of tall datura, waxed and waned   495
The lamp-fly lured there, wanting the white flower.
Over the roof o' the lighted church I looked
A bowshot to the street's end, north away
Out of the Roman gate to the Roman road
By the river, till I felt the Apennine.   500
And there would lie Arezzo, the man's town,
The woman's trap and cage and torture-place,
Also the stage where the priest played his part,
A spectacle for angels,—ay, indeed,
There lay Arezzo! Farther then I fared,   505
Feeling my way on through the hot and dense,

488 MS In   MS ^quick^   MS sky>heaven   489 MS silently>silent>
silently   491 MS {commas added later}   493 MS between>beneath   MS
feet,   496 MS lampfly   497 MS of   498 MS end   north
500 MS Apennine,   503 MS part   504 MS {dash added later}
506 MS ^way^   MS dense

490 *gold snow*: recalling Pindar, *Olympian Odes*, 7. 34: βρέχε θεῶν βασιλεὺς ὁ
μέγας χρυσέαις νιφάδεσσι πόλιν: 'the great King of the gods showered the city
with golden snowflakes'. Here the 'gold snow' is occasional rays of a setting sun
breaking between banks of cloud.

495 *datura*: EBB, in particular, greatly loved the datura with its lily-like flowers.

496 *lamp-fly*: firefly.

497–500 *I...Apennine*: not literally, since the Roman gate was not visible from the
terrace. In his mind Browning looks south-west down the Via Romana to the Porta
Romana ('the Roman gate'). Then he travels 'north away' (actually ENE) along the
city wall, over the river Arno, and onto the main road to Arezzo ('the Roman road'
because via Arezzo and Perugia was one of the routes to Rome). The road follows the
Arno briefly in a NE direction before heading south along the edge of the Apennine
mountains to Arezzo.

501 *Arezzo, the man's town*: Arezzo, Guido Franceschini's home town, lies about 40
miles south-east of Florence.

504 *A spectacle for angels*: cf. 1 Cor. 4: 9.

Romeward, until I found the wayside inn
By Castelnuovo's few mean hut-like homes
Huddled together on the hill-foot bleak,
Bare, broken only by that tree or two   510
Against the sudden bloody splendour poured
Cursewise in day's departure by the sun
O'er the low house-roof of that squalid inn
Where they three, for the first time and the last,
Husband and wife and priest, met face to face.   515
Whence I went on again, the end was near,
Step by step, missing none and marking all,
Till Rome itself, the ghastly goal, I reached.
Why, all the while,—how could it otherwise?—
The life in me abolished the death of things,   520
Deep calling unto deep: as then and there
Acted itself over again once more
The tragic piece. I saw with my own eyes
In Florence as I trod the terrace, breathed
The beauty and the fearfulness of night,   525

---

507 *MS* Romewards>Romeward,   508 *MS* {beginning of fo. 19}   511
MS splendor   512 *MS 1868 1872* his departure by the day   513 *MS* On the
low house-roofs and ignoble>On the low house-roofs and the squalid   *1868 1872*
On   514 *MS* time as   515 *Yale 2* Husband and wife and priest, met face
to face.>Husband, wife, priest, next morn met face to face. {see note below}
518 *MS* reached: 519 *MS* while,   *MS* otherwise,   520 *MS* things
521 *MS* deep,   523 *MS* piece:

508 *Castelnuovo*: a hamlet 15 miles from Rome, and the last stopping-place of
Pompilia and Caponsacchi.
512 *Cursewise*: like a curse.
515 *Husband . . . face*: in 1881 Leonard Courtney, journalist and Liberal MP, suggested to Browning that this passage from l. 505 implied that the encounter of Guido,
Pompilia, and Caponsacchi at the inn took place at evening, whereas their monologues
affirm that it took place at morning. Even though Courtney was wrong in his
assumption, Browning felt that the passage could be made clearer and so altered this
line in the Yale proofs: see *Yale 2* above and Appendix E. Like the other *Yale 2*
alterations, he forgot it, and it was not adopted in *1888*. In 1909 Courtney repeated
his point in a long letter to *The Times*, in which he discussed his earlier exchange with
Browning. See Leonard Courtney to RB, 12 May 1881: ABL; RB's reply, 14 May
1881: ABL; and Leonard Courtney to the Editor of *The Times*: TLS, 25 Feb. 1909, pp.
72–3.
521 *Deep . . . deep*: cf. Ps. 42: 7.

How it had run, this round from Rome to Rome—
Because, you are to know, they lived at Rome,
Pompilia's parents, as they thought themselves,
Two poor ignoble hearts who did their best
Part God's way, part the other way than God's,   530
To somehow make a shift and scramble through
The world's mud, careless if it splashed and spoiled,
Provided they might so hold high, keep clean
Their child's soul, one soul white enough for three,
And lift it to whatever star should stoop,   535
What possible sphere of purer life than theirs
Should come in aid of whiteness hard to save.
I saw the star stoop, that they strained to touch,
And did touch and depose their treasure on,
As Guido Franceschini took away   540
Pompilia to be his for evermore,
While they sang "Now let us depart in peace,
"Having beheld thy glory, Guido's wife!"
I saw the star supposed, but fog o' the fen,
Gilded star-fashion by a glint from hell;   545
Having been heaved up, haled on its gross way,
By hands unguessed before, invisible help
From a dark brotherhood, and specially
Two obscure goblin creatures, fox-faced this,
Cat-clawed the other, called his next of kin   550

527 *MS* {no commas}   528 *MS* parents as   529 *MS* The poor ignoble
pair   532 *MS* This   535 *MS* {beginning of fo. 20}   536 *MS* First
>What   537 *MS* help>aid   538 *MS* stoop that   540 *MS* Franceshini
541 *MS* forevermore   542 *MS* cried   *MS* peace   542–3 {inverted
commas added later}   544 *MS* of   *MS* fen   545 *MS* hell,
546 *MS* Which had   *MS* way   550 *MS* the>his

542–3 *"Now . . . wife*: parodying the Song of Simeon (Luke 2: 29–30), this is an ironic
comment on the Comparini's concern with social status: to see Pompilia married to an
aristocrat is the equivalent of seeing the Christchild. A further irony is that Simeon's song
is one of peace before death, very different from the future of the Comparini.

544 *fog o' the fen*: this may be the *ignis fatuus* or will-o'-the-wisp, but is more likely a
fog that is poisonous but not phosphorescent, after *King Lear*, II. iv. 167: 'fen-suck'd
fogs'. Only the light from Hell makes the fog appear shining, like a star.

By Guido the main monster,—cloaked and caped,
Making as they were priests, to mock God more,—
Abate Paul, Canon Girolamo.
These who had rolled the starlike pest to Rome
And stationed it to suck up and absorb   555
The sweetness of Pompilia, rolled again
That bloated bubble, with her soul inside,
Back to Arezzo and a palace there—
Or say, a fissure in the honest earth
Whence long ago had curled the vapour first,   560
Blown big by nether fires to appal day:
It touched home, broke, and blasted far and wide.
I saw the cheated couple find the cheat
And guess what foul rite they were captured for,—
Too fain to follow over hill and dale   565
That child of theirs caught up thus in the cloud
And carried by the Prince o' the Power of the Air
Whither he would, to wilderness or sea.
I saw them, in the potency of fear,
Break somehow through the satyr-family   570

551 *MS* To>By   *MS* monster, cloaked and caped   552 *MS* more,   553 *MS*
Girolamo;   556 *MS* roll>rolled   557 *MS* {no commas}   558 *MS*
there   560 *MS* vapor first   562 *MS* {beginning of fo. 21}   562 *MS*
broke and   564 *MS* for,   566 *MS* The heart of them caught up there>
That heart of theirs caught up thus   567 *MS* of the power of the air
568 *MS* would to   569 *MS* them in the agony of fear

  553 *Paul . . . Girolamo*: Guido's younger brothers. They were both priests, Paul in
Rome, Girolamo (like Caponsacchi) in Arezzo. Abate (abbot) was a courtesy title.
  554 *starlike pest*: a noxious thing or plague that is like a star in appearance; equivalent
to l. 544 (see note).
  561 *nether fires*: cf. *Paradise Lost*, i. 346.
  562 *blasted*: blighted, destroyed (as by the action of lightning or plague).
  564 *foul rite*: this passage develops a surreal version of the story, in which a satanic
rite is acted out against Pompilia by the Franceschini family, who appear in the form of
animal devils: fox, cat, goats, and a monkey: see ll. 549–50, 570–1. It vaguely recalls the
Witch's Kitchen in *Faust: Part One* with its female monkey ('a grey mother with a
monkey-mien', l. 571), its cauldron, and its satanic circle drawn on the ground round
the victim ('the obscene ring traced', l. 581). Guido, then, is both the devil, and the
dragon of the Perseus–St George story: see l. 585 n.
  567 *Prince o' the Power of the Air*: Satan. Cf. Eph. 2: 2.

(For a grey mother with a monkey-mien,
Mopping and mowing, was apparent too,
As, confident of capture, all took hands
And danced about the captives in a ring)
—Saw them break through, breathe safe, at Rome again,   575
Saved by the selfish instinct, losing so
Their loved one left with haters. These I saw,
In recrudescency of baffled hate,
Prepare to wring the uttermost revenge
From body and soul thus left them: all was sure,   580
Fire laid and cauldron set, the obscene ring traced,
The victim stripped and prostrate: what of God?
The cleaving of a cloud, a cry, a crash,
Quenched lay their cauldron, cowered i' the dust the crew,
As, in a glory of armour like Saint George,   585
Out again sprang the young good beauteous priest
Bearing away the lady in his arms,
Saved for a splendid minute and no more.

---

571 *MS* monkey-mien   572 *MS* mowing was   *MS* too)>too   574 *MS*
victims>captives   *MS* ring.>ring)   575 *MS* Break through and breathe safe,
back at Rome again,>—Break....again,   577 *MS* The>Their   *MS* saw
578 *MS* rage>hate   580 *MS* sure: 581 *MS* traced   582 *MS*
where was God?   584 *MS* in   585 *MS* {no commas}   586 *MS*
young, good, potent>young good potent   588 *MS* moment>minute

572 *Mopping and mowing*: gesturing and making ugly faces. Cf. *Tempest*, IV. i. 47.

578 *recrudescency*: a breaking out afresh, usually used of a disease or infection, here of
'baffled hate'; the phrase is an Anglicizing of 'recrudescentibus odiis': OYB lxxi (78).

585 *Saint George*: Caponsacchi is often compared to St George, the mythical knight
who rescued maidens from dragons, himself a Christianization of the Greek hero
Perseus. In the comparison here Pompilia is the rescued maiden and Guido (implicitly)
the dragon. From a small number of references in OYB it is possible to establish that
Caponsacchi and Pompilia's flight took place between early on Monday, 29 April 1697
till capture by Guido on the dawn of Wednesday, 1 May. From the autograph
chronologies (Appendix C), however, it would appear that when trying to place the
dates of the flight Browning made a fortuitous mistake, and shifted the flight back a
week to the morning of Monday, 22 April, the day before St George's Day (23 April),
hence establishing in his mind a symbolic link between Caponsacchi and St George.
In *1868*, and subsequently, he set the flight as actually beginning on 23 April,
making the link more explicit: see VI. 1110. For his wider interest in the Perseus–
Andromeda story, see W. C. DeVane, 'The Virgin and the Dragon', *Yale Review*, NS 37
(1947), 33–46.

For, whom i' the path did that priest come upon,
He and the poor lost lady borne so brave,   590
—Checking the song of praise in me, had else
Swelled to the full for God's will done on earth—
Whom but a dusk misfeatured messenger,
No other than the angel of this life,
Whose care is lest men see too much at once.   595
He made the sign, such God-glimpse must suffice,
Nor prejudice the Prince o' the Power of the Air,
Whose ministration piles us overhead
What we call, first, earth's roof and, last, heaven's floor,
Now grate o' the trap, then outlet of the cage: 600
So took the lady, left the priest alone,
And once more canopied the world with black.
But through the blackness I saw Rome again,
And where a solitary villa stood
In a lone garden-quarter: it was eve,   605
The second of the year, and oh so cold!
Ever and anon there flittered through the air
A snow-flake, and a scanty couch of snow
Crusted the grass-walk and the garden-mould.
All was grave, silent, sinister,—when, ha?   610
Glimmeringly did a pack of were-wolves pad
The snow, those flames were Guido's eyes in front,
And all five found and footed it, the track,

589 *MS* {beginning of fo. 22}   *MS* in   591 *MS* that>the   *MS* me
had   594 *MS* life   596 *MS* {no commas}   597 *MS* of the power
of the air,   599 *MS* {no commas except after floor}   600 *MS* grate of
602 *MS* And canopied the world with black once more.>And once more canopied
the world with black.   605 *MS* In a lone suburb>In a lone garden-quarter: it
was eve   606 *MS* year and   607 *MS* quivered>flittered   609 *MS*
garden mould   610 *MS* {dash added later}   612 *MS* and those were>
those flames were   613 *MS* footed it and found the track

593 *dusk*: dim, shadowy.
  misfeatured: having bad features; probably based on Keats's coinage of the noun: 'He
[man] has his winter, too, of pale misfeature': 'Four Seasons', 13.
  596–600 *He . . . cage*: cf. *The Inn Album*, 1831–2: 'prison-roof / Shall break one day
and Heaven beam overhead'.
  607 *flittered*: fluttered.

To where a threshold-streak of warmth and light
Betrayed the villa-door with life inside,   615
While an inch outside were those blood-bright eyes,
And black lips wrinkling o'er the flash of teeth,
And tongues that lolled—Oh God that madest man!
They parleyed in their language. Then one whined—
That was the policy and master-stroke—   620
Deep in his throat whispered what seemed a name—
"Open to Caponsacchi!" Guido cried:
"Gabriel!" cried Lucifer at Eden-gate.
Wide as a heart, opened the door at once,
Showing the joyous couple, and their child   625
The two-weeks' mother, to the wolves, the wolves
To them. Close eyes! And when the corpses lay
Stark-stretched, and those the wolves, their wolf-work done,
Were safe-embosomed by the night again,
I knew a necessary change in things;   630
As when the worst watch of the night gives way,
And there comes duly, to take cognizance,
The scrutinizing eye-point of some star—
And who despairs of a new daybreak now?
Lo, the first ray protruded on those five!   635
It reached them, and each felon writhed transfixed.
Awhile they palpitated on the spear

---

614 *MS* the threshold streak   616 *MS* {beginning of fo. 23}   *MS* eyes
617 *MS* teeth   618 *MS* lolled . .   622 *MS* {line added later}   *MS*
cried—   624 *MS* heart opened   625 *MS* couple and   626 *MS*
mother to   627 *MS* these corpses   628 *MS* wolfwork   629 *MS*
safe, embosomed   630 *MS* things   631 *MS* way   632 *MS* duly to
take cognisance   *1868 1872* cognisance   636 *MS* them and

---

623 *"Gabriel!" cried Lucifer.* for Guido to use Caponsacchi's name is as though
Lucifer (the fallen archangel become Satan) were to use the archangel Gabriel's
name to get into paradise.

633 *eye-point*: eye-spot, a spot resembling an eye. After the completely dark night
(the evil) of the murders, the light of this symbolic star is the first sign of change. The
star (the eye) sees the murderers, and then its ray of light becomes like a spear of justice
that transfixes them.

635 *protruded on*: thrust out upon; after OED² v. 3 *intr.*, but an unusual use with 'on'.

Motionless over Tophet: stand or fall?
"I say, the spear should fall—should stand, I say!"
Cried the world come to judgment, granting grace   640
Or dealing doom according to world's wont,
Those world's-bystanders grouped on Rome's cross-road
At prick and summons of the primal curse
Which bids man love as well as make a lie.
There prattled they, discoursed the right and wrong,   645
Turned wrong to right, proved wolves sheep and
      sheep wolves,
So that you scarce distinguished fell from fleece;
Till out spoke a great guardian of the fold,
Stood up, put forth his hand that held the crook,
And motioned that the arrested point decline: 650
Horribly off, the wriggling dead-weight reeled,
Rushed to the bottom and lay ruined there.
Though still at the pit's mouth, despite the smoke
O' the burning, tarriers turned again to talk
And trim the balance, and detect at least   655
A touch of wolf in what showed whitest sheep,
A cross of sheep redeeming the whole wolf,—
Vex truth a little longer:—less and less,
Because years came and went, and more and more
Brought new lies with them to be loved in turn.   660
Till all at once the memory of the thing,—
The fact that, wolves or sheep, such creatures were,—
Which hitherto, however men supposed,
Had somehow plain and pillar-like prevailed

---

639 *MS* say the   *MS* say"   641 *MS* its>their   642 *MS* at>on   644 *MS*
{beginning of fo. 24}   646 *MS* wrong and right,   647 *MS* Until>So
that   *MS* fleece   648 *MS* outspoke   650 *MS* decline,   651 *MS*
And horribly off the wriggling deadweight rolled,>reeled,   652 *MS* was ruined
there,   654 *MS* Of   658 *MS* Vexed>Vex   *MS* longer—   *MS* less
660 *MS* turn,

638 *Tophet*: Hell. Cf. 'Childe Roland', 143.
644 *love . . . lie*: cf. Rev. 22: 15.
647 *fell*: coat of a wolf.
651 *dead-weight*: heavy, inert weight (the bodies of Guido and his fellow murderers).

I' the midst of them, indisputably fact,   665
Granite, time's tooth should grate against, not graze,—
Why, this proved sandstone, friable, fast to fly
And give its grain away at wish o' the wind.
Ever and ever more diminutive,
Base gone, shaft lost, only entablature,   670
Dwindled into no bigger than a book,
Lay of the column; and that little, left
By the roadside 'mid the ordure, shards and weeds.
Until I haply, wandering that lone way,
Kicked it up, turned it over, and recognized,   675
For all the crumblement, this abacus,
This square old yellow book,—could calculate
By this the lost proportions of the style.

This was it from, my fancy with those facts,
I used to tell the tale, turned gay to grave,   680
But lacked a listener seldom; such alloy,
Such substance of me interfused the gold
Which, wrought into a shapely ring therewith,
Hammered and filed, fingered and favoured, last

---

665 *MS* In   *MS* truth>true,   666 *MS* Granite   time's   667 *MS* Why
this   *MS* was>proved   *MS* fugitive,>fast to fly,   668 *MS* That gives   *MS*
to the wish of the wind,   670 *MS* entablature   671 *MS* {beginning of fo.
25}   672 *MS* column,   *MS* little left   673 *MS* mid   674 *MS 1868
1872* that way,   675 *MS* over and   677 *MS* book, could   679 *MS*
{New paragraph indicated with line and 'N.P.' in left-hand margin}   680 *MS*
a tale turned   *MS* grave   682 *MS* And>Such   *MS* gold,   683 *MS*
^into a shapely ring^   *MS* thereby,—>therewith,

   667 *friable*: 'easily crumbled; easily reduced to powder': Johnson.
   670 *entablature*: top part of a classical column (usually comprising architrave, frieze,
and cornice), but Browning uses it loosely as the equivalent of 'abacus': see l. 676 n.
The crumbling of the imagined column, representing the historical fading of the
murder case, takes place from the base up. When the column itself is dust (when the
murder is forgotten) only one square slab of stone survives (equivalent to OYB).
   676 *crumblement*: crumbling, crumbling condition: OED² gives only this instance.
   abacus: the top slab of a capital of a column, hence like OYB in appearance. In
'calculate' (next line) there is a pun on the other sense of abacus, i.e. calculating frame.
   681 *lacked a listener seldom*: presumably Isa Blagden, Anthony Trollope, the Benzons,
and others: see Introduction.
   684 *favoured*: ornamented (as described in l. 16).

Lay ready for the renovating wash 685
O' the water. "How much of the tale was true?"
I disappeared; the book grew all in all;
The lawyers' pleadings swelled back to their size,—
Doubled in two, the crease upon them yet,
For more commodity of carriage, see!— 690
And these are letters, veritable sheets
That brought posthaste the news to Florence, writ
At Rome the day Count Guido died, we find,
To stay the craving of a client there,
Who bound the same and so produced my book. 695
Lovers of dead truth, did ye fare the worse?
Lovers of live truth, found ye false my tale?

Well, now; there's nothing in nor out o' the world
Good except truth: yet this, the something else,
What's this then, which proves good yet seems untrue?
This that I mixed with truth, motions of mine 701
That quickened, made the inertness malleolable

686 *MS* Of   687 *MS* disappeared: *MS* all,   688 *MS* pleading's
690 *MS* see—   692 *MS* ^post haste>posthaste^   *MS* Florence writ
693 *MS* you know,   696 *MS* Lover . . . . didst thou   697 *MS* Lover
MS find it in my tale.>in my tale 'twas found.   698 *MS* {beginning of fo. 26.
New paragraph indicated by 'New P.' in left-hand margin}   *MS* out the
world   700 *MS* then which   702 *MS* quicken and make>quickened and
made   *Yale 2* malleolable>malleable {see note}

685–6 *renovating wash / O' the water*: this was a spirt of acid at ll. 23–4. Perhaps we
are meant to understand 'the water' as *aquafortis* or a similar acid.

689–90 *crease . . . carriage*: OYB is a neat volume in appearance, but strong creases on
the individual pamphlets make it evident that before being bound into book form they
were indeed folded 'for more commodity of carriage', i.e. to be carried by post from
Rome to Florence.

694 *a client*: Francesco Cencini, a Florentine lawyer. The three manuscript letters to
Cencini, OYB ccxxxv–ccxl (237–8), imply that, at a distance in Florence, he helped
with Guido's defence, and that he was sent separate copies of the original printed legal
pamphlets. These letters are the basis of Browning's reasonable conjecture that it was
Cencini who had the legal pamphlets bound together to make up OYB.

702 *malleolable*: in *Yale 2* Browning corrected this to the normal spelling. Cook
makes the following suggestion to account for this coinage: '*Malleus* = hammer,
malleolus = little hammer; "malleolable". . . is therefore more suitable here than the
usual "malleable", the workmanship of the poet's fancy being delicate like that
required in fashioning an Etruscan ring': Cook, 19.

O' the gold was not mine,—what's your name for this?
Are means to the end, themselves in part the end?
Is fiction which makes fact alive, fact too?   705
The somehow may be thishow.
                                    I find first
Writ down for very A B C of fact,
"In the beginning God made heaven and earth;"
From which, no matter with what lisp, I spell   710
And speak you out a consequence—that man,
Man,—as befits the made, the inferior thing,—
Purposed, since made, to grow, not make in turn,
Yet forced to try and make, else fail to grow,—
Formed to rise, reach at, if not grasp and gain   715
The good beyond him,—which attempt is growth,—
Repeats God's process in man's due degree,
Attaining man's proportionate result,—
Creates, no, but resuscitates, perhaps.
Inalienable, the arch-prerogative   720
Which turns thought, act—conceives, expresses too!
No less, man, bounded, yearning to be free,
May so project his surplusage of soul
In search of body, so add self to self
By owning what lay ownerless before,—   725
So find, so fill full, so appropriate forms—
That, although nothing which had never life
Shall get life from him, be, not having been,
Yet, something dead may get to live again,

---

703 *MS* Of   *MS* {dash added later}   704 *MS* Are the means to the end, in
part the end?   *MS* end,>end?   707 *MS* {New paragraph indicated by 'N.P.'
in left-hand margin}   708 *MS 1868 1872* A.B.C.   *MS* {comma added later}
709 *MS* Heaven and Earth:">Heaven and Earth;"   711 *MS* Man   712 *MS*
{dashes added later}   714 *MS* {dash added later}   717 *MS* the arch-
process>God's process   718 *MS* Attains thus   *MS* result,   719 *MS*
may resuscitate,>but resuscitates,   720 *MS* {no comma}   721 *MS*
too.>too: 722 *MS* {first comma added later}   725 *MS* {beginning of
fo. 27}   *MS* till then,—   *MS* {dash added later}

---

    723 *surplusage*: surplus, excess.

Something with too much life or not enough, 730
Which, either way imperfect, ended once:
An end whereat man's impulse intervenes,
Makes new beginning, starts the dead alive,
Completes the incomplete and saves the thing.
Man's breath were vain to light a virgin wick,— 735
Half-burned-out, all but quite-quenched wicks o' the lamp
Stationed for temple-service on this earth,
These indeed let him breathe on and relume!
For such man's feat is, in the due degree,
—Mimic creation, galvanism for life, 740
But still a glory portioned in the scale.
Why did the mage say,—feeling as we are wont
For truth, and stopping midway short of truth,
And resting on a lie,—"I raise a ghost"?
"Because," he taught adepts, "man makes not man. 745
"Yet by a special gift, an art of arts,
"More insight and more outsight and much more
"Will to use both of these than boast my mates,

---

731 *MS* once; 735 *MS* the virgin 736 *MS* {comma added later} *MS*
of 737 *MS* earth; 738 *MS* relume, 739 *MS* For there>For here
740 *MS* {dash added later} 743 *MS* and, stopping>and stopping 744 *MS*
1868 ghost?" 745 *MS* {no commas} *MS* man; 746–59 *MS* {quotation
marks at beginnings of lines added later} 746 *MS* the>an 747 *MS*
outsight than>outsight and much more

736–7 *lamp . . temple-service*: recalling the lamps in the temple at Jerusalem: cf. 2 Chr.
4: 20.

738 *relume*: rekindle, cause to burn afresh.

740 *galvanism for life*: galvanism, the use of electric current to stimulate weak or
inactive limbs, is different from the actual creation of those limbs (just as the power of
human imagination is different in kind from God's original creative power).

742 *mage*: magician (a serious magician of old). Browning is thinking of a magician
like John of Halberstadt in 'Transcendentalism', 37, only in this instance the mage is
less powerful.

744 *"I raise a ghost"*: a statement by the mage; the stress is on 'raise' (as against an
implied 'create'). In the following speech the mage expands the statement: he can
reanimate or extend a 'rag of flesh' into a living body, but cannot perform an act of
original creation from nothing, like God. Even the mage must concede the limits of his
power (as must the poet).

747 *outsight*: the perception of external things, a keen faculty of observing the
natural world.

"I can detach from me, commission forth
"Half of my soul; which in its pilgrimage   750
"O'er old unwandered waste ways of the world,
"May chance upon some fragment of a whole,
"Rag of flesh, scrap of bone in dim disuse,
"Smoking flax that fed fire once: prompt therein
"I enter, spark-like, put old powers to play,   755
"Push lines out to the limit, lead forth last
"(By a moonrise through a ruin of a crypt)
"What shall be mistily seen, murmuringly heard,
"Mistakenly felt: then write my name with Faust's!"
Oh, Faust, why Faust? Was not Elisha once?—   760
Who bade them lay his staff on a corpse-face.
There was no voice, no hearing: he went in
Therefore, and shut the door upon them twain,
And prayed unto the Lord: and he went up
And lay upon the corpse, dead on the couch,   765
And put his mouth upon its mouth, his eyes
Upon its eyes, his hands upon its hands,
And stretched him on the flesh; the flesh waxed warm:
And he returned, walked to and fro the house,
And went up, stretched him on the flesh again,   770
And the eyes opened. 'T is a credible feat
With the right man and way.
                              Enough of me!

---

750 *MS* soul, which   751 *MS* waste>old   *MS* over>waste   752 {beginning
of fo. 28}   754 *MS* A smoking flax that once fed fire—therein>Smoking flax that
fed fire once:—prompt therein   755 *MS* powers>power   756 *MS* at>
forth   757 *MS* in a vault)>of a crypt)   759 *MS* touched>felt   760 *MS*
once?>once,   761 *MS* corpse-face?   763 *MS* {line added later}   768 *MS*
flesh, *MS* warm;   769 *1872* {New paragraph} *Yale 2* {New paragraph
removed. In *1888* and *1889* the pagination obscures the paragraphing}   *MS*
house   773 *MS* {New paragraph indicated by 'N.P.' in left-hand margin}

760–71 *Faust . . . opened*: Browning Christianizes the image of the mage, getting
away from the gothic atmosphere of the preceding passage and the sinister overtones of
the Faust story (in which Faust raises up the ghost of Helen of Troy with the help of a
devil). He holds with his point that the poet's imagination resuscitates life but does not
create it. The holy man Elisha brought back to life the Shunammite woman's son: 2
Kgs. 4: 18–37.

The Book! I turn its medicinable leaves
In London now till, as in Florence erst,   775
A spirit laughs and leaps through every limb,
And lights my eye, and lifts me by the hair,
Letting me have my will again with these
—How title I the dead alive once more?

Count Guido Franceschini the Aretine,   780
Descended of an ancient house, though poor,
A beak-nosed bushy-bearded black-haired lord,
Lean, pallid, low of stature yet robust,
Fifty years old,—having four years ago
Married Pompilia Comparini, young,   785
Good, beautiful, at Rome, where she was born,
And brought her to Arezzo, where they lived
Unhappy lives, whatever curse the cause,—
This husband, taking four accomplices,
Followed this wife to Rome, where she was fled   790
From their Arezzo to find peace again,
In convoy, eight months earlier, of a priest,
Aretine also, of still nobler birth,
Giuseppe Caponsacchi,—caught her there
Quiet in a villa on a Christmas night,   795
With only Pietro and Violante by,
Both her putative parents; killed the three,

---

775 *MS* first>erst,   777 *MS* Lights my eye, lifts me by the very hair,>And lights
my eye, and lifts me by the hair,   780 *MS* {beginning of fo. 29. New paragraph
indicated by 'N.P.' in left-hand margin.}   782 *MS* bushy-bearded, black-haired
790 *MS* that wife   *MS* Rome where   791 *MS* again   792 *MS* priest
794 *MS 1868 1872* Caponsacchi,—and caught   797 *MS* all three,

774 *medicinable leaves*: medicinable = medicinal, having healing or curative proper-
ties. A pun: the 'leaves' (pages) of OYB are like the leaves of a healing plant or herb,
reviving Browning's spirits.
775 *erst*: previously.
777 *lifts me by the hair*: cf. Ezek. 8: 3.
780 *Aretine*: citizen of Arezzo.
782–4 *beak-nosed . . . old*: adapting SS 23, a description of Guido at the time of his
execution: 'Franceschini was short of stature, thin and pale, with a sharp nose, black
hair and a heavy beard, about 50 years of age.'

Aged, they, seventy each, and she, seventeen,
And, two weeks since, the mother of his babe
First-born and heir to what the style was worth   800
O' the Guido who determined, dared and did
This deed just as he purposed point by point.
Then, bent upon escape, but hotly pressed,
And captured with his co-mates that same night,
He, brought to trial, stood on this defence—   805
Injury to his honour caused the act;
And since his wife was false, (as manifest
By flight from home in such companionship,)
Death, punishment deserved of the false wife
And faithless parents who abetted her   810
I' the flight aforesaid, wronged nor God nor man.
"Nor false she, nor yet faithless they," replied
The accuser; "cloaked and masked this murder glooms;
"True was Pompilia, loyal too the pair;
"Out of the man's own heart a monster curled   815
"Which—crime coiled with connivancy at crime—
"His victim's breast, he tells you, hatched and reared;
"Uncoil we and stretch stark the worm of hell!"
A month the trial swayed this way and that
Ere judgment settled down on Guido's guilt;   820
Then was the Pope, that good Twelfth Innocent,

---

798 *MS* seventeen   800 *MS* Firstborn   801 *MS* Of   803 *MS*
escape but   805 *MS* defence,   806 *MS* act:>act;   807 *MS* {begin-
ning of fo. 30}   *MS 1868 1872* That   *MS* false, as   808 *MS* companionship,
810 *MS* And faithless parents, wronged nor God nor man.   811 *MS* {line not
found}   812–18 *MS* {quotation marks added later}   814 *MS* loyal was
the pair,   815 *MS 1868 1872* this monster curled,   *816 *MS 1868 1872*
"This crime   *1888* "Which crime   *DC Br U* "Which crime>"Which—
crime   *1889* "Which—crime   *MS 1868 1872* at crime,   817 *Yale 2* "His . . . .
reared;>"—His . . . . reared;—   820 *MS* guilt.   821 *MS* Innocent

800 *style*: title.
813 *glooms*: has a dark appearance: OED² v.¹ 3.
815 *a monster curled*: the worm of hell (l. 818) emerges from Guido's breast. Cf.
Paradise Lost, ix. 1068.

Appealed to: who well weighed what went before,
Affirmed the guilt and gave the guilty doom.

Let this old woe step on the stage again!
Act itself o'er anew for men to judge, 825
Not by the very sense and sight indeed—
(Which take at best imperfect cognizance,
Since, how heart moves brain, and how both move hand,
What mortal ever in entirety saw?)
—No dose of purer truth than man digests, 830
But truth with falsehood, milk that feeds him now,
Not strong meat he may get to bear some day—
To-wit, by voices we call evidence,
Uproar in the echo, live fact deadened down,
Talked over, bruited abroad, whispered away, 835
Yet helping us to all we seem to hear:
For how else know we save by worth of word?

Here are the voices presently shall sound
In due succession. First, the world's outcry
Around the rush and ripple of any fact 840
Fallen stonewise, plumb on the smooth face of things;
The world's guess, as it crowds the bank o' the pool,
At what were figure and substance, by their splash:
Then, by vibrations in the general mind,
At depth of deed already out of reach. 845
This threefold murder of the day before,—

---

822 *MS* to, 824 *MS* {New paragraph (already written thus) indicated by 'N.P.'
in left-hand margin} *MS* again, 828 *MS* Since how 830 *Yale 2*
digests,>digests—>digests, 834 *MS* {beginning of fo. 31} 836 *MS*
hear— 838 *MS* {New paragraph (already written thus) indicated by 'N.P.' in
left-hand margin} *MS* to sound 841 *MS* things: 842 *MS* of 843 *MS*
substance by their splash, 844 *MS* And,

839–43 *world's . . . splash*: the event of the murder falls 'plumb' (vertically) on the
'smooth face' of ordinary life, like a stone falling into a pool. As it passes on its way, it
leaves the movement and ripples of the water. The world, seeing only these signs of its
fall, and not the event itself, tries to guess at the 'figure and substance' (the shape and
size) of the event by interpreting the kind of disturbance it leaves.

Say, Half-Rome's feel after the vanished truth;
Honest enough, as the way is: all the same,
Harbouring in the centre of its sense
A hidden germ of failure, shy but sure, 850
To neutralize that honesty and leave
That feel for truth at fault, as the way is too.
Some prepossession such as starts amiss,
By but a hair's breadth at the shoulder-blade,
The arm o' the feeler, dip he ne'er so bold; 855
So leads arm waveringly, lets fall wide
O' the mark its finger, sent to find and fix
Truth at the bottom, that deceptive speck.
With this Half-Rome,—the source of swerving, call
Over-belief in Guido's right and wrong 860
Rather than in Pompilia's wrong and right:
Who shall say how, who shall say why? 'T is there—
The instinctive theorizing whence a fact
Looks to the eye as the eye likes the look.
Gossip in a public place, a sample-speech. 865
Some worthy, with his previous hint to find
A husband's side the safer, and no whit
Aware he is not Æacus the while,—

---

847 *MS* Half Rome's *Yale 1* Half Rome's>Half-Rome's *MS* truth,—
848 *MS* is; 850 *MS* The *MS* shy and 851 *MS* Shall *1868 1872*
Should 852 *MS* too: 853 *MS* amiss 854, 855 *MS* {These lines
stand in the reverse order} 855 *MS* of *MS* brave, *1868 1872* brave;
856 *MS 1868 1872* And so leads 857 *MS* Of *MS* his finger meant *1868
1872* his finger meant to find, 859 *MS* Half Rome,— *Yale 1* Half Rome,—>
Half-Rome,— *MS* ,>,— 860 *MS* {beginning of fo. 32} 861 *MS* right,
862 *MS* 'Twas>'Tis 865 *MS* sample-speech; 866 *MS* worthy with
868 *MS* while,

---

853 *prepossession*: preconceived opinion or prejudice (which tends to bias the mind).

855 *dip he ne'er so bold*: continuing the image of 839–43: see note. Half-Rome, the speaker of Book II, reaches with his arm into the pool to try and recover the stone (the event), but misses it.

866 *worthy*: in its first sense this means 'a distinguished or eminent person', but here, as commonly in the 19th century, it is 'applied colloquially or facetiously to any person, esp. one having a marked personality': OED² C. sb. 1.e.

867 *no whit*: not at all.

868 *Æacus*: i.e. a good judge. Æacus was the king of Aegina who, because of his reputation for impartiality, became one of the three judges of Hades.

How such an one supposes and states fact
To whosoever of a multitude   870
Will listen, and perhaps prolong thereby
The not-unpleasant flutter at the breast,
Born of a certain spectacle shut in
By the church Lorenzo opposite. So, they lounge
Midway the mouth o' the street, on Corso side,   875
'Twixt palace Fiano and palace Ruspoli,
Linger and listen; keeping clear o' the crowd,
Yet wishful one could lend that crowd one's eyes,
(So universal is its plague of squint)
And make hearts beat our time that flutter false: 880
—All for the truth's sake, mere truth, nothing else!
How Half-Rome found for Guido much excuse.

Next, from Rome's other half, the opposite feel
For truth with a like swerve, like unsuccess,—
Or if success, by no skill but more luck   885
This time, through siding rather with the wife,
Because a fancy-fit inclined that way,

871 *MS* listen and   872 *MS* breast   874 *MS* opposite; so they   875 *MS*
of   877 *MS* listen,   *MS* of   879 *MS* So   *MS* squint,   880 *MS* false
881 *MS* else.   882 *MS* Half Rome   *Yale 1* Half Rome>Half-Rome
883 *MS* {New paragraph (already written thus) indicated by 'N.P.' in left-hand
margin}   885 *MS* {line not found}   *1868 1872* more skill but luck: *Yale 2*
by no more skill but luck:>by skill no more but luck: 886 *MS 1868 1872* rather
siding   887 *MS* {beginning of fo. 33}   *MS* Whatever the>However the
1868 1872 However the

875–6 *Midway...Ruspoli*: Browning gives an exact location for Book II. The
Corso is the two-mile long, main north–south road of Rome. About half-way
down, on the west side, is a road that develops immediately into the small Piazza di
San Lorenzo in Lucina. The church where the bodies of the Comparini are laid out ('a
certain spectacle') is on the south side. Half-Rome (the speaker of II) and his
companion stand just off the Corso, in the middle of the opening into the piazza,
with Palazzo Ruspoli on their right and Palazzo Fiano on their left. Also on their left,
they can see the crowd outside the church. The inspiration for this scene is SS 17.

878–80 *lend...false*: ironically Half-Rome and his companion think that the crowd
suffers a 'plague of squint' (that it does not see the murders straight or in a true way);
the hearts of the crowd 'flutter false' (their judgement is unreliable and emotional).

Than with the husband. One wears drab, one pink;
Who wears pink, ask him "Which shall win the race,
"Of coupled runners like as egg and egg?"   890
"—Why, if I must choose, he with the pink scarf."
Doubtless for some such reason choice fell here.
A piece of public talk to correspond
At the next stage of the story; just a day
Let pass and new day brings the proper change.   895
Another sample-speech i' the market-place
O' the Barberini by the Capucins;
Where the old Triton, at his fountain-sport,
Bernini's creature plated to the paps,
Puffs up steel sleet which breaks to diamond dust,   900
A spray of sparkles snorted from his conch,
High over the caritellas, out o' the way
O' the motley merchandizing multitude.
Our murder has been done three days ago,
The frost is over and gone, the south wind laughs,   905
And, to the very tiles of each red roof
A-smoke i' the sunshine, Rome lies gold and glad:

---

888 *MS 1868 1872* one, pink;   889 *MS* him which>him, "which   *MS* race
890 *MS* Of the coupled   *MS* egg.>egg?"   891 *MS* {quotation marks added
later}   894 *MS* story, just   895 *Yale 2* and>till   *MS 1868 1872* bring
MS change;   896 *MS* in   897 *MS* {line not found}   901 *MS* conch
902 *MS* of   903 *MS* Of   907 *MS* Asmoke in

---

888 *drab*: dull light-brown colour. A person wearing a particular colour chooses the
jockey wearing the same colour to win a race.

896–901 *market-place / O' the Barberini . . . conch*: another exact location. The Other
Half-Rome (the speaker of Book III) and his companion are about half a mile to the
east of San Lorenzo Church, in the Piazza Barberini (with, on its east side, the church
of the Capuchins) by the great Triton fountain by Gian Lorenzo Bernini. 'The sea-god
is plunging up to the waist in a double shell, supported by four dolphins. He is in the
act of sounding his marine trumpet [a huge sea shell]; instead, however, of air, he
discharges a very fine jet of water': Chevalier de Chatelain, *Rambles through Rome*
(1851), 36.

902 *caritellas*: light horse-drawn carriages (gigs or chaises); an odd spelling of *carrettella*
(It.). A buggy was 'carrettella a un cavallo solo', a phaeton 'carrettella scoperta'. 'I have
no doubt myself that the "*i*" ought to have been an *e* in "*caritella*"': Pen Browning to
W. H. Griffin, 7 Feb. 1898: Griffin Collections, vi. 84[v]. The effect here, of the fountain
water rising high above the carriages in the piazza, is well illustrated by a photograph in
F. M. Crawford, *Ave Roma Immortalis* (2 vols., 1898): i. 188.

So, listen how, to the other half of Rome,
Pompilia seemed a saint and martyr both!

Then, yet another day let come and go,   910
With pause prelusive still of novelty,
Hear a fresh speaker!—neither this nor that
Half-Rome aforesaid; something bred of both:
One and one breed the inevitable three.
Such is the personage harangues you next;   915
The elaborated product, *tertium quid:*
Rome's first commotion in subsidence gives
The curd o' the cream, flower o' the wheat, as it were,
And finer sense o' the city. Is this plain?
You get a reasoned statement of the case,   920
Eventual verdict of the curious few
Who care to sift a business to the bran
Nor coarsely bolt it like the simpler sort.
Here, after ignorance, instruction speaks;
Here, clarity of candour, history's soul,   925
The critical mind, in short: no gossip-guess.
What the superior social section thinks,
In person of some man of quality
Who,—breathing musk from lace-work and brocade,
His solitaire amid the flow of frill,   930

---

908 *MS* how to   *MS* Rome   909 *MS* too.>both.   910 *MS* {New paragraph (already written thus) indicated by 'N.P.' in left-hand margin}   912 *MS* speaker, neither   913 *Yale 1* Half Rome>Half-Rome   *MS* both;   914 *MS* {beginning of fo. 34}   *MS* three: 915 *MS* next,   916 *MS tertium quid.* 918 *MS* of   919 *MS* of   924 *MS* speaks,   925 *MS* story's   926 *MS* gossip's-guess.   927 *MS* thinks

911 *prelusive*: serving as a prelude.
916 *elaborated*: worked up, highly developed.
tertium quid: literally 'a third thing' (L.), a common phrase meaning a third different thing, usually produced by the mixture of two other things. The speaker of Book IV, Tertium Quid, is a mixture of Half-Rome and Other Half-Rome, but a mixture that produces his own unique character and viewpoint: see Introduction to Book IV.
918 *curd . . . wheat*: richest of the cream, best of the wheat.
930 *solitaire*: diamond or other gem set by itself, presumably here a brooch.

Powdered peruke on nose, and bag at back,
And cane dependent from the ruffled wrist,—
Harangues in silvery and selectest phrase
'Neath waxlight in a glorified saloon
Where mirrors multiply the girandole: 935
Courting the approbation of no mob,
But Eminence This and All-Illustrious That
Who take snuff softly, range in well-bred ring,
Card-table-quitters for observance' sake,
Around the argument, the rational word—   940
Still, spite its weight and worth, a sample-speech.
How Quality dissertated on the case.

So much for Rome and rumour; smoke comes first:
Once let smoke rise untroubled, we descry
Clearlier what tongues of flame may spire and spit   945
To eye and ear, each with appropriate tinge
According to its food, or pure or foul.
The actors, no mere rumours of the act,
Intervene. First you hear Count Guido's voice,
In a small chamber that adjoins the court,   950
Where Governor and Judges, summoned thence,
Tommati, Venturini and the rest,
Find the accused ripe for declaring truth.
Soft-cushioned sits he; yet shifts seat, shirks touch,
As, with a twitchy brow and wincing lip   955
And cheek that changes to all kinds of white,
He proffers his defence, in tones subdued

---

936 *MS* mob   941 *MS* {beginning of fo. 35}   942 *MS* quality disertated
1868 quality   943 MS {New paragraph (already written thus) indicated by 'N.P.'
in left-hand margin}   *MS* rumour: smoke comes first—   944 *MS 1868 1872*
the smoke risen   945 *MS* the tongues   *MS* that spire   947 *MS 1868 1872*
food, pure or impure.   949 *MS* voice   *Yale 2* voice,>voice.   953 *Yale 2*
truth.>truth,   954 *MS* he,   955 *MS* As with   957 *MS* defence in

931 *peruke . . . back*: a grand wig with the hair at the front overhanging the nose, and
the hair at the back tied into a small silk pouch ('bag').
935 *girandole*: holder for candles, fitted to the wall.

Near to mock-mildness now, so mournful seems
The obtuser sense truth fails to satisfy;
Now, moved, from pathos at the wrong endured,   960
To passion; for the natural man is roused
At fools who first do wrong then pour the blame
Of their wrong-doing, Satan-like, on Job.
Also his tongue at times is hard to curb;
Incisive, nigh satiric bites the phrase,   965
Rough-raw, yet somehow claiming privilege
—It is so hard for shrewdness to admit
Folly means no harm when she calls black white!
—Eruption momentary at the most,
Modified forthwith by a fall o' the fire,   970
Sage acquiescence; for the world's the world,
And, what it errs in, Judges rectify:
He feels he has a fist, then folds his arms
Crosswise and makes his mind up to be meek.
And never once does he detach his eye   975
From those ranged there to slay him or to save,
But does his best man's-service for himself,
Despite,—what twitches brow and makes lip wince,—
His limbs' late taste of what was called the Cord,

---

959 *MS* satisfy,   960 *MS* moved from   *MS* endured   961 *MS* passion,   962 *MS 1868 1872* wrong,   964 *MS* curb,   967 *MS* {begin-
ning of fo. 36}   *MS* {dash added later}   968 *Yale 2* Folly means no harm>No
harm means Folly   *MS* ,>!   969 *MS* {dash added later}   970 *MS* of
971 *MS* Meek>Sage   *MS* acquiescence,   972 *MS* judges   976 *MS*
those,   *Yale 1* those,>those   978 *MS* For all>Despite   979 *MS* limbs

---

958–9 *mock-mildness . . . satisfy*: Guido speaks in a mock mild way, as though sad-
dened by the judges' failure to understand his 'truthful' story. The passage that follows
describes his devious changes of voice and manner.

961–3 *natural man . . . Job*: Guido casts himself as the natural man (one free from
false sophistication), and Pompilia and the Comparini as those who did wrong, who
are in effect responsible for their own murder. They foolishly fail to acknowledge
this; instead (Satan-like) they have cast the blame on him, the innocent and suffering
Job.

979–80 *the Cord, / Or Vigil-torture*: in this form of torture the victim was stripped
naked, tied to an awkwardly topped bench; his hands were tied behind his back with
'the Cord'; the bench was raised 6 ft off the ground, and then the victim's bound arms

Or Vigil-torture more facetiously.   980
Even so; they were wont to tease the truth
Out of loth witness (toying, trifling time)
By torture: 't was a trick, a vice of the age,
Here, there and everywhere, what would you have?
Religion used to tell Humanity   985
She gave him warrant or denied him course.
And since the course was much to his own mind,
Of pinching flesh and pulling bone from bone
To unhusk truth a-hiding in its hulls,
Nor whisper of a warning stopped the way,   990
He, in their joint behalf, the burly slave,
Bestirred him, mauled and maimed all recusants,
While, prim in place, Religion overlooked;
And so had done till doomsday, never a sign
Nor sound of interference from her mouth,   995
But that at last the burly slave wiped brow,
Let eye give notice as if soul were there,
Muttered "'T is a vile trick, foolish more than vile,

---

981 *MS* teaze   982 *MS 1868 1872* loath   *MS* witness toying, trifling time,
983 *MS 1888 1889* 't was   *MS* trick we>trick, vice   *MS* age   986 *MS*
way;>course;   987 *MS* this way>the course   989 *MS* have out>unhusk
MS close->a-   *MS* his   991 *MS* slave   992 *MS* racked>mauled
993 *MS* While prim in place Religion overlooked,   994 *MS* {beginning of fo.
37}   997 *MS* wink somewhat>give notice   998 *MS* Said   *MS 1888*
1889 "'T is

---

were pulled upwards by a rope on a pulley and held in position. The torture lasted
from five to ten hours. The Vigil was simply a form of sleep deprivation, the victim
being seated on a bench (on the ground) and then kept awake and upright by a torturer
on either side. Browning is only thinking of the Cord, which was originally a
development of the Vigil. He says it was called Vigil-torture 'facetiously', because
rather incidentally it kept the victim awake. He had investigated torture in the works
of the Italian jurist Prospero Farinacci (1544–1618) in the British Museum: see
Introduction, xix.

985–6 *Religion . . . course*: Religion used to tell mankind what it could and could not
do.

989 *unhusk . . . hulls*: the image is of wheat: to uncover the inside grain (the truth) by
taking off the outer shells or cuticles ('hulls') of the grain.

992 *recusants*: dissidents; people who refuse to submit to some authority, particularly
religious authority.

"Should have been counted sin; I make it so:
"At any rate no more of it for me—   1000
"Nay, for I break the torture-engine thus!"
Then did Religion start up, stare amain,
Look round for help and see none, smile and say
"What, broken is the rack? Well done of thee!
"Did I forget to abrogate its use?   1005
"Be the mistake in common with us both!
"—One more fault our blind age shall answer for,
"Down in my book denounced though it must be
"Somewhere. Henceforth find truth by milder means!"
Ah but, Religion, did we wait for thee   1010
To ope the book, that serves to sit upon,
And pick such place out, we should wait indeed!
That is all history: and what is not now,
Was then, defendants found it to their cost.
How Guido, after being tortured, spoke.   1015

Also hear Caponsacchi who comes next,
Man and priest—could you comprehend the coil!—
In days when that was rife which now is rare.
How, mingling each its multifarious wires,
Now heaven, now earth, now heaven and earth at once,
Had plucked at and perplexed their puppet here,   1021
Played off the young frank personable priest;
Sworn fast and tonsured plain heaven's celibate,
And yet earth's clear-accepted servitor,

999–1001 *MS* {initial quotation marks added later}   1005–8 *MS* {quotation marks added later}   1006 *MS* ,>!   1007 *MS* {dash added later}   *MS* must>shall   1009 *MS* mode!>means!   1010 *MS* Ah, but Religion did   1013 *Yale 2* and what>what   1014 *MS* and Guido>defendants   *MS* his> their   1016 *MS* {New paragraph (already written thus) indicated by 'N.P.' in left-hand margin}   1017 *MS* coil—>coil   1018 *MS* rare;   1020 *MS* {beginning of fo. 38}   1022 *MS* young, frank,>young frank   *MS* priest   1023 *MS* Heaven's   1024 *MS* Earth's

1002 *amain*: greatly.
1017 *coil*: tangle, mix-up. Caponsacchi is caught between his role as priest and his role as society beau or 'squire of dames'.

A courtly spiritual Cupid, squire of dames   1025
By law of love and mandate of the mode.
The Church's own, or why parade her seal,
Wherefore that chrism and consecrative work?
Yet verily the world's, or why go badged
A prince of sonneteers and lutanists,   1030
Show colour of each vanity in vogue
Borne with decorum due on blameless breast?
All that is changed now, as he tells the court
How he had played the part excepted at;
Tells it, moreover, now the second time: 1035
Since, for his cause of scandal, his own share
I' the flight from home and husband of the wife,
He has been censured, punished in a sort
By relegation,—exile, we should say,
To a short distance for a little time,—   1040
Whence he is summoned on a sudden now,
Informed that she, he thought to save, is lost,
And, in a breath, bidden re-tell his tale,
Since the first telling somehow missed effect,
And then advise in the matter. There stands he,   1045
While the same grim black-panelled chamber blinks
As though rubbed shiny with the sins of Rome
Told the same oak for ages—wave-washed wall
Against which sets a sea of wickedness.
There, where you yesterday heard Guido speak,   1050
Speaks Caponsacchi; and there face him too

1027 *MS* Churches   1028 *MS* consecration   1029 *MS* World's   1030 *MS*
lord   1033 *MS* now as   *MS* Court   1034 *MS* at,   1035 *MS*
time,   1037 *MS* In   1045 *MS* he stands>stands he   1046 *MS*
black-panneled   1047 *MS* {beginning of fo. 39}   1049 *MS* Whereto
had set   *1868 1872* Whereto has set   1051 *MS* Caponsacchi,

1025 *squire of dames*: a devotee of ladies; a servant, as it were, paying marked attention to
them. Spenser's Squire of Dames has 'a comely personage, / And louely face, made fit for
to deceiue / Fraile Ladies hart with loues consuming rage': *Faerie Queene*, III. vii, st. 46.
1026 *mandate of the mode*: order of convention.
1034 *excepted at*: taken exception to.
1046 *blinks*: gleams, gives off momentary gleams of light: see OED^2 v. 5.

Tommati, Venturini and the rest
Who, eight months earlier, scarce repressed the smile,
Forewent the wink; waived recognition so
Of peccadillos incident to youth,   1055
Especially youth high-born; for youth means love,
Vows can't change nature, priests are only men,
And love likes stratagem and subterfuge:
Which age, that once was youth, should recognize,
May blame, but needs not press too hard upon.   1060
Here sit the old Judges then, but with no grace
Of reverend carriage, magisterial port:
For why? The accused of eight months since,—the same
Who cut the conscious figure of a fool,
Changed countenance, dropped bashful gaze to ground,   1065
While hesitating for an answer then,—
Now is grown judge himself, terrifies now
This, now the other culprit called a judge,
Whose turn it is to stammer and look strange,
As he speaks rapidly, angrily, speech that smites: 1070
And they keep silence, bear blow after blow,
Because the seeming-solitary man,
Speaking for God, may have an audience too,
Invisible, no discreet judge provokes.
How the priest Caponsacchi said his say.   1075

Then a soul sighs its lowest and its last
After the loud ones,—so much breath remains
Unused by the four-days'-dying; for she lived

1053 *MS* smile   1054 *MS* wink,   1058 *MS 1868* needs   *MS 1888 1889*
subterfuge   *1868   1872* subterfuge: 1059 *MS* Age,   *MS* Youth, will
1060 *MS* Must blame but   *MS 1868 1872* against.   1062 *MS* lordly>reverend
MS port—   *1868 1872* port.   1067 *MS* menaces   1070 *MS* words that
smite.   1072 *MS* man   1073 *MS* God might>God may   1074 *MS*
{beginning of fo. 40}   1075 *MS* says>said   1076 *MS* {New paragraph
(already written thus) indicated by 'N.P.' in left-hand margin}   1078 *MS* four
days' dying

  1062 *port*: deportment, the manner in which one bears oneself; here the equivalent
of 'carriage'.
  1073–4 *audience too, / Invisible*: i.e. of angels: cf. l. 504 n.

Thus long, miraculously long, 't was thought,
Just that Pompilia might defend herself.   1080
How, while the hireling and the alien stoop,
Comfort, yet question,—since the time is brief,
And folk, allowably inquisitive,
Encircle the low pallet where she lies
In the good house that helps the poor to die,—   1085
Pompilia tells the story of her life.
For friend and lover,—leech and man of law
Do service; busy helpful ministrants
As varied in their calling as their mind,
Temper and age: and yet from all of these,   1090
About the white bed under the arched roof,
Is somehow, as it were, evolved a one,—
Small separate sympathies combined and large,
Nothings that were, grown something very much:
As if the bystanders gave each his straw,   1095
All he had, though a trifle in itself,
Which, plaited all together, made a Cross
Fit to die looking on and praying with,
Just as well as if ivory or gold.
So, to the common kindliness she speaks,   1100
There being scarce more privacy at the last
For mind than body: but she is used to bear,
And only unused to the brotherly look.
How she endeavoured to explain her life.

[—]

1079 *1872* 'twas   1082 *MS* question, since   *MS* brief   1083 *MS* folk
allowably   1086 *MS* {line added later}   1087 *Yale 2* For friend and>Nor
friend nor   1088 *MS* service, busy, helpful   1090 *MS* these   1091 *MS*
roof   1094 *MS* much,   1095 *MS* standers by   1097 *MS* altogether
MS cross ⟨—⟩   1098 *MS* with   1100 *MS* So to   1101 *MS* {beginning of
fo. 41}   1102 *MS* body,   *MS* bear

  1081 *hireling*: hired person, i.e. doctor or lawyer.
  alien: stranger.
  1087 *leech*: doctor.
  1097 *made a Cross*: i.e. the sympathy of the bystanders came together to form a
symbolic crucifix, an image consoling to the dying.

Then, since a Trial ensued, a touch o' the same   1105
To sober us, flustered with frothy talk,
And teach our common sense its helplessness.
For why deal simply with divining-rod,
Scrape where we fancy secret sources flow,
And ignore law, the recognized machine,   1110
Elaborate display of pipe and wheel
Framed to unchoke, pump up and pour apace
Truth till a flowery foam shall wash the world?
The patent truth-extracting process,—ha?
Let us make that grave mystery turn one wheel,   1115
Give you a single grind of law at least!
One orator, of two on either side,
Shall teach us the puissance of the tongue
—That is, o' the pen which simulated tongue
On paper and saved all except the sound   1120
Which never was. Law's speech beside law's thought?
That were too stunning, too immense an odds:
That point of vantage law lets nobly pass.
One lawyer shall admit us to behold
The manner of the making out a case,   1125
First fashion of a speech; the chick in egg,

1105 MS {New paragraph (already written thus) indicated by 'N.P.' in left-hand margin} MS of 1109 MS truth may>sources 1110 MS Law 1112 MS 1868 1872 unchoak, 1113 MS 1868 1872 Truth in 1115 MS 1868 1872 all that mystery 1117 MS {no commas} 1119 MS {dash added later} MS of MS simulates the tongue 1120 MS saves 1121 MS was: law's 1122 MS and>too 1123 MS Law let 1868 1872 vantage, law let 1126 MS speech,

1106 flustered: 'made half drunk, made hot and rosy with drinking': Johnson; adding to the image implied in 'sober' and 'frothy'.

1108–10 divining-rod . . . recognized machine: a divining-rod is a forked stick by which diviners can trace underground supplies of water. The contrast is between this personal, intuitive way of finding water (hidden truth)—as in the early monologues—and the professional, complex method of law, as seen in the lawyers' rhetoric and legal citations in Books VIII and IX. The image of law as the 'recognized machine', some elaborate mechanical pump for bringing up the underground water, is satirical.

1118 puissance: probably trisyllabic, with stress on the second syllable 'puíssance'; see OED². Cf. the four-syllable pronunciation of 'impuissance' in 'Saul', 294.

The masterpiece law's bosom incubates.
How Don Giacinto of the Arcangeli,
Called Procurator of the Poor at Rome,
Now advocate for Guido and his mates,—   1130
The jolly learned man of middle age,
Cheek and jowl all in laps with fat and law,
Mirthful as mighty, yet, as great hearts use,
Despite the name and fame that tempt our flesh,
Constant to that devotion of the hearth,   1135
Still captive in those dear domestic ties!—
How he,—having a cause to triumph with,
All kind of interests to keep intact,
More than one efficacious personage
To tranquillize, conciliate and secure,   1140
And above all, public anxiety
To quiet, show its Guido in good hands,—
Also, as if such burdens were too light,
A certain family-feast to claim his care,
The birthday-banquet for the only son—   1145
Paternity at smiling strife with law—
How he brings both to buckle in one bond;
And, thick at throat, with waterish under-eye,
Turns to his task and settles in his seat
And puts his utmost means in practice now: 1150
Wheezes out law-phrase, whiffles Latin forth,
And, just as though roast lamb would never be,

1127 *MS* {beginning of fo. 42}   *MS A*   *1868 1872* And   1129 *MS* High>
Hight   *MS* Rome   1130 *MS* And   *MS* mates,   1133 *MS* potent
1136 *MS A*   *MS* ties,—   1137 *MS* he,   1138 *MS* kinds   1140 *MS*
tranquilize   1142 *MS* quiet and show   1145 *MS* birthday banquet
1147 *MS* bond,   *1148 *1888 1889* {line indented}   *MS* throat with   *MS*
undereye   1149 *MS* chair   1150 *1868 1872* to practice *MS* to practise
now,   1151 *MS 1868 1872* law and whiffles   *MS* latin

1132 *jowl*: jaw.

1139 *efficacious*: influential. Browning uses the word to mean this rather than
'effective': cf. III. 1471, VI. 443.

1151 *whiffles*: speaks in a whistling, breathy way. The description makes great play
with Arcangeli being fat and rheumy.

Makes logic levigate the big crime small:
Rubs palm on palm, rakes foot with itchy foot,
Conceives and inchoates the argument,   1155
Sprinkling each flower appropriate to the time,
—Ovidian quip or Ciceronian crank,
A-bubble in the larynx while he laughs,
As he had fritters deep down frying there.
How he turns, twists, and tries the oily thing   1160
Shall be—first speech for Guido 'gainst the Fisc.

Then with a skip as it were from heel to head,
Leaving yourselves fill up the middle bulk
O' the Trial, reconstruct its shape august,
From such exordium clap we to the close;   1165
Give you, if we dare wing to such a height,
The absolute glory in some full-grown speech
On the other side, some finished butterfly,

1153 *MS* the crime away.   1154 *MS* {beginning of fo. 43}   1158 *MS*
laughs   1160 *MS* does turn, twist, try   1161 *MS* First Speech   *MS*
against   *1162 *MS* {New paragraph (already written thus) indicated by 'N.P.'
in left-hand margin. Paragraphing obscured in *1868* and *1872* by this line's being at the
head of the page}   *1888 1889* {no new paragraph}   1163 *MS* man   1164 *MS*
Of   1165 *MS* come>clap   *MS* close,   1168 *MS* butterfly

1153 *levigate*: break down (into fragments), rub or grind (to a fine powder), from
Med. L. *levigabilis*; cf. 'Christmas-Eve', 1078.

1155 *inchoates*: begins, commences, from L. *incohare* or *inchoare*. This self-
consciously Latinate word, like 'levigate' before, is a comic suggestion of Arcangeli's
obsession with Latinity and his rhetorical pomp. OED[2] records uses by Donne and
Henry More, two of Browning's favourite writers: see Ian Jack, 'Some Reflections on
the Words in *Sordello*', BIS 6 (1978), 79–80.

1156 *flower*: flower of rhetoric, an ornament of speech.

1157 *Ovidian quip or Ciceronian crank*: cf. 'Quips and cranks': Milton, 'L'Allegro', 27.
A crank is a twist or fanciful turn of speech. Arcangeli's speech has both the wit of one
of Rome's greatest poets, Ovid (43 BC–AD 17), and the rhetorical elegance of one of
her greatest orators, Cicero (106–43 BC).

1159 *fritters*: small pieces of potato cut to be fried in oil. The image suggests the
catarrh-ridden nature of Arcangeli's throat, and goes appropriately with his obsession
with food.

1160 *the oily thing*: i.e. the smooth, unctuous speech; there is also a pun on oily =
greasy, picking up on 'fritters'.

1165 *exordium*: introduction.
clap: hurry.

Some breathing diamond-flake with leaf-gold fans,
That takes the air, no trace of worm it was,   1170
Or cabbage-bed it had production from.
Giovambattista o' the Bottini, Fisc,
Pompilia's patron by the chance of the hour,
To-morrow her persecutor,—composite, he,
As becomes who must meet such various calls—   1175
Odds of age joined in him with ends of youth.
A man of ready smile and facile tear,
Improvised hopes, despairs at nod and beck,
And language—ah, the gift of eloquence!
Language that goes, goes, easy as a glove,   1180
O'er good and evil, smoothens both to one.
Rashness helps caution with him, fires the straw,
In free enthusiastic careless fit,
On the first proper pinnacle of rock
Which offers, as reward for all that zeal,   1185
To lure some bark to founder and bring gain:
While calm sits Caution, rapt with heavenward eye,
A true confessor's gaze, amid the glare
Beaconing to the breaker, death and hell.
"Well done, thou good and faithful!" she approves: 1190
"Hadst thou let slip a faggot to the beach,

1169 *MS* vans,   1172 *MS* of   *1174 *1888 1889* {line indented}   *MS*
composite he,   1176 *MS* youth,   1180 *MS* {beginning of fo. 44}   *MS 1868*
1872 goes as easy   *MS 1868 1872* glove   1181 *MS* them   1182 *MS* straw
1183 *MS* fit   1185 *MS 1868 1872* happens,   1186 *MS* split>founder   *MS*
the gain,>gain,   1187 *MS* caution   1188 *MS* gaze amid the glare   *1868*
1872 gaze amid the glare,   1189 *MS* While beaconing   *1190 *MS* faithful,>
faithful!   *1868 1872* faithful!"   *1888 1889* faithful" {space indicates broken sort}
MS law approves   1191 *MS* fall>slip   *MS* beach

   1174 *To-morrow her persecutor*: at the end of this trial Bottini, here the defender
of Pompilia and her reputation, undertook a case presupposing her adultery: see XII.
622–750.   *composite*: made up of various parts or elements.
   1182–95 *Rashness . . . time!"*: Bottini—a character of contradictory attributes—
employs both rashness and caution in his attacks. The image is that of a wrecking,
where a ship was lured onto a rocky beach by a false beacon on a cliff in order to
plunder its cargo. 'Rashness' (personified) is seen as the initiator of the fire, a reckless
beacon-lighter. (Wrecking was punishable by hanging.) 'Caution', on the other hand,
plays the part of those who allow the wreckers to act, and then share the plunder from

"The crew might surely spy thy precipice
"And save their boat; the simple and the slow
"Might so, forsooth, forestall the wrecker's fee!
"Let the next crew be wise and hail in time!"   1195
Just so compounded is the outside man,
Blue juvenile pure eye and pippin cheek,
And brow all prematurely soiled and seamed
With sudden age, bright devastated hair.
Ah, but you miss the very tones o' the voice,   1200
The scrannel pipe that screams in heights of head,
As, in his modest studio, all alone,
The tall wight stands a-tiptoe, strives and strains,
Both eyes shut, like the cockerel that would crow,
Tries to his own self amorously o'er   1205
What never will be uttered else than so—
Since to the four walls, Forum and Mars' Hill,
Speaks out the poesy which, penned, turns prose.

1192 *MS 1868 1872* had surely spied   1193 *MS 1868 1872* saved   *MS* boat,   *MS* mariners,>and the slow,   *1868 1872* slow,   1194 *MS* "Who should have prompt forestalled the wrecker's fee.   *1868 1872* "Who should have prompt forestalled the wrecker's fee: 1196 *MS* was   1197 *MS* His   1199 *MS* With age,>With sudden age,   *MS* and devastated   1200 *MS* of him,>of the man,   1201 *MS* voice   *MS* screamed>screams   1202 *MS* {no commas}   1203 *MS* a tiptoe   *MS* strains   1207–16 *MS* {lines not found}   1207 *1868 1872* To the four walls, for

the ship, without feeling responsible for the crime. Caution applies also to the 'careful' use of rashness: the wild 'fire-lighting' of Bottini is not so careless as it appears (l. 1191); it is governed by caution in some sense.

1197 *pippin cheek*: round, red cheek (like the apple).

1199 *bright devastated*: i.e. white and thinning; maybe, also, a mess.

1201 *scrannel pipe*: thin, harsh wind instrument; cf. 'their lean and flashy songs / Grate on their scrannel pipes of wretched straw': Milton, 'Lycidas', 123–4.

1203–4 *wight . . . crow*: the archaism 'wight' (person) signals the comic and moral allusion to Chaucer's cock called Chauntecleer and his vain obsession with his own crowing. Bottini is as ludicrous as the cock straining to sing sweetly: 'This Chauntecleer stood hye upon his toos, / Strecchynge his nekke, and heeld his eyen cloos, / And gan to crowe loude for the nones': *The Nun's Priest's Tale*, 4521–3.

1207 *Forum and Mars' Hill*: the two great places of debate and speech-making in ancient Rome and Greece. Mars' Hill (the Areopagus) was the site of St Paul's great speech to the Athenians: Acts 17: 22; cf. 'Mr Sludge', 742–4. For Bottini, the four walls of his room have to act as an equivalent, though he fantasizes a wider audience.

Clavecinist debarred his instrument,
He yet thrums—shirking neither turn nor trill,   1210
With desperate finger on dumb table-edge—
The sovereign rondo, shall conclude his *Suite*,
Charm an imaginary audience there,
From old Corelli to young Haendel, both
I' the flesh at Rome, ere he perforce go print   1215
The cold black score, mere music for the mind—
The last speech against Guido and his gang,
With special end to prove Pompilia pure.
How the Fisc vindicates Pompilia's fame.

Then comes the all but end, the ultimate   1220
Judgment save yours. Pope Innocent the Twelfth,
Simple, sagacious, mild yet resolute,
With prudence, probity and—what beside
From the other world he feels impress at times,
Having attained to fourscore years and six,—   1225
How, when the court found Guido and the rest
Guilty, but law supplied a subterfuge
And passed the final sentence to the Pope,
He, bringing his intelligence to bear
This last time on what ball behoves him drop   1230
In the urn, or white or black, does drop a black,

1218 *MS* {beginning of fo. 45}   1220 *MS* {New paragraph (already written
thus) indicated by 'N.P.' in left-hand margin}   *MS* the>and   1221 *MS*
Twelfth   1226 *MS* Court   1231 *MS* he drops

1209 *Clavecinist*: player on the clavecin (Fr. harpsichord). This use, and the musical
comparison, are intended to give a late-seventeenth, early-eighteenth-century feel;
Browning played the harpsichord and may have been thinking of Handel's *Suites de
pieces pour le clavecin* (1720).
    1212 *sovereign rondo*: grand, supreme rondo (a stirring piece of music to end his suite).
Suite: a group of musical pieces, usually in contrasting fashions.
    1214 *old Corelli to young Haendel*: Arcangelo Corelli (1653–1713), the Italian com-
poser, spent most of his working life in Rome. George Frideric Handel (1685–1759),
born in Germany, only came to Italy in 1706 when he was 21; he spent part of his time
in Rome, leaving Italy in 1710. Browning uses historical licence to place him with
Corelli in Rome in 1698. Presumably the spelling 'Haendel' is deliberately adopted to
suit the time when George Frideric Handel was still Georg Friedrich Händel.
    1230–1 *ball . . . black*: the practice of voting in ancient Greece, with white and black
balls for innocent and guilty, has become proverbial.

Send five souls more to just precede his own,
Stand him in stead and witness, if need were,
How he is wont to do God's work on earth.
The manner of his sitting out the dim   1235
Droop of a sombre February day
In the plain closet where he does such work,
With, from all Peter's treasury, one stool,
One table and one lathen crucifix.
There sits the Pope, his thoughts for company;   1240
Grave but not sad,—nay, something like a cheer
Leaves the lips free to be benevolent,
Which, all day long, did duty firm and fast.
A cherishing there is of foot and knee,   1244
A chafing loose-skinned large-veined hand with hand,—
What steward but knows when stewardship earns its wage,
May levy praise, anticipate the lord?
He reads, notes, lays the papers down at last,
Muses, then takes a turn about the room;
Unclasps a huge tome in an antique guise,   1250

1232 *MS* Sends   1233 *MS* {no commas}   1234 *MS* was   1240 *MS* company,   1243 *MS* {no commas}   1244 *MS* {beginning of fo. 46}   1245 *MS* chafe of   1247 *MS* And levies>May levy   *MS* anticipates>anticipate   1248 *MS* reads, writes, lays   1249 *MS* room,

1236 *Droop*: end; perhaps a memory of the verb use in *Paradise Lost*, xi. 178.
1239 *lathen*: made of lath: crude, thin wood.
1240–7 *There . . . lord?*: the pope is relaxing after a long, hard day—implicitly also at the end of long, dutiful life. His small gentlenesses with himself (his relaxed smile, his cherishing of aching legs) indicate his sense that he has served his master (God) well. A good servant knows when he may expect his master's praise.
1250 *huge tome*: this is usually taken to be the ancient history of the popes referred to in the opening lines of Book X. By this reading, the 'evening's chance' would be what is revealed in x. 24–6, 157–61: that the extract of papal history that the Pope reads is from A D 891–8, eight hundred years before his own pontificate, and that one major judgement made by John IX took place eight hundred years to the day of his own pronouncing on the murder trial. It is difficult to see how ll. 1253–4 fit with this, since it would make the Pope's act a personal one, not something decreed by 'an order long in use'. It seems simpler to think that what we have here is confirming evidence that Book I was written before Book X. Browning is imagining the Pope reading his Vulgate Bible or his breviary, seeing some chance application of the set passages to the murder trial. He had not yet settled on the passage or its application, and later changed the Pope's reading to the history of the popes.

Primitive print and tongue half obsolete,
That stands him in diurnal stead; opes page,
Finds place where falls the passage to be conned
According to an order long in use:
And, as he comes upon the evening's chance,   1255
Starts somewhat, solemnizes straight his smile,
Then reads aloud that portion first to last,
And at the end lets flow his own thoughts forth
Likewise aloud, for respite and relief,
Till by the dreary relics of the west   1260
Wan through the half-moon window, all his light,
He bows the head while the lips move in prayer,
Writes some three brief lines, signs and seals the same,
Tinkles a hand-bell, bids the obsequious Sir
Who puts foot presently o' the closet-sill   1265
He watched outside of, bear as superscribed
That mandate to the Governor forthwith:
Then heaves abroad his cares in one good sigh,
Traverses corridor with no arm's help,
And so to sup as a clear conscience should.   1270
The manner of the judgment of the Pope.

Then must speak Guido yet a second time,
Satan's old saw being apt here—skin for skin,
All a man hath that will he give for life.
While life was graspable and gainable,   1275

1252 *MS* stead,   1253 *MS* read>conned   1254 *MS* use,   1259 *MS*
relief.   *Yale 1* relief.>relief,   1260 *MS* West   *Yale 1* West>west   1265 *MS*
on   1267 *MS* forthwith,   1268 *MS* with>in   1269 *MS* help
1271 *MS* {line added later}   1272 *MS* {beginning of fo. 47. New paragraph
indicated by 'N.P.' in left-hand margin}   *MS* Th[ ]>Then   1273 *MS* skin for
skin   1275 *MS 1868 1872* gainable, free

1252 *diurnal*: daily.
   1273–4 *skin . . . life*: 'And Satan answered the Lord, and said, Skin for skin, yea, all
that a man hath will he give for his life': Job 2: 4.
   1275–81 *While . . . last*: Guido's 'web of words' for catching the bird (i.e. life) is
partly like a net, partly like a piece of woven material or tapestry ('web'). The
imminence of death, like fire, shrinks up all of the web that is lies, leaving shining
just the gold threads of truth.

And bird-like buzzed her wings round Guido's brow,
Not much truth stiffened out the web of words
He wove to catch her: when away she flew
And death came, death's breath rivelled up the lies,
Left bare the metal thread, the fibre fine   1280
Of truth, i' the spinning: the true words shone last.
How Guido, to another purpose quite,
Speaks and despairs, the last night of his life,
In that New Prison by Castle Angelo
At the bridge-foot: the same man, another voice.   1285
On a stone bench in a close fetid cell,
Where the hot vapour of an agony,
Struck into drops on the cold wall, runs down—
Horrible worms made out of sweat and tears—
There crouch, well nigh to the knees in dungeon-straw,
Lit by the sole lamp suffered for their sake,   1291
Two awe-struck figures, this a Cardinal,
That an Abate, both of old styled friends
O' the thing part man part monster in the midst,
So changed is Franceschini's gentle blood.   1295
The tiger-cat screams now, that whined before,
That pried and tried and trod so gingerly,

1276 *MS* To bird-like buz   *Yale 1* buz>buzz   *1868 1872* To bird-like buzz
1280 *MS* f>bare   1281 *MS* truth in   *MS* at>come   *1868 1872* come
1282 *MS* {no commas}   1285 *MS* Bridge-foot. The   *MS* a novel>
another   1286 *MS* cell   1287 *MS* Down>Where   *MS* agony
1288 *MS* wall ran down   *1868 1872* down   1290, 1291 *MS* {These lines
stand in the reverse order}   1291 *MS* sake   1292 *MS* awestruck
1293 *MS* Abate both   1294 *MS* Of the part man part monster   *1868 1872* Of
the part-man part-monster   1295 *MS* blood: 1296 *MS* now that
1297 *MS* gingerly

1279 *rivelled*: shrivelled; used in such contexts as Time setting wrinkles on a face, or
the sun's heat shrinking up a flower. Cf. 'Or Alom-*Stypticks* with contracting Power /
Shrink his thin Essence like a rivell'd Flower': Pope, *The Rape of the Lock* (1714), ii.
131–2. The use is different from that in *Paracelsus*, i. 481.

1296–9 *tiger-cat . . . foams*: in Book V Guido seemed quite a delicate creature, only
whining and treading carefully through the arguments. Now he has been caught by the
trap of justice ('the trap-teeth joined') which bites through his 'silkiness' (his silky fur,
his smooth manner) he is revealed as a tiger-cat, screaming his true nature in pain and
fear.

Till in its silkiness the trap-teeth joined;
Then you know how the bristling fury foams.
They listen, this wrapped in his folds of red,   1300
While his feet fumble for the filth below;
The other, as beseems a stouter heart,
Working his best with beads and cross to ban
The enemy that comes in like a flood
Spite of the standard set up, verily   1305
And in no trope at all, against him there:
For at the prison-gate, just a few steps
Outside, already, in the doubtful dawn,
Thither, from this side and from that, slow sweep
And settle down in silence solidly,   1310
Crow-wise, the frightful Brotherhood of Death.
Black-hatted and black-hooded huddle they,
Black rosaries a-dangling from each waist;
So take they their grim station at the door,
Torches lit, skull-and-cross-bones-banner spread,   1315
And that gigantic Christ with open arms,
Grounded. Nor lacks there aught but that the group
Break forth, intone the lamentable psalm,
"Out of the deeps, Lord, have I cried to thee!"—
When inside, from the true profound, a sign   1320

1298 *MS* join,   *1868 1872* join;   1299 *MS* {beginning of fo. 48}   1301 *MS*
below,   *1306 *1888 1889* there· {broken sort}   *MS 1868 1872* there:
1308 *MS* already in   1310 *MS* solidly   1311 *MS* Crow-wise the   *MS*
Death,   1313 *MS* the waist.   1315 *MS 1868* Torches alight and
cross-bones-banner   *MS* spread   1316 *MS* arms   1317 *MS* Grounded:
nor   1319 *MS* Thee!"

1304–5 *enemy . . . up*: cf. 'When the enemy shall come in like a flood, the Spirit of
the Lord shall lift up a standard against him': Isa. 59: 19. The literal 'standard' here is the
crucifix of l. 1316.

1311 *Brotherhood of Death*: the Confraternity of Death and Pity, or brothers of
mercy, who helped criminals prepare for death, and who accompanied them to their
executions: see SS 19. They were secular volunteers from all spheres of society.
Because of their striking black hats and hoods with eye-slits, the poet imagines them
as a flock of crows, sensing the imminence of death, and gathering to eat the corpses.

1319 *"Out . . . thee!*: the opening line of Ps. 130, commonly known after its opening
in Latin as the 'De Profundis' (Out of the deep).

1320 *profound*: deep; punning on the previous line.

Shall bear intelligence that the foe is foiled,
Count Guido Franceschini has confessed,
And is absolved and reconciled with God.
Then they, intoning, may begin their march,
Make by the longest way for the People's Square,   1325
Carry the criminal to his crime's award:
A mob to cleave, a scaffolding to reach,
Two gallows and Mannaia crowning all.
How Guido made defence a second time.

Finally, even as thus by step and step   1330
I led you from the level of to-day
Up to the summit of so long ago,
Here, whence I point you the wide prospect round—
Let me, by like steps, slope you back to smooth,
Land you on mother-earth, no whit the worse,   1335
To feed o' the fat o' the furrow: free to dwell,
Taste our time's better things profusely spread
For all who love the level, corn and wine,
Much cattle and the many-folded fleece.
Shall not my friends go feast again on sward,   1340
Though cognizant of country in the clouds
Higher than wistful eagle's horny eye

1322 *MS* And   1324 *MS* And   *MS* intoning may   1326 *MS* {beginning
of fo. 49}   *MS* award—   1327 *MS* scaffolding>scaffoldage>scaffolding
MS climb,>mount,>reach,   1329 *MS* tried   1330 *MS* {New paragraph
(already written thus) indicated by 'N.P.' in left-hand margin}   *MS* Finally even
1332 *MS* Up this the   1333 *MS* Where I have pointed you the prospect
round—>This, where I pointed you the prospect round—   1336 *MS* But fed
with fat of   1337 *MS* Mid>Taste   1339 *MS* fleece,   1340 *MS* {line
not found}

1328 *Mannaia*: guillotine: from SS 19. This is the It. name for a version of this, used
in Italy from the thirteenth century for the execution of criminals of noble birth.
1330–9 *Finally. . .fleece*: the image is vaguely biblical: cf. Deut. 34: 1–4, Gen. 27: 28.
1340 *sward*: rich green grass; part of the image of the easy present-day time, as
opposed to the difficult, aspiring act of historical imagining, 'the summit of so long ago'.
1341 *country in the clouds*: 'heaven' in l. 1345; in terms of the image, the perfectly
imagined historical past.
1342 *horny*: the slightly hard appearance of the eagle's eyelid, with also a suggestion
of its old age.

Ever unclosed for, 'mid ancestral crags,
When morning broke and Spring was back once more,
And he died, heaven, save by his heart, unreached?   1345
Yet heaven my fancy lifts to, ladder-like,—
As Jack reached, holpen of his beanstalk-rungs!

A novel country: I might make it mine
By choosing which one aspect of the year
Suited mood best, and putting solely that   1350
On panel somewhere in the House of Fame,
Landscaping what I saved, not what I saw:
—Might fix you, whether frost in goblin-time
Startled the moon with his abrupt bright laugh,
Or, August's hair afloat in filmy fire,   1355
She fell, arms wide, face foremost on the world,
Swooned there and so singed out the strength of things.
Thus were abolished Spring and Autumn both,
The land dwarfed to one likeness of the land,
Life cramped corpse-fashion. Rather learn and love   1360
Each facet-flash of the revolving year!—
Red, green and blue that whirl into a white,
The variance now, the eventual unity,
Which make the miracle. See it for yourselves,
This man's act, changeable because alive!   1365

1343 *MS* mid   1344 *MS* back again,   1345 *MS* unreached,
1347 *MS* Yet   1348 *MS* {New paragraph (already written thus) indicated by
'N.P.' in left-hand margin}   1350 *MS* Suits my   1351 *MS* pannel
1352 *MS* {beginning of fo. 50}   1357 *MS* things: 1361 *MS* year,
1364 *MS* miracle: see   1365 *MS* Man's Act   *MS* alive;

1347 *holpen*: helped (archaic).

1348–61 *I . . . year!*: Browning justifies his approach to the past: he has given us 'the
revolving year'—all the seasons (all the variety and confused variation of the life of the
murder-case)—and not just one or two static and careful vignettes of winter and
summer.

1351 *House of Fame*: cf. Chaucer, *The House of Fame* (*c.*1370).

1353 *goblin-time*: i.e. winter, or long winter nights, a time attractive to goblins. Cf.
The Winter's Tale, 11. i. 25–6.

Action now shrouds, now shows the informing thought;
Man, like a glass ball with a spark a-top,
Out of the magic fire that lurks inside,
Shows one tint at a time to take the eye:
Which, let a finger touch the silent sleep,   1370
Shifted a hair's-breadth shoots you dark for bright,
Suffuses bright with dark, and baffles so
Your sentence absolute for shine or shade.
Once set such orbs,—white styled, black stigmatized,—
A-rolling, see them once on the other side   1375
Your good men and your bad men every one
From Guido Franceschini to Guy Faux,
Oft would you rub your eyes and change your names.

Such, British Public, ye who like me not,
(God love you!)—whom I yet have laboured for,   1380
Perchance more careful whoso runs may read
Than erst when all, it seemed, could read who ran,—
Perchance more careless whoso reads may praise
Than late when he who praised and read and wrote
Was apt to find himself the self-same me,—   1385

*1366 *MS* shrouds now shows   *1868* now shows   *1872 1888 1889* nor
shows   *MS* thought,   1367 *MS* Lies like   *MS* a-top   1368 *MS* rolls>
lurks   1369 *MS* The   *MS* that takes   1371 *MS* gives   1374 *MS*
orbs, styled white, black stigmatized,>orbs, white styled, black stigmatized,
1376 *MS* men, every   *1868* one,   1378 *MS* shift   1379 *MS* {beginning
of fo. 51. New paragraph indicated by 'N.P.' in left-hand margin.}   *MS* you
1382 *MS* Than late   1385 *MS* selfsame

   1367 *glass ball*: Browning is thinking of a glass ball, or 'electric egg'—a glass bulb
with two metal or carbon rods going into it. This was used to demonstrate an electric
current through a vacuum or through different gases. A pump takes the air out of the
'egg', and an electric machine passes a current through it. The current, crossing the gap
between the rods, creates variable patterns of light and dark in the ball; a finger moved
on the outside of the ball (l. 1370) creates even more variation. The image illustrates
the difficulty in evaluating a man by the ever-changing impression made by his actions
and speech.
   1381–2 *Perchance . . . ran*: cf. Hab. 2: 2 'he may run that readeth it', used proverbially
about something that is easy to read (that can be read by a man running). In l. 1382 the
proverb is playfully inverted. Previously, Browning assumed that everybody would be
able to understand his poetry on first reading it. Now, in writing R&B, he has been
perhaps more aware of the need to make it clear to others.

Such labour had such issue, so I wrought
This arc, by furtherance of such alloy,
And so, by one spirt, take away its trace
Till, justifiably golden, rounds my ring.

A ring without a posy, and that ring mine?   1390

O lyric Love, half angel and half bird
And all a wonder and a wild desire,—
Boldest of hearts that ever braved the sun,
Took sanctuary within the holier blue,
And sang a kindred soul out to his face,—   1395
Yet human at the red-ripe of the heart—
When the first summons from the darkling earth
Reached thee amid thy chambers, blanched their blue,
And bared them of the glory—to drop down,
To toil for man, to suffer or to die,—   1400

1388 *1872* spirit,   *Yale 2* spirit,>spirt,   *MS* its trace away   1390 *MS*
{New paragraph (already written thus) indicated by 'N.P.' in left-hand margin}
1391 *MS* {New paragraph (already written thus) indicated by 'N.P.' in left-hand
margin}   *MS* love, half-angel and half-bird   1394 *MS* blue   1395 *MS*
in his face,   1399 *MS* down   1400 *MS* To toil, to suffer or to die for
man,—>To toil for man, to suffer or to die,—

1390 *posy*: motto or love-verse (inscribed on a ring); cf. *Hamlet*, III. ii. 152. The
posy written for the poet's ring of verse (the completed poem) is the loving invocation
to EBB that follows.

1391 *lyric Love*: Love that is like lyric poetry, i.e. passionate and heaven-aspiring: a
name for EBB herself.

1393 *Boldest . . . sun*: EBB was like the angel and bird (of l. 1391) flying upward
towards the sun, which is life-giving, pure, and bright (symbolic of God, truth, and
heaven).

1395 *his face*: i.e. the sun's face.

1398 *thy chambers*: the heavenly spaces of thought and feeling that EBB naturally
inhabited, from which she responded to the 'summons' (l. 1397) to come down into
the world. The phrase also has a biographical resonance: EBB's upstairs room at 50
Wimpole Street.

blanched: took the colour out of.

1399–1400 *drop . . . die*: cf. Phil. 2: 5–8. EBB came down to respond to suffering,
like the supreme 'lyric Love', Christ, who, though God, was born into the world. The
biographical parallel is EBB's entry into married life, her work and sufferings within
this, her political commitments, and her eventual death.

This is the same voice: can thy soul know change?
Hail then, and hearken from the realms of help!
Never may I commence my song, my due
To God who best taught song by gift of thee,
Except with bent head and beseeching hand—   1405
That still, despite the distance and the dark,
What was, again may be; some interchange
Of grace, some splendour once thy very thought,
Some benediction anciently thy smile:
—Never conclude, but raising hand and head   1410
Thither where eyes, that cannot reach, yet yearn
For all hope, all sustainment, all reward,
Their utmost up and on,—so blessing back
In those thy realms of help, that heaven thy home,

1401 *MS* voice—can   1402 *MS* then and   1404 *MS* {beginning of
fo. 52}   1405 *MS* hand   1407 *MS* be, some   1410 *MS* conclude
but   1411 *MS* {no commas}   *MS* strain>yearn   1413 *MS* on, so
1416 *MS* guess>think   *MS* fall.

1401 *same voice*: i.e. Browning's voice, the same voice that summoned her from her
'chambers' before.

1402 *realms of help*: heaven.

1405 *bent . . . hand*: a posture of prayer.

1408 *splendour*: brightness.

1409 *benediction*: blessing. To inspire him to his work, Browning cannot receive
EBB's 'thought' and 'smile' directly, as when she was on earth, but he hopes at least to
feel this 'splendour' and 'benediction' coming down from heaven from her soul.

1410 *conclude*: finish (his work on the poem).

1411 *Thither*: i.e. to heaven.

1413 *blessing back*: Browning will reciprocate the blessing he hopes to receive in ll.
1407–9.

1410–16 *Never . . . fall*: in 1870 Bloomfield Parker wrote to Browning asking the
meaning of this passage, and Browning sent him a paraphrase. The original of this letter
is lost. We give it here from a surviving transcript, RB to Revd. Bloomfield Parker, 11
Jan. 1870: California State University, Hayward:

My dear Sir,

Thank you [so] much for your kind letter. I dare say there is a real fault of obscurity
in the passage you desire to be elucidated. Such a paraphrase as you want, would, I
suppose, be the following.

"May I never conclude a song but,—in return to what has been conceded to bent
head & beseeching hand,—to wit some interchange etc.,—but by raising hand & head
to heaven, so to conclude in gratefully blessing back—or returning a blessing for—
whatever manifestation in that heaven shall have seemed to earthly eyes a token of real

Some whiteness which, I judge, thy face makes proud,
Some wanness where, I think, thy foot may fall!   1416

presence—whether some whiteness, the brighter of the starry clusters, which etc. etc.,
or even, in the lowest degree, some wanness, merest suspicion of light, where etc. etc."
The force of "I judge" & "I think" being proportioned to the assurance in the one case
& the doubt in the other.

May I add that the indisposition to write this "plainly" even now, seems to account
for the original failure: & I only trust this to your own sympathy of course.

I am, Dear Sir,
Yours very truly
Robert Browning

1416 *wanness*: see Browning to Mr Leonard: 'Wanness should be taken as meaning
simply *less bright* than absolute whiteness as Keats speaks of "wannish fire"'. Cf. Keats,
'Lamia', i. 57. This fragment of a letter is imbedded in a postcard from Edward Berdoe
to F. J. Furnivall, 20 Feb. 1896, which commences as follows: 'A Mr Leonard of 19
Oakfield Rd. Clifton writes to say re "Lyric Love" in *Br. Studies* that he has an original
letter from R.B. in which he says . . .': Furnivall holding, King's College, London. The
original letter is lost.

Browning cannot see EBB in heaven, but he will bless that which he can see: a
bright starry cluster ('some whiteness') that he imagines has been distinguished by her
gaze, and a less bright spot ('some wanness') perhaps marked out by her footstep.

INTRODUCTION TO BOOK II

HALF-ROME

The dramatic monologue of Book II was probably suggested by, and is partly based upon, the Italian pamphlet 'Notizie di fatto, e di ragioni per la Causa Franceschini' ('An Account of the Facts and Grounds of the Franceschini Case'), OYB cxli–cliv (145–56), though, in the way its material is shaped to Browning's dramatic ends, it leaves the pamphlet far behind. Half-Rome, the speaker of the monologue, is representative of a large segment of the citizens of Rome, while at the same time also a striking individual in his own right. The murders of Violante and Pietro, and the fatal stabbing of Pompilia, have taken place on the evening of 2 January 1698. Now, it is the dusk of the next day. The gossiping citizens have come to view the corpses laid out in the Church of San Lorenzo in Lucina, to give their views on the murder-case, 'granting grace / Or dealing doom' (I. 640–1). Half-Rome, one of their number, stands on the edge of the Piazza di San Lorenzo in Lucina—described by Treves as 'small, oddly shaped and very still . . . a placid backwater to the rushing stream of the Corso';[1] from here he delivers his verdict on the murder-case, one favourable to Count Guido Franceschini: see I. 875–6 n.

The setting and characterization of the monologue are masterful, particularly at the beginning. Half-Rome has spent the day in and around the Church of San Lorenzo, viewing the corpses laid out since early morning, and picking up the gossip concerning the murders. He seems an expert on such scenes (101–5), in a state of excitement and impatience. The man he has run into—to whom he directs his speech—is a cousin of the 'jackanapes' who is trying to seduce his wife (I, 16, 190, etc.), and the apparent aim of the monologue is to issue, via the cousin, a warning to the would-be seducer. As he sees it, Count Guido Franceschini's drama is bound up with his own. Just as Guido is a pathetic nobleman cuckolded by a glamorous priest, he too could be a victim of adultery, but only if he allows it: his implication at the end of the monologue is that he will, if necessary, follow Guido's example of violence, and maim or kill the would-be seducer if he does not desist.

[1] Treves, 118.

There are few reasons to believe this scenario, and many to disbelieve it. The threat of seduction seems a fantasy, one held almost self-consciously, an excuse to vent a powerful set of obsessions, and indicative of a mind-set in which sadism and sexism have reinforced each other. Half-Rome upholds the 'Cause of Honour' (29), the code of 'gallants' and 'gentlemen' (30, 1529), ideas of 'birth and breeding' (639), and these complement his conservative views concerning violence: his admiration for the era 'when men were men' (1524) and women better controlled. These beliefs are the assertion of a profound egotism which influences all his ideas of the feminine. Later, at the heart of *The Ring and the Book*, there are hints of the relationship of love which could have existed, under different circumstances, between Pompilia and Caponsacchi, a relationship of tenderness and mutuality. In this sense the poem hinges on what Henry James calls 'the great constringent relation of man and woman', the 'relation most worth while in life for either party'.[2] Half-Rome's dominative mind-set, with its rooted sense of social hierarchy and superiority—class over class, and man over woman—precludes such love:

Half-Rome is both the embodiment and the exponent of a male sexism so virulent and disguised that it pollutes the world in which he himself exists and transforms life at its potentially tenderest and most re-creative centre . . . into one of the most psychologically, morally, and aesthetically imprisoning realities of the culture the poem probes, into one of its greatest sources of human cruelty, self-righteousness, and injustice.[3]

This is not evident at the beginning. In a novelistic way, we are gradually involved further and further in Half-Rome's characteristic thought-patterns and the mannerisms of speech that reflect these. We learn about his fascination with the murdered corpses, his vicarious interest in their disfigurement, his relish concerning the exact manner of their death. Having been crowded in the Church of San Lorenzo all day, he is excited to note that Violante's face is so torn up with stab-wounds that her eyes are indistinguishable from her mouth (613–18).

Sullivan notes the continually demeaning effect of his style of speech: 'The most characteristic elements of his diction are the use of colloquialisms and slang, and of epithets and undignified descriptive words . . . which shrink everything he touches on'.[4] He has, we may say, the verbal energy of an Iago, and the way he builds up the image of Guido into that of a pathetic nobleman so wronged that his 'overburdened mind / Broke

---

[2] James, 409.   [3] Buckler, 67.   [4] Sullivan, 28.

down' (1389–90) makes Guido into a kind of justified Othello figure. There are hints of Iago's lubricity, his power of innuendo: as, for example, in the figure of Caponsacchi as Apollo shooting the arrow of love 'while the snake / Pompilia writhed transfixed through all her spires' (794–5), and the picture of him as Ovid, seducing the women of Civitavecchia (1216–28). Either through direct speech, or through the speeches he imagines for others, we are made aware that Half-Rome is attracted to the idea of public whipping for women (1244), and would like to see Caponsacchi dead (1536). Though his monologue is clearly impatient and tense in tone, his wit, his apparent reasonableness, and his ranging irony and sarcasm hold at bay a complete awareness of his character. Perhaps our impressions crystallize in the final heightened passages concerning the murders, particularly in the fantasy of how Guido should have split open the skulls of Pompilia and Caponsacchi, and stuffed the love-letters inside them (1488–1504). Far in the background, we can sense the Duke of 'My Last Duchess', another man who expected to exercise a domineering authority over a wife. In Half-Rome's cherishing admiration of Guido Reni's painting of the crucifixion, 'Second to nought observable in Rome' (85), there is even an echo of the Duke's connoisseurship of art.

II.

HALF-ROME.

WHAT, you, Sir, come too? (Just the man I'd meet.)
Be ruled by me and have a care o' the crowd:
This way, while fresh folk go and get their gaze:
I'll tell you like a book and save your shins.
Fie, what a roaring day we've had! Whose fault?   5
Lorenzo in Lucina,—here's a church
To hold a crowd at need, accommodate
All comers from the Corso! If this crush
Make not its priests ashamed of what they show
For temple-room, don't prick them to draw purse   10
And down with bricks and mortar, eke us out
The beggarly transept with its bit of apse
Into a decent space for Christian ease,
Why, to-day's lucky pearl is cast to swine.

---

1 *MS* {fo. 53. At the head of the page is the title '2. Half-Rome' in RB's hand}
2 *MS* of   7 *MS* accomodate>accommodate   14 *MS* to day's

5 *roaring*: noisy, riotous.

6 *Lorenzo in Lucina*: Henry James described it as 'that banal little church in the old upper Corso—banal, that is, at the worst, with the rare Roman *banalité*': James, 321. The details about the church, here and elsewhere in the poem, were supplied by Frederic Leighton: see RB to Frederic Leighton, 17 Oct. 1864: 'A favour, if you have time for it. Go into the church St. Lorenzo in Lucina in the Corso—and look attentively at it—so as to describe it to me on your return. The general arrangement of the building, if with a nave—pillars or not—the number of altars, and any particularity there may be—over the High Altar is a famous Crucifixion by Guido. It will be of great use to me. I don't care about the *outside*': Orr, 273. For an account of their friendship, see Leonée and Richard Ormond, *Lord Leighton* (New Haven and London, 1975), 76–82.

8 *Corso*: the main north–south thoroughfare of Rome.

11 *eke us out*: extend, supplement.

12 *transept*: area of the cruciform church lying at right angles to the principal axis, including the area in front of the main altar, which in this case is not big enough to hold the crowd that wants to see the Comparini's bodies.

apse: semicircular domed area, behind the altar.

14 *pearl . . . swine*: cf. Matt. 7: 6.

Listen and estimate the luck they've had!   15
(The right man, and I hold him.)
                       Sir, do you see,
They laid both bodies in the church, this morn
The first thing, on the chancel two steps up,
Behind the little marble balustrade;   20
Disposed them, Pietro the old murdered fool
To the right of the altar, and his wretched wife
On the other side. In trying to count stabs,
People supposed Violante showed the most,
Till somebody explained us that mistake;   25
His wounds had been dealt out indifferent where,
But she took all her stabbings in the face,
Since punished thus solely for honour's sake,
Honoris causâ, that's the proper term.
A delicacy there is, our gallants hold,   30
When you avenge your honour and only then,
That you disfigure the subject, fray the face,
Not just take life and end, in clownish guise.
It was Violante gave the first offence,
Got therefore the conspicuous punishment: 35
While Pietro, who helped merely, his mere death
Answered the purpose, so his face went free.
We fancied even, free as you please, that face
Showed itself still intolerably wronged;
Was wrinkled over with resentment yet,   40
Nor calm at all, as murdered faces use,
Once the worst ended: an indignant air

---

15 *MS* had.   16 *MS* {no comma}   18 *MS* {no comma}   21 *MS*
man   24 *MS* thought   *Yale 1* thought>supposed   28 *MS* {beginning of
fo. 54}   *MS* honor's   29 *MS* term: 31 *MS* honor   32 *MS* face
33 *MS* guise: 34 *MS* 'Twas   *Yale 1* 'Twas>It was   35 *MS* punishment
37 *MS* purpose and   39 *MS* wronged   41 *MS* all as

19 *chancel*: the altar area.
29 *Honoris causâ*: for the sake of honour (L.).
30 *gallants*: fine gentlemen, men of fashion and pleasure.
33 *in clownish guise*: in a clown-like or peasant-like way (as opposed to the gallants).
41 *use*: usually are.

O' the head there was—'t is said the body turned
Round and away, rolled from Violante's side
Where they had laid it loving-husband-like.   45
If so, if corpses can be sensitive,
Why did not he roll right down altar-step,
Roll on through nave, roll fairly out of church,
Deprive Lorenzo of the spectacle,
Pay back thus the succession of affronts   50
Whereto this church had served as theatre?
For see: at that same altar where he lies,
To that same inch of step, was brought the babe
For blessing after baptism, and there styled
Pompilia, and a string of names beside,   55
By his bad wife, some seventeen years ago,
Who purchased her simply to palm on him,
Flatter his dotage and defraud the heirs.
Wait awhile! Also to this very step
Did this Violante, twelve years afterward,   60
Bring, the mock-mother, that child-cheat full-grown,
Pompilia, in pursuance of her plot,
And there brave God and man a second time
By linking a new victim to the lie.
There, having made a match unknown to him,   65
She, still unknown to Pietro, tied the knot
Which nothing cuts except this kind of knife;
Yes, made her daughter, as the girl was held,
Marry a man, and honest man beside,

---

43 *MS* Of   *MS* 'tis   44 *MS* away from   *Yale 1* ^, rolled^   46 *MS* and
corpses   47 *MS* {no comma}   48 *MS* Roll through the   *MS* church
49 *MS* his   51 *MS* Whereof>Whereto   53 *MS* {no comma}   54 *MS* {no
comma}   55 *MS* {beginning of fo. 55}   *MS* {no commas}   59 *MS*
awhile: also   *MS* on>to   60 *MS* Did Violante,   64 *MS* lie,
65 *MS* him   67 *MS* knife—   69 *MS* beside

  55 *string of names*: Francesca Camilla Vittoria Angela Pompilia Comparini: cf. VII.
5–7.
  66 *the knot*: the proverbial 'marriage-knot' (the legal bond of marriage), but in the
next line punning on a knot in string. The marriage-knot can only be ended by death
or 'this kind of knife' (the knife of murder).

And man of birth to boot,—clandestinely 70
Because of this, because of that, because
O' the devil's will to work his worst for once,—
Confident she could top her part at need
And, when her husband must be told in turn,
Ply the wife's trade, play off the sex's trick 75
And, alternating worry with quiet qualms,
Bravado with submissiveness, prettily fool
Her Pietro into patience: so it proved.
Ay, 't is four years since man and wife they grew,
This Guido Franceschini and this same 80
Pompilia, foolishly thought, falsely declared
A Comparini and the couple's child:
Just at this altar where, beneath the piece
Of Master Guido Reni, Christ on cross,
Second to nought observable in Rome, 85
That couple lie now, murdered yestereve.
Even the blind can see a providence here.

From dawn till now that it is growing dusk
A multitude has flocked and filled the church,
Coming and going, coming back again, 90
Till to count crazed one. Rome was at the show.
People climbed up the columns, fought for spikes
O' the chapel-rail to perch themselves upon,
Jumped over and so broke the wooden work

---

70 *MS* to-boot,— 72 *MS* Of 75 *MS* sexes 77 *MS 1868 1872*
quick fool 81 *MS* falsely called 82 *MS* {beginning of fo. 56} *MS*
child, *88 MS 1868 1872 1888* dusk, *DC Br U* dusk,>dusk *1889* dusk
89 *MS* {no comma} 93 *MS* Of

73 *top her part*: a theatrical phrase: '*to top one's part* is to play one's part to its utmost
possibilities or to perfection; also, to transcend the character assigned to one': OED[2]
top v.[1] 15.

75 *play... trick*: act up in a particularly female way; cf. *Paracelsus*, iv. 83–5: 'Just so
long as I was pleased / To play off the mere antics of my art, / Fantastic gambols
leading to no end'.

84 *Guido Reni*: Italian painter (1575–1642): see l. 6 n.

Painted like porphyry to deceive the eye;   95
Serve the priests right! The organ-loft was crammed,
Women were fainting, no few fights ensued,
In short, it was a show repaid your pains:
For, though their room was scant undoubtedly,
Yet they did manage matters, to be just,   100
A little at this Lorenzo. Body o' me!
I saw a body exposed once . . . never mind!
Enough that here the bodies had their due.
No stinginess in wax, a row all round,
And one big taper at each head and foot.   105

So, people pushed their way, and took their turn,
Saw, threw their eyes up, crossed themselves, gave place
To pressure from behind, since all the world
Knew the old pair, could talk the tragedy
Over from first to last: Pompilia too,   110
Those who had known her—what 't was worth to them!
Guido's acquaintance was in less request;
The Count had lounged somewhat too long in Rome,
Made himself cheap; with him were hand and glove
Barbers and blear-eyed, as the ancient sings.   115

---

95 *MS* eye—   98 *MS* pains,   101 *MS* of   102 *MS* once .. never
105 *MS* two>one   *MS* tapers>taper   106 *MS* So people   108 {beginning
of fo. 57}   112 *MS* request,   113 *MS* man   *MS* {no comma}
114 *MS* cheap, were him were   115 *MS* sings:

---

95 *porphyry*: valuable, deep-red or purple stone. Leighton's artist's eye would have caught this detail: wood painted to look like porphyry.

101 *Body o' me*: my body! (an oath).

102 *I . . . once*: Half-Rome's implication is that, in times past, he has seen something horrific in relation to an exposed body, some mistreatment of the corpse, or lack of control in the crowd.

111 *what . . . them*: i.e. people who knew Pompilia enjoyed showing off their knowledge in the circumstances.

114 *hand and glove*: on intimate terms.

115 *Barbers and blear-eyed*: i.e. the common gossips; from Horace, *Satires*, I. vii. 3: 'omnibus et lippis notum et tonsoribus': '[a tale] well-known to everyone with sore eyes and to every barber'. Sore eyes were a common complaint in ancient Italy; sufferers would collect and talk in chemists' shops (*medicinae*) while buying ointment. Barbers' shops were also proverbially places for gossip.

ancient: Horace.

Also he is alive and like to be:
Had he considerately died,—aha!
I jostled Luca Cini on his staff,
Mute in the midst, the whole man one amaze,
Staring amain and crossing brow and breast.   120
"How now?" asked I. " 'T is seventy years," quoth he,
"Since I first saw, holding my father's hand,
"Bodies set forth: a many have I seen,
"Yet all was poor to this I live and see.
"Here the world's wickedness seals up the sum: 125
"What with Molinos' doctrine and this deed,
"Antichrist surely comes and doomsday's near.
"May I depart in peace, I have seen my see."
"Depart then," I advised, "nor block the road
"For youngsters still behindhand with such sights!"   130
"Why no," rejoins the venerable sire,
"I know it's horrid, hideous past belief,
"Burdensome far beyond what eye can bear;
"But they do promise, when Pompilia dies
"I' the course o' the day,—and she can't outlive night,—
"They'll bring her body also to expose   136
"Beside the parents, one, two, three a-breast;

---

117 *MS* aha,   120 *MS* Staring and crossing brow and breast amain.   121 *MS* quoth I. "Tis   *1868* "Tis   *MS* {no commas}   122–8 *MS* {no quotation marks} 127 *MS* Antichrist's surely come and doomsday near.   *1868 1872* "Antichrist's surely come and doomsday near.   130 *MS* {no quotation mark}   *MS* sights."   131 *MS* sire   133–9 *MS* {no quotation marks}   133 *MS* bear, 135 *MS* {beginning of fo. 58}   *MS* In the course of   *Yale 1* of>o'   137 *MS* a-breast,

---

118 *Luca Cini*: a character not in OYB. Half-Rome's account of the old man's manner and speech (118–28) make him into a parodic version of Simeon, amazed, however, not by the Christ child, but by the Comparini's dead bodies: cf. Luke 2: 25–35.
   119 *amaze*: confusion of fear and awe.
   120 *amain*: a great deal.
   125 *seals up the sum*: fixes the seal completing the totality (of wickedness): cf. Ezek. 28: 12.
   128 *depart in peace*: a version of the Song of Simeon (Luke 2: 29), deflated by Half-Rome in the next lines.
   see: rare as a noun: OED[2].

"That were indeed a sight, which might I see,
"I trust I should not last to see the like!"
Whereat I bade the senior spare his shanks,   140
Since doctors give her till to-night to live,
And tell us how the butchery happened.   "Ah,
"But you can't know!" sighs he, "I'll not despair:
"Beside I'm useful at explaining things—
"As, how the dagger laid there at the feet,   145
"Caused the peculiar cuts; I mind its make,
"Triangular i' the blade, a Genoese,
"Armed with those little hook-teeth on the edge
"To open in the flesh nor shut again:
"I like to teach a novice: I shall stay!"   150
And stay he did, and stay be sure he will.

A personage came by the private door
At noon to have his look: I name no names:
Well then, His Eminence the Cardinal,
Whose servitor in honourable sort   155
Guido was once, the same who made the match,
(Will you have the truth?) whereof we see effect.
No sooner whisper ran he was arrived
Than up pops Curate Carlo, a brisk lad,
Who never lets a good occasion slip,   160
And volunteers improving the event.
We looked he'd give the history's self some help,

---

138 *MS 1868 1872* sight which,   140 *MS* save his time   141 *MS* ^doctors^
MS half a week>till to night   *MS 1868 1872* {no comma}   142 *MS* happened:
143 *MS* know" sighs he "   144 *MS* Besides   *MS* things   146 *MS* cuts,
147 *MS* in   150 *MS* stay."   151 *MS* {no new paragraph}   155 *MS*
honorable   157 *MS* Will   *MS* truth?,—   *MS* effect;   160 *MS* let
161 *MS* volunteered   162 *MS* {beginning of fo. 59}   *MS* history some

---

140 *shanks*: legs; Half-Rome's use is colloquial and contemptuous.

147–9 *Triangular . . . again*: adapting SS 14: 'Franceschini's knife was in the Genoese
style, triangular, with barbed hooks on the back of the blade that made fatal any wound
from which it was withdrawn.'

159 *Curate Carlo*: another character not in OYB.

brisk: lively, quick-witted.

Treat us to how the wife's confession went
(This morning she confessed her crime, we know)
And, may-be, throw in something of the Priest—   165
If he's not ordered back, punished anew,
The gallant, Caponsacchi, Lucifer
I' the garden where Pompilia, Eve-like, lured
Her Adam Guido to his fault and fall.
Think you we got a sprig of speech akin   170
To this from Carlo, with the Cardinal there?
Too wary he was, too widely awake, I trow.
He did the murder in a dozen words;
Then said that all such outrages crop forth
I' the course of nature when Molinos' tares   175
Are sown for wheat, flourish and choke the Church:
So slid on to the abominable sect
And the philosophic sin—we've heard all that,
And the Cardinal too, (who book-made on the same)
But, for the murder, left it where he found.   180
Oh but he's quick, the Curate, minds his game!
And, after all, we have the main o' the fact:
Case could not well be simpler,—mapped, as it were,

---

164 MS {no comma}   165 MS may be,   Yale 1 may be>may-be   MS
Priest   168 MS In   169 MS fall: 170 MS like this>akin   171 MS
{no comma}   172 MS Too wary, I trow, too widely awake he was.>Too wary,
he was, too widely awake, I trow.   1868 1872 wary, he   173 MS words,
175 MS In   1868 1872 nature,   176 MS Church,   182 MS of

164 confessed her crime: Pompilia never confesses herself guilty of any crime: this is
Half-Rome's bias.

172 trow: believe.

175 tares: weeds (Molinos's heretical teachings): cf. Matt. 13: 24–30.

177 abominable sect: the Molinists, followers of Molinos's ideas: see I. 307 n. The
Ohio editor believes that this refers to the Jesuits on account of the 'philosophic sin' in
the next line, which he understands as a reference to the heretical thesis proposed by
the Jesuit François Musnier in 1686. Comparison, however, with III. 96–7 and I. 309
makes clear that Browning means Molinists. He regards Molinism as the 'philosophic
sin' because it was an idea of inner quietness and prayer that involved no obvious
immorality. His source is OYB cxlvi (150).

183–5 mapped . . . mistake: the puzzling course of the murder is like a red (bloody)
river that has been mapped on a continent. The image may have been suggested by

We follow the murder's maze from source to sea,
By the red line, past mistake: one sees indeed   185
Not only how all was and must have been,
But cannot other than be to the end of time.
Turn out here by the Ruspoli! Do you hold
Guido was so prodigiously to blame?
A certain cousin of yours has told you so?   190
Exactly! Here's a friend shall set you right,
Let him but have the handsel of your ear.

These wretched Comparini were once gay
And galliard, of the modest middle class:
Born in this quarter seventy years ago   195
And married young, they lived the accustomed life,
Citizens as they were of good repute:
And, childless, naturally took their ease
With only their two selves to care about
And use the wealth for: wealthy is the word,   200
Since Pietro was possessed of house and land—
And specially one house, when good days smiled,
In Via Vittoria, the aspectable street

---

185 *MS* {no comma}   188 *MS* Ruspoli: so you   189 *MS* {beginning of
fo. 60}   190 *MS* friend   194 *MS 1868 1872* galiard,   *Yale 2* class:>
class.   195 *MS 1868 1872* ago,   201 *MS* land   202 *MS 1868 1872*
were,   203 *MS* an

'main' in l. 182. The first meaning of main is 'the chief part', but another is 'mainland',
'continent'.

188 *Ruspoli*: Palazzo Ruspoli, on the north side of the piazza. Half-Rome is getting
his companion out of the immediate push of the crowd.

192 *handsel*: earnest money, the first instalment of payment in a transaction. Half-
Rome asks for the 'ear' of his companion as earnest money, in return for which he will
give the true story of the murder.

194 *galliard*: lively; adj. derived from French *gaillard*.

203 *aspectable*: attractive, agreeable to look upon; the Brownings stressed the first
syllable in pronunciation: OED². This unusual word occurs three times in *Aurora
Leigh*: v. 627 n., vi. 195, ix. 569.

In OYB two road names are associated with the Comparini's home: in one
reference it is 'sitam in via Paulina', in another Pompilia directs a letter 'alla strada
Vittoria': OYB clv (159), clvi (160). In fact there was only one house, located at the
intersection of these roads: see Treves, 101. Browning assumes there were two houses
and so creates the contrast between the fashionable town house in the Via Vittoria, in

Where he lived mainly; but another house
Of less pretension did he buy betimes,   205
The villa, meant for jaunts and jollity,
I' the Pauline district, to be private there—
Just what puts murder in an enemy's head.
Moreover,—here's the worm i' the core, the germ
O' the rottenness and ruin which arrived,—   210
He owned some usufruct, had moneys' use
Lifelong, but to determine with his life
In heirs' default: so, Pietro craved an heir,
(The story always old and always new)
Shut his fool's-eyes fast on the visible good   215
And wealth for certain, opened them owl-wide
On fortune's sole piece of forgetfulness,
The child that should have been and would not be.

Hence, seventeen years ago, conceive his glee
When first Violante, 'twixt a smile and blush,   220
With touch of agitation proper too,
Announced that, spite of her unpromising age,

---

204 *MS* mainly, and   205 *1872* lees   *Yale 2* lees>less   206 *MS* Villa,
207 *MS* In   *MS* there,   209 *MS* and here's the worm in   210 *MS* Of
211 *MS* monies'   *Yale 1* monies'>moneys'   212 *MS* {no comma}   213 *MS*
so Pietro   214 *MS* The   *MS* new,   215 *MS* {beginning of fo. 61}   *MS*
fool's eyes   *MS* good,   216 *MS* And   217 *MS* {no comma}   219 *MS*
{no new paragraph}   220 *MS 1868 1872* a blush,

---

the heart of Rome, and the more modest villa near the edge of town, in a location
vulnerable to attack. By Browning's time Via Paolina had taken its popular name of
Via del Babuino: see III. 391–3 n.

205 *betimes*: later, in due time.

211 *usufruct*: usufruct is the right to enjoy the fruits of property or investment one
does not own, the 'principal' of l.582. Cf. SS 1 and nn.

212 *determine*: end (a legal use).

216 *owl-wide*: in a solemn, but foolish, wide-eyed way. Owl has its sense of 'solemn
dullard': a person with a figurative repugnance to light, really foolish, but with an
appearance of wisdom. Pietro shuts his eyes to the obvious daytime good of the
usufruct, and, like an owl straining to see in the dark, concentrates on his lack of an
heir. Cf. VI. 1759, and also 'Valiant Wisdom... escorted by owl-eyed Pedantry, by
owlish and vulturish and many other forms of Folly': Carlyle, *Past and Present*, II. xvii:
Works, X. 132.

The miracle would in time be manifest,
An heir's birth was to happen: and it did.
Somehow or other,—how, all in good time!   225
By a trick, a sleight of hand you are to hear,—
A child was born, Pompilia, for his joy,
Plaything at once and prop, a fairy-gift,
A saints' grace or, say, grant of the good God,—
A fiddle-pin's end! What imbeciles are we!   230
Look now: if some one could have prophesied,
"For love of you, for liking to your wife,
"I undertake to crush a snake I spy
"Settling itself i' the soft of both your breasts.
"Give me yon babe to strangle painlessly!   235
"She'll soar to the safe: you'll have your crying out,
"Then sleep, then wake, then sleep, then end your days
"In peace and plenty, mixed with mild regret,
"Thirty years hence when Christmas takes old folk"—
How had old Pietro sprung up, crossed himself,   240
And kicked the conjuror! Whereas you and I,
Being wise with after-wit, had clapped our hands;
Nay, added, in the old fool's interest,
"Strangle the black-eyed babe, so far so good,
"But on condition you relieve the man   245
"O' the wife and throttle him Violante too—
"She is the mischief!"

            We had hit the mark.
She, whose trick brought the babe into the world,

228 MS ^at once^   MS fairy-gift   229 MS or say grant   MS God,
230 MS fiddlepin's   231 MS {no comma}   233–9 MS {no quotation
marks}   234 MS in   MS breasts,   MS {between 234 and 235 deleted line:
For that's a snake the thing you fondle so—}   235 MS painlessly,   236 MS
{no comma}   241 MS {beginning of fo. 62}   MS {no comma}   242 MS
{no comma, no semi-colon}   243 MS added in   MS interest   245–7 MS
{no quotation marks}   246 MS Of   MS his   248 MS {no new paragraph}

230 *A fiddle-pin's end*: i.e. 'What nonsense!', a coinage based on the usual exclamation 'fiddlestick's end'.

241 *conjuror*: magician; here a person foretelling the future.

She it was, when the babe was grown a girl, 250
Judged a new trick should reinforce the old,
Lend vigour to the lie now somewhat spent
By twelve years' service; lest Eve's rule decline
Over this Adam of hers, whose cabbage-plot
Throve dubiously since turned fools'-paradise, 255
Spite of a nightingale on every stump.
Pietro's estate was dwindling day by day,
While he, rapt far above such mundane care,
Crawled all-fours with his baby pick-a-back,
Sat at serene cats'-cradle with his child, 260
Or took the measured tallness, top to toe,
Of what was grown a great girl twelve years old:
Till sudden at the door a tap discreet,
A visitor's premonitory cough,
And poverty had reached him in her rounds. 265

This came when he was past the working-time,
Had learned to dandle and forgot to dig,
And who must but Violante cast about,
Contrive and task that head of hers again?
She who had caught one fish, could make that catch
A bigger still, in angler's policy: 271
So, with an angler's mercy for the bait,
Her minnow was set wriggling on its barb

---

*252 MS Lend   1868 1872 1888 1889 Send {the word has been misread in MS}   253 MS service,   254 MS {no commas}   256 MS stump: 257 MS {no comma}   258 MS care   259 MS pick a back   260 MS Sate   262 MS ^what^   MS old,   263 MS distinct>discreet,   265 MS Poverty   266 MS {no new paragraph}   268 MS but his Violante must 269 MS {beginning of fo. 63}

253–6 *lest . . . stump*: Violante's 'lie' (Pompilia) gives Pietro a false view of the world: he thinks his financial estate ('cabbage-plot') is thriving, though he does no real work on it; he lives in a fools' paradise, as though a tuneful nightingale were on every cabbage stump. This illusion is now under threat.

260 *cats'-cradle*: an absorbing game played with children in which patterns made with string are transferred between the fingers of the two players.

And tossed to mid-stream; which means, this grown girl
With the great eyes and bounty of black hair   275
And first crisp youth that tempts a jaded taste,
Was whisked i' the way of a certain man, who snapped.

Count Guido Franceschini the Aretine
Was head of an old noble house enough,
Not over-rich, you can't have everything,   280
But such a man as riches rub against,
Readily stick to,—one with a right to them
Born in the blood: 't was in his very brow
Always to knit itself against the world,
Beforehand so, when that world stinted due   285
Service and suit: the world ducks and defers.
As such folks do, he had come up to Rome
To better his fortune, and, since many years,
Was friend and follower of a cardinal;
Waiting the rather thus on providence   290
That a shrewd younger poorer brother yet,
The Abate Paolo, a regular priest,
Had long since tried his powers and found he swam
With the deftest on the Galilean pool:
But then he was a web-foot, free o' the wave,   295
And no ambiguous dab-chick hatched to strut,

---

274 *MS 1868 1872* the mid-stream; that is,   *Yale 2* the mid-stream; that is,>mid-
stream; that is,   275 *MS* the two great   276 *MS* {no comma}   277 *MS*
in   *MS* an old man,   283 *MS* blood, 'twas   284 *MS* {no comma}
285 *MS 1868* So be beforehand when that stinted due   289 *MS* cardinal—
290 *MS* Providence   *1868 1872* providence,   291 *MS* {no comma}
293 *MS* webs>powers   294 *MS* pool,   295 *MS* {beginning of fo.
64}   *MS* of   296 *MS* dabchick   *MS* {no comma}

286 *Service and suit*: service and attendance (as of an inferior to a lord); the normal
order of the phrase is 'suit and service'.
294 *Galilean pool*: Christian pool; after Christ, who is sometimes called 'the Galilean'. The allusion is to 'the Galilean lake': Milton, 'Lycidas', 109, but Half-Rome's
version is typically debunking: here the 'Galilean pool' is a duckpond, i.e. the Church,
the 'pool' of good ecclesiastical jobs.
295 *web-foot*: a duck, with real webbed feet.
296 *dab-chick*: usually a Little Grebe, but in Half-Rome's use essentially a bird that is
neither a proper cock (a land bird) nor a proper duck (a water bird), hence a comic

Humbled by any fond attempt to swim
When fiercer fowl usurped his dunghill top—
A whole priest, Paolo, no mere piece of one
Like Guido tacked thus to the Church's tail!   300
Guido moreover, as the head o' the house,
Claiming the main prize, not the lesser luck,
The centre lily, no mere chickweed fringe.

He waited and learned waiting, thirty years;
Got promise, missed performance—what would you have?
No petty post rewards a nobleman   306
For spending youth in splendid lackey-work,
And there's concurrence for each rarer prize;
When that falls, rougher hand and readier foot
Push aside Guido spite of his black looks.   310
The end was, Guido, when the warning showed,
The first white hair i' the glass, gave up the game,
Determined on returning to his town,
Making the best of bad incurable,
Patching the old palace up and lingering there   315
The customary life out with his kin,
Where honour helps to spice the scanty bread.

Just as he trimmed his lamp and girt his loins
To go his journey and be wise at home,
In the right mood of disappointed worth,   320
Who but Violante sudden spied her prey

---

297 *MS* such attempt   298 *MS* dunghill-top;   *1868* dunghill-top—
299 *MS* Pal>Paolo   300 *MS* Churches   301 *MS* of   302 *MS* and>not
MS middle>lesser   304 *MS* {no new paragraph}   *MS* waiting twenty years,
Yale 1 twenty>thirty   307 *MS* lackey's-work,   312 *MS* in   315 *MS* place
318 *MS* {no new paragraph}   320 *MS* gay   *MS* man,

---

image of Guido, who is caught between his desire to succeed as an aristocrat and his
desire to succeed in the Church. Cf. Pope, *The Dunciad* (1742), ii. 63–4: 'As when a
dab-chick waddles thro' the copse / On feet and wings, and flies, and wades, and hops'.

298 *dunghill*: proverbial: 'A cock is bold on his own dunghill': ODEP, 130.

300 *tacked . . . tail*: for Guido's church status see 1. 263–5 n.

308 *concurrence*: competition.

318 *Just . . . loins*: cf. Luke 12: 35.

(Where was I with that angler-simile?)
And threw her bait, Pompilia, where he sulked—
A gleam i' the gloom!

What if he gained thus much,
Wrung out this sweet drop from the bitter Past,   326
Bore off this rose-bud from the prickly brake
To justify such torn clothes and scratched hands,
And, after all, brought something back from Rome?
Would not a wife serve at Arezzo well   330
To light the dark house, lend a look of youth
To the mother's face grown meagre, left alone
And famished with the emptiness of hope,
Old Donna Beatrice? Wife you want
Would you play family-representative,   335
Carry you elder-brotherly, high and right
O'er what may prove the natural petulance
Of the third brother, younger, greedier still,
Girolamo, also a fledgeling priest,
Beginning life in turn with callow beak   340
Agape for luck, no luck had stopped and stilled.
Such were the pinks and greys about the bait
Persuaded Guido gulp down hook and all.

What constituted him so choice a catch,
You question? Past his prime and poor beside!   345
Ask that of any she who knows the trade.
Why first, here was a nobleman with friends,
A palace one might run to and be safe

322 MS {beginning of fo. 65}   323 MS {no commas}   324 MS in
325 MS {no new paragraph}   328 MS {no comma}   329 MS {no
commas}   330 MS Arezzo now   332 MS long>grown   337 MS might
339 MS A priest, too, if you please! Girolamo,>Also a fledgeling priest, Girolamo,
341 MS stilled?   *344 MS 1868 1872 {new paragraph. Paragraphing obscured in
1888 and 1889 by this line's being at the head of the page}   345 MS beside:
1868 1872 beside?   346 MS anyone

333 *famished . . . hope*: proverbial: 'Who lives by hope will die by hunger': ODEP, 475.
340 *callow*: inexperienced.

When presently the threatened fate should fall,
A big-browed master to block door-way up,   350
Parley with people bent on pushing by
And praying the mild Pietro quick clear scores:
Is birth a privilege and power or no?
Also,—but judge of the result desired,
By the price paid and manner of the sale.   355
The Count was made woo, win and wed at once:
Asked, and was haled for answer, lest the heat
Should cool, to San Lorenzo, one blind eve,
And had Pompilia put into his arms
O' the sly there, by a hasty candle-blink,   360
With sanction of some priest-confederate
Properly paid to make short work and sure.

So did old Pietro's daughter change her style
For Guido Franceschini's lady-wife
Ere Guido knew it well; and why this haste   365
And scramble and indecent secrecy?
"Lest Pietro, all the while in ignorance,
"Should get to learn, gainsay and break the match:
"His peevishness had promptly put aside
"Such honour and refused the proffered boon,   370
"Pleased to become authoritative once.
"She remedied the wilful man's mistake—"
Did our discreet Violante. Rather say,

---

349 *MS* {beginning of fo. 66}   350 *MS* With   *MS* doorway   *MS* {no comma}   352 *MS* Master Pietro   354 *MS* Also . .   *MS* {no comma} 355 *MS* paid down and   356 *MS* The man   358 *MS* Lorenzo one blind eve   359 *MS* have>had   360 *MS* On the sly, by a hasty candle's blink,   363 *MS* {no new paragraph}   366 *MS* scramble? and>scramble and   *MS* secrecy   368–72 *MS* {no quotation marks at beginnings of lines} 368 *Yale 2* match:>match!   369 *MS* prompty>promptly   370 *MS* honor 372 *Yale 2* mistake—">mistake—   373 *MS* Said>Did   *Yale 2* Violante.> Violante."   *Yale 2* {in left-hand margin deleted question mark}

---

358 *blind*: dark.
363 *style*: name.
368 *gainsay*: speak against, oppose.
371 *authoritative*: entitled to obedience, aristocratic.

Thus did she, lest the object of her game,
Guido the gulled one, give him but a chance,   375
A moment's respite, time for thinking twice,
Might count the cost before he sold himself,
And try the clink of coin they paid him with.

But coin paid, bargain struck and business done,
Once the clandestine marriage over thus,   380
All parties made perforce the best o' the fact;
Pietro could play vast indignation off,
Be ignorant and astounded, dupe, poor soul,
Please you, of daughter, wife and son-in-law,
While Guido found himself in flagrant fault,   385
Must e'en do suit and service, soothe, subdue
A father not unreasonably chafed,
Bring him to terms by paying son's devoir.
Pleasant initiation!

The end, this: 390
Guido's broad back was saddled to bear all—
Pietro, Violante, and Pompilia too,—
Three lots cast confidently in one lap,
Three dead-weights with one arm to lift the three
Out of their limbo up to life again.   395
The Roman household was to strike fresh root

374 *MS* game   376 *MS* {beginning of fo. 67}   377 *MS* {no comma}
379 *MS* 'Twas pursed, the bargain struck, the business done.   *1868* But passed, the
bargain struck, the business done,   381 *MS* of   *Yale 2* fact;> fact.   383 *MS*
1868 1872 dupe alike   384 *MS* Of wife, of daughter and of son-in-law,>At need, of
wife, daughter and son-in-law,   *1868 1872* At need, of wife, daughter and son-in-
law,   385 *MS* {no comma}   386 *MS* make submission,>e'en do suit and
service,   388 *MS* devoir—   390 *MS* {no new paragraph}   *MS* The
end was this—   392 *MS* ^and^   *MS* too—   394 *MS* deadweights
395 *1868* again:

382 *play . . . off*: play off vast indignation, i.e. Pietro could display, perform as in a
play, his part of 'vast indignation', his role as 'dupe': cf. OED² *play* v. 24.c. and l. 75 n.
386 *suit and service*: cf. l. 286 n.
387 *chafed*: angered.
388 *devoir*: dutiful respect.

In a new soil, graced with a novel name,
Gilt with an alien glory, Aretine
Henceforth and never Roman any more,
By treaty and engagement; thus it ran: 400
Pompilia's dowry for Pompilia's self
As a thing of course,—she paid her own expense;
No loss nor gain there: but the couple, you see,
They, for their part, turned over first of all
Their fortune in its rags and rottenness   405
To Guido, fusion and confusion, he
And his with them and theirs,—whatever rag
With coin residuary fell on floor
When Brother Paolo's energetic shake
Should do the relics justice: since 't was thought,   410
Once vulnerable Pietro out of reach,
That, left at Rome as representative,
The Abate, backed by a potent patron here,
And otherwise with purple flushing him,
Might play a good game with the creditor,   415
Make up a moiety which, great or small,
Should go to the common stock—if anything,
Guido's, so far repayment of the cost
About to be,—and if, as looked more like,
Nothing,—why, all the nobler cost were his   420

399 *MS* more.   400 *MS 1868* engagement: 402 *MS* expense,   403 *MS*
{beginning of fo. 68}   *MS* Couple   408 *MS 1868 1872* a coin   409 *MS*
brother   410 *MS* {no comma}   412 *MS* {no commas}   413 *MS*
here   420 *MS* why all

398 *Gilt*: revives in 'glory' the sense of 'aureole, gold halo'.
alien: foreign, belonging rightly to the Franceschini.
408 *residuary*: remaining, left over.
410 *relics*: remains (of the Comparini's wealth). Also, since Paolo is a priest, a pun on
'relics' in the religious sense: the bodily remains, parts of those remains, clothing, etc.
of a saint.
414 *with purple flushing him*: with influential people—particularly (purple-wearing)
cardinals—encouraging him. 'Purple' is suggested by It. *porporato* = 'cardinal' (*porpora* =
purple), as in SS 1. Also with the sense that purple (the colour of the cardinalate) is flushing
(suffusing, rushing into) him: Paolo has a confident air: cf. III. 375. There may also be a
concealed pun between 'flush' (the term from cards) and the image of the next line.
416 *moiety*: share, portion.

Who guaranteed, for better or for worse,
To Pietro and Violante, house and home,
Kith and kin, with the pick of company
And life o' the fat o' the land while life should last.
How say you to the bargain at first blush?   425
Why did a middle-aged not-silly man
Show himself thus besotted all at once?
Quoth Solomon, one black eye does it all.

They went to Arezzo,—Pietro and his spouse,
With just the dusk o' the day of life to spend,   430
Eager to use the twilight, taste a treat,
Enjoy for once with neither stay nor stint
The luxury of lord-and-lady-ship,
And realize the stuff and nonsense long
A-simmer in their noddles; vent the fume   435
Born there and bred, the citizen's conceit
How fares nobility while crossing earth,
What rampart or invisible body-guard
Keeps off the taint of common life from such.
They had not fed for nothing on the tales   440
Of grandees who give banquets worthy Jove,
Spending gold as if Plutus paid a whim,
Served with obeisances as when... what God?
I'm at the end of my tether; 't is enough

---

421 *MS* worse   423 *MS* {no comma}   424 *MS* on   *MS* of   426 *MS*
not silly   428 *MS* One   429 *MS* {beginning of fo. 69}   *MS* spouse
430 *MS* of   434 *MS* realise   435 *MS* noddles,   438 *MS* bodyguard
439 *MS* common things   441 *MS* grandees and their   443 *MS* when..
Yale 2 God?>god?   444 *MS* 'tis

428 *Quoth . . . all*: cf. S. of S. 4: 9: 'thou hast ravished my heart with one of thine eyes'.
435 *vent the fume*: literally 'discharge the steam (in their heads)'; fig. 'give expression
to their illusion'.
442 *as . . . whim*: i.e. as if Wealth paid for any desire. In Greek myth Plutus, the son
of Demeter and Iasion, was the personification of wealth.
443 *obeisances*: bows.
as . . . God?: following the previous two lines: 'in the Comparini's fantasy of aristocratic life, they imagine that nobles give banquets as good as Jove, their spending is
backed by Plutus (Wealth), and they are served with bows as when [another god did

You understand what they came primed to see: 445
While Guido who should minister the sight,
Stay all this qualmish greediness of soul
With apples and with flagons—for his part,
Was set on life diverse as pole from pole:
Lust of the flesh, lust of the eye,—what else   450
Was he just now awake from, sick and sage,
After the very debauch they would begin?—
Suppose such stuff and nonsense really were.
That bubble, they were bent on blowing big,
He had blown already till he burst his cheeks,   455
And hence found soapsuds bitter to the tongue.
He hoped now to walk softly all his days
In soberness of spirit, if haply so,
Pinching and paring he might furnish forth
A frugal board, bare sustenance, no more,   460
Till times, that could not well grow worse, should mend.

Thus minded then, two parties mean to meet
And make each other happy. The first week,
And fancy strikes fact and explodes in full.
"This," shrieked the Comparini, "this the Count,   465
"The palace, the signorial privilege,
"The pomp and pageantry were promised us?

---

445 *MS* see   452 *MS* begin   454 *MS* {no commas}   455 *MS*
been blowing till   *MS* cheeks   456 *MS* {beginning of fo. 70}   *MS* the
soapsuds bitter on his   458 *MS* spirit if   462 *MS* {no new paragraph}
MS There, minded thus,   464 *MS* meets fact   465 *MS* "This"
shrieked   466–84 *MS* {initial quotation marks added by a pencil line in the
left-hand margin and a single pair of pencil quotation marks}   467 *MS*
And>The   *MS* wealth and pageantry was

---

something].' Half-Rome casts about for another mythological illustration, but, in his
impatience with what he sees as the Comparini's idiocy, he fails to find one.

445 *primed*: prepared.

448 *apples ... flagons*: cf. S. of S. 2: 5: 'Stay me with flagons, comfort me with
apples'.

450 *Lust ... eye*: cf. 1 John 2: 16.

457–8 *walk ... spirit*: cf. Isa. 38: 15: 'I shall go softly all my years in the bitterness of
my soul.'

"For this have we exchanged our liberty,
"Our competence, our darling of a child?
"To house as spectres in a sepulchre   470
"Under this black stone-heap, the street's disgrace,
"Grimmest as that is of the gruesome town,
"And here pick garbage on a pewter plate
"Or cough at verjuice dripped from earthenware?
"Oh Via Vittoria, oh the other place   475
"I' the Pauline, did we give you up for this?
"Where's the foregone housekeeping good and gay,
"The neighbourliness, the companionship,
"The treat and feast when holidays came round,
"The daily feast that seemed no treat at all,   480
"Called common by the uncommon fools we were!
"Even the sun that used to shine at Rome,
"Where is it? Robbed and starved and frozen too,
"We will have justice, justice if there be!"
Did not they shout, did not the town resound!   485
Guido's old lady-mother Beatrice,
Who since her husband, Count Tommaso's death,
Had held sole sway i' the house,—the doited crone
Slow to acknowledge, curtsey and abdicate,—
Was recognized of true novercal type,   490
Dragon and devil. His brother Girolamo
Came next in order: priest was he? The worse!
No way of winning him to leave his mumps

---

469 *MS* child,   471 *MS* stone heap the   *1868 1872* stone heap,   476 *MS*
In   478 *MS* neighbourliness and   479 *MS* {no comma}   480 *MS*
{no comma}   483 *MS* {beginning of fo. 71}   484 *MS* be."   486 *MS* {no
comma}   488 *MS* in   *1868* i' the   *MS* house, the   489 *MS* abdicate,
490 *MS* recognized, the   491 *MS* devil: his   492 *MS* worse: 493 *MS*
sulks

---

474 *verjuice . . . earthenware*: sour wine, made from crab-apples, in niggardly quant-
ities, poured from earthenware (instead of silver). Johnson notes that verjuice 'is
vulgarly pronounced *varges*'.
488 *doited*: with impaired faculties (due to age).
490 *novercal*: stepmotherly, in the derogatory sense of 'cruel, malicious, hostile'.
493 *mumps*: ill humour.

And help the laugh against old ancestry
And formal habits long since out of date,   495
Letting his youth be patterned on the mode
Approved of where Violante laid down law.
Or did he brighten up by way of change,
Dispose himself for affability?
The malapert, too complaisant by half   500
To the alarmed young novice of a bride!
Let him go buzz, betake himself elsewhere
Nor singe his fly-wings in the candle-flame!

Four months' probation of this purgatory,
Dog-snap and cat-claw, curse and counterblast,   505
The devil's self were sick of his own din;
And Pietro, after trumpeting huge wrongs
At church and market-place, pillar and post,
Square's corner, street's end, now the palace-step
And now the wine-house bench—while, on her side,   510
Violante up and down was voluble
In whatsoever pair of ears would perk
From goody, gossip, cater-cousin and sib,
Curious to peep at the inside of things
And catch in the act pretentious poverty   515
At its wits' end to keep appearance up,
Make both ends meet,—nothing the vulgar loves

---

494 *MS* his ancestry   495 *MS* For rustic   497 *MS* the Comparini
498 *MS 1868* change?   501 *MS* beauty of the   504 *MS* {no new para-
graph}   505 *Yale 2* counterblast,>counterblast,—   506 *MS 1868* had
been *MS* din,   *Yale 2* din;>din!   507 *MS* of wrongs   510 *MS*
{beginning of fo. 72}   *MS* side   513 *MS* catercousin and sib   517 *MS*
meet:

---

500 *malapert*: impudent person.
complaisant: disposed to please, obliging.
513 *goody, gossip, cater-cousin and sib*: synonyms for 'a friend who enjoys gossip'. In
its context, this line shows Half-Rome using language to typically demeaning
and contemptuous effect. 'Goody' implies a married woman in humble life. 'Cater-
cousin' and 'sib' imply a relation, here relative in a figurative sense. Cf. 'Fust and His
Friends', 12.

Like what this couple pitched them right and left.
Then, their worst done that way, both struck tent, marched:
—Renounced their share o' the bargain, flung what dues
Guido was bound to pay, in Guido's face,   521
Left their hearts'-darling, treasure of the twain
And so forth, the poor inexperienced bride,
To her own devices, bade Arezzo rot,
Cursed life signorial, and sought Rome once more.   525

I see the comment ready on your lip,
"The better fortune, Guido's—free at least
"By this defection of the foolish pair,
"He could begin make profit in some sort
"Of the young bride and the new quietness,   530
"Lead his own life now, henceforth breathe unplagued."
Could he? You know the sex like Guido's self.
Learn the Violante-nature!

                    Once in Rome,
By way of helping Guido lead such life,   535
Her first act to inaugurate return
Was, she got pricked in conscience: Jubilee
Gave her the hint. Our Pope, as kind as just,
Attained his eighty years, announced a boon

---

518 *MS 1868 1872* left,—   *Yale 2* left,—>left.   519 *MS* struck tent and
marched: *1868 1872* they struck   520 *MS* of   524 *MS* left Arezzo thus
1868 rot   525 *MS 1868* And the   526 *MS* tremble>ready   528–31 {initial
quotation marks added by a line in the left-hand margin}   529 *MS* ^make
profit in^   531 *MS* in peace."   533 *MS* Violante-nature.   534 *MS*
{no new paragraph}   535 *MS* his life,   537 *MS* {beginning of fo.
73}   *MS* Was to get   538 *MS* as good as

---

   537 *Jubilee*: Jubilee or 'Holy Year', a time of spiritual renewal proclaimed by the
Pope. A Jubilee Indulgence was granted to the faithful who came to Rome, confessed
their sins, and prayed at specified churches. The Indulgence was a special form of
forgiveness for sins which cancelled the penalties due for them under canon law.
Jubilee was generally a time for getting especially bad sins off the conscience: see III.
555–8. Innocent XII held extraordinary Jubilees in 1691, 1694, and 1696, and the full
Jubilee in 1700; Violante made her confession in 1694. People confessing their sins at
Jubilee would often give alms.

Should make us bless the fact, held Jubilee—   540
Short shrift, prompt pardon for the light offence,
And no rough dealing with the regular crime
So this occasion were not suffered slip—
Otherwise, sins commuted as before,
Without the least abatement in the price.   545
Now, who had thought it? All this while, it seems,
Our sage Violante had a sin of a sort
She must compound for now or not at all.
Now be the ready riddance! She confessed
Pompilia was a fable not a fact: 550
She never bore a child in her whole life.
Had this child been a changeling, that were grace
In some degree, exchange is hardly theft,
You take your stand on truth ere leap your lie:
Here was all lie, no touch of truth at all,   555
All the lie hers—not even Pietro guessed
He was as childless still as twelve years since.
The babe had been a find i' the filth-heap, Sir,
Catch from the kennel! There was found at Rome,
Down in the deepest of our social dregs,   560
A woman who professed the wanton's trade
Under the requisite thin coverture,

---

540 *MS* his Jubilee—   *541 *MS 1868 1872* offence,   *1888* offence
DC Br U offence>offence,   *1889* offence,   548 *MS 1868* all: 551 *MS*
had   *MS* life;   552 *MS* there were   553 *MS 1868* theft;   556 *MS*
of>the   *MS* [?he]>lie   558 *MS* in   559 *MS* kennel.   *MS* {no
comma}   560 *MS* the social   *MS* {no comma}

---

541 *Short shrift*: i.e. quick amends (by confession).

544 *commuted*: bought off. Cf. 'little sums paid . . . by women who wish to . . . commute a penance with a small present': J. C. Hobhouse, *Italy* (2 vols., 1859), ii. 247: cited OED².

548 *compound for*: settle up for; a word with financial overtones similar to 'commute': see previous note.

552 *changeling*: 'A child secretly substituted for another in infancy; especially a child (usually stupid or ugly) supposed to have been left by fairies in exchange for one stolen': OED².

559 *Catch from the kennel*: a thing taken up from the gutter (the surface drain of the street); the phrase is in parallel with 'find i' the filth-heap'.

Communis meretrix and washer-wife:
The creature thus conditioned found by chance
Motherhood like a jewel in the muck,   565
And straightway either trafficked with her prize
Or listened to the tempter and let be,—
Made pact abolishing her place and part
In womankind, beast-fellowship indeed.
She sold this babe eight months before its birth   570
To our Violante, Pietro's honest spouse,
Well-famed and widely-instanced as that crown
To the husband, virtue in a woman's shape.
She it was, bought, paid for, passed off the thing
As very flesh and blood and child of her   575
Despite the flagrant fifty years,—and why?
Partly to please old Pietro, fill his cup
With wine at the late hour when lees are left,
And send him from life's feast rejoicingly,—
Partly to cheat the rightful heirs, agape,   580
Each uncle's cousin's brother's son of him,
For that same principal of the usufruct
It vext him he must die and leave behind.

Such was the sin had come to be confessed.
Which of the tales, the first or last, was true?   585
Did she so sin once, or, confessing now,
Sin for the first time? Either way you will.

564 *MS* {beginning of fo. 74}   565 *MS* {no comma}   567 *MS* be
568 *MS* A pact   569 *MS* beast fellowship indeed— *1868* indeed—
572 *MS* widely instanced   574 *MS* was bought and paid for, passed the
thing *1868 1872* bought and paid for, passed the thing   575 *MS* Off as the
flesh and blood, the *1868 1872* Off as the   *Yale 2* her>her,   580 *MS* agape
583 *MS* vexed   584 *MS* {no new paragraph}   585 *MS* last was true,
587 *MS* please>will.

563 *Communis meretrix*: common prostitute (L.).
564 *conditioned*: circumstanced.
565–9 *Motherhood . . . indeed*: i.e. the prostitute is so poor she either actively seeks to
sell the child in her womb or, more passively, does not resist when tempted to sell it.
572–3 *that crown / To the husband*: cf. Prov. 12: 4.
576 *flagrant*: notorious.

One sees a reason for the cheat: one sees
A reason for a cheat in owning cheat
Where no cheat had been. What of the revenge?   590
What prompted the contrition all at once,
Made the avowal easy, the shame slight?
Why, prove they but Pompilia not their child,
No child, no dowry! this, supposed their child,
Had claimed what this, shown alien to their blood,   595
Claimed nowise: Guido's claim was through his wife,
Null then and void with hers. The biter bit,
Do you see! For such repayment of the past,
One might conceive the penitential pair
Ready to bring their case before the courts,   600
Publish their infamy to all the world
And, arm in arm, go chuckling thence content.

Is this your view? 'T was Guido's anyhow
And colourable: he came forward then,
Protested in his very bride's behalf   605
Against this lie and all it led to, least
Of all the loss o' the dowry; no! From her
And him alike he would expunge the blot,
Erase the brand of such a bestial birth,
Participate in no hideous heritage   610
Gathered from the gutter to be garnered up
And glorified in a palace. Peter and Paul!
But that who likes may look upon the pair
Exposed in yonder church, and show his skill

---

591 *MS* {beginning of fo. 75}   *MS* {no comma}   594 *MS 1868* dowry;
596 *MS* no wise: *MS* {no comma}   598 *MS* {no comma}   603 *MS* {no
new paragraph}   604 *MS* too,   607 *MS* of   610 *MS* Participate no
611 *MS* Gathered in   612 *MS* Glorified in

597 *The biter bit*: proverbial: ODEP, 62. Probably suggested by 'ars deluditur arte':
'craft is deluded by craft': OYB ccxii (214).
604 *colourable*: plausible.
613–18   *But...Sir*: i.e. only the pitiful sight of the Comparini's stabbed bodies
prevents Half-Rome cursing them as liars.

By saying which is eye and which is mouth   615
Thro' those stabs thick and threefold,—but for that—
A strong word on the liars and their lie
Might crave expression and obtain it, Sir!
—Though prematurely, since there's more to come,
More that will shake your confidence in things   620
Your cousin tells you,—may I be so bold?

This makes the first act of the farce,—anon
The sombre element comes stealing in
Till all is black or blood-red in the piece.
Guido, thus made a laughing-stock abroad,   625
A proverb for the market-place at home,
Left alone with Pompilia now, this graft
So reputable on his ancient stock,
This plague-seed set to fester his sound flesh,
What does the Count? Revenge him on his wife?   630
Unfasten at all risks to rid himself
The noisome lazar-badge, fall foul of fate,
And, careless whether the poor rag was 'ware
O' the part it played, or helped unwittingly,
Bid it go burn and leave his frayed flesh free?   635
Plainly, did Guido open both doors wide,
Spurn thence the cur-cast creature and clear scores

---

617 *MS* there>their   618 *MS* {beginning of fo. 76}   619 *MS* All   620 *MS*
things.   621 *MS* {line not found}   622 *MS* {no new paragraph}   623 *MS*
The sombre element comes stealing in>Comes stealing in the sombre element   *1868*
1872 The stealing sombre element comes in   *Yale 2* The stealing sombre element
comes in>The sombre element comes stealing in   624 *MS* bloodred   625 *MS*
laughing stock   627 *MS* this lady   630 *MS* did the man?   *1868 1872*
did   633 *MS* {no comma}   **MS* 1868 1872 1888* ware   *DC Br U* ware>'
ware   *1889* 'ware   634 *MS* Of   *MS* played or   635 *MS* let his flesh
alone?   636 *MS* wide·   637 *MS* be free

631–3 *Unfasten . . . rag*: Guido finds himself wearing Pompilia like a 'poor rag' of
diseased clothing. Half-Rome wonders if he will tear this off so as to get rid of the
'noisome lazar-badge': the repugnant sign marking him as a leper, a socially unaccept-
able person.

637 *cur-cast*: dropped, born prematurely, from a low-bred dog; here figurative. The
energy of this contemptuous adjective is typical of Half-Rome's style of speech. Cf.
IV. 611.

As man might, tempted in extreme like this?
No, birth and breeding, and compassion too
Saved her such scandal. She was young, he thought,
Not privy to the treason, punished most   641
I' the proclamation of it; why make her
A party to the crime she suffered by?
Then the black eyes were now her very own,
Not any more Violante's: let her live,   645
Lose in a new air, under a new sun,
The taint of the imputed parentage
Truly or falsely, take no more the touch
Of Pietro and his partner anyhow!
All might go well yet.   650

         So she thought, herself,
It seems, since what was her first act and deed
When news came how these kindly ones at Rome
Had stripped her naked to amuse the world
With spots here, spots there and spots everywhere?
—For I should tell you that they noised abroad   656
Not merely the main scandal of her birth,
But slanders written, printed, published wide,
Pamphlets which set forth all the pleasantry
Of how the promised glory was a dream,   660
The power a bubble, and the wealth—why, dust.
There was a picture, painted to the life,
Of those rare doings, that superlative
Initiation in magnificence
Conferred on a poor Roman family   665
By favour of Arezzo and her first
And famousest, the Franceschini there.

<hr>

640 *MS* this scandal   641 *MS* punished too   642 *MS* In   *MS* it,
why   646 *MS* {beginning of fo. 77}   648 *MS* Truely   649 *MS*
anyhow.   651 *MS* {no new paragraph}   *MS* thought herself,   652 *MS*
this>what   653 *MS* ones contrived   654 *MS* To strip her naked and
656 *MS* {line added later}   *MS* For   660 *MS* {no comma}   661 *MS*
1868 bubble and   666 *MS* favor

You had the Countship holding head aloft
Bravely although bespattered, shifts and straits
In keeping out o' the way o' the wheels o' the world,
The comic of those home-contrivances   671
When the old lady-mother's wit was taxed
To find six clamorous mouths in food more real
Than fruit plucked off the cobwebbed family-tree,
Or acorns shed from its gilt mouldered frame—   675
Cold glories served up with stale fame for sauce.
What, I ask,—when the drunkenness of hate
Hiccuped return for hospitality,
Befouled the table they had feasted on,
Or say,—God knows I'll not prejudge the case,—   680
Grievances thus distorted, magnified,
Coloured by quarrel into calumny,—
What side did our Pompilia first espouse?
Her first deliberate measure was—she wrote,
Pricked by some loyal impulse, straight to Rome   685
And her husband's brother the Abate there,
Who, having managed to effect the match,
Might take men's censure for its ill success.
She made a clean breast also in her turn,
And qualified the couple properly,   690
Since whose departure, hell, she said, was heaven,
And the house, late distracted by their peals,
Quiet as Carmel where the lilies live.

668 MS keeping   670 MS of.... of.... of   675 MS {beginning of fo.
78}   MS let fall>shed   MS its mouldered   676 MS 1868 1872 three-
pauls' worth'   678 MS {no comma}   679 MS Bespewed   681 MS
magnified   683 MS part>side   684 MS was to write,   1868 1872 was,
687 MS {no commas}   688 MS the>men's   MS success,   689 MS
And   MS 1868 1872 turn;   690 MS 1868 1872 She   MS 1868 1872 hand-
somely!

668 *Countship*: the office or dignity of a Count; here a sardonic name for Guido.
671 *The comic*: the comedy; quasi-sb.: OED² sb.3.
690 *qualified*: characterized.
693 *Quiet as Carmel*: i.e. quiet as a holy, monastic place. Mount Carmel, now in
Israel, the site of Elijah's defeat of the prophets of Baal, was from that time through to
the 12th century traditionally the site of a community of hermits, which eventually

Herself had oftentimes complained: but why?
All her complaints had been their prompting, tales   695
Trumped up, devices to this very end.
Their game had been to thwart her husband's love
And cross his will, malign his words and ways,
To reach this issue, furnish this pretence
For impudent withdrawal from their bond,—   700
Theft, indeed murder, since they meant no less
Whose last injunction to her simple self
Had been—what parents'-precept do you think?
That she should follow after with all speed,
Fly from her husband's house clandestinely,   705
Join them at Rome again, but first of all
Pick up a fresh companion in her flight,
So putting youth and beauty to fit use,—
Some gay dare-devil cloak-and-rapier spark
Capable of adventure,—helped by whom   710
She, some fine eve when lutes were in the air,
Having put poison in the posset-cup,
Laid hands on money, jewels and the like,
And, to conceal the thing with more effect,
By way of parting benediction too,   715
Fired the house,—one would finish famously
I' the tumult, slip out, scurry off and away
And turn up merrily at home once more.
Fact this, and not a dream o' the devil, Sir!

---

694 *MS* {line added later}   695 *MS* lies   696 *MS* end,   699 *1868*
So {"To" in *MS* has been misread}   700 *MS* bond,   703 *MS* {beginning
of fo. 79}   *MS* been . . what   705 *MS* {no comma}   706 *MS* And join
them (merrily) at Rome again, first of all   707 *MS* Picking up as companion
708 *MS* Putting her youth   *1868* Putting so   *MS 1868* use,   709 *MS* Some
gay, bold gallant,   *1868* gay, dare-devil,   711 *MS* lutes where {evidently a
mistranscription}   714 *MS* And to   716 *MS* Fire   717 *MS* In
718 *MS* at Rome   719 *MS* of

---

became the Carmelite Order of monks. It is renowned in the Bible for its fertility and
beauty. Cf. 'And *Carmel's* flow'ry Top perfumes the skies': Pope, *Messiah*, 28.

712 *posset-cup*: a cup containing a posset: a drink made with wine and hot milk, with
added sugar and spices. Cf. 'I have drugg'd their possets': *Macbeth*, II. ii. 6.

715 *benediction*: blessing.

And more than this, a fact none dare dispute,   720
Word for word, such a letter did she write,
And such the Abate read, nor simply read
But gave all Rome to ruminate upon,
In answer to such charges as, I say,
The couple sought to be beforehand with.   725

The cause thus carried to the courts at Rome,
Guido away, the Abate had no choice
But stand forth, take his absent brother's part,
Defend the honour of himself beside.
He made what head he might against the pair,   730
Maintained Pompilia's birth legitimate
And all her rights intact—hers, Guido's now:
And so far by his policy turned their flank,
(The enemy being beforehand in the place)
That,—though the courts allowed the cheat for fact,   735
Suffered Violante to parade her shame,
Publish her infamy to heart's content,
And let the tale o' the feigned birth pass for proved,—
Yet they stopped there, refused to intervene
And dispossess the innocents, befooled   740
By gifts o' the guilty, at guilt's new caprice.
They would not take away the dowry now

720 *MS* than that   *MS* dare>dares   *MS* {commas added later}   721 *1868*
1872 write.   723 *MS* give   724 *MS* {no comma}   726 *MS* {no
new paragraph}   *MS* Courts   729 *MS* beside;   730 *MS* {beginning
of fo. 80}   732 *MS* and Guido's now—   *1868* now—   733 *MS 1868*
tactics   *MS* {no comma}   734 *MS 1868 1872* The   *MS 1868 1872* place,
735 *MS 1868* That, though   *MS* Court   736 *MS* the woman   *MS* {no
comma}   737 *MS* Profess>Publish   *MS* content,—   738 *MS* of   *MS*
proved   739 *MS* interpose   740 *MS* innocent, abused   741 *MS*
of   *MS* now at guilt's caprice: *1868* caprice:

725 *beforehand*: first, earliest.

735 *allowed the cheat for fact*: i.e. accepted that Violante *had* cheated about Pompilia's
birth.

740 *the innocents*: the Franceschini; following OYB ccxii (214): 'Although the same
judge [Tommati] saw fit to decide the case only on the most summary possessory
footing, by granting that the said Francesca Pompilia should remain in quasi-possession
of her status as daughter.'

Wrongfully given at first, nor bar at all
Succession to the aforesaid usufruct,
Established on a fraud, nor play the game   745
Of Pietro's child and now not Pietro's child
As it might suit the gamester's purpose.   Thus
Was justice ever ridiculed in Rome:
Such be the double verdicts favoured here
Which send away both parties to a suit   750
Nor puffed up nor cast down,—for each a crumb
Of right, for neither of them the whole loaf.
Whence, on the Comparini's part, appeal—
Counter-appeal on Guido's,—that's the game:
And so the matter stands, even to this hour,   755
Bandied as balls are in a tennis-court,
And so might stand, unless some heart broke first,
Till doomsday.

               Leave it thus, and now revert
To the old Arezzo whence we moved to Rome.   760
We've had enough o' the parents, false or true,
Now for a touch o' the daughter's quality.
The start's fair henceforth, every obstacle
Out of the young wife's footpath, she's alone,
Left to walk warily now: how does she walk?   765
Why, once a dwelling's threshold marked and crossed
In rubric by the enemy on his rounds
As eligible, as fit place of prey,

745 *MS* lie,   747 *MS* purpose: thus   749 *MS* One of   754 *MS*
game   757 *MS* {beginning of fo. 81}   758 *MS* {no new para-
graph}   *MS* doomsday: leave   761 *MS* of   *MS* parents false   762 *MS*
of   763 *MS* *1868* henceforth—every   764 *MS* *1868* footpath—she's
alone—   *Yale 2* [? wife s>wife's]   765 *MS* how with her?   766 *MS*
1868 doorpost   768 *MS* his place

   766–7 *dwelling's threshold . . . rubric*: here the marking in 'rubric' (red) of the threshold is done by 'the enemy' (the devil). 'Threshold' originally read 'doorpost' (*MS,
1868*): the passage is inverting the significance of Exod. 12: 7, where the
Israelites marked their doorposts with lambs' blood, identifying themselves amid the
Egyptians.

Baffle him henceforth, keep him out who can!
Stop up the door at the first hint of hoof,   770
Presently at the window taps a horn,
And Satan's by your fireside, never fear!
Pompilia, left alone now, found herself;
Found herself young too, sprightly, fair enough,
Matched with a husband old beyond his age   775
(Though that was something like four times her own)
Because of cares past, present and to come:
Found too the house dull and its inmates dead,
So, looked outside for light and life.
                              And love   780
Did in a trice turn up with life and light,—
The man with the aureole, sympathy made flesh,
The all-consoling Caponsacchi, Sir!
A priest—what else should the consoler be?
With goodly shoulderblade and proper leg,   785
A portly make and a symmetric shape,
And curls that clustered to the tonsure quite.
This was a bishop in the bud, and now
A canon full-blown so far: priest, and priest
Nowise exorbitantly overworked,   790
The courtly Christian, not so much Saint Paul
As a saint of Cæsar's household: there posed he
Sending his god-glance after his shot shaft,

776 MS Though   MS own,   779 MS {no new paragraph}   MS So looked
MS life, and lo   780 1868 1872 And lo   781 MS There in a trice turned up
the life and light   1868 1872 There in a trice did turn up life and light,   783 MS
sir!   785 MS presence and a   786 MS {beginning of fo. 82}   789 MS
Canon fullblown   MS far—>far: 793 MS {no comma}

782 *aureole*: crown or golden halo, set round the heads of saints by painters. Cf.
'Angels, with aureoles like golden quoits / Pitched home': *Sordello*, iv. 610–11.
sympathy made flesh: a parody of 'Word made flesh': John 1: 14. Half-Rome is highly
sarcastic about Caponsacchi's priesthood.
786 *portly make*: handsome build.
792 *saint of Cæsar's household*: i.e. a perfect, worldly courtier; an ironic allusion to
Phil. 4: 22. Half-Rome paints Caponsacchi as refined and aristocratic, unlike the
humble St Paul.

Apollos turned Apollo, while the snake
Pompilia writhed transfixed through all her spires.   795
He, not a visitor at Guido's house,
Scarce an acquaintance, but in prime request
With the magnates of Arezzo, was seen here,
Heard there, felt everywhere in Guido's path
If Guido's wife's path be her husband's too.   800
Now he threw comfits at the theatre
Into her lap,—what harm in Carnival?
Now he pressed close till his foot touched her gown,
His hand brushed hers,—how help on promenade?
And, ever on weighty business, found his steps   805
Incline to a certain haunt of doubtful fame
Which fronted Guido's palace by mere chance;
While—how do accidents sometimes combine!—
Pompilia chose to cloister up her charms
Just in a chamber that o'erlooked the street,   810
Sat there to pray, or peep thence at mankind.

This passage of arms and wits amused the town.
At last the husband lifted eyebrow,—bent
On day-book and the study how to wring
Half the due vintage from the worn-out vines   815

---

796 *MS* He was no   797 *MS* but, in   800 *MS* was her   802 *MS*
carnival?   803 *MS* {no comma}   807 *MS* chance   808 *MS 1868*
combine!   810 *MS* same,   811 *MS* pray and peep   812 *MS* {no
new paragraph}   813 *MS* {beginning of fo. 83}   815 *MS* wornout

794 *Apollos turned Apollo*: i.e. a mild Christian transformed into a handsome Greek
god. This is a contemptuous and sarcastic pun by Half-Rome. In 1 Cor. 4: 6 Apollos is
a friend of St Paul. Apollo was the perfect type of male beauty, god of the lyre and bow
(music and archery), hence an apt parallel for Half-Rome's version of Caponsacchi,
dashing poet and courtier. Caponsacchi stands 'posed' like the Apollo Belvedere with
his bow, 'slaying' with his arrow and his looks the serpent Python (Pompilia), i.e.
overcoming her with his beauty.

795 *spires*: coils; cf. *Paradise Lost*, ix. 502.

801 *comfits*: sweets; small pieces of candied fruit, etc.

812 *passage of arms*: amorous fencing.

814 *day-book*: account book.

At the villa, tease a quarter the old rent
From the farmstead, tenants swore would tumble soon,—
Pricked up his ear a-singing day and night
With "ruin, ruin;"—and so surprised at last—
Why, what else but a titter? Up he jumps.   820
Back to mind come those scratchings at the grange,
Prints of the paw about the outhouse; rife
In his head at once again are word and wink,
Mum here and *budget* there, the smell o' the fox,
The musk o' the gallant. "Friends, there's falseness here!"

The proper help of friends in such a strait   826
Is waggery, the world over. Laugh him free
O' the regular jealous-fit that's incident
To all old husbands that wed brisk young wives,
And he'll go duly docile all his days.   830
"Somebody courts your wife, Count? Where and when?
"How and why? Mere horn-madness: have a care!
"Your lady loves her own room, sticks to it,
"Locks herself in for hours, you say yourself.
"And—what, it's Caponsacchi means you harm?   835
"The Canon? We caress him, he's the world's,
"A man of such acceptance—never dream,

---

816 *MS* Villa, teaze   *1868 1872* teaze   817 *MS* Farmstead tenants   819 *MS*
ruin",—   *MS* last   821 *MS* came   *MS* gate>grange   822 *MS* hen
roost,>outhouse,   823 *MS* were   824 *MS* of   825 *MS* trace>
musk   *MS* of   *MS* here."   826 *MS* {no new paragraph}   *MS* use of
MS case   827 *MS* {no comma}   828 *MS* Of   831 *MS* the Countess?>
your wife, Count?   832–40 *MS* {no quotation marks at beginning of lines}
837 *MS* acceptance,—   *MS* fear>dream,

---

816 *villa*: the location of this villa, at Vittiano, is mentioned only once: OYB cxxviii
(136).

821 *scratchings at the grange*: noises of a fox. Caponsacchi is the cunning fox, trying to
steal Guido's hen (Pompilia).

824 *Mum . . . budget*: calls for silence, 'shhhhhh', from the children's game mum-
budget. Cf. *Merry Wives*, v. ii. 5–7, where the supposed lovers Slender and Anne Page
arrange the words as a secret call: 'I come to her in white, and cry "mum"; she cries
"budget"; and by that we know one another.'

827 *waggery*: mischievous joking.

832 *horn-madness*: fear of cuckoldry.

837 *acceptance*: popularity.

"Though he were fifty times the fox you fear,
"He'd risk his brush for your particular chick,
"When the wide town's his hen-roost! Fie o' the fool!"   840
So they dispensed their comfort of a kind.
Guido at last cried "Something is in the air,
"Under the earth, some plot against my peace.
"The trouble of eclipse hangs overhead;
"How it should come of that officious orb   845
"Your Canon in my system, you must say:
"I say—that from the pressure of this spring
"Began the chime and interchange of bells,
"Ever one whisper, and one whisper more,
"And just one whisper for the silvery last,   850
"Till all at once a-row the bronze-throats burst
"Into a larum both significant
"And sinister: stop it I must and will.
"Let Caponsacchi take his hand away
"From the wire!—disport himself in other paths   855
"Than lead precisely to my palace-gate,—
"Look where he likes except one window's way
"Where, cheek on hand, and elbow set on sill,
"Happens to lean and say her litanies
"Every day and all day long, just my wife—   860
"Or wife and Caponsacchi may fare the worse!"

Admire the man's simplicity, "I'll do this,
"I'll not have that, I'll punish and prevent!"—

839 *MS* He'll   840 *MS* {beginning of fo. 84}   *MS* henroost. Fie on
843–61 *MS* {no quotation marks at beginning of lines}   843 *MS* a plot   *MS*
1868 peace: *844 *MS* is overhead,   *1868* overhead,   *1888* overheard;   *DC*
Br U overheard;>overhead;   *1889* overhead;   846 *MS* {no comma}
851 *MS* the bronze throats burst a-row>a-row the bronze throats burst   855 *MS*
wire! Disport   856 *MS* palace-gate: 858 *MS* Where cheek   862 *MS*
{no new paragraph}   863 *MS* prevent,—"

844 *trouble of eclipse*: shadow of an eclipse, an omen of bad events. Guido concludes
that Caponsacchi must somehow be the 'officious orb' (the meddlesome planet) that
has come into his system (solar system, his life), threatening ill luck to his marriage.

847–52 *spring . . . larum*: a system of alarm bells warning of adultery. The spring sets
small silver bells ringing, and these set off louder bells ('bronze-throats') to sound the
alarm ('larum'). Caponsacchi has set the warning bells ringing.

'T is easy saying. But to a fray, you see,
Two parties go. The badger shows his teeth: 865
The fox nor lies down sheep-like nor dares fight.
Oh, the wife knew the appropriate warfare well,
The way to put suspicion to the blush!
At first hint of remonstrance, up and out
I' the face of the world, you found her: she could speak,
State her case,—Franceschini was a name,   871
Guido had his full share of foes and friends—
Why should not she call these to arbitrate?
She bade the Governor do governance,
Cried out on the Archbishop,—why, there now,   875
Take him for sample! Three successive times,
Had he to reconduct her by main-force
From where she took her station opposite
His shut door,—on the public steps thereto,
Wringing her hands, when he came out to see,   880
And shrieking all her wrongs forth at his foot,—
Back to the husband and the house she fled:
Judge if that husband warmed him in the face
Of friends or frowned on foes as heretofore!
Judge if he missed the natural grin of folk,   885
Or lacked the customary compliment
Of cap and bells, the luckless husband's fit!

So it went on and on till—who was right?
One merry April morning, Guido woke

---

865 *MS* teeth—   866 *MS* Does the fox lie down sheeplike or show fight?
867 *MS* {beginning of fo. 85}   *MS* too,   870 *MS* In   876 *MS* {no comma}   877 *MS* main force   879 *MS* door on   881 *MS* foot,
Yale 2 foot,—>foot.   885 *MS* {no comma}   888 *MS* {no new paragraph}
889 *MS* {no comma}

864–5 *to a fray . . . Two parties go*: proverbial: 'It takes two to make a quarrel': ODEP,
852.
869 *remonstrance*: reproof, protest (from Guido).
877 *main-force*: overpowering force.
887 *cap and bells*: head-dress of a fool.

After the cuckoo, so late, near noonday,   890
With an inordinate yawning of the jaws,
Ears plugged, eyes gummed together, palate, tongue
And teeth one mud-paste made of poppy-milk;
And found his wife flown, his scritoire the worse
For a rummage,—jewelry that was, was not,   895
Some money there had made itself wings too,—
The door lay wide and yet the servants slept
Sound as the dead, or dosed which does as well.
In short, Pompilia, she who, candid soul,
Had not so much as spoken all her life   900
To the Canon, nay, so much as peeped at him
Between her fingers while she prayed in church,—
This lamb-like innocent of fifteen years
(Such she was grown to by this time of day)
Had simply put an opiate in the drink   905
Of the whole household overnight, and then
Got up and gone about her work secure,
Laid hand on this waif and the other stray,
Spoiled the Philistine and marched out of doors
In company of the Canon who, Lord's love,   910
What with his daily duty at the church,

---

893 *MS* poppy-milk,   894 *MS* {beginning of fo. 86}   *MS 1868 1872* scrutoire
895 *MS* not,—   897 *Yale 2* wide and>wide, and   901 *MS* nay so
902 *MS* church,   907 *MS* went   909 *MS* Philistines   911 *MS*
{no comma}

---

890 *cuckoo*: associated with adultery because it lays its eggs in other birds' nests. Its
song 'Cuckoo, cuckoo' was therefore a warning of adultery to married men, a 'word of
fear / Unpleasing to a married ear': *Love's Labour's Lost*, v. ii. 901–2. The primary
meaning is that Guido has failed to hear the cuckoo's warning song. Cook suggests a
second meaning: that the cuckoo is the adulterer, i.e. Caponsacchi; Guido wakes after
Caponsacchi has done his work.

893 *poppy-milk*: milky juice of the poppy, a sleep-inducing drug.

894 *scritoire*: writing-desk.

908 *waif and . . . stray*: (a legal term) lost property, apparently ownerless goods waiting to be claimed. Half-Rome's use is ironic.

909 *Spoiled the Philistine*: despoiled the Philistine: cf. 1 Sam. 17: 50–3. A withering
mock-heroic image by Half-Rome: like an Israelite soldier despoiling his enemy,
Pompilia self-righteously plunders Guido's possessions.

Nightly devoir where ladies congregate,
Had something else to mind, assure yourself,
Beside Pompilia, paragon though she be,
Or notice if her nose were sharp or blunt!   915
Well, anyhow, albeit impossible,
Both of them were together jollily
Jaunting it Rome-ward, half-way there by this,
While Guido was left go and get undrugged,
Gather his wits up, groaningly give thanks   920
When neighbours crowded round him to condole.
"Ah," quoth a gossip, "well I mind me now,
"The Count did always say he thought he felt
"He feared as if this very chance might fall!
"And when a man of fifty finds his corns   925
"Ache and his joints throb, and foresees a storm,
"Though neighbours laugh and say the sky is clear,
"Let us henceforth believe him weatherwise!"
Then was the story told, I'll cut you short:
All neighbours knew: no mystery in the world.   930
The lovers left at nightfall—over night
Had Caponsacchi come to carry off
Pompilia,—not alone, a friend of his,
One Guillichini, the more conversant
With Guido's housekeeping that he was just   935
A cousin of Guido's and might play a prank—
(Have not you too a cousin that's a wag?)

---

915 *MS* blunt.   918 *MS* Romewards, halfway   919 *MS* to go get
920   *MS* return>give   921 *MS* {beginning of fo. 87}   922 *MS*
now   923–8 *MS* {no quotation marks at beginning of lines}   924 *MS*
fall: 926 *MS* storm   931 *MS* had left at nightfall—at night at least
936 *MS* prank,   937 *MS* {line not found}

912 *devoir*: duty.

934 *Guillichini*: Signor Gregorio Guillichini, relative and friend of Guido, was
charged by the prosecution with complicity in the elopement and adultery with
Pompilia. The defence, accepting his complicity in the elopement, argued that it
showed Pompilia's innocence: Guillichini, as Guido's relative, would not have con-
nived at his dishonour unless he believed Pompilia was in mortal danger: see OYB v
(5), cxcv (199–200).

—Lord and a Canon also,—what would you have?
Such are the red-clothed milk-swollen poppy-heads
That stand and stiffen 'mid the wheat o' the Church!—   940
This worthy came to aid, abet his best.
And so the house was ransacked, booty bagged,
The lady led downstairs and out of doors
Guided and guarded till, the city passed,
A carriage lay convenient at the gate.   945
Good-bye to the friendly Canon; the loving one
Could peradventure do the rest himself.
In jumps Pompilia, after her the priest,
"Whip, driver! Money makes the mare to go,
"And we've a bagful. Take the Roman road!"   950
So said the neighbours. This was eight hours since.

Guido heard all, swore the befitting oaths,
Shook off the relics of his poison-drench,
Got horse, was fairly started in pursuit
With never a friend to follow, found the track   955

---

938 *MS* (Lord and a canon   939 *MS* ^red-clothed^   940 *MS* mid   *MS*
of   *MS* Church)   941 *MS* best,   945 *MS* gate   948 *MS* Priest,
949 *MS* {beginning of fo. 88}   *MS* {no quotation mark at beginning of line}
950 *MS* {no quotation mark at beginning of line}   *MS* bagfull   953 *MS*
{no comma}

939–40 *red-clothed . . . Church*: a memory of Nathaniel Lee, *Caesar Borgia*, i. i. 376–7,
the first play Browning ever read: see our Vol. II, p. 1. The lines are also recalled in RB
to EBB, 27 Feb. 1846: 'Do you know anything of Nat Lee's Tragedies? In one of them
a man angry with a Cardinal, cries—"Stand back, and let me mow this poppy down, /
This rank red weed that spoils the Churches' corn!" Is not that good?': *Correspondence*,
xii. 110. The transfer of this image to Half-Rome at a moment of anger and high irony,
when he is thinking of the man who would seduce his wife, is a master-stroke.
Caponsacchi and Guillichini, who are both Canons, are, in Half-Rome's abusive
language, 'poppy-heads' because of their red ecclesiastical dress, and also because
they are like weeds in the wheatfield of the true church. 'Milk-swollen' is both a
description of the milky juice of the poppy-heads, and the implication that
Caponsacchi and Guillichini are big-headed because of their rank, swollen with
preferment.

949 *Money makes the mare to go*: proverbial, meaning 'Money makes things happen':
ODEP, 539.

953 *poison-drench*: large drink of poison; 'drench' is more usually applied to medi-
cine for animals.

Fast enough, 't was the straight Perugia way,
Trod soon upon their very heels, too late
By a minute only at Camoscia, reached
Chiusi, Foligno, ever the fugitives
Just ahead, just out as he galloped in,   960
Getting the good news ever fresh and fresh,
Till, lo, at the last stage of all, last post
Before Rome,—as we say, in sight of Rome
And safety (there's impunity at Rome
For priests, you know) at—what's the little place?—   965
What some call Castelnuovo, some just call
The Osteria, because o' the post-house inn,
There, at the journey's all but end, it seems,
Triumph deceived them and undid them both,
Secure they might foretaste felicity   970
Nor fear surprisal: so, they were surprised.
There did they halt at early evening, there
Did Guido overtake them: 't was day-break;
He came in time enough, not time too much,
Since in the courtyard stood the Canon's self   975
Urging the drowsy stable-grooms to haste
Harness the horses, have the journey end,
The trifling four-hours'-running, so reach Rome.
And the other runaway, the wife? Upstairs,
Still on the couch where she had spent the night,   980
One couch in one room, and one room for both.
So gained they six hours, so were lost thereby.

[—]

957 *MS* Was   958 *MS 1868* Camoscia, at   960 *MS* in   964 *MS*
safety—there's   965 *MS* know—at, what's the little place,   *1868* place?
967 *MS* of   *MS* Inn,   970 *MS* Secure,   971 *MS* {no comma}
974 *MS* enough not time too much: 975 *MS* {beginning of fo. 89}   *MS*
There   978 *MS* four hours' running,   982 *1868* thereby,

959 *Chiusi*: the road from Arezzo to Foligno and Rome in fact goes nowhere near
Chiusi. Either Browning deliberately lets his speaker be impressionistic, or, more
likely, his own memories of his 1860 journey from Rome to Florence via Chiusi are
again surfacing here: see Appendix D.
967 *Osteria*: hostel, inn: see SS 8.
970 *felicity*: i.e. sexual intercourse.

Sir, what's the sequel? Lover and beloved
Fall on their knees? No impudence serves here?
They beat their breasts and beg for easy death, 985
Confess this, that and the other?—anyhow
Confess there wanted not some likelihood
To the supposition so preposterous,
That, O Pompilia, thy sequestered eyes
Had noticed, straying o'er the prayerbook's edge, 990
More of the Canon than that black his coat,
Buckled his shoes were, broad his hat of brim:
And that, O Canon, thy religious care
Had breathed too soft a *benedicite*
To banish trouble from a lady's breast 995
So lonely and so lovely, nor so lean!
This you expect? Indeed, then, much you err.
Not to such ordinary end as this
Had Caponsacchi flung the cassock far,
Doffed the priest, donned the perfect cavalier. 1000
The die was cast: over shoes over boots:
And just as she, I presently shall show,
Pompilia, soon looked Helen to the life,
Recumbent upstairs in her pink and white,
So, in the inn-yard, bold as 't were Troy-town, 1005
There strutted Paris in correct costume,
Cloak, cap and feather, no appointment missed,
Even to a wicked-looking sword at side,

---

983 *MS* Then,   984 *MS* knees: no   *MS* here: 986 *MS* other, anyhow—   990 *MS* edge   991 *MS* {no comma}   992 *MS* and
broad   995 *MS* Satan   1000 *MS 1868* cavalier;   1001 *MS* {begin-
ning of fo. 90}   1003 *MS* Pompilia now   1005 *MS* as in Troy-town
1006 *MS* {no comma}   1008 *MS* {no comma}

994 *benedicite*: blessing (L.).

1001 *over shoes over boots*: proverbial, meaning 'no half measures': ODEP, 603. Both
Caponsacchi and Pompilia are fully committed to their actions. Cf. *Two Gentlemen of
Verona*, 1. i. 24–5.

1003 *Helen*: a withering mock-epic allusion comparing the flight of Pompilia and
Caponsacchi with that of Helen and Paris. Guido is implicitly the righteous husband,
Menelaus.

1007 *appointment*: detail of outfit or equipment.

He seemed to find and feel familiar at.
Nor wanted words as ready and as big   1010
As the part he played, the bold abashless one.
"I interposed to save your wife from death,
"Yourself from shame, the true and only shame:
"Ask your own conscience else!—or, failing that,
"What I have done I answer, anywhere,   1015
"Here, if you will; you see I have a sword:
"Or, since I have a tonsure as you taunt,
"At Rome, by all means,—priests to try a priest.
"Only, speak where your wife's voice can reply!"
And then he fingered at the sword again.   1020
So, Guido called, in aid and witness both,
The Public Force. The Commissary came,
Officers also; they secured the priest;
Then, for his more confusion, mounted up
With him, a guard on either side, the stair   1025
To the bed-room where still slept or feigned a sleep
His paramour and Guido's wife: in burst
The company and bade her wake and rise.

Her defence? This. She woke, saw, sprang upright
I' the midst and stood as terrible as truth,   1030
Sprang to her husband's side, caught at the sword
That hung there useless,—since they held each hand
O' the lover, had disarmed him properly,—
And in a moment out flew the bright thing
Full in the face of Guido: but for help   1035

1009 *MS* feel, familiar   1011 *MS* A[ ]>As   1013–19 *MS* {no quotation
marks at beginning of lines}   1014 *MS* else, or,   1015 *MS* anywhere
1018 *MS* ;>,—   1019 *1872* 'Only,   1021 *MS* So Guido   1027 *MS*
wife, in   1028 *MS* {beginning of fo. 91}   1029 *MS* This: she   1030 *MS*
In   1031 *MS* lover's   1032 *MS* useless while they held his hands,   *1868*
useless, since   1033 *MS* {line not found}   *1868* properly,   1034 *MS*
there flew   1035 *MS 1868* Guido,—

1011 *abashless*: shameless; a rare word, perhaps a coinage: OED^2 gives only this and
III. 897.
1022 *Public Force*: the police; from 'la Forza': SS 12, 13.
Commissary: chief officer or governor.

O' the guards who held her back and pinioned her
With pains enough, she had finished you my tale
With a flourish of red all round it, pinked her man
Prettily; but she fought them one to six.
They stopped that,—but her tongue continued free: 1040
She spat forth such invective at her spouse,
O'erfrothed him with such foam of murderer,
Thief, pandar—that the popular tide soon turned,
The favour of the very *sbirri*, straight
Ebbed from the husband, set toward his wife,   1045
People cried "Hands off, pay a priest respect!"
And "persecuting fiend" and "martyred saint"
Began to lead a measure from lip to lip.

But facts are facts and flinch not; stubborn things,
And the question "Prithee, friend, how comes my purse
"I' the poke of you?"—admits of no reply.   1051
Here was a priest found out in masquerade,
A wife caught playing truant if no more;
While the Count, mortified in mien enough,
And, nose to face, an added palm in length,   1055

1036 *MS* Of   1037 *MS* the tale   1038 *MS* the man   1041 *MS* {no
comma}   1042 *MS* Murderer   1043 *MS* Pandar—   *MS* was changed,
1044 *MS* feeling   1045 *MS* towards   1046 *MS* the priest   1050 *Yale 1*
purse,>purse   1051 *MS* In   *MS* but one reply.   1052 *MS* plainly in
1053 *MS* at the least,   1054 *MS* man mortified   1055 *MS* {beginning of
fo. 92}   *MS* And nose

1037–8 *finished . . . it*: 'ended my story with a flourish of red handwriting; i.e. made
a bloody end of things by killing Guido.'
1038 *pinked*: stabbed.
1044 *sbirri*: police officers (It.).
1048 *lead a measure*: dance.
1051 *I' the poke of you*: in your pocket.
1055 *nose . . . length*: i.e. made to look ridiculous; from the It. idiom 'rimanere con
un palmo di naso': to be left with a hand's length of nose, i.e. 'to be astonished,
bewildered, stupefied, balked': John Millhouse, *New Pronouncing and Explanatory
English–Italian and Italian–English Dictionary* (3rd ed., 2 vols., 1866), ii. 526. Browning
also uses the idiom in *Red Cotton Night-Cap Country*, 2782–4: 'Cousin regarded cousin,
turned up eye, / And took departure, as our Tuscans laugh, / Each with his added
palm-breadth of long nose'.

Was plain writ "husband" every piece of him:
Capture once made, release could hardly be.
Beside, the prisoners both made appeal,
"Take us to Rome!"
                              Taken to Rome they were;   1060
The husband trooping after, piteously,
Tail between legs, no talk of triumph now—
No honour set firm on its feet once more
On two dead bodies of the guilty,—nay,
No dubious salve to honour's broken pate   1065
From chance that, after all, the hurt might seem
A skin-deep matter, scratch that leaves no scar:
For Guido's first search,—ferreting, poor soul,
Here, there and everywhere in the vile place
Abandoned to him when their backs were turned,   1070
Found,—furnishing a last and best regale,—
All the love-letters bandied 'twixt the pair
Since the first timid trembling into life
O' the love-star till its stand at fiery full.
Mad prose, mad verse, fears, hopes, triumph, despair,   1075
Avowal, disclaimer, plans, dates, names,—was nought
Wanting to prove, if proof consoles at all,
That this had been but the fifth act o' the piece
Whereof the due proemium, months ago
These playwrights had put forth, and ever since   1080
Matured the middle, added 'neath his nose.
He might go cross himself: the case was clear.

[—]

1057 *MS* was made,   1058 *MS* Beside the   1063 *MS* honor   1065 *MS* honor's   1066 *MS* By>From   *MS* its hurt   1067 *MS* instead of>that leaves   *MS* scar,—   1071 *MS* best>last   1072 *MS* *1868 1872* twixt 1074 *MS* Of   1075 *MS* hopes, fears,>fears, hopes,   1076 *MS* names, nought   1078 *MS* been the   *MS* of

1065 *salve*: healing ointment.
1071 *regale*: feast, refreshment (ironic): the food found by Guido the 'ferret', l. 1068.
1079 *proemium*: beginning.
1082 *go cross himself*: make the sign of the cross, in recognition that something is finished. As the priest and congregation cross themselves at the end of mass, so Guido

Therefore to Rome with the clear case; there plead
Each party its best, and leave law do each right,
Let law shine forth and show, as God in heaven,   1085
Vice prostrate, virtue pedestalled at last,
The triumph of truth! What else shall glad our gaze
When once authority has knit the brow
And set the brain behind it to decide
Between the wolf and sheep turned litigants?   1090
"This is indeed a business!" law shook head:
"A husband charges hard things on a wife,
"The wife as hard o' the husband: whose fault here?
"A wife that flies her husband's house, does wrong:
"The male friend's interference looks amiss,   1095
"Lends a suspicion: but suppose the wife,
"On the other hand, be jeopardized at home—
"Nay, that she simply hold, ill-groundedly,
"An apprehension she is jeopardized,—
"And further, if the friend partake the fear,   1100
"And, in a commendable charity
"Which trusteth all, trust her that she mistrusts,—
"What do they but obey law—natural law?
"Pretence may this be and a cloak for sin,
"And circumstances that concur i' the close   1105
"Hint as much, loudly—yet scarce loud enough
"To drown the answer 'strange may yet be true:'

1083 *MS* {beginning of fo. 93; the foliation conceals whether *MS* had a new paragraph here}   1084 *MS* the Law her rights,   *1868 1872* the law do   1085 *MS*
1868 1872 Let her   *MS* show us   1088 *MS* her   1089 *MS* her>the
1090 *MS* now litigants?   1091 *MS* business" quoth the Dame: *1868 1872*
business"   1092 *MS* the wife,   1092–1132 *MS* {no quotation marks at
beginnings of lines}   1093 *MS* on   *Yale 1* on>o'   1099 *MS* That>
An   1100 *MS* {no commas}   1101 *MS* commendably   1103 *MS*
1868 1872 the natural law?   1105 *MS* at   1107 *MS* "strange   *MS* true:

can cross himself in recognition that the five-act play of the love affair is completed.
Cf. the Italian idiom *fateci una croce*, make a cross on it, i.e. forget about it.

1101–2 *charity / Which trusteth all*: imitating 1 Cor. 13: 4–7; also alluded to at l. 1116.
1103 *natural law*: the sense of good and evil arising naturally in the human mind, as
distinguished from law coming from legislation.

"Innocence often looks like guiltiness.
"The accused declare that in thought, word and deed,
"Innocent were they both from first to last   1110
"As male-babe haply laid by female-babe
"At church on edge of the baptismal font
"Together for a minute, perfect-pure.
"Difficult to believe, yet possible,
"As witness Joseph, the friend's patron-saint.   1115
"The night at the inn—there charity nigh chokes
"Ere swallow what they both asseverate;
"Though down the gullet faith may feel it go,
"When mindful of what flight fatigued the flesh
"Out of its faculty and fleshliness,   1120
"Subdued it to the soul, as saints assure:
"So long a flight necessitates a fall
"On the first bed, though in a lion's den,
"And the first pillow, though the lion's back:
"Difficult to believe, yet possible.   1125
"Last come the letters' bundled beastliness—
"Authority repugns give glance to—nay,
"Turns head, and almost lets her whip-lash fall;
"Yet here a voice cries 'Respite!' from the clouds—
"The accused, both in a tale, protest, disclaim,   1130

1110 *MS* {beginning of fo. 94}   1112 *MS* On>At   1114 *MS* possible
1115 *MS* Joseph the   1116 *MS* Inn   1117 *MS* asseverate,   1118 *MS* {no
comma}   1119 *MS* that>what   1120 *MS* {no comma}   1122 *MS*
Long>So long a   1127 *MS* to twice   *1868 1872* to twice,   1128 *MS*
fall—   1129 *MS* too there cries "Respite!"

1115 *Joseph*: St Joseph. Joseph came to believe, against probability, in Mary's
chastity: see Matt. 1: 18–25.
1117 *asseverate*: solemnly affirm.
1126 *beastliness*: beastly quality, here lust.
1127 *repugns give glance to*: repugns [to] give glance to = refuses to look at.
'Repugns' is not usually used with the infinitive ('to give'). Authority is so disgusted
by the implication of the 'beastliness' of the letters that she refuses to examine them
closely, turns her head away, and instantly prepares to punish Pompilia and Caponsacchi.
1130 *in a tale*: in a (=one) tale, i.e. in agreement, as opposed to 'in two tales'. Cf.
Much Ado, IV. ii. 31; *Luria*, IV. 125 n.

"Abominate the horror: 'Not my hand'
"Asserts the friend—'Nor mine' chimes in the wife,
" 'Seeing I have no hand, nor write at all.'
"Illiterate—for she goes on to ask,
"What if the friend did pen now verse now prose,   1135
"Commend it to her notice now and then?
" 'Twas pearls to swine: she read no more than wrote,
"And kept no more than read, for as they fell
"She ever brushed the burr-like things away,
"Or, better, burned them, quenched the fire in smoke.
"As for this fardel, filth and foolishness,   1141
"She sees it now the first time: burn it too!
"While for his part the friend vows ignorance
"Alike of what bears his name and bears hers:
" 'Tis forgery, a felon's masterpiece,   1145
"And, as 'tis said the fox still finds the stench,
"Home-manufacture and the husband's work.
"Though he confesses, the ingenuous friend,
"That certain missives, letters of a sort,
"Flighty and feeble, which assigned themselves   1150
"To the wife, no less have fallen, far too oft,
"In his path: wherefrom he understood just this—
"That were they verily the lady's own,
"Why, she who penned them, since he never saw
"Save for one minute the mere face of her,   1155

1131 MS "not my hand"   1132 MS "Nor mine"   MS {no comma}
1133 MS "Seeing   MS all."   1134 MS {line added later}   MS {no quotation mark}   MS say   1135 MS {no comma}   1136 MS then,
1136–1212 MS {no quotation marks at beginnings of lines}   1138 MS {begin-
ning of fo. 95}   MS it came>they fell   1145 MS forger's work,>forgery,
1146 MS since   1151 MS wife no   MS had   1152 MS path—wherefrom
MS this   *1153 1868 1872 own,   1888 1889 own.

1131 hand: handwriting.
1137 pearls to swine: cf. Matt. 7: 6.
1141 fardel: parcel, pack (of letters).
1146 fox ... stench: proverbial, a version of 'The fox is the finder': ODEP, 284.
Guido finds the letters he has hidden himself.
1150 assigned: ascribed, attributed.

"Since never had there been the interchange
"Of word with word between them all their life,
"Why, she must be the fondest of the frail,
"And fit, she for the '*apage*' he flung,
"Her letters for the flame they went to feed!   1160
"But, now he sees her face and hears her speech,
"Much he repents him if, in fancy-freak
"For a moment the minutest measurable,
"He coupled her with the first flimsy word
"O' the self-spun fabric some mean spider-soul   1165
"Furnished forth: stop his films and stamp on him!
"Never was such a tangled knottiness,
"But thus authority cuts the Gordian through,
"And mark how her decision suits the need!
"Here's troublesomeness, scandal on both sides,   1170
"Plenty of fault to find, no absolute crime:
"Let each side own its fault and make amends!
"What does a priest in cavalier's attire
"Consorting publicly with vagrant wives
"In quarters close as the confessional,   1175
"Though innocent of harm? 'T is harm enough:
"Let him pay it,—say, be relegate a good
"Three years, to spend in some place not too far

1158 *MS* frail   1159 *MS* "apage"   1160 *MS 1868 1872* feed.   1161 *MS*
since he saw her face, and heard   1165 *MS* {beginning of fo. 96}   *MS* Of
1166 *MS* ^stop his films and^   *MS* him.   1168 *MS* Authority   *MS* it
Gordian-wise—   1169 *MS* case.   1171 *MS* crime.   1172 *MS*
amends.   1175 *MS* {no comma}   1177 *MS* it, and be relegate a year,
1868 1872 it, and be   1178 *MS* Two

1158 *fondest of the frail*: most foolish of the morally weak.
1159 '*apage*': 'Get thee hence, [Satan]', from the Greek New Testament, Matt. 4: 10.
1166 *films*: threads, from Guido's 'web' of lies in the forged letters.
1168 *Gordian*: = Gordian knot, i.e. 'complicated matter'. 'To cut a Gordian knot' is
to get rid of a complicated matter in a simple or forceful way, evading the supposed
complexities of its solution. The original Gordian knot was tied by Gordius, an ancient
king of Phrygia; instead of untying it, Alexander cut it with his sword.
1177 *relegate*: banished, from OYB 'relegatus'. Ancient Roman law distinguished
between 'relegatio', in which a person retained property and civic rights at Rome, and
the more severe 'exilium'. A similar distinction is made here at l. 1183. See also l. 1221 n.

"Nor yet too near, midway 'twixt near and far,
"Rome and Arezzo,—Civita we choose,   1180
"Where he may lounge away time, live at large,
"Find out the proper function of a priest,
"Nowise an exile,—that were punishment,—
"But one our love thus keeps out of harm's way
"Not more from the husband's anger than, mayhap
"His own . . . say, indiscretion, waywardness,   1186
"And wanderings when Easter eves grow warm.
"For the wife,—well, our best step to take with her,
"On her own showing, were to shift her root
"From the old cold shade and unhappy soil   1190
"Into a generous ground that fronts the south
"Where, since her callow soul, a-shiver late,
"Craved simply warmth and called mere passers-by
"To the rescue, she should have her fill of shine.
"Do house and husband hinder and not help?   1195
"Why then, forget both and stay here at peace,
"Come into our community, enroll
"Herself along with those good Convertites,
"Those sinners saved, those Magdalens re-made,
"Accept their ministration, well bestow   1200
"Her body and patiently possess her soul,
"Until we see what better can be done.
"Last for the husband: if his tale prove true,
"Well is he rid of two domestic plagues—

1179 *MS* twixt here and there,   *1868 1872* twixt   1180 *MS* we'll say,
1182 *MS* {no comma}   1183 *MS* Not as   *MS 1868* punishment,
1186 *MS* own—say,   1188 *MS* ^well,^   *MS* her   1189 *MS* {no
comma}   1191 *MS* south,   *1868 1872* south: 1192 *MS* {beginning
of fo. 97}   1193 *MS* guidance, called   1194 *MS* thereof.   1195 *MS*
The   1196 *MS* again,   1198 *MS* Yourself   *MS* {no comma}   1200 *MS*
and bestow   1201 *MS* Your   *MS* your   1203 *MS* Husband: *MS* be
MS {no comma}   1204 *MS* a domestic plague

1180 *Civita*: Civitavecchia, a seaport 40 miles NW of Rome.
1198 *Convertites*: an order of nuns, originally formed from reformed prostitutes,
'converts' from sin.
1201 *patiently . . . soul*: cf. Luke 21: 19.

"Both wife that ailed, do whatsoever he would,   1205
"And friend of hers that undertook the cure.
"See, what a double load we lift from breast!
"Off he may go, return, resume old life,
"Laugh at the priest here and Pompilia there
"In limbo each and punished for their pains,   1210
"And grateful tell the inquiring neighbourhood—
"In Rome, no wrong but has its remedy."
The case was closed. Now, am I fair or no
In what I utter? Do I state the facts,
Having forechosen a side? I promised you!   1215

The Canon Caponsacchi, then, was sent
To change his garb, re-trim his tonsure, tie
The clerkly silk round, every plait correct,
Make the impressive entry on his place
Of relegation, thrill his Civita,   1220
As Ovid, a like sufferer in the cause,
Planted a primrose-patch by Pontus: where,—

1205 *MS 1868 1872* The   *MS* whatsoe'er   1207 *MS* a load   *MS* from off his
1209 *MS* Priest   1211 *1872* 'And   *MS* tell   enquiring   neighbours
this—   1212 *1872* 'In   *MS* remedy.   1214 *MS* utter,—do I state the
case,   1215 *MS* you.   1218 *MS* {beginning of fo. 98}   *MS* on,   1220 *MS*
His   *MS* Civita   1222 *MS* [ ]>—where,   *1868 1872* where,

1215 *forechosen*: already chosen. Ironically, this is exactly what Half-Rome has done.
1218 *clerkly silk*: his priest's robes (as opposed to his cavalier costume). 'Silk' suggests
that even in his proper dress Caponsacchi will be a beau.
1221 *Ovid*: the Latin poet (43 BC–AD 17) was relegated from Rome in AD 8 by
order of the emperor and sent into banishment at Tomi on Pontus (the Black Sea): see
l. 1177 n. He himself gives two reasons for his exile: his writing of *Ars Amatoria*, an
erotic poem that apparently taught sexual immorality, and some 'mistake' or indiscretion, perhaps his complicity in the adultery of the emperor's daughter. Half-Rome
portrays Caponsacchi sardonically as Ovid, another 'sufferer' in the cause of sex and
adultery.
1222 *primrose-patch*: a small piece of ground with primroses, a flower associated with
pleasure: cf. 'a puff'd and reckless libertine, / Himself the primrose path of dalliance
treads': *Hamlet*, I. iii. 49–50. Half-Rome is very cynical: Ovid did not continue a life of
easy love-making in exile, as this implies, but was constantly sad about the harshness of
his situation; also, the severity of his banishment is an unequal comparison to Caponsacchi's 40-mile removal to the coast at Civita.

What with much culture of the sonnet-stave
And converse with the aborigines,
Soft savagery of eyes unused to roll   1225
And hearts that all awry went pit-a-pat
And wanted setting right in charity,—
What were a couple of years to while away?
Pompilia, as enjoined, betook herself
To the aforesaid Convertites, soft sisterhood   1230
In Via Lungara, where the light ones live,
Spin, pray, then sing like linnets o'er the flax.
"Anywhere, anyhow, out of my husband's house
"Is heaven," cried she,—was therefore suited so.
But for Count Guido Franceschini, he—   1235
The injured man thus righted—found no heaven
I' the house when he returned there, I engage,
Was welcomed by the city turned upside down
In a chorus of inquiry. "What, back—you?
"And no wife? Left her with the Penitents?   1240
"Ah, being young and pretty, 't were a shame
"To have her whipped in public: leave the job
"To the priests who understand! Such priests as yours—
"(Pontifex Maximus whipped Vestals once)

1223 MS with culture   1225 MS with eyes   MS 1868 1872 roll,   1226 MS
pit-a-pat,   1227 MS {line added later}   MS 1868 1872 charity,   1228 MS
wile   1230 MS 1868 1872 the sisterhood   1234 MS {no quotation mark at
beginning of line}   MS and therefore   1235 MS And he,   MS he
1236 MS now righted,—   1237 MS In   1239 MS back you?   1240–
59 MS {no quotation marks at beginnings of lines}   1243 MS understand.
1244 MS {line not found}

   1223 *sonnet-stave*: the sonnet stanza, associated with love poetry. The remark is
suggested by the improper 'ottave' that Caponsacchi is supposed to have sent Pompilia:
OYB xciii (100), ccxiv (216).
   1224–7 *aborigines . . . charity*: Ovid complained of the barbarity of the people in
Tomi; Half-Rome twists this into a witty, lubricious image of Caponsacchi sexually
awakening the 'savages', the chaste women of Civitavecchia.
   1232 *linnets o'er the flax*: song-birds attracted to the seeds of the flax plant = nuns
singing as they weave fibre made from flax.
   1244 *Pontifex . . . once*: in ancient Rome a Vestal Virgin who let the sacred fire go
out was whipped by the chief priest or Pontifex Maximus. This line is not in *MS*. The

"Our madcap Caponsacchi: think of him!   1245
"So, he fired up, showed fight and skill of fence?
"Ay, you drew also, but you did not fight!
"The wiser, 't is a word and a blow with him,
"True Caponsacchi, of old Head-i'-the-Sack
"That fought at Fiesole ere Florence was: 1250
"He had done enough, to firk you were too much.
"And did the little lady menace you,
"Make at your breast with your own harmless sword?
"The spitfire! Well, thank God you're safe and sound,
"Have kept the sixth commandment whether or no   1255
"The lady broke the seventh: I only wish
"I were as saint-like, could contain me so.
"I, the poor sinner, fear I should have left
"Sir Priest no nose-tip to turn up at me!"
You, Sir, who listen but interpose no word,   1260

1246 *MS* So he   *MS* fence-   1247 *MS* {beginning of fo. 99}   *MS*
fight.   1248 *MS* him   1249 *MS* Head-in-the-sack   1250 *MS* in
1253 *MS* her breast with Caponsacchi's   1254 *MS* sound   1255 *MS*
And   *MS* eighth   1256 *MS* Lady   *MS* sixth: 1258 *MS* *1868 1872* I
am a sinner, I fear   1259 *MS* me."

speaker appears to endorse Guido's giving of Pompilia into the hands of the church
authorities, giving ancient precedent for priests disciplining women; really he is
ironically suggesting that Guido has consented to give his wife into the hands of her
seducer, a priest, and failed to exercise husbandly discipline.

    1249 *of old Head-i'-the-Sack*: descended from old Caponsacco (i.e. *capo 'n sacco*, 'head
in sack'), the ferocious founder of the family; see next note. Cf. vi. 228–38.

    1250 *at Fiesole ere Florence was*: the Caponsacchi family were originally from Fiesole
and then Florence. Browning knew this from well-known sources, from early Florentine history, and from Dante, *Paradiso*, xvi. 121–2: 'Già era il Caponsacco nel
mercato / disceso giù da Fiesole': 'Already had Caponsacco to the market / from
Fiesole descended'. Fiesole, now covered with fine villas, was the hill-fort town that
preceded the building of Florence down in the valley. The founder of the Caponsacchi
family, the original winner of the name 'Head-in-the-sack', is imagined fighting
against Julius Caesar's Roman troops at the siege of Fiesole in 72 BC, before the first
building of Florence. For an account of the siege see Giovanni Villani, *Croniche
fiorentine*, i. 38. In a highly ironic vein, the speaker is praising Caponsacchi's long-
descended aristocratic spirit, and taunting Guido's feebleness.

    1251 *firk*: beat, chastise.

    1255–6 *sixth commandment ... seventh*: 'Thou shalt not kill. Thou shalt not commit
adultery': Exod. 20: 13–14.

Ask yourself, had you borne a baiting thus?
Was it enough to make a wise man mad?
Oh, but I'll have your verdict at the end!

Well, not enough, it seems: such mere hurt falls,
Frets awhile, aches long, then grows less and less,   1265
And so gets done with. Such was not the scheme
O' the pleasant Comparini: on Guido's wound
Ever in due succession, drop by drop,
Came slow distilment from the alembic here
Set on to simmer by Canidian hate,   1270
Corrosives keeping the man's misery raw.
First fire-drop,—when he thought to make the best
O' the bad, to wring from out the sentence passed,
Poor, pitiful, absurd although it were,
Yet what might eke him out result enough   1275
And make it worth while to have had the right
And not the wrong i' the matter judged at Rome.
Inadequate her punishment, no less
Punished in some slight sort his wife had been;
Then, punished for adultery, what else?   1280
On such admitted crime he thought to seize,

1261 *MS* yourself had   *MS* thus,   1264 *MS* {no new paragraph}   *MS* the
mere   1265 *MS* awile, and aches long, then less   *1868 1872* and aches long,
then less   1266 *MS* *1868 1872* is done   1267 *MS* Of   *MS* people here:
1269 *MS* distilments   1270 *MS* Kept>Set   1272 *MS* fire-drop was,—
he   1273 *MS* Of   *MS* passed   1274 *MS* {beginning of fo. 100}   *MS*
inadequate>absurd although   *MS* r[ ]>although   1276 *MS* To   *MS* *1868*
1872 his   while   he   had   1277 *MS* in   *MS* Rome: 1279 *MS*
been,   1281 *MS* could>thought   *MS* {no comma}

1262 *wise man mad*: proverbial: 'Oppression makes a wise man mad', from Eccl. 7:
7: ODEP, 600.

1269 *alembic*: distilling apparatus: a gourd-shaped vessel, with a head and beak
through which the vapours are condensed.

1270 *Canidian hate*: a hate like that of Canidia, the malicious witch of poisons and
spells in Horace's *Epodes*. Half-Rome's phrase is modelled on 'Vatinian hate', the
hatred allegedly borne by P. Vatinius for C. Calvus (Catullus 14.3).

1272 *First fire-drop*: 'We do not discover what this fire-drop was till we reach the
next paragraph [l. 1286]; the speaker loses himself in the circumstances which preceded
its application': Cook, 50.

And institute procedure in the courts
Which cut corruption of this kind from man,
Cast loose a wife proved loose and castaway:
He claimed in due form a divorce at least.   1285

This claim was met now by a counterclaim:
Pompilia sought divorce from bed and board
Of Guido, whose outrageous cruelty,
Whose mother's malice and whose brother's hate
Were just the white o' the charge, such dreadful depths
Blackened its centre,—hints of worse than hate,   1291
Love from that brother, by that Guido's guile,
That mother's prompting. Such reply was made,
So was the engine loaded, wound up, sprung
On Guido, who received bolt full in breast;   1295
But no less bore up, giddily perhaps.
He had the Abate Paolo still in Rome,
Brother and friend and fighter on his side:
They rallied in a measure, met the foe
Manlike, joined battle in the public courts,   1300
As if to shame supine law from her sloth:
And waiting her award, let beat the while
Arezzo's banter, Rome's buffoonery,
On this ear and on that ear, deaf alike,
Safe from worse outrage. Let a scorpion nip,   1305
And never mind till he contorts his tail!

1282 *MS* Courts   1283 *MS* in this kind   1286 *MS* {no new paragraph}
1289 *MS* hate,   1290 *MS* of   1291 *MS* hate   1292 *MS* {? ruse,>
guile,}   1293 *MS* malice: such   1295 *MS* Guido who   *MS* the bolt in
breast,   *1868 1872* the bolt in breast;   1296 *MS* perhaps   1297 *MS* here
in Rome   1300 *MS* Courts,   1301 *MS* {beginning of fo. 101}   *MS*
sloth,   1303 *MS* buffoonery   1305 *MS* nip   1306 *MS* his tail,—as
well you said!

1284 *castaway*: reprobate; from the noun use in 1 Cor. 9: 27. Cf. Emily Brontë,
Wuthering Heights, ed. Hilda Marsden and Ian Jack (Oxford, 1976), 18.

1301 *supine*: Johnson stresses 'supíne'.

1305–6 *Let . . . tail*: i.e. 'the scorpion's claws can do no real harm (just as Guido
believes the gossip of Rome and Arezzo cannot harm him); you need only worry
about a scorpion's poison when you see its tail move ("contort") over its back to sting.'
Guido thinks the problem is all claws and no sting, but it proves otherwise.

But there was sting i' the creature; thus it struck.
Guido had thought in his simplicity—
That lying declaration of remorse,
That story of the child which was no child   1310
And motherhood no motherhood at all,
—That even this sin might have its sort of good
Inasmuch as no question more could be,—
Call it false, call the story true,—no claim
Of further parentage pretended now: 1315
The parents had abjured all right, at least,
I' the woman owned his wife: to plead right still
Were to declare the abjuration false:
He was relieved from any fear henceforth
Their hands might touch, their breath defile again   1320
Pompilia with his name upon her yet.
Well, no: the next news was, Pompilia's health
Demanded change after full three long weeks
Spent in devotion with the Sisterhood,—
Which rendered sojourn,—so the court opined,—   1325
Too irksome, since the convent's walls were high
And windows narrow, nor was air enough
Nor light enough, but all looked prison-like,
The last thing which had come in the court's head.
Propose a new expedient therefore,—this!   1330
She had demanded—had obtained indeed,
By intervention of her pitying friends
Or perhaps lovers—(beauty in distress,
Beauty whose tale is the town-talk beside,

1307 *MS* There was a sting in   *MS* struck: 1308 *MS* simplicity   1310 *MS* that was   1312 *MS* That   *MS* had its   1313 *MS 1868 1872* could be more,   *Yale 2* Inasmuch as no question could be more,>Inasmuch as no more could question be,   1314 *MS 1868 1872* true, no   1315 *Yale 2* now:> now.   1317 *MS* In   *MS 1868 1872* still   *MS* fres[ ]>right   *MS 1868 1872* now   1324 *MS* :>,—   1325 *MS* Rendered her   *1868 1872* Rendering   *MS* Court   1326 *MS* Convent's   *MS* high,   1328 *MS* {beginning of fo. 102}   1329 *MS* Court's head: 1330 *MS* this.   1331 *MS* {no comma}   1332 *MS 1868 1872* whatever friends   1333 *MS* lovers—beauty   1334 *MS 1868 1872* In one

Never lacks friendship's arm about her neck)—   1335
Obtained remission of the penalty,
Permitted transfer to some private place
Where better air, more light, new food might soothe—
Incarcerated (call it, all the same)
At some sure friend's house she must keep inside,   1340
Be found in at requirement fast enough,—
Domus pro carcere, in Roman style.
You keep the house i' the main, as most men do
And all good women: but free otherwise,
Should friends arrive, to lodge them and what not?   1345
And such a *domum*, such a dwelling-place,
Having all Rome to choose from, where chose she?
What house obtained Pompilia's preference?
Why, just the Comparini's—just, do you mark,
Theirs who renounced all part and lot in her   1350
So long as Guido could be robbed thereby,
And only fell back on relationship
And found their daughter safe and sound again
When that might surelier stab him: yes, the pair
Who, as I told you, first had baited hook   1355
With this poor gilded fly Pompilia-thing,
Then caught the fish, pulled Guido to the shore
And gutted him,—now found a further use
For the bait, would trail the gauze wings yet again
I' the way of what new swimmer passed their stand.

1335 *MS* neck—   1336 *MS* —Not freedom, scarce remitted   *1868 1872* Not
freedom, scarce remitted   1337 *MS 1868 1872* Solely the   1338 *MS* air
and light and food might be—   *1868 1872* might be—   1339 *MS* {no
comma}   1341 *MS* enough,   1342 *MS* the Roman mode.   1343 *MS* in
1344 *MS* {no comma}   1345 *MS* arrive to entertain the same. *1868 1872*
lodge and entertain.   *DC* {pencil note "Wrong spacing" between 1345 and 1346.
This note does not appear to have been acted on}   1346 *MS domus,*   1349 *MS*
see,   1354 *MS 1868 1872* So soon as that might   1355 *MS* {beginning of
fo. 103}   1358 *MS* him,   1359 *MS* [?]oer>yet   1360 *MS* In
MS [ ]>swimmer   *MS* creel—

1342 *Domus pro carcere*: house arrest (L.), literally 'a house for a prison'.
1346 *domum*: house (L.); in the Latin accusative, picking up the legal phrase.
1360 *stand*: fishing-place.

They took Pompilia to their hiding-place—   1361
Not in the heart of Rome as formerly,
Under observance, subject to control—
But out o' the way,—or in the way, who knows?
That blind mute villa lurking by the gate   1365
At Via Paulina, not so hard to miss
By the honest eye, easy enough to find
In twilight by marauders: where perchance
Some muffled Caponsacchi might repair,
Employ odd moments when he too tried change,   1370
Found that a friend's abode was pleasanter
Than relegation, penance and the rest.

Come, here's the last drop does its worst to wound:
Here's Guido poisoned to the bone, you say,
Your boasted still's full strain and strength: not so!   1375
One master-squeeze from screw shall bring to birth
The hoard i' the heart o' the toad, hell's quintessence.
He learned the true convenience of the change,
And why a convent lacks the cheerful hearts
And helpful hands which female straits require,   1380
When, in the blind mute villa by the gate,
Pompilia—what? sang, danced, saw company?
—Gave birth, Sir, to a child, his son and heir,

1361 *MS* hiding-place   1362 *MS* {no comma}   1364 *MS* of   1365 *MS*
blind, mute Villa   1368 *MS* marauders—   1370 *MS* {no comma}
*1373 *MS 1868 1872* wound,   *1888* wound   *DC Br U* wound>wound: *1889*
wound: *1374 *MS 1868 1872* say,   *1888* say   *DC Br U* say>say,   *1889* say,
1376 *MS* master squeeze   *MS* its birth,   1377 *MS* in   *MS* of   1379 *MS*
Convent wants   *1868 1872* convent wants   1381 *MS* {beginning of fo. 104}
MS Villa   *MS* {no commas}   1383 *MS* Gave

1365 *blind*: dark.
1365–6 *by the gate / At Via Paulina*: see l. 203 n.
1375 *still*: the alembic of l. 1269.
1377 *hoard i' the heart o' the toad*: the store of poison in the centre of a toad. Toads
were thought to be full of deadly poison: see Juvenal, *Satires*, i. 70, vi. 659. Horace's
Canidia has the toad as an ingredient for her cauldron: see *Epodes*, v. 19, and also
above, l. 1270 n.

Or Guido's heir and Caponsacchi's son.
I want your word now: what do you say to this?   1385
What would say little Arezzo and great Rome,
And what did God say and the devil say
One at each ear o' the man, the husband, now
The father? Why, the overburdened mind
Broke down, what was a brain became a blaze.   1390
In fury of the moment—(that first news
Fell on the Count among his vines, it seems,
Doing his farm-work,)—why, he summoned steward,
Called in the first four hard hands and stout hearts
From field and furrow, poured forth his appeal,   1395
Not to Rome's law and gospel any more,
But this clown with a mother or a wife,
That clodpole with a sister or a son:
And, whereas law and gospel held their peace,
What wonder if the sticks and stones cried out?   1400

All five soon somehow found themselves at Rome,
At the villa door: there was the warmth and light—
The sense of life so just an inch inside—
Some angel must have whispered "One more chance!"

He gave it: bade the others stand aside: 1405
Knocked at the door,—"Who is it knocks?" cried one.
"I will make," surely Guido's angel urged,
"One final essay, last experiment,
"Speak the word, name the name from out all names

1387 *MS* Devil   1388 *MS* of   1389 *MS* father.   *MS* {no comma}
1392 *MS* man   1393 *MS* Steward,   1396 *MS* Law and Gospel   1397 *MS*
{no comma}   1398 *MS* son,   1399 *MS* Law and Gospel   1401 *MS* {no
new paragraph}   *MS* Rome—   1402 *MS* Villa   1405 *MS* {no new
paragraph}   1406 *MS* door.   1407 *MS* Guido must have said,   *1868*
1872 said,   1408 *MS* {beginning of fo. 105}   *MS* wise experiment,   1408–
18 *MS* {no quotation marks at beginnings of lines}

1398 *clodpole*: stupid rustic.
    1399–1400 *held . . . out*: cf. Luke 19: 40, but 'sticks and stones' (ordinary things, i.e.
the farm labourers) replaces 'stones' in the biblical text.

"Which, if,—as doubtless strong illusions are,   1410
"And strange disguisings whereby truth seems false,
"And, since I am but man, I dare not do
"God's work until assured I see with God,—
"If I should bring my lips to breathe that name
"And they be innocent,—nay, by one mere touch   1415
"Of innocence redeemed from utter guilt,—
"That name will bar the door and bid fate pass.
"I will not say 'It is a messenger,
"'A neighbour, even a belated man,
"'Much less your husband's friend, your husband's self:'
"At such appeal the door is bound to ope.   1421
"But I will say"—here's rhetoric and to spare!
Why, Sir, the stumbling-block is cursed and kicked,
Block though it be; the name that brought offence
Will bring offence: the burnt child dreads the fire   1425
Although that fire feed on some taper-wick
Which never left the altar nor singed a fly:
And had a harmless man tripped you by chance,
How would you wait him, stand or step aside,
When next you heard he rolled your way? Enough.   1430

"Giuseppe Caponsacchi!" Guido cried;
And open flew the door: enough again.
Vengeance, you know, burst, like a mountain-wave

1411 *MS* disguising whence even   *1868 1872* whence even   1412 *MS 1868*
1872 for I am a   1414 *MS* the same   1415 *MS 1868 1872* one touch
1417 *MS* Will bar the door and bid fate pass this time   1418 *MS* "It
1419 *MS* {no double quotation marks}   1420 *MS* {no double quotation
marks at beginning of line and no quotation mark at end}   1421 *MS* {no
quotation mark}   1423 *MS* sir,   *MS* kicked   1424 *MS* be,   *MS*
brings   1425 *MS* Is the   *MS* fire,   1426 *MS 1868 1872* a taper-wick
1427 *MS* That   *MS* did harm   *1868 1872* singed fly: 1431 *MS* {no new
paragraph}   *MS* cried: 1432 *MS* went   1433 *MS* mountain wave

  1423 *stumbling-block*: cf. 1 Cor. 1: 23.
  1425 *burnt . . . fire*: proverbial: ODEP, 92.
  1433–7 *Vengeance . . . blood*: cf. OYB cxlix (152): 'As he looked all around at those
walls encrusted with his heaviest insults and with his infamy, the dams of his reason

That holds a monster in it, over the house,
And wiped its filthy four walls free at last   1435
With a wash of hell-fire,—father, mother, wife,
Killed them all, bathed his name clean in their blood,
And, reeking so, was caught, his friends and he,
Haled hither and imprisoned yesternight
O' the day all this was.   1440
                    Now, Sir, tale is told,
Of how the old couple come to lie in state
Though hacked to pieces,—never, the expert say,
So thorough a study of stabbing—while the wife
(Viper-like, very difficult to slay)   1445
Writhes still through every ring of her, poor wretch,
At the Hospital hard by—survives, we'll hope,
To somewhat purify her putrid soul
By full confession, make so much amends
While time lasts; since at day's end die she must.   1450

For Caponsacchi,—why, they'll have him here,
As hero of the adventure, who so fit
To figure in the coming Carnival?
'Twill make the fortune of whate'er saloon

1435 *MS* {beginning of fo. 106}   *MS 1868* free again   1436 *MS* hellfire,   *MS*
wife   1439 *MS* yesterday   1440 *MS* The day   *MS* {no new paragraph}
1441 *MS 1868 1872* Now the whole is known,   1442 *MS 1868 1872* And
1444 *MS* stabbing. While   1445 *MS 1868 1872* Viper-like,   *MS 1868 1872*
slay,   1450 *MS* lasts—   1451 *MS* {no new paragraph}   *MS* why, you'll
see, they'll have him here,   1452 *MS 1868 1872* The   *MS* novel,   1453 *MS*
1868 1872 To tell it

gave way and he fell headlong into that miserable ruin of plunging himself with deadly
catastrophe into the blood of the oppressors of his reputation.' Sullivan (26) notes that
Half-Rome 'rises to an unusual pitch of passion in describing the murder scene'.

   1439–40 *yesternight / O' the day*: from SS 16: the imprisonment took place at 4 p.m.,
3 January.
   1445 *Viper-like*: folk belief held that snakes were difficult to kill and could make
themselves whole again: 'We have scorch'd the snake, not kill'd it; / She'll close and be
herself': *Macbeth*, III. ii. 13–14. A related belief was that a wounded snake would
survive until after sunset, hence l. 1450. Half-Rome continues the imagery associating
Pompilia with witches, poisoning, and toads.

Hears him recount, with helpful cheek, and eye   1455
Hotly indignant now, now dewy-dimmed,
The incidents of flight, pursuit, surprise,
Capture, with hints of kisses all between—
While Guido, wholly unromantic spouse,
No longer fit to laugh at since the blood   1460
Gave the broad farce an all too brutal air,
Why, he and those four luckless friends of his
May tumble in the straw this bitter day—
Laid by the heels i' the New Prison, I hear,
To bide their trial, since trial, and for the life,   1465
Follows if but for form's sake: yes, indeed!

But with a certain issue: no dispute,
"Try him," bids law: formalities oblige:
But as to the issue,—look me in the face!—
If the law thinks to find them guilty, Sir,   1470
Master or men—touch one hair of the five,
Then I say in the name of all that's left
Of honour in Rome, civility i' the world
Whereof Rome boasts herself the central source,—
There's an end to all hope of justice more.   1475
Astræa's gone indeed, let hope go too!
Who is it dares impugn the natural law,
Deny God's word "the faithless wife shall die"?
What, are we blind? How can we fail to learn
This crowd of miseries make the man a mark,   1480
Accumulate on one devoted head

1457 *MS* moving incidents of flight, surprise,   1459 *MS 1868 1872* the most
1462 *MS* five   *1868 1872* our luckless   1463   *MS* {beginning of fo. 107}
1464 *MS* in   1466 *MS* indeed.   1467 *MS* {no comma} 1468 *MS* Law:
MS have force: 1469 *MS* face,—   1472 *MS* {Then added later}
1473 *MS* in   *MS* world,   1475 *MS* more,   1476 *MS* too.   1477 *MS*
1868 law?   1478 *MS* "The   *1868 1872* die?"   1479 *MS* see   *1868 1872* see,

1473 *civility*: the civilized ideal; cf. 1. 287 n.
1476 *Astræa's gone*: i.e. Justice has gone. Astraea, goddess of justice, departed from
earth at the end of the Golden Age and became the constellation Virgo.
1478 *faithless wife shall die*: cf. Lev. 20: 10, Deut. 22: 22–4.
1480 *mark*: target.

For our example?—yours and mine who read
Its lesson thus—"Henceforward let none dare
"Stand, like a natural in the public way,
"Letting the very urchins twitch his beard   1485
"And tweak his nose, to earn a nickname so,
"Be styled male-Grissel or else modern Job!"
Had Guido, in the twinkling of an eye,
Summed up the reckoning, promptly paid himself,
That morning when he came up with the pair   1490
At the wayside inn,—exacted his just debt
By aid of what first mattock, pitchfork, axe
Came to hand in the helpful stable-yard,
And with that axe, if providence so pleased,
Cloven each head, by some Rolando-stroke,   1495
In one clean cut from crown to clavicle,
—Slain the priest-gallant, the wife-paramour,
Sticking, for all defence, in each skull's cleft
The rhyme and reason of the stroke thus dealt,
To-wit, those letters and last evidence   1500

1482 *MS 1868* example, yours   1483 *MS* "Heneforf[ ]>"Henceforward
1484–1487 *MS* {no quotation marks at beginnings of lines}   1484 *MS* {no
commas}   1487 *MS* Of the   *MS* the modern Job.   *1868 1872* "Of the
male-Grissel or the modern Job!"   1489 *MS* {beginning of fo. 108}   *MS* himself
1491 *MS* Inn,—   1494 *MS* Providence   1495 *MS* skull,>head,   *MS*
Rolando-stroke   1497 *MS* The priest-gallant the wife his paramour,
1499 *MS* and the reason   *MS* {no comma}   1500 *MS* To whit,   *Yale 1*
To wit,>To-wit

1484 *natural*: fool.
1487 *male-Grissel*: Griselda, the model wife, proverbial type of patience and submissiveness in the face of suffering. Her story, told in Boccaccio's *Decameron* (x. 10) and
Chaucer's *Clerk's Tale*, of apparent sufferings inflicted by her husband, is an allegory of
human trials set by a loving God; hence she is a parallel figure to Job. There is irony,
however, in 'male-Grissel': Half-Rome implies that Guido has been 'womanly' in his
patient response to events. In a letter of 22 Sept. 1864, Browning recalls an interesting
discussion with Julia Wedgwood about the figure of Griselda, and praises to her the
unusual version of the story in the play *Griseldis* (1835) by the German writer Friedrich
Halm (1806–71) in which Griselda in the end rejects her husband: see *Wedgwood*, 90–1.
1495 *Rolando-stroke*: i.e. massive sword-stroke. Roland, the hero of the Old French
epic *La Chanson de Roland*, wielded the famous sword Durendal. The *Chanson* revels in
descriptions of spectacular, body-cleaving sword-strokes, inflicted by Roland and
others, like that described in the next line.
1496 *clavicle*: collar-bone.

Of shame, each package in its proper place,—
Bidding, who pitied, undistend the skulls,—
I say, the world had praised the man. But no!
That were too plain, too straight, too simply just!
He hesitates, calls law forsooth to help.   1505
And law, distasteful to who calls in law
When honour is beforehand and would serve,
What wonder if law hesitate in turn,
Plead her disuse to calls o' the kind, reply
(Smiling a little) " 'T is yourself assess   1510
"The worth of what's lost, sum of damage done.
"What you touched with so light a finger-tip,
"You whose concern it was to grasp the thing,
"Why must law gird herself and grapple with?
"Law, alien to the actor whose warm blood   1515
"Asks heat from law whose veins run lukewarm milk,—
"What you dealt lightly with, shall law make out
"Heinous forsooth?"
                            Sir, what's the good of law
In a case o' the kind? None, as she all but says.   1520
Call in law when a neighbour breaks your fence,
Cribs from your field, tampers with rent or lease,
Touches the purse or pocket,—but wooes your wife?
No: take the old way trod when men were men!
Guido preferred the new path,—for his pains,   1525

1501 *MS* place,   1502 *MS* And let,   1503 *MS* man: but no—   1504 *MS*
just—   1505 *MS* hesitates—calls   *MS* at last   1506 *MS* what   1509 *MS*
of   1510 *MS 1868* {no parentheses}   *MS* "Tis   1511–18 *MS* {no quotation marks at beginnings of lines}   1511 *MS 1868* done: 1512 *MS*
touch   1513 *MS* is   1514 *MS* to grapple   *MS* ?>,   1516 *MS*
{beginning of fo. 109}   *MS* Law   *MS* milk.   1519 *MS* {no new paragraph}
MS Why,   1520 *MS* of   1522 *MS* lease   1523 *MS* but, takes
1524 *MS* tried   *MS* men.   1525 *MS* pains

   1502 *undistend*: push back together: Browning's coinage, the reversal of the action
of 'distend'. This passage is a good instance of Half-Rome's sadism.
   1505 *forsooth*: truly, in truth (a sarcastic use).
   1507 *When honour is beforehand*: when honour has priority, i.e. when considerations
of honour come before considerations of law.
   1515 *alien to*: unsympathetic to.

Stuck in a quagmire, floundered worse and worse
Until he managed somehow scramble back
Into the safe sure rutted road once more,
Revenged his own wrong like a gentleman.
Once back 'mid the familiar prints, no doubt   1530
He made too rash amends for his first fault,
Vaulted too loftily over what barred him late,
And lit i' the mire again,—the common chance,
The natural over-energy: the deed
Maladroit yields three deaths instead of one,   1535
And one life left: for where's the Canon's corpse?

All which is the worse for Guido, but, be frank—
The better for you and me and all the world,
Husbands of wives, especially in Rome.
The thing is put right, in the old place,—ay,   1540
The rod hangs on its nail behind the door,
Fresh from the brine: a matter I commend
To the notice, during Carnival that's near,
Of a certain what's-his-name and jackanapes
Somewhat too civil of eves with lute and song   1545
About a house here, where I keep a wife.
(You, being his cousin, may go tell him so.)

1526 *MS* sank there   1528 *MS* again,   1530 *MS* mid   1531 *MS*
{no comma}   1532 *MS* {no comma}   1533 *MS* in   *MS* again, the
1534 *MS* over energy: 1535 *MS* [ ]>three   *MS* {no comma}   1536 *MS*
Canon now?>Canon's corpse?   *1537 *MS* {new paragraph. Paragraphing
obscured in *1868* and *1872* by this line's being at the head of the page}   *1888*
1889{no new paragraph}   *MS* but—   1538 *MS* {no comma}   1541 *MS*
{no comma}   1543 *MS* {beginning of fo. 110}   *MS* notice during   *MS*
close,   1546 *MS* {no comma}

   1530 *prints*: footprints; continuing the image of the 'rutted road' of honorable revenge.
   1532–3 *Vaulted . . . again*: cf. *Macbeth* I. vii. 27–8.
   1534–5 *deed / Maladroit*: clumsy, badly executed deed.
   1541–2 *rod . . . brine*: developing the proverbial 'To have rods in pickle' = to have
punishment in store: ODEP, 682. Birch-rods were preserved in brine to keep the twigs
pliable. This is Half-Rome's threat of violence: the instrument of punishment has been
used justly, he thinks, against Pompilia and the Comparini; now, he implies, it hangs
ready to be used against his listener's cousin, unless the latter desists from trying to
seduce his wife: see Introduction above.
   1544 *jackanapes*: upstart, impertinent fellow.

INTRODUCTION TO BOOK III

THE OTHER HALF-ROME

THE dramatic monologue of Book III was probably suggested to
Browning by the anti-Guido pamphlet 'Risposta Alle notizie di fatto,
e di ragioni nella Causa Franceschini' ('A Response to the Account of
the Facts and Grounds in the Franceschini Case'), OYB ccvii–ccxxv
(209–26), though—even more than in the case of the previous monologue—its drama, characterization, and substance leave the pamphlet far
behind. The monologue is imagined as spoken in the Piazza Barberini,
near the Bernini fountain, and also near the crowds attending the market:
see I. 896–901 n. The probable date on which we should imagine it is 4
January 1698, two days after the murders;[1] like Half-Rome's monologue,
it is near to the heat and confusion of the events it describes.

Other Half-Rome, the speaker of the monologue, takes up a position
against Guido in relation to the murder-case, and in this respect is
representative of the 'Other Half' of the gossiping population of Rome.
To some critics his monologue is the least satisfying of the first three, less
vivid for example than Half-Rome's. Partly this seems to be the point.
We are being invited to attune ourselves to a different range of tones,
verbal gestures, and mannerisms. There is little irony or sarcasm in Other
Half-Rome's speech when compared with Half-Rome's. He uses gentler
imagery, a muted form of exclamation, and milder ways of introducing
arguments: 'Will you go somewhat back to understand?' (964), or
'Whither it leads is what remains to tell' (1418). Occasionally, he creates
a very beautiful image (1533–8). Some critics have read his character in
positive ways. Cook, agreeing with much of his judgement of the rights
and wrongs of the murder-case, says that he shows 'a reflectiveness and a
sensibility which are absent from the coarser nature [of Half-Rome]':
'His speech is not merely a more or less honest, and a more or less
successful, attempt to get at the truth from the evidence before him; it

---

[1] There is an element of inconsistency in the timetable of the first three monologues. Tertium Quid (Book IV) speaks when Pompilia is still alive, i.e. at the latest on
the day of her death, 6 Jan. This, combined with I. 846, 894–5, 904, and 910 would
tend to suggest 4 Jan.; but III. 867 would suggest 5 or 6 Jan.

is on the whole a very scrupulous attempt.'[2] Sullivan says he has an 'idealistic', 'sensitive', and 'imaginative' nature.[3] Later assessments of him are more critical. Ann Brady calls him 'fuzzy-minded' and 'double-tongued', since from his advocacy Pompilia inadvertently emerges as a potential adulteress.[4] Buckler speaks of his falsely 'romanticizing' narrative which, while it enshrines Pompilia as a saint and martyr, 'cannot encompass her as a woman'.[5] These later readings of Other Half-Rome seem to engage more closely with the implications of his sentimentality. Behind the monologue we may sense the Romantic judgement that awe or delight—and the commitment to the world that they imply—are a prerequisite for intellectual or moral perception: in the words of 'Andrea del Sarto', 'a man's reach should exceed his grasp', and here it evidently does not. Indeed, if Half-Rome is partly a reworking of the Duke of 'My Last Duchess', then we can appropriately consider Other Half-Rome as a version of Andrea del Sarto: as with the latter, his quality of pathos is a weakening of significant truth.

Where Half-Rome is a pastiche of the 'masculine', Other Half-Rome is a pastiche of the 'feminine'; where Half-Rome gloats with energetic sadism over the corpses in San Lorenzo church, Other Half-Rome takes his cue from the scene of Pompilia's deathbed which he has just attended in the hospital of Santa Anna. Pompilia is 'little', with a 'flower-like body' (5), a soul that has bloodied 'its last thorn with unflinching foot' (23). She lies in the 'long white lazar-house' (35), 'the most lamentable of things' (224). The tug of these adjectives is characteristic. At the deathbed Other Half-Rome has noticed the old woman, Monna Baldi, who thinks that Pompilia's body is saint-like: could she but touch it she would be cured of her illnesses. He has also noticed the visit to the deathbed by the famous painter, Carlo Maratta, and records the painter's emotional comments. These are hints of Other Half-Rome's religiosity and artistic aspiration, and indications of the ways in which the monologue is much subtler, in moral terms, than simply the debunking of a cloying sentimentalism. Whereas Half-Rome wrests the story into the aggressive patterns of his own mind, conversely Other Half-Rome lacks a necessary measure of energy, and consequently of moral and emotional perception.

Parts of his monologue show a witty and ironic stance—as, for example, his portrayal of Paolo seducing Violante with the idea of an aristo-

---

[2] Cook, 34, 54.   [3] Sullivan, 40, 47.

[4] Ann P. Brady, *Pompilia: A Feminist Reading of Robert Browning's The Ring and the Book* (Ohio University Press, Athens, 1988), 16–17.

[5] Buckler, 82.

cratic marriage for her daughter (249–376). But when he approaches the centre of the story, the discrepancies between Caponsacchi and Pompilia's accounts confuse him, and he refers to 'the tenebrific passage of the tale' (789). He cannot really see into it; he cannot apprehend the lives of Pompilia and Caponsacchi as complex realities, two different people finding their way with considerable difficulty towards good and heroic actions. He insidiously erodes them, so that Caponsacchi becomes, partly, a romantically minded priest in love with Pompilia's 'youth and beauty' (835)—'priests are merely flesh and blood' (830)—and Pompilia a vulnerable teenager 'helpless, simple-sweet / Or silly-sooth' (805–6). By the same token, Caponsacchi's action in rescuing Pompilia can be accommodated to 'the regular way o' the world' (1048). Other Half-Rome's mentality is genial but low-pulsed, and it prevents him grasping the real spiritual dimensions of good and evil present in the murder-case. His is a classic instance of a kind of deficiency, reducing a dramatic, rich and—to Browning—awe-inspiring series of events, to the limitations of his own mind.

Other Half-Rome's status as a bachelor is significant in this respect. While Half-Rome is a jealous husband who commands and distorts the realm of sexual love, Other Half-Rome is anaemic with regard to it. In the close of his monologue he accepts, apparently for the sake of argument, that Guido might be right in thinking of his wife and Caponsacchi as adulterers, and then—in a quietly amazing analogy—compares what Guido might have felt as an outraged and sexually betrayed husband to his own feelings in relation to some small annoyances caused by business. He seems unconscious of the unequal nature of the comparison. In fact, as he returns to his own bourgeois concerns, the syntax and vocabulary enact a measure of pettiness that is symptomatic of his wider moral mediocrity: the large bounds of the murder-case are suddenly reduced to talk of 'my contract's clause', 'co-heir in a will', 'my administration of effects' (1685–8). His argument at this point—'Even if Guido was completely right in his analysis of adultery, he should still keep his actions within the law'—posits a mind as comfortable as his own. What Buckler calls his 'desexualizing' of the story, corresponds with his failure of moral perception: his blandness smooths out the nature of events, robbing them of their full dimensions of morality and passion.

THE OTHER HALF-ROME.

ANOTHER day that finds her living yet,
Little Pompilia, with the patient brow
And lamentable smile on those poor lips,
And, under the white hospital-array,
A flower-like body, to frighten at a bruise   5
You'd think, yet now, stabbed through and through again,
Alive i' the ruins. 'T is a miracle.
It seems that, when her husband struck her first,
She prayed Madonna just that she might live
So long as to confess and be absolved;   10
And whether it was that, all her sad life long
Never before successful in a prayer,
This prayer rose with authority too dread,—
Or whether, because earth was hell to her,
By compensation, when the blackness broke   15
She got one glimpse of quiet and the cool blue,
To show her for a moment such things were,—
Or else,—as the Augustinian Brother thinks,

---

1 *MS* {beginning of fo. 111. At the head of the page is the title '3. The Other Half Rome.' in RB's hand}   *Yale 1* THE OTHER HALF ROME>THE OTHER HALF-ROME {At the foot of the page RB has written "Q^y Should not the words be corrected throughout (in the Heading) as in the [text lost]"}   4 *MS* {no commas}   5 *MS* with>at   10 *MS* absolved: 11 *MS 1868* long, 15 *MS* {no comma}   18 *MS* Augustine   *MS* thought,

---

1 *Another day*: 4 Jan. 1698. Pompilia does not die until 6 Jan.

3 *lamentable*: pitiable, sorrow-provoking.

4 *hospital-array*: see ll. 35, 37. Pompilia is imagined dying in St Anna's hospital, though elsewhere her death is set in the Convertites' convent. Browning took the idea of the hospital from Fra Celestino's affidavit, which refers to the medical treatment received by Pompilia in her last days, and which is signed 'Fra Celestino Angelo of St Anna, barefooted Augustinian': OYB lviii (58). Celestino testified movingly to Pompilia's innocence.

18 *Augustinian Brother*: Fra Celestino.

The friar who took confession from her lip,—
When a probationary soul that moved   20
From nobleness to nobleness, as she,
Over the rough way of the world, succumbs,
Bloodies its last thorn with unflinching foot,
The angels love to do their work betimes,
Staunch some wounds here nor leave so much for God.   25
Who knows? However it be, confessed, absolved,
She lies, with overplus of life beside
To speak and right herself from first to last,
Right the friend also, lamb-pure, lion-brave,
Care for the boy's concerns, to save the son   30
From the sire, her two-weeks' infant orphaned thus,
And—with best smile of all reserved for him—
Pardon that sire and husband from the heart.
A miracle, so tell your Molinists!

There she lies in the long white lazar-house.   35
Rome has besieged, these two days, never doubt,
Saint Anna's where she waits her death, to hear
Though but the chink o' the bell, turn o' the hinge
When the reluctant wicket opes at last,
Lets in, on now this and now that pretence,   40

---

19 *MS* lips,—>lip,—   20 *MS 1868 1872* moves   22 *MS* succumbs—   23 *MS* foot,—   28 *MS* {beginning of fo. 112}   *MS* speak [ ]>speak   29 *MS* lamb-pure   30 *MS* boys   35 *MS* {no new paragraph}   36 *MS* flocked these two last days,>besieged, these two days,   37 *MS* To the place>Saint Anna's   *MS* where thus she>where she   38 *MS* of .... of

---

   23 *Bloodies . . . foot*: the image continues from the preceding line: Pompilia, walking over the rough path of the world to heaven ('the strait and narrow way'), treads on thorns (trials and sufferings), enduring them bravely, even to this last thorn (her murder).
   30–1 *Care . . . sire*: on her deathbed Pompilia made a will in her son's favour. Earlier she had taken precautions to protect him from his father: OYB cxiii (121).
   32 *him*: i.e. Guido.
   35 *lazar-house*: a house for lepers, i.e. a hospital.
   36–42 *Rome . . . plight*: the sense is: 'The people of Rome have besieged St Anna's, eager to hear anything: even the sound of the door admitting other, more favoured people—still too many, say the doctors—is newsworthy for them.'
   39 *wicket*: small door (often within a larger, formal door).

Too many by half,—complain the men of art,—
For a patient in such plight. The lawyers first
Paid the due visit—justice must be done;
They took her witness, why the murder was.
Then the priests followed properly,—a soul   45
To shrive; 't was Brother Celestine's own right,
The same who noises thus her gifts abroad.
But many more, who found they were old friends,
Pushed in to have their stare and take their talk
And go forth boasting of it and to boast.   50
Old Monna Baldi chatters like a jay,
Swears—but that, prematurely trundled out
Just as she felt the benefit begin,
The miracle was snapped up by somebody,—
Her palsied limb 'gan prick and promise life   55
At touch o' the bedclothes merely,—how much more
Had she but brushed the body as she tried!
Cavalier Carlo—well, there's some excuse
For him—Maratta who paints Virgins so—
He too must fee the porter and slip by   60
With pencil cut and paper squared, and straight
There was he figuring away at face:
"A lovelier face is not in Rome," cried he,

41 *MS* Two   *MS* art   44 *MS 1868* was;   46 *MS* shrive,   47 *MS*
1868 abroad: 55 *MS* {beginning of fo. 113}   56 *MS* of   58 *MS*
Carlo,—   62 *MS 1868* face—   63 *MS* he

41 *men of art*: doctors.
46 *shrive*: hear the confession of.
Brother Celestine's own right: because he was the priest working at St Anna's.
50 *boasting . . . boast*: two different senses of 'boast': people go out boasting of having
seen Pompilia, and boasting of themselves in consequence.
51 *Monna Baldi*: Monna (It.) = Dame or Lady; an invented character, though the
name probably comes from 'Signora Maddalena Baldi Albergotti', mentioned
incidentally at OYB xlix (49). Cf. George Eliot, *Romola* (1863), bk. 1, ch. 1:
'"Monna Trecca" (equivalent to "Dame Greengrocer")'. The old woman thinks
Pompilia's body is saint-like: a touch of it will cure her ills.
58–9 *Carlo . . . Maratta*: Carlo Maratta (1625–1713), the once celebrated Roman
painter, was called Carluccio delle Madonne ('Little Carlo of the Madonnas') because
of his many pictures of the Virgin. Arcangeli thinks of him as 'first in reputation'
among portrait-painters in 1698: VIII. 639.
61 *paper squared*: the artistic technique of a grid of squares, to assist accurate drawing.

"Shaped like a peacock's egg, the pure as pearl,
"That hatches you anon a snow-white chick."   65
Then, oh that pair of eyes, that pendent hair,
Black this and black the other! Mighty fine—
But nobody cared ask to paint the same,
Nor grew a poet over hair and eyes
Four little years ago when, ask and have,   70
The woman who wakes all this rapture leaned
Flower-like from out her window long enough,
As much uncomplimented as uncropped
By comers and goers in Via Vittoria: eh?
'T is just a flower's fate: past parterre we trip,   75
Till peradventure someone plucks our sleeve—
"Yon blossom at the briar's end, that's the rose
"Two jealous people fought for yesterday
"And killed each other: see, there's undisturbed
"A pretty pool at the root, of rival red!"   80
Then cry we "Ah, the perfect paragon!"
Then crave we "Just one keepsake-leaf for us!"

Truth lies between: there's anyhow a child
Of seventeen years, whether a flower or weed,
Ruined: who did it shall account to Christ—   85
Having no pity on the harmless life
And gentle face and girlish form he found,
And thus flings back. Go practise if you please

65 *MS* {no quotation mark at beginning of line}   66 *MS* hair   67 *MS*
1868 this,   *MS* other: mighty   68 *MS* draw>paint   72 *MS* of   *MS*
{no comma}   76 *MS* some one   *MS* sleeve   78–80 *MS* {no quotation
marks}   78 *MS* rival lovers>jealous people   79 *MS* other—   *MS*
still>there's   82 *MS* {beginning of fo. 114}   *1868* we,   *MS* keepsake leaf
83 *MS* {no new paragraph}   84 {not found in *MS*}   86 *MS* Who had
88 *1868* back: go

64 *like a peacock's egg*: i.e. very white, pure, and oval.
70 *ask and have*: proverbial: ODEP, 20.
73 *uncropped*: not cut or plucked (used of flowers). Cf. *All's Well*, v. iii. 327–8: 'If
thou beest yet a fresh uncropped flower, / Choose thou thy husband, and I'll pay thy
dower.'
75 *parterre*: formal garden.

With men and women: leave a child alone
For Christ's particular love's sake!—so I say.   90

Somebody, at the bedside, said much more,
Took on him to explain the secret cause
O' the crime: quoth he, "Such crimes are very rife,
"Explode nor make us wonder now-a-days,
"Seeing that Antichrist disseminates   95
"That doctrine of the Philosophic Sin:
"Molinos' sect will soon make earth too hot!"
"Nay," groaned the Augustinian, "what's there new?
"Crime will not fail to flare up from men's hearts
"While hearts are men's and so born criminal;   100
"Which one fact, always old yet ever new,
"Accounts for so much crime that, for my part,
"Molinos may go whistle to the wind
"That waits outside a certain church, you know!"

Though really it does seem as if she here,   105
Pompilia, living so and dying thus,

---

90 *MS* sake: so   91 *MS* {no new paragraph}   93 *MS* Of   *MS* he
"such crimes are rife,   94–7 *MS* {no quotation marks at beginnings of
lines}   94 *MS* nowadays,   95 *Yale 1* Antichrist>Antichrist   98 *MS*
"Nay, brother,"   *Yale 1* "Nay, groaned>"Nay," groaned   *MS* Augustine,   *MS*
whats   *MS* then>there   99–104 *MS* {no quotation marks at beginnings of
lines}   100 *MS* the hearts   *MS* and born criminal,   103 *MS* for the
wind   104 *MS* {no quotation mark at end of line}   105 *MS* {no new
paragraph}   *MS* {no comma}

---

96 *Philosophic Sin*: cf. 11. 177 n.

98 *groaned the Augustinian*: in accordance with the thinking of St Augustine, the
patron saint of his order, Fra Celestino thinks that it is trivial to ascribe the murders to
the climate created by Molinism; he looks to man's deeper alienation from God, the
doctrine of original sin: men's hearts are 'born criminal'.

103–4 *Molinos . . . church*: a conflation of the phrase 'to go whistle': to go and do
what you will, a contemptuous dismissal, and the proverbial 'to whistle for a wind':
traditionally sailors whistle to summon the wind: ODEP, 884. The sense therefore is
'Molinos can go hang, go and whistle in an already windy place', i.e. his doctrine is
irrelevant to the case. The 'certain church' is the Jesuits' church, the Gesù, whose
square was considered the most draughty place in Rome: 'The legend runs that the
devil and the wind were one day taking a walk together. When they came to this

Has had undue experience how much crime
A heart can hatch. Why was she made to learn
—Not you, not I, not even Molinos' self—
What Guido Franceschini's heart could hold?   110
Thus saintship is effected probably;
No sparing saints the process!—which the more
Tends to the reconciling us, no saints,
To sinnership, immunity and all.

For see now: Pietro and Violante's life   115
Till seventeen years ago, all Rome might note
And quote for happy—see the signs distinct
Of happiness as we yon Triton's trump.
What could they be but happy?—balanced so,
Nor low i' the social scale nor yet too high,   120
Nor poor nor richer than comports with ease,
Nor bright and envied, nor obscure and scorned,
Nor so young that their pleasures fell too thick,
Nor old past catching pleasure when it fell,
Nothing above, below the just degree,   125
All at the mean where joy's components mix.
So again, in the couple's very souls
You saw the adequate half with half to match,
Each having and each lacking somewhat, both
Making a whole that had all and lacked nought.   130
The round and sound, in whose composure just

---

109 *MS* {line added later}   *MS* Not   *MS* self,   111 *MS* {beginning of fo.
115}   *MS* probably,   112 *MS* Which   114 *MS* immunities
118 *MS* As>Of happiness as   *MS* [ ]>we   *MS* see Triton's   *MS* [ ]>
trump.   119 *MS* happy,   120 *MS* in   123 *MS* {no comma}
126 *MS* Just   *MS* all joy's   *MS* mixed.   130 *MS* nought,   *1868* nought;

square, the devil, who seemed to be very devout, said to the wind, "Just wait a minute,
mio caro, while I go into this church." So the wind promised, and the devil went into
the Gesù, and has never come out again—and the wind is blowing about in the Piazza
del Gesù to this day': Augustus J. C. Hare, *Walks in Rome* (2 vols., 1871), i. 82.

118 *yon Triton's trump*: the sea shell held up by the Triton, through which he blows
the fountain's jet of water: see 1. 896–901 n.

131 *round . . . just*: complete and healthy (whole), in whose balanced composition.

The acquiescent and recipient side
Was Pietro's, and the stirring striving one
Violante's: both in union gave the due
Quietude, enterprise, craving and content,   135
Which go to bodily health and peace of mind.
But, as 't is said a body, rightly mixed,
Each element in equipoise, would last
Too long and live for ever,—accordingly
Holds a germ—sand-grain weight too much i'
   the scale—   140
Ordained to get predominance one day
And so bring all to ruin and release,—
Not otherwise a fatal germ lurked here:
"With mortals much must go, but something stays;
"Nothing will stay of our so happy selves."   145
Out of the very ripeness of life's core
A worm was bred—"Our life shall leave no fruit."
Enough of bliss, they thought, could bliss bear seed,
Yield its like, propagate a bliss in turn
And keep the kind up; not supplant themselves   150
But put in evidence, record they were,
Show them, when done with, i' the shape of a child.
"'T is in a child, man and wife grow complete,
"One flesh: God says so: let him do his work!"

Now, one reminder of this gnawing want,   155
One special prick o' the maggot at the core,

133 *MS* stirring,   134 *MS* Violantes;   137 *MS* {beginning of fo.
116}   138 *MS* {no comma}   139 *MS* To   *Yale 1* To>Too   *MS*
accordingly,   140 *MS* in   141 *MS* O'erdained   *MS* day,   144 *MS* stays,
145 *MS* {no quotation mark at beginning of line}   147 *MS* fruit"   150 *MS*
up,   152 *MS* in   154 *MS* {no quotation mark at beginning of line}
155 *MS* {no new paragraph}   *MS* Now one   *Yale 1* Now one>Now, one
156 *MS* of   *MS* {no comma}

137–8 *as ... equipoise*: the more the four ancient elements (fire, earth, air, and water)
were balanced in a given body or substance, the longer it was supposed to endure.
   144–5 *"With ... selves."*: the imagined thoughts of the Comparini, as at ll. 153–4.
   153–4 *'T is ... so*: the Comparini twist Matt. 19: 5; the biblical text does not
mention 'a child'.

Always befell when, as the day came round,
A certain yearly sum,—our Pietro being,
As the long name runs, an usufructuary,—
Dropped in the common bag as interest   160
Of money, his till death, not afterward,
Failing an heir: an heir would take and take,
A child of theirs be wealthy in their place
To nobody's hurt—the stranger else seized all.
Prosperity rolled river-like and stopped,   165
Making their mill go; but when wheel wore out,
The wave would find a space and sweep on free
And, half-a-mile off, grind some neighbour's corn.

Adam-like, Pietro sighed and said no more:
Eve saw the apple was fair and good to taste,   170
So, plucked it, having asked the snake advice.
She told her husband God was merciful,
And his and her prayer granted at the last:
Let the old mill-stone moulder,—wheel unworn,
Quartz from the quarry, shot into the stream   175
Adroitly, as before should go bring grist—
Their house continued to them by an heir,
Their vacant heart replenished with a child.
We have her own confession at full length
Made in the first remorse: 't was Jubilee   180
Pealed in the ear o' the conscience and it woke.
She found she had offended God no doubt,

---

159 *MS* runs an Usufructuary,—   161 *MS* monies>money   *MS* afterward—   163 *MS* happy   164 *MS* {beginning of fo. 117}   166 *MS*
go,   168 *MS* bring some neighbour grist.>grind some neighbour's corn.
169 *MS* {no new paragraph}   171 *MS* And plucked   *Yale 1* So plucked>So,
plucked   173 *MS* His>And his   *MS* was granted>granted   176 *MS*
Adroitly should go bring grist as before—   *1868 1872* Adroitly, should go bring grist
as before—   181 *MS* of

---

159 *usufructuary*: someone who gains the benefit of a usufruct: cf. ll. 211 n.
168 *grind . . . corn*: note *MS*. Here, and at ll. 174–6, the imagery derives from the
proverb 'To bring grist to one's mill', i.e. to bring business into one's hands, to be a
source of profit or advantage: ODEP, 339. 'Grist'= corn for grinding.

So much was plain from what had happened since,
Misfortune on misfortune; but she harmed
No one i' the world, so far as she could see.   185
The act had gladdened Pietro to the height,
Her spouse whom God himself must gladden so
Or not at all: thus much seems probable
From the implicit faith, or rather say
Stupid credulity of the foolish man   190
Who swallowed such a tale nor strained a whit
Even at his wife's far-over-fifty years
Matching his sixty-and-under. Him she blessed;
And as for doing any detriment
To the veritable heir,—why, tell her first   195
Who was he? Which of all the hands held up
I' the crowd, one day would gather round their gate,
Did she so wrong by intercepting thus
The ducat, spendthrift fortune thought to fling
For a scramble just to make the mob break shins? ·   200
She kept it, saved them kicks and cuffs thereby.
While at the least one good work had she wrought,
Good, clearly and incontestably! Her cheat—
What was it to its subject, the child's self,
But charity and religion? See the girl!   205
A body most like—a soul too probably—
Doomed to death, such a double death as waits
The illicit offspring of a common trull,
Sure to resent and forthwith rid herself

185 *MS* man in   187 *MS* husband God   *1868* husband—God   188 *MS*
1868 all—(thus   190 *MS* soul   191 *MS* {beginning of fo. 118}   *MS*
cheat nor choked at all>tale nor choked a whit   193 *MS* own: such fools we
make ourselves)   *1868* sixty-and-under.)   *1868* blessed,   197 *MS* In   *MS*
1868 would one day   200 *MS* shins: 201 *MS* and saved   203 *MS*
Good,>Oh,   *MS* her   205 *MS* girl   206 *MS* probably   208 *MS*
{no comma}

191 *swallowed . . . whit*: cf. Matt. 23: 24: 'Ye blind guides, which strain at a gnat, and
swallow a camel.'
207 *double death*: of body and of soul; i.e. the prostitute would throw the baby in the
Tiber without baptizing it.
208 *trull*: prostitute.

Of a mere interruption to sin's trade,   210
In the efficacious way old Tiber knows.
Was not so much proved by the ready sale
O' the child, glad transfer of this irksome chance?
Well then, she had caught up this castaway:
This fragile egg, some careless wild bird dropped,   215
She had picked from where it waited the foot-fall,
And put in her own breast till forth broke finch
Able to sing God praise on mornings now.
What so excessive harm was done?—she asked.

To which demand the dreadful answer comes—   220
For that same deed, now at Lorenzo's church,
Both agents, conscious and inconscious, lie;
While she, the deed was done to benefit,
Lies also, the most lamentable of things,
Yonder where curious people count her breaths,   225
Calculate how long yet the little life
Unspilt may serve their turn nor spoil the show,
Give them their story, then the church its group.

Well, having gained Pompilia, the girl grew
I' the midst of Pietro here, Violante there,   230
Each, like a semicircle with stretched arms,
Joining the other round her preciousness—
Two walls that go about a garden-plot
Where a chance sliver, branchlet slipt from bole

---

210 *MS* such an   *MS* her   *MS* {no comma}   213 *MS* Of   *MS* the
transfer   214 *MS* [ ]>Well   215 *MS* {no commas}   217 *MS* this
bird   218 *MS* {beginning of fo. 119}   219 *MS* done, she   220 *MS* {no
new paragraph}   221 *MS* lie>now,   225 *MS* {no comma}   227 *MS*
show.   228 {not found in *MS*}   229 *MS* there she grew   230 *MS*
In   231 *MS* {no commas}   233 *MS* Walls>Two walls   *MS* went
234 *MS* branch   *MS* the bole

211 *the efficacious way*: i.e. by drowning.
222 *inconscious*: unaware; Pietro did not know about the buying of the baby.
227 *the show*: the spectacle of the bodies in San Lorenzo church.

Of some tongue-leaved eye-figured Eden tree,   235
Filched by two exiles and borne far away,
Patiently glorifies their solitude,—
Year by year mounting, grade by grade surmounts
The builded brick-work, yet is compassed still,
Still hidden happily and shielded safe,—   240
Else why should miracle have graced the ground?
But on the twelfth sun that brought April there
What meant that laugh? The coping-stone was reached;
Nay, above towered a light tuft of bloom
To be toyed with by butterfly or bee,   245
Done good to or else harm to from outside:
Pompilia's root, stalk and a branch or two
Home enclosed still, the rest would be the world's.
All which was taught our couple though obtuse,
Since walls have ears, when one day brought a priest,   250
Smooth-mannered soft-speeched sleek-cheeked visitor,
The notable Abate Paolo—known
As younger brother of a Tuscan house

---

235 *MS* eye-blossomed   236 *MS* an exile>two exiles   237 *MS* solitude,
*238 *MS 1868 1872* surmounts   *1888 1889* surmount   239 *MS* brickwork yet
241 *MS* For   *Yale 2* ground>ground?   243 *MS* was   *MS* copingstone *MS*
reached   244 *MS 1868 1872* a light tuft of bloom towered above   *Yale 2*
bloom>blossom   245 *MS* {beginning of fo. 120}   247 *MS 1868 1872*
stem   249 *MS* {no comma}   250 *MS* ears when   251 *MS* Smooth-
mannered, soft-speeched,

---

235 *some . . . Eden tree*: an unusual image. Cook conjectures the influence of an
allegorical Renaissance woodcut. There is perhaps the suggestion of a slight pun:
'tongue-leaved' and *oculus* (L.) = an eye, i.e. a leaf-bud, were botanical terms.

236 *two exiles*: Adam and Eve: like them, Pietro and Violante find themselves
guardians of a piece of paradise—in the Comparinis' case, Pompilia. The allusion
here is to the medieval legend of the Tree of Life. When Eve picked the apple in Eden
from the Tree of Knowledge, the fruit came away with a small piece of branch
attached. She unconsciously kept this in her hand, and, after she and Adam had been
expelled from Eden, she planted it in the ground. It rooted and grew into a tree, the
Tree of Life, which eventually supplied the wood for Christ's cross. The most obvious
source for Browning's knowledge of the legend is Malory's 'The Quest of the Holy
Grail': see *The Works of Sir Thomas Malory*, ed. Eugène Vinaver, revised P. J. C. Field (3
vols., 1990), ii. 990–4.

252 *notable*: worthy of note, eminent.

Whereof the actual representative,
Count Guido, had employed his youth and age   255
In culture of Rome's most productive plant—
A cardinal: but years pass and change comes,
In token of which, here was our Paolo brought
To broach a weighty business. Might he speak?
Yes—to Violante somehow caught alone   260
While Pietro took his after-dinner doze,
And the young maiden, busily as befits,
Minded her broider-frame three chambers off.

So—giving now his great flap-hat a gloss
With flat o' the hand between-whiles, soothing now   265
The silk from out its creases o'er the calf,
Setting the stocking clerical again,
But never disengaging, once engaged,
The thin clear grey hold of his eyes on her—
He dissertated on that Tuscan house,   270
Those Franceschini,—very old they were—
Not rich however—oh, not rich, at least,
As people look to be who, low i' the scale
One way, have reason, rising all they can
By favour of the money-bag! 't is fair—   275
Do all gifts go together? But don't suppose
That being not so rich means all so poor!
Say rather, well enough—i' the way, indeed,

254 *MS* {no comma}   *Yale 1* representative>representative,   255 *MS* {no comma}   *Yale 1* Guido had>Guido, had   *MS* till now   256 *MS* plant 257 *MS* Cardinal: 261 *MS* {no comma}   262 *MS* befits   264 *MS* {no new paragraph}   *MS* black hat   265 *MS* of the hand,   271 *MS* The   272 *MS* {beginning of fo. 121}   273 *MS* in   *MS* scale,>scale 275 *MS 1868* money-bag: 276 *1868 1872* do n't   277 *MS* poor— 278 *MS* in

264 *flap-hat*: i.e. one having a flapping brim; Paolo wears something like a cardinal's hat.

273–5 *As . . . money-bag*: an image of a weighing-scale: people 'low in the scale one way' (i.e. with no aristocratic blood) need lots of money to help them rise in prestige. Paolo implies that the Franceschini are so aristocratic they do not need this kind of wealth.

Ha, ha, to fortune better than the best:
Since if his brother's patron-friend kept faith,   280
Put into promised play the Cardinalate,
Their house might wear the red cloth that keeps warm,
Would but the Count have patience—there's the point!
For he was slipping into years apace,
And years make men restless—they needs must spy   285
Some certainty, some sort of end assured,
Some sparkle, tho' from topmost beacon-tip,
That warrants life a harbour through the haze.
In short, call him fantastic as you choose,
Guido was home-sick, yearned for the old sights   290
And usual faces,—fain would settle himself
And have the patron's bounty when it fell
Irrigate far rather than deluge near,
Go fertilize Arezzo, not flood Rome.
Sooth to say, 't was the wiser wish: the Count   295
Proved wanting in ambition,—let us avouch,
Since truth is best,—in callousness of heart,
And winced at pin-pricks whereby honours hang
A ribbon o'er each puncture: his—no soul
Ecclesiastic (here the hat was brushed)   300
Humble but self-sustaining, calm and cold,
Having, as one who puts his hand to the plough,

---

279 *MS 1868* better fortune   *MS 1868* best,   280 *MS* {no comma}   282 *MS*
House   *MS* get   *MS* warm[ ]>warm,   283 *MS* point.   285 *MS 1868*
1872 see   287 *MS* Sparkle tho' only from the beacon-top   *1868* Sparkle, tho'
from the topmost beacon-tip   290 *MS* homesick,   292 *MS* patrons'
293 *MS* here,   296 *MS* Was   298 *MS* Winced at those pinpricks   *1868*
Winced at those pin-pricks   *MS* hang,   299 *MS* {beginning of fo. 122}

282 *red cloth*: clothing of a cardinal. Guido has toadied to his 'patron-friend', his
cardinal, in the hope that Paolo too will be made a cardinal. If he attains the
cardinalate, Paolo will use his influence to ensure the comfort of his family.
302-3 *puts . . . family-feel*: cf. Luke 9: 61-2: 'And another also said, Lord, I will
follow thee; but let me first go bid them farewell, which are at home at my house.
And Jesus said unto him, No man, having put his hand to the plough, and looking
back, is fit for the kingdom of God.' Paolo characterizes himself as a true priest, a
disciple of Christ—single, chaste, and separated from family—and Guido as weakly
attracted to the satisfactions of home and marriage.

Renounced the over-vivid family-feel—
Poor brother Guido! All too plain, he pined
Amid Rome's pomp and glare for dinginess   305
And that dilapidated palace-shell
Vast as a quarry and, very like, as bare—
Since to this comes old grandeur now-a-days—
Or that absurd wild villa in the waste
O' the hill side, breezy though, for who likes air,   310
Vittiano, nor unpleasant with its vines,
Outside the city and the summer heats.
And now his harping on this one tense chord
The villa and the palace, palace this
And villa the other, all day and all night   315
Creaked like the implacable cicala's cry
And made one's ear-drum ache: nought else would serve
But that, to light his mother's visage up
With second youth, hope, gaiety again,
He must find straightway, woo and haply win   320
And bear away triumphant back, some wife.
Well now, the man was rational in his way:
He, the Abate,—ought he to interpose?
Unless by straining still his tutelage
(Priesthood leaps over elder-brothership)   325
Across this difficulty: then let go,
Leave the poor fellow in peace! Would that be wrong?
There was no making Guido great, it seems,

---

304 *MS* Guido!—all   305 *MS* the pomp   306 *MS* delapidated   307 *MS*
bare   308 *MS* nowadays—   309 *MS* Villa   310 *MS* On   *MS*
though for   312 *MS* Out   314 *MS* Villa   *MS* Palace, Palace   315 *MS*
Villa   316 *MS* Raked   ★317 *MS* ear drum raw: *1868 1872* ear-drum
1888 ear drum   *DC Br U* ear drum>ear-drum   *1889* ear-drum   320 *MS*
[ ]>He   321 *MS* {no comma}   322 *MS 1868* way—   326 *MS*
{beginning of fo. 123}   *MS* Over   *MS* difficulty,   *MS* go   327 *MS*
peace.

311 *Vittiano*: see II. 816 n.
316 *cicala*: (It.) = cicada.
324 *Unless by*: only to the extent of.

Spite of himself: then happy be his dole!
Indeed, the Abate's little interest   330
Was somewhat nearly touched i' the case, they saw:
Since if his simple kinsman so were bent,
Began his rounds in Rome to catch a wife,
Full soon would such unworldliness surprise
The rare bird, sprinkle salt on phœnix' tail,   335
And so secure the nest a sparrow-hawk.
No lack of mothers here in Rome,—no dread
Of daughters lured as larks by looking-glass!
The first name-pecking credit-scratching fowl
Would drop her unfledged cuckoo in our nest   340
To gather greyness there, give voice at length
And shame the brood... but it was long ago
When crusades were, and we sent eagles forth!
No, that at least the Abate could forestall.
He read the thought within his brother's word,   345
Knew what he purposed better than himself.
We want no name and fame—having our own:

---

330 *MS* {no comma}   331 *MS* in   *MS* you see: 332 *MS* was   334 *MS*
his unworldliness surprize   336 *MS* [?him]>his House a sparrow hawk.   337
Yale 2 dread>lack   338 *MS* looking glass.   339 *MS* honor-scratching
342 *MS* brood..but that was long ago..   *1868 1872* brood..   343 *MS* {no
comma}   *MS* they>it   *MS* forth.   344 *MS* would   346 *MS* it
purposed

329 *happy be his dole*: proverbial, i.e. may happiness be his portion: ODEP, 352. Cf.
Taming of the Shrew, i. i. 139–40.

335 *sprinkle...tail*: proverbial: 'to cast salt on a bird's tail'. ODEP explains that this
is in allusion 'to the jocular advice given to children to catch birds by putting salt on
their tails': 697. Guido is characterized as a naïf, who will think he has cleverly and
quickly caught himself a rare wife (a phoenix), when really he has been pounced on by
someone vulgar and opportunistic (a sparrow-hawk).

338 *as larks by looking-glass*: this is probably recalled from William Wetmore Story's
Roba di Roma (1863), which Browning helped to edit: see *Story*, ii. 143. One way in
which the Romans hunted was to place an owl on a pole and a mirror beneath: 'the
owl fluttering on the pole, and the glitter of the mirror, attract scores of larks, for these
are very curious birds.... From his hiding-place the sportsman shoots one after
another of them without scaring the rest, for their curiosity entirely overcomes their
fear': *Roba di Roma*, ii. 78.

339 *name-pecking credit-scratching fowl*: Paolo's characterization of the Roman mother,
as eager to pick up an aristocratic name and money as a hen to peck up food.

No worldly aggrandizement—such we fly:
But if some wonder of a woman's-heart
Were yet untainted on this grimy earth,   350
Tender and true—tradition tells of such—
Prepared to pant in time and tune with ours—
If some good girl (a girl, since she must take
The new bent, live new life, adopt new modes)
Not wealthy (Guido for his rank was poor)   355
But with whatever dowry came to hand,—
There were the lady-love predestinate!
And somehow the Abate's guardian eye—
Scintillant, rutilant, fraternal fire,—
Roving round every way had seized the prize   360
—The instinct of us, we, the spiritualty!
Come, cards on table; was it true or false
That here—here in this very tenement—
Yea, Via Vittoria did a marvel hide,
Lily of a maiden, white with intact leaf   365
Guessed thro' the sheath that saved it from the sun?
A daughter with the mother's hands still clasped
Over her head for fillet virginal,
A wife worth Guido's house and hand and heart?
He came to see; had spoken, he could no less—   370
(A final cherish of the stockinged calf)

349 *MS* woman's heart   350 *MS* earth of ours,>grimy earth,   353 *MS*
{beginning of fo. 124}   354 *MS* lead>live   *MS* laws)   355 *MS* *1868*
wealthy—Guido   *MS* *1868* poor—   356 *MS* *1868* hand,   357 *MS* the
the lady-love   358 *MS* guardian-eye—   361 *MS* we the   364 *MS*
hide   366 *MS* sheathe   *MS* sun: 369 *MS* for Guido's   371 {not
found in *MS*}

351 *tradition tells of such*: probably an allusion to Griselda, the model wife: see II.
1487 n.

358–60 *guardian . . . prize*: the image is of Paolo as a dragon, protecting Guido and
seizing the 'prize' of the maiden Pompilia. His eye is like a dragon's, gleaming
('scintillant') and shining red ('rutilant').

361 *spiritualty*: clergy.

365 *intact leaf*: also suggests 'virgo intacta'.

368 *fillet virginal*: thin band tying back the loose hair of a young girl. Such loose hair,
not 'put up', signified virginity and innocence.

371 *cherish*: caress.

If harm were,—well, the matter was off his mind.

Then with the great air did he kiss, devout,
Violante's hand, and rise up his whole height
(A certain purple gleam about the black)   375
And go forth grandly,—as if the Pope came next.
And so Violante rubbed her eyes awhile,
Got up too, walked to wake her Pietro soon
And pour into his ear the mighty news
How somebody had somehow somewhere seen   380
Their tree-top-tuft of bloom above the wall,
And came now to apprize them the tree's self
Was no such crab-sort as should go feed swine,
But veritable gold, the Hesperian ball
Ordained for Hercules to haste and pluck,   385
And bear and give the Gods to banquet with—
Hercules standing ready at the door.
Whereon did Pietro rub his eyes in turn,
Look very wise, a little woeful too,
Then, periwig on head, and cane in hand,   390
Sally forth dignifiedly into the Square

---

372 MS was,—   373 MS {no new paragraph}   374 MS did>and   376 MS
as the   377 MS And Violante   378 MS Pietro up   381 MS {begin-
ning of fo. 125}   MS tree-top tuft   MS {no comma}   382 MS 1868 1872
apprise   383 MS drop its fruit,   1868 feed the swine,   389 MS Look
wise>Look very wise   390 MS head and   391 MS square,

375 purple . . . black: this wryly comic line is typical of Other Half-Rome: though
Paolo wears the black of an abate, his manner is so grand he seems to have a halo of
purple, as though he thinks he will soon be made a cardinal: cf. II. 414 n. Paolo walks
out of the room as if he were next going to visit the Pope (376).

383 no such crab-sort: not a crab-apple tree (a tree with sour apples).

384 Hesperian ball: gold apple of the Hesperides. The Greek hero Hercules, in his
tenth labour, had to pluck it from the tree in the Garden of the Hesperides, having first
killed the guardian dragon. The allusion suggests Violante's sudden sense of Pompilia's
value in the marriage-market, and her naïve view of Guido (Hercules).

391-3 Square . . . Boat-fountain: Pietro walks just round the corner. As Other Half-
Rome imagines it, he walks to the end of Via Vittoria, into Via del Babuino (a main
road), crosses this in 'six steps', and is soon in Piazza di Spagna ('Spanish Square'). His

Of Spain across Babbuino the six steps,
Toward the Boat-fountain where our idlers lounge,—
Ask, for form's sake, who Hercules might be,
And have congratulation from the world.   395

Heartily laughed the world in his fool's-face
And told him Hercules was just the heir
To the stubble once a corn-field, and brick-heap
Where used to be a dwelling-place now burned.
Guido and Franceschini; a Count,—ay: 400
But a cross i' the poke to bless the Countship? No!
All gone except sloth, pride, rapacity,
Humours of the imposthume incident
To rich blood that runs thin,—nursed to a head
By the rankly-salted soil—a cardinal's court   405
Where, parasite and picker-up of crumbs,
He had hung on long, and now, let go, said some,
Shaken off, said others,—but in any case

392–3 {not found in MS}   396 *MS* And heartily   398 *MS* cornfield,
MS brick heap   399 *MS* be dwellingplace   400 *MS* aye: 401 *MS*
in   *MS* Count?>Countship?   402 *MS* rapacity—   405 *MS* Cardinal's
406 *MS* picker up of crumbs   408 *MS 1868 1872* But shaken off, said
others,—in any case

---

friends are near the fountain called 'La Barcaccia' (old, useless boat) by Pietro or Gian
Lorenzo Bernini, a low-lying fountain in the shape of a stone boat which lies half-
submerged in a shallow pool.

401 *cross i' the poke*: money in the pocket. 'Cross' = coin, from the silver coin with a
cross marked on one side. Cf. *As You Like It*, II. iv. 12–14.

403 *Humours*: mental dispositions, characteristics. In ancient and medieval physiol-
ogy humours were originally the four chief fluids of the body which determined a
person's physical and mental disposition.
imposthume: abscess, boil. Far removed from his noble ancestor, Guido no longer
has any true aristocratic qualities; he is a diseased idea of aristocracy—a boil made up of
laziness, pride, and greed.

404 *head*: fully developed top (of the boil).

405 *rankly-salted*: over-salted, corrupt. The bad 'soil' of the cardinal's court helps to
grow a deformed crop: the boil that is Guido. 'Head' (preceding line) and 'rankly' also
play on the idea of Guido as head (= leading representative) of his family, and man of
rank.

406 *picker-up of crumbs*: cf. Luke 16: 21; the allusion then develops into the picture of
Guido as a scavenging mouse. 'Parasite' similarly develops into the image of Guido as a
blood-sucking insect, hanging on as long as he can.

Tired of the trade and something worse for wear,
Was wanting to change town for country quick,   410
Go home again: let Pietro help him home!
The brother, Abate Paolo, shrewder mouse,
Had pricked for comfortable quarters, inched
Into the core of Rome, and fattened so;
But Guido, over-burly for rat's hole   415
Suited to clerical slimness, starved outside,
Must shift for himself: and so the shift was this!
What, was the snug retreat of Pietro tracked,
The little provision for his old age snuffed?
"Oh, make your girl a lady, an you list,   420
"But have more mercy on our wit than vaunt
"Your bargain as we burgesses who brag!
"Why, Goodman Dullard, if a friend must speak,
"Would the Count, think you, stoop to you and yours
"Were there the value of one penny-piece   425
"To rattle 'twixt his palms—or likelier laugh,
"Bid your Pompilia help you black his shoe?"

[—]

---

409 *MS* {beginning of fo. 126}   *MS* trade,   *MS* wear   410 *MS* now,
411 *MS* there!   412 *MS* mouse   413 *MS* cared   415 *MS* over burly
for the   417 *MS* H>Must   419 *MS* store of pursed-up ducats> provision
for his old age   420–7 *MS* {no quotation marks at beginnings of lines}
420 *MS* if   422 *MS* count gain.   425 *MS* pennypiece 426 *MS* palms
and let him   427 *MS* {no quotation mark at end of line}

---

410 *town for country*: from here to l. 417 the imagery is partly from Aesop's fable of
the town mouse and the country mouse. Paolo is the town mouse who has found
himself a snug home in the Church; Guido is the dissatisfied country mouse heading
back into the country. Browning's mother read Croxall's version of Aesop to him as a
child; there are many references in the poems: Orr, 26–7.

413 *pricked for*: chosen: OED² *prick* v. 4.b., which also cites the nautical phrase 'to
prick for a soft plank': to select a place on the deck for sleeping on.

413–14 *inched . . . so*: perhaps alluding to the proverb 'As snug as a mouse in a
cheese': ODEP, 691.

420 *an you list*: if you like.

423 *Goodman Dullard*: Mr Stupid. 'Goodman' was a formal prefix to the name of a
yeoman, or more generally anyone below the rank of gentleman; here its use is ironic.
Cf. 'Dictynna, goodman Dull, Dictynna, goodman Dull': *Love's Labour's Lost*, IV. ii. 36.

Home again, shaking oft the puzzled pate,
Went Pietro to announce a change indeed,
Yet point Violante where some solace lay   430
Of a rueful sort,—the taper, quenched so soon,
Had ended merely in a snuff, not stink—
Congratulate there was one hope the less
Not misery the more: and so an end.

The marriage thus impossible, the rest   435
Followed: our spokesman, Paolo, heard his fate,
Resignedly Count Guido bore the blow:
Violante wiped away the transient tear,
Renounced the playing Danae to gold dreams,
Praised much her Pietro's prompt sagaciousness,   440
Found neighbours' envy natural, lightly laughed
At gossips' malice, fairly wrapped herself
In her integrity three folds about,
And, letting pass a little day or two,
Threw, even over that integrity,   445
Another wrappage, namely one thick veil
That hid her, matron-wise, from head to foot,
And, by the hand holding a girl veiled too,
Stood, one dim end of a December day,
In Saint Lorenzo on the altar-step—   450
Just where she lies now and that girl will lie—
Only with fifty candles' company
Now, in the place of the poor winking one

428 *MS* pate   429 *MS* {no comma}   432 *MS* {no comma}   435 *MS*
{beginning of fo. 127}   436 *MS* spokesman Paolo heard   439 *MS*
Confessed   *MS* herself a>the playing   444 *MS* two   445 *MS* integrity
Yale 1 integrity>integrity,   447 *MS* matronwise,   453 *MS* Now—in
place   *Yale 1* ^the^   *1868* Now—in

439 *playing Danae to gold dreams*: i.e. seeking their fortune. In Greek legend, Danaë
was shut up in a brass tower by her father Acrisius, because an oracle had warned that
she would bear a son who would kill him. Zeus visited her in the form of a shower of
gold and impregnated her, and she bore him a son, Perseus. In paintings, Danaë
sometimes seems eager to embrace the shower.
    442-3 *fairly…about*: cf. 'I put on righteousness, and it clothed me': Job 29: 14.

Which saw,—doors shut and sacristan made sure,—
A priest—perhaps Abate Paolo—wed   455
Guido clandestinely, irrevocably
To his Pompilia aged thirteen years
And five months,—witness the church register,—
Pompilia, (thus become Count Guido's wife
Clandestinely, irrevocably his,)   460
Who all the while had borne, from first to last,
As brisk a part i' the bargain, as yon lamb,
Brought forth from basket and set out for sale,
Bears while they chaffer, wary market-man
And voluble housewife, o'er it,—each in turn   465
Patting the curly calm inconscious head,
With the shambles ready round the corner there,
When the talk's talked out and a bargain struck.

Transfer complete, why, Pietro was apprised.
Violante sobbed the sobs and prayed the prayers   470
And said the serpent tempted so she fell,
Till Pietro had to clear his brow apace
And make the best of matters: wrath at first,—
How else? pacification presently,

---

456 *MS* irrevocably,   459 *MS* Pompilia, thus   460 *MS* his,   462 *MS*
{beginning of fo. 128}   *MS* in   *MS* {no commas}   463 *MS* [ ]>basket
MS sale   464 *MS* marketman   467 *MS* {no comma}   *469 *MS*
1868 1872 {new paragraph. Paragraphing obscured in *1888* and *1889* by this
line's being at the head of the page}   *MS* apprised: 471 *MS* {no comma}
473 *MS* wroth   474 *MS* but rightly pacified presently   *MS* anon>
presently

454 *sacristan*: priest in charge of vestments, chalices, etc., and generally the practical
affairs of a particular church.
462 *brisk*: active, lively.
yon lamb: Other Half-Rome points to a lamb in the market-place of Piazza Barberini, reminding us that he and his listener stand watching the 'motley merchandizing
multitude': I. 903. His image of Pompilia as an innocent lamb to the slaughter is a
bathetic climax to the sentimentality of this passage.
467 *shambles*: slaughter-house, place where animals are killed for meat.
471 *said the serpent tempted*: Violante paints herself as a foolish Eve: Gen. 3: 13.

Why not?—could flesh withstand the impurpled one,   475
The very Cardinal, Paolo's patron-friend?
Who, justifiably surnamed "a hinge,"
Knew where the mollifying oil should drop
To cure the creak o' the valve,—considerate
For frailty, patient in a naughty world.   480
He even volunteered to supervise
The rough draught of those marriage-articles
Signed in a hurry by Pietro, since revoked:
Trust's politic, suspicion does the harm,
There is but one way to brow-beat this world,   485
Dumb-founder doubt, and repay scorn in kind,—
To go on trusting, namely, till faith move
Mountains.

          And faith here made the mountains move.
Why, friends whose zeal cried "Caution ere too late!"—   490
Bade "Pause ere jump, with both feet joined, on slough!"—
Counselled "If rashness then, now temperance!"—
Heard for their pains that Pietro had closed eyes,
Jumped and was in the middle of the mire,
Money and all, just what should sink a man.   495
By the mere marriage, Guido gained forthwith
Dowry, his wife's right; no rescinding there:

---

475 *MS* Impurpled One,   476 *MS* patron-friend,   477 *MS* declared "a
hinge"   479 *MS* of   480 *1868* world,   482 *MS* first>rough   *MS*
marriage articles   484 *MS* politic: *MS* harm.   485 *MS* browbeat
486 *MS* Dumbfounder   *MS* kind,   487 *MS* moves>move   488 *MS*
{beginning of fo. 129}   *MS* {no new paragraph}   *MS* What   *MS* move?
490 *MS* late!"   491 *MS* Bade pause   *MS* slough   492 *MS* now temperance
>more temperance now"—   493 *MS* {no comma}   495 *MS* Casket
496 *MS* {no comma}   *Yale 1* marriage Guido>marriage, Guido   497 *MS* right,

---

475 *impurpled one*: i.e. the cardinal. A spelling of 'empurpled', i.e. robed in purple;
again suggested by It. *porporato* = adj. clothed in purple, n. cardinalate, cardinal. Cf. 11.
414 n.

477 *"a hinge"*: the title 'Cardinal' is derived from *cardo* (L.), a hinge.

479 *valve*: one of the halves or leaves of a double or folding door, from *valva* (L.).
Pietro and Violante are the two halves of this folding door, but Pietro is creaking and
requires the Cardinal's 'oil'.

487–8 *till faith move / Mountains*: proverbial, from Matt. 17: 20.

But Pietro, why must he needs ratify
One gift Violante gave, pay down one doit
Promised in first fool's-flurry? Grasp the bag   500
Lest the son's service flag,—is reason and rhyme,
Above all when the son's a son-in-law.
Words to the wind! The parents cast their lot
Into the lap o' the daughter: and the son
Now with a right to lie there, took what fell,   505
Pietro's whole having and holding, house and field,
Goods, chattels and effects, his worldly worth
Present and in perspective, all renounced
In favour of Guido. As for the usufruct—
The interest now, the principal anon,   510
Would Guido please to wait, at Pietro's death:
Till when, he must support the couple's charge,
Bear with them, housemates, pensionaries, pawned
To an alien for fulfilment of their pact.
Guido should at discretion deal them orts,   515
Bread-bounty in Arezzo the strange place,—
They who had lived deliciously and rolled
Rome's choicest comfit 'neath the tongue before.
Into this quag, "jump" bade the Cardinal!

---

500 *MS* Bear the bag>Grasp the purse   501 *MS* And keep the son kind, quoth
the rhyming saw   *MS* child>son   502 *MS* child's>son's   *MS* son-in-
law."   503 *MS* Sir, he gave all: the   504 *MS* of   *MS* daughter—
Yale 2 son>son,   505 *MS* take what fell.   509 *MS* Guido,—as   *MS*
usufruct   511 *MS* death   512 *MS* Couple's   *MS* {no commas}
514 *MS* pact,   515 *MS* One who should,   *MS* bread   516 *MS* {begin-
ning of fo. 130}   *MS* Of bounty   *MS* pla[ ]>place,   517 *MS* deliciously,
519 *MS* Cardinal:

---

499 *doit*: tiny sum of money (from an old Dutch coin of very little value).

500–1 *Grasp . . . flag*: the *MS* reading 'Bear the bag / And keep the child kind' shows
more clearly the origin in *King Lear*, II. iv. 48–51. 'Bag' = money-bag. Likewise the
MS reading in l. 503 recalls Lear's 'I gave you all'.

513 *pensionaries*: i.e. living on Guido's charity to them.

514 *alien*: stranger.

515 *orts*: left-overs, bits of food.

518 *comfit*: sweet (a preserved fruit, sugar-almond, etc.).

519 *quag*: marsh or bog, especially one covered with a layer of turf that collapses
when walked on.

And neck-deep in a minute there flounced they. 520

But they touched bottom at Arezzo: there—
Four months' experience of how craft and greed
Quickened by penury and pretentious hate
Of plain truth, brutify and bestialize,—
Four months' taste of apportioned insolence, 525
Cruelty graduated, dose by dose
Of ruffianism dealt out at bed and board,
And lo, the work was done, success clapped hands.
The starved, stripped, beaten brace of stupid dupes
Broke at last in their desperation loose, 530
Fled away for their lives, and lucky so;
Found their account in casting coat afar
And bearing off a shred of skin at least:
Left Guido lord o' the prey, as the lion is,
And, careless what came after, carried their wrongs 535
To Rome,—I nothing doubt, with such remorse
As folly feels, since pain can make it wise,
But crime, past wisdom, which is innocence,
Needs not be plagued with till a later day.

Pietro went back to beg from door to door, 540
In hope that memory not quite extinct
Of cheery days and festive nights would move

---

520 *MS* stood   521 *MS* there   522 *MS* months   524 *MS* truth—
MS bestialize.   525 *MS* cruelty,   526 *MS* Insolence   528 *MS* hands;
529 *MS* ones   530 *MS* {no comma}   531 *MS* lives and   *MS* so,
533 *MS* So   534 *MS* of the prey as   537 *MS* feels because pain
makes   *MS* {no commas}   538 *MS* But wickedness, past growing innocent,   540 *MS* {no comma}   *Yale 1* door>door,   541 *MS* {begin-
ning of fo. 131}

529 *brace*: pair, couple (usually of dogs or game birds). The image is from shooting
or hunting.

536-9 *with . . . day*: the sense is: 'Criminals, in losing their innocence, have also lost
the capacity to gain wisdom, as fools can do through the suffering and remorse which
their folly brings them. Criminals need feel no remorse until Judgement Day': cf.
Cook, 60.

Friends and acquaintance—after the natural laugh,
And tributary "Just as we foretold—"
To show some bowels, give the dregs o' the cup,   545
Scraps of the trencher, to their host that was,
Or let him share the mat with the mastiff, he
Who lived large and kept open house so long.
Not so Violante: ever a-head i' the march,
Quick at the bye-road and the cut-across,   550
She went first to the best adviser, God—
Whose finger unmistakably was felt
In all this retribution of the past.
Here was the prize of sin, luck of a lie!
But here too was what Holy Year would help,   555
Bound to rid sinners of sin vulgar, sin
Abnormal, sin prodigious, up to sin
Impossible and supposed for Jubilee' sake:
To lift the leadenest of lies, let soar
The soul unhampered by a feather-weight.   560
"I will" said she "go burn out this bad hole
"That breeds the scorpion, baulk the plague at least
"Of hope to further plague by progeny:
"I will confess my fault, be punished, yes,
"But pardoned too: Saint Peter pays for all."   565

                         [—]

---

543 *MS* acquaintance,   *Yale 1* acquaintance,>acquaintance—   545 *MS*
Might>To   *MS* of the wine   549 *MS* in the race,   550 *MS* nigh
road   553 *MS* old crime.   555 *MS* the Holy Year in   *1868 1872* the
Holy   560 *MS* featherweight.   562–5 *MS* {no quotation marks at beginnings of lines}   563 *MS* Its hope of further creeping progeny: *1868 1872* "Its
hope of further creeping progeny: 565 *MS* Peter, prays for me."   *MS* pray>
prays

---

545 *bowels*: i.e. compassion. Cf. Col. 3: 12.
550 *cut-across*: short cut; not in OED².
555 *Holy Year*. Jubilee: see II. 537 n.
556 *vulgar*: common.
565 *Saint Peter pays for all*: i.e. the Church forgives me. The Catholic Church
(represented by St Peter, the first Pope), out of the treasury of mercies stored up by
holy lives, 'pays' the debt due to divine justice incurred by sinners. More especially, in
Jubilee, sins can be confessed without the usual penalties ('payment') due under canon
law. Cf. II. 537 n.

So, with the crowd she mixed, made for the dome,
Through the great door new-broken for the nonce
Marched, muffled more than ever matron-wise,
Up the left nave to the formidable throne,
Fell into file with this the poisoner   570
And that the parricide, and reached in turn
The poor repugnant Penitentiary
Set at this gully-hole o' the world's discharge
To help the frightfullest of filth have vent,
And then knelt down and whispered in his ear   575
How she had bought Pompilia, palmed the babe
On Pietro, passed the girl off as their child
To Guido, and defrauded of his due
This one and that one,—more than she could name,
Until her solid piece of wickedness   580

---

566 *MS* {no new paragraph}   *MS* So with   *Yale 1* So with>So, with   *MS*
church,   567 {not found in *MS*}   568 *MS* covered over once more
matronwise,   569 *MS* {beginning of fo. 132}   *MS* {no comma}   572 *MS*
penententiary   573 *MS* of   574 *MS* see the frightfulest of filth had   576 *MS*
"How   577 *MS* {? child.>child}   580 *MS* So had her single

567 *for the nonce*: for this occasion. Cardinal Wiseman describes the ceremony of the
breaking of the *Porta Sancta* (L. 'Holy Door'): 'The visitor of Rome may easily have
noticed, that, of the five great doors opening from the porch into St Peter's, the one
nearest to the palace is walled up, and has a gilt metal cross upon it. Only during the
year of Jubilee is this gate unclosed, as symbolical of the commencement of the
Jubilee.... After preliminary prayers from scripture singularly apt, the Pope goes
down from his throne, and, armed with a silver hammer, strikes the wall in the
door-way, which, having been cut round from its jambs and lintel, falls at once
inwards, and is cleared away in a moment by the active Sanpietrini. The Pope, then,
bare-headed and torch in hand, first enters the door, and is followed by the cardinals
and his other attendants to the high altar, where the first vespers of Christmas Day are
chaunted as usual': Wiseman, *Recollections of the Four Last Popes* (1859), 270–1. All
subsequent penitents of the Jubilee, like Violante, pass through the door to symbolize
their movement from sin to grace. The depiction of this incident is in keeping with
Other Half-Rome's vague religiosity.

572 *repugnant*: unwilling, resisting: cf. *Dramatis Personæ*, 'Epilogue', 65.
Penitentiary: chief confessor, for Jubilee usually a Cardinal. Here the Penitentiary is
overwhelmed by the press of unsavoury characters attracted into St Peter's by the
Jubilee.

573 *gully-hole*: sewer hole (from a street's waste channel into the sewer beneath).

Happened to split and spread woe far and wide:
Contritely now she brought the case for cure.

Replied the throne—"Ere God forgive the guilt,
"Make man some restitution! Do your part!
"The owners of your husband's heritage,   585
"Barred thence by this pretended birth and heir,—
"Tell them, the bar came so, is broken so,
"Theirs be the due reversion as before!
"Your husband who, no partner in the guilt,
"Suffers the penalty, led blindfold thus   590
"By love of what he thought his flesh and blood
"To alienate his all in her behalf,—
"Tell him too such contract is null and void!
"Last, he who personates your son-in-law,
"Who with sealed eyes and stopped ears, tame and mute,
"Took at your hand that bastard of a whore   596
"You called your daughter and he calls his wife,—
"Tell him, and bear the anger which is just!
"Then, penance so performed, may pardon be!"

Who could gainsay this just and right award?   600
Nobody in the world: but, out o' the world,
Who knows?—might timid intervention be
From any makeshift of an angel-guide,
Substitute for celestial guardianship,
Pretending to take care of the girl's self: 605

581 *MS* lies   582 *MS* cure."   583 *MS* priest—   *MS* sin,   584–
99 *MS* {no quotation marks at beginnings of lines}   584 *MS* Man some restitution. Do your part.   585 *MS* {no comma}   586 *MS* heir,   587 *MS*
was>is   *MS*   so: 588 *MS*   before.   590 *MS*   penalty,—   *MS*
thus,   592 *MS* behalf,   593 *MS* Tell him, declare his contract null and
void.   594 *MS* son-in-law   595 *MS* {beginning of fo. 133}   596 *MS*
the bastard   597 *MS* wife—   598 *MS* his anger   *MS* just.   599 *MS*
let   601 *MS* of   602 *MS* knows,

592 *alienate*: transfer ownership of.
595 *sealed eyes and stopped ears*: the image is of a hawk in training.

"Woman, confessing crime is healthy work,
"And telling truth relieves a liar like you,
"But how of my quite unconsidered charge?
"No thought if, while this good befalls yourself,
"Aught in the way of harm may find out her?"   610
No least thought, I assure you: truth being truth,
Tell it and shame the devil!
                          Said and done:
Home went Violante, disbosomed all:
And Pietro who, six months before, had borne   615
Word after word of such a piece of news
Like so much cold steel inched through his breast-blade,
Now at its entry gave a leap for joy,
As who—what did I say of one in a quag?—
Should catch a hand from heaven and spring thereby   620
Out of the mud, on ten toes stand once more.
"What? All that used to be, may be again?
"My money mine again, my house, my land,
"My chairs and tables, all mine evermore?
"What, the girl's dowry never was the girl's,   625
"And, unpaid yet, is never now to pay?
"Then the girl's self, my pale Pompilia child
"That used to be my own with her great eyes—
"He who drove us forth, why should he keep her
"When proved as very a pauper as himself?   630
"Will she come back, with nothing changed at all,
"And laugh 'But how you dreamed uneasily!
"'I saw the great drops stand here on your brow—

---

606 *MS* "Oh yes—   607–10 *MS* {no quotation marks at beginnings of lines}   608 *MS* But, what of this my unconsidered charge,   *1868 1872* "But what of her my   609 *MS 1868 1872* of,   610 *MS* What   *1868 1872* "What   614 *MS 1868 1872* Violante and disbosomed   617 *MS* breastbone, 618 *MS* clapped his hands   619 *MS* quag?   621 *MS* {beginning of fo. 134}   *MS* solidly stand   623–45 *MS* {no quotation marks at beginnings of lines}   625 *MS* Next,   627 *MS* Pompilia thing   629–30 *MS* {lines added later}   632 *MS* "But

---

612 *Tell . . . devil*: proverbial: 'Tell truth and shame the devil': ODEP, 807.
614 *disbosomed*: confessed; a coinage based on 'unbosomed' or 'disembosomed'.

" 'Did I do wrong to wake you with a kiss?'
"No, indeed, darling! No, for wide awake   635
"I see another outburst of surprise:
"The lout-lord, bully-beggar, braggart-sneak,
"Who not content with cutting purse, crops ear—
"Assuredly it shall be salve to mine
"When this great news red-letters him, the rogue!   640
"Ay, let him taste the teeth o' the trap, this fox,
"Give us our lamb back, golden fleece and all,
"Let her creep in and warm our breasts again!
"Why care for the past? We three are our old selves,
"And know now what the outside world is worth."   645
And so, he carried case before the courts;
And there Violante, blushing to the bone,
Made public declaration of her fault,
Renounced her motherhood, and prayed the law
To interpose, frustrate of its effect   650
Her folly, and redress the injury done.

[—]

634 *MS* kiss?"   636 *MS* splendor   637 *MS* mock-lord,   638 *MS*
cropt ears—>crops ear—   639 *MS* I see his worship at the whipping-post!>
Assuredly it shall be salve to mine   640 *MS* {line added when 639 was rewrit-
ten}   641 *MS* Aye,   *MS* of   *MS* fox: 643 *MS* again;   644 *MS*
What   *1868 1872* "What   *1868 1872* past?—we   *MS* selves;   645 *MS*
Who   *1868 1872* "Who   *MS* ^outside^ wintry world   646 *MS* {no
comma}   *Yale 1* so he>so, he   *MS* carried the case   *MS* Courts   647 *MS*
[ ] shame>blushing to the bone,   650 *MS* hinder,>interpose,   651 *MS*
{beginning of fo. 135}

637 *lout-lord . . . braggart-sneak*: a series of paradoxes: Guido is ill-mannered yet an
aristocrat, a bully yet a wheedling beggar, a boaster yet mean-spirited.
638 *cutting purse, crops ear*: Guido is a criminal who yet exploits the law: he steals
your purse and then sides with law and gets *your* ear cropped for the crime.
640 *red-letters him*: marks him, brands him (as a rogue): not the use in OED[2].
Browning is probably thinking of Hawthorne's *The Scarlet Letter* (1850), where Hester
Prynne has the red letter 'A' marked on the bosom of her dress, indicating she is an
adulteress. Guido will be clearly branded as a rogue because (so Pietro thinks) once
Pompilia brings no money, Guido will reject her, showing the baseness of his motives
in the marriage. Browning is said to have described Hawthorne as 'the finest genius
that had appeared in English literature for many years': E. P. Gould, *The Brownings and
America* (Boston, USA, 1904), 65.

Whereof was the disastrous consequence,
That though indisputably clear the case
(For thirteen years are not so large a lapse,
And still six witnesses survived in Rome   655
To prove the truth o' the tale)—yet, patent wrong
Seemed Guido's; the first cheat had chanced on him:
Here was the pity that, deciding right,
Those who began the wrong would gain the prize.
Guido pronounced the story one long lie   660
Lied to do robbery and take revenge:
Or say it were no lie at all but truth,
Then, it both robbed the right heirs and shamed him
Without revenge to humanize the deed:
What had he done when first they shamed him thus?
But that were too fantastic: losels they,   666
And leasing this world's-wonder of a lie,
They lied to blot him though it brand themselves.

So answered Guido through the Abate's mouth.
Wherefore the court, its customary way,   670
Inclined to the middle course the sage affect.
They held the child to be a changeling,—good:
But, lest the husband got no good thereby,
They willed the dowry, though not hers at all,
Should yet be his, if not by right then grace—   675

---

652 *MS* And this   656 *MS* of   657 *MS* Guido's,   *MS* him,   658 *MS*
right   659 *MS* gain thereby.   *1868 1872* good.   661 *MS* revenge
662 *MS* Or,   663 *MS* Why,   *Yale 1* Then it>Then, it   664 deed
669 *MS* {no new paragraph}   *MS* mouth,   670 *MS* And so the Court,
671 *MS 1868* affect—

658-9 *Here . . . prize*: i.e. if the court acknowledges that Pompilia should not have
the dowry (so 'deciding right'), then Violante and Pietro, who began the deceit, will
none the less win.

665 *What . . . thus?*: i.e. originally, Guido had done nothing to offend the Comparini. Why should they have wanted to shame him by marrying him to a bastard?

666 *losels*: scoundrels.

671 *middle . . . affect*: the middle course which wise people show an ostentatious
liking for.

Part-payment for the plain injustice done.
As for that other contract, Pietro's work,
Renunciation of his own estate,
That must be cancelled—give him back his gifts,
He was no party to the cheat at least!   680
So ran the judgment:—whence a prompt appeal
On both sides, seeing right is absolute.
Cried Pietro "Is the child no child of mine?
"Why give her a child's dowry?"—"Have I right
"To the dowry, why not to the rest as well?"   685
Cried Guido, or cried Paolo in his name:
Till law said "Reinvestigate the case!"
And so the matter pends, to this same day.

Hence new disaster—here no outlet seemed;
Whatever the fortune of the battle-field,   690
No path whereby the fatal man might march
Victorious, wreath on head and spoils in hand,
And back turned full upon the baffled foe,—
Nor cranny whence, desperate and disgraced,
Stripped to the skin, he might be fain to crawl   695
Worm-like, and so away with his defeat
To other fortune and a novel prey.
No, he was pinned to the place there, left alone
With his immense hate and, the solitary
Subject to satisfy that hate, his wife.   700

---

676 *MS* a plain   677 *MS* {beginning of fo. 136}   *MS 1868 1872* But
then,   678 {not found in *MS*}   679 *MS 1868 1872* goods,   680 *MS*
least.   681 *MS* Such was   *MS* sentence—>judgment:—   683 *MS*
Pompilia not my child?   *1868 1872* "Is Pompilia not my child?   684 *MS* {no
quotation mark at beginning of line}   *MS 1868 1872* my child's   685 *MS* {no
quotation mark at beginning of line}   687 *MS* {line added later}   *MS* So Law
MS case: 688 *MS* pends unto this   *1868 1872* unto this day.   689 *MS 1868
1872* that no   *MS* came,—>seemed,—   690 {not found in *MS*}   691 *Yale
1* Nor>No   692 *MS* Victoriously,   *MS* with all his gains confirmed>wreath
on head and spoils in hand,   693 *MS* Turning his back upon>And back turned
full upon   694 *MS* No   696 *MS* Wormlike,   697 *MS* the other
Yale 1 the other>other   *MS 1868 1872* the novel

---

691 *fatal*: deadly or destined.

"Cast her off? Turn her naked out of doors?
"Easily said! But still the action pends,
"Still dowry, principal and interest,
"Pietro's possessions, all I bargained for,—
"Any good day, be but my friends alert,   705
"May give them me if she continue mine.
"Yet, keep her? Keep the puppet of my foes—
"Her voice that lisps me back their curse—her eye
"They lend their leer of triumph to—her lip
"I touch and taste their very filth upon?"   710

In short, he also took the middle course
Rome taught him—did at last excogitate
How he might keep the good and leave the bad
Twined in revenge, yet extricable,—nay
Make the very hate's eruption, very rush   715
Of the unpent sluice of cruelty relieve
His heart first, then go fertilize his field.
What if the girl-wife, tortured with due care,
Should take, as though spontaneously, the road
It were impolitic to thrust her on?   720
If, goaded, she broke out in full revolt,
Followed her parents i' the face o' the world,
Branded as runaway not castaway,
Self-sentenced and self-punished in the act?
So should the loathed form and detested face   725
Launch themselves into hell and there be lost
While he looked o'er the brink with folded arms;

702–10 MS {no quotation marks at beginnings of lines}   702 MS said
when   MS {no comma}   703 MS When   704 MS {line added later}
MS for,   706 MS continues   707 MS {beginning of fo. 137}   MS darling
710 MS I only touch, to taste their filth upon?">I touch, and taste their very filth
upon?"   714 MS Blent>Twined   MS extricable [?so],>extricable,—nay
715 MS Nay, make>Make   MS eruption, rush   719 MS as if   721 MS
If goaded she broke out in open flight,   722 MS [ ]>her   MS in   MS
of   MS {no comma}   724 MS self punished   727 MS arms.

712 *excogitate*: think out.

So should the heaped-up shames go shuddering back
O' the head o' the heapers, Pietro and his wife,
And bury in the breakage three at once: 730
While Guido, left free, no one right renounced,
Gain present, gain prospective, all the gain,
None of the wife except her rights absorbed,
Should ask law what it was law paused about—
If law were dubious still whose word to take,   735
The husband's—dignified and derelict,
Or the wife's—the . . . what I tell you. It should be.

Guido's first step was to take pen, indite
A letter to the Abate,—not his own,
His wife's,—she should re-write, sign, seal and send.
She liberally told the household-news,   741
Rejoiced her vile progenitors were gone,
Revealed their malice—how they even laid
A last injunction on her, when they fled,
That she should forthwith find a paramour,   745
Complot with him to gather spoil enough,
Then burn the house down,—taking previous care
To poison all its inmates overnight,—
And so companioned, so provisioned too,
Follow to Rome and there join fortunes gay.   750
This letter, traced in pencil-characters,
Guido as easily got re-traced in ink

729 *MS* On   *MS* of   *MS* {no commas}   730 *MS* breaking   *MS* once,
731 *MS* [?coin]>no   *MS* renounced   732 *MS* gain   733 *MS* {begin-
ning of fo. 138}   *MS* but all her   734 *MS* ask Law what it was she   735 *MS*
she was   *Yale 1* she>law   *MS* which word   *MS* {no comma}   737 *MS*
The wife's..what I shall show you. It should be. *1868 1872* the..
what   740 *MS* wife's,   *MS* and seal>sign seal   741 *MS* household
news,   742 *1868 1872* fled,   743 *MS* malice who had   744 *MS* This
Yale 1 A last injunction, when they fled, on her>A last injunction on her, when they
fled,   745 *MS* {no comma}   746 *MS 1868 1872* {no comma}   750 *MS*
all join fortunes there.   *1868* all join   751 *MS* pencil-characters   752 *MS*
1868 1872 retraced

736 *derelict*: deserted.
746 *Complot*: plot together.

By his wife's pen, guided from end to end,
As if it had been just so much Chinese.
For why? That wife could broider, sing perhaps,   755
Pray certainly, but no more read than write
This letter "which yet write she must," he said,
"Being half courtesy and compliment,
"Half sisterliness: take the thing on trust!"
She had as readily re-traced the words   760
Of her own death-warrant,—in some sort 't was so.
This letter the Abate in due course
Communicated to such curious souls
In Rome as needs must pry into the cause
Of quarrel, why the Comparini fled   765
The Franceschini, whence the grievance grew,
What the hubbub meant: "Nay,—see the wife's own word,
"Authentic answer! Tell detractors too
"There's a plan formed, a programme figured here
"—Pray God no after-practice put to proof,   770
"This letter cast no light upon, one day!"

So much for what should work in Rome: back now
To Arezzo, follow up the project there,
Forward the next step with as bold a foot,
And plague Pompilia to the height, you see!   775
Accordingly did Guido set himself
To worry up and down, across, around,

753 *MS* wife, pen in hand, from end to end,   *Yale 1* pen guided,>pen, guided   754 *MS* As it had been just so much Latin, ⟨Greek⟩ Sir,   *1868 1872* As it had been just so much Hebrew, Sir: 757 *MS* {no quotation marks}   *MS 1868 1872* said   758 *MS* {no quotation mark at beginning of line}   *MS* kindness>courtesy   *MS* half compliment>compliment   759 *MS* {beginning of fo. 139}   *MS* {no quotation marks}   *MS* sisterliness—   760 *MS* as as   761 *MS* 'twas   767 *MS* scandal   768–70 *MS* {no quotation marks at beginnings of lines}   768 *MS* answer: 770 *MS* proof,— 771 *MS* {no quotation marks}   *MS* {no comma}   772 *MS 1868* Rome,—   773 *MS 1868 1872* go on with   774 *MS* {no comma} 775 *MS* know: 776 *MS* And thereupon>Accordingly   777 *MS* here,>up and   *MS* around

770 *put to proof:* put into action.

The woman, hemmed in by her household-bars,—
Chase her about the coop of daily life,
Having first stopped each outlet thence save one   780
Which, like bird with a ferret in her haunt,
She needs must seize as sole way of escape
Though there was tied and twittering a decoy
To seem as if it tempted,—just the plume
O' the popinjay, not a real respite there   785
From tooth and claw of something in the dark,—
Giuseppe Caponsacchi.
                          Now begins
The tenebrific passage of the tale:
How hold a light, display the cavern's gorge?   790
How, in this phase of the affair, show truth?
Here is the dying wife who smiles and says
"So it was,—so it was not,—how it was,
"I never knew nor ever care to know—"
Till they all weep, physician, man of law,   795
Even that poor old bit of battered brass
Beaten out of all shape by the world's sins,
Common utensil of the lazar-house—

---

778 *MS* household bars,   779 *MS* Chased   *MS* {no comma}   781 *MS*
That,   birdlike   782 *MS* the   sole   783 *MS* There,   where   was
tied   785 *MS* {beginning of fo. 140}   *MS* Of the popinjay,—and not the
respite there   *Yale 1* Of>O'   *1868 1872* and not a   793 *MS* was   794 *MS*
{no quotation mark at beginning of line}   *MS* know"—   795 *MS* doctor>
physician,   797 *MS* {no comma}   798 *MS* The common   *MS* Lazar-
house

---

785 *popinjay*: parrot, (figuratively) fop: someone vainly dressed and stupid (in
reference to the parrot's garish plumage and repetitive squawk). The use here keeps
a shade of the original meaning: 'plume of the popinjay' is both the bright feather of a
parrot and the feathered hat of the fop.

789 *tenebrific*: 'causing or producing darkness; obscuring': OED[2]. A favourite word
of Carlyle's. It also occurs in the epigraph to one of Alfred Domett's poems, which
may have drawn Browning's attention to it: *Poems* (1833), 73. The epigraph is from
Burns's 'Epistle to Davie', 138: 'It lightens—it brightens / The tenebrific scene!' For
Browning's copy, see Kelley and Coley, A807.

796-8 *battered . . . utensil*: a description of Fra Celestino: as confessor in the hospital,
he exists there like a familiar, cheap pot, one that has been beaten out of shape by
hearing people's sins. Other Half-Rome is surprised that this unromantic figure, with
few illusions, is making large claims for Pompilia's innocence.

Confessor Celestino groans " 'T is truth,
"All truth and only truth: there's something here,   800
"Some presence in the room beside us all,
"Something that every lie expires before:
"No question she was pure from first to last."
So far is well and helps us to believe:
But beyond, she the helpless, simple-sweet   805
Or silly-sooth, unskilled to break one blow
At her good fame by putting finger forth,—
How can she render service to the truth?
The bird says "So I fluttered where a springe
"Caught me: the springe did not contrive itself,   810
"That I know: who contrived it, God forgive!"
But we, who hear no voice and have dry eyes,
Must ask,—we cannot else, absolving her,—
How of the part played by that same decoy
I' the catching, caging? Was himself caught first?   815
We deal here with no innocent at least,
No witless victim,—he's a man of the age
And priest beside,—persuade the mocking world
Mere charity boiled over in this sort!
He whose own safety too,—(the Pope's apprised—
Good-natured with the secular offence,   821

799 *MS* "Tis   800–3 *MS* {no quotation marks at beginnings of lines}
800 *MS 1868 1872* else,   801 *MS* you   804 *MS* well, and   805 *MS*
beyond she is   807 *MS* On   *MS* forth.   808 {not found in *MS*}   810–
11 *MS* {no quotation marks at beginnings of lines}   813 *MS* {beginning of fo.
141}   *MS* Must ask, cannot but ask, absolving her,   815 *MS* In   817 *MS*
world>age   818 *MS 1868 1872* a priest   819 *MS* wise>   820 *MS*
He,   *MS* priests>(The Pope's apprised)   *Yale 1* Pope's>Pope 's   821–3 {not
found in *MS*}

799–800 '*T is . . . truth*: echoing the legal oath and proverb 'The truth, the whole
truth, and nothing but the truth'.
805–6 *simple-sweet / Or silly-sooth*: innocent or naïve. In the use of 'silly-sooth',
which occurs several times in the poem, Browning is probably recalling *Twelfth Night*,
II. iv. 46, where it means 'simple truth'. In his use it usually implies a naïvety bordering
on the foolish.
809–10 *springe / "Caught me*: cf. 'springes to catch woodcocks': *Hamlet*, I. iii. 115.
Other Half-Rome is thinking of Pompilia as a naïve Ophelia figure.
812 *hear . . . eyes*: i.e. not in the immediate presence of the death-bed.

The Pope looks grave on priesthood in a scrape)
Our priest's own safety therefore, may-be life,
Hangs on the issue! You will find it hard.
Guido is here to meet you with fixed foot,   825
Stiff like a statue—"Leave what went before!
"My wife fled i' the company of a priest,
"Spent two days and two nights alone with him:
"Leave what came after!" He stands hard to throw.
Moreover priests are merely flesh and blood;   830
When we get weakness, and no guilt beside,
'T is no such great ill-fortune: finding grey,
We gladly call that white which might be black,
Too used to the double-dye. So, if the priest
Moved by Pompilia's youth and beauty, gave   835
Way to the natural weakness.... Anyhow
Here be facts, charactery; what they spell
Determine, and thence pick what sense you may!

There was a certain young bold handsome priest
Popular in the city, far and wide   840
Famed, since Arezzo's but a little place,
As the best of good companions, gay and grave
At the decent minute; settled in his stall,

---

823 *Yale 1* may be>may-be   824 *MS* He will   825 *MS* him   826 *MS*
Stands   *MS* before,—   827-9 *MS* {no quotation marks at beginnings of
lines}   827 *MS* in   829 *MS* after." He is hard   *1868 1872* is hard
830 *MS* men   *MS* blood,   831 *MS* {no comma}   832 *MS* We have no
such ill fortune: *1868 1872* We have no   *MS* {no comma}   *Yale 1* grey>
grey,   834 *MS* Here anyhow   835-6 {not found in *MS*}   836 *1868*
1872 weakness . . . . .   837 *MS* Are the facts, the charactery;   838 *MS* {no
comma}   *MS* may.   ★839 *MS* {new paragraph. Paragraphing obscured in *1868*
and *1872* by this line's being at the head of the page}   *1888 1889* {no new para-
graph}   *MS* young and handsome   841 *MS* since>for   *1868 1872* for Arezzo's

---

829 *He stands hard to throw:* he (and his accusation) are hard to overturn or evade.
This continues the image of Guido as a staunch wrestler 'with fixed foot, / Stiff like a
statue' (825-6).

837 *charactery:* handwritten letters (of the alphabet).

843 *decent:* appropriate.

stall: one of a row of enclosed seats in the choir of the church, where Caponsacchi
would take part in the sung offices.

Or sidling, lute on lap, by lady's couch,
Ever the courtly Canon; see in him   845
A proper star to climb and culminate,
Have its due handbreadth of the heaven at Rome,
Though meanwhile pausing on Arezzo's edge,
As modest candle does 'mid mountain fog,
To rub off redness and rusticity   850
Ere it sweep chastened, gain the silver-sphere!
Whether through Guido's absence or what else,
This Caponsacchi, favourite of the town,
Was yet no friend of his nor free o' the house,
Though both moved in the regular magnates' march:
Each must observe the other's tread and halt   856
At church, saloon, theatre, house of play.
Who could help noticing the husband's slouch,
The black of his brow—or miss the news that buzzed
Of how the little solitary wife   860
Wept and looked out of window all day long?
What need of minute search into such springs
As start men, set o' the move?—machinery
Old as earth, obvious as the noonday sun.
Why, take men as they come,—an instance now,—   865
Of all those who have simply gone to see
Pompilia on her deathbed since four days,
Half at the least are, call it how you please,
In love with her—I don't except the priests
Nor even the old confessor whose eyes run   870

---

844 *MS* {beginning of fo. 142}   *1868 1872* sideling,   845 *MS 1868 1872*
Canon: see in such   846 *MS 1868 1872* A star shall climb apace and   847 *MS*
{no comma}   848 *MS* {no comma}   849 *MS* taper>candle   *MS* mid
the mountain-fog   *1868 1872* candle 'mid the mountain   850 *MS* rusticity,
851 *MS* Ere, gold thrice chastened, it>Ere it [?spin] chastened, to the silver-sphere>
Ere it sweep chastened, to the silver-sphere   *1868* silver-sphere.   852 *MS* {no
comma}   853 *MS* favorite   854 *MS* of   855 *MS* magnate's
march—   *1868* march—   863 *MS* on   864 *MS* sun?   870 *MS* Confessor

---

846 *culminate*: reach its highest altitude, its highest point in the sky.

850 *redness and rusticity*: earth-colour or rawness, and what is countrified, lacking
refinement. The star (Caponsacchi) appears red on the horizon because seen through
haze; having been tested in obscurity, it rises to appear brilliant in the height of the sky.

Over at what he styles his sister's voice
Who died so early and weaned him from the world.
Well, had they viewed her ere the paleness pushed
The last o' the red o' the rose away, while yet
Some hand, adventurous 'twixt the wind and her,　　875
Might let shy life run back and raise the flower
Rich with reward up to the guardian's face,—
Would they have kept that hand employed all day
At fumbling on with prayer-book pages? No!
Men are men: why then need I say one word　　880
More than that our mere man the Canon here
Saw, pitied, loved Pompilia?

　　　　　　　　　This is why;
This startling why: that Caponsacchi's self—
Whom foes and friends alike avouch, for good　　885
Or ill, a man of truth whate'er betide,
Intrepid altogether, reckless too
How his own fame and fortune, tossed to the winds,
Suffer by any turn the adventure take,
Nay, more—not thrusting, like a badge to hide,　　890
'Twixt shirt and skin a joy which shown is shame—
But flirting flag-like i' the face o' the world
This tell-tale kerchief, this conspicuous love
For the lady,—oh, called innocent love, I know!

---

871 *MS* {beginning of fo. 143}　　872 *MS* world:　*Yale 1* world;>
world.　874 *MS* of the red of　875 *MS* sort of screen was>hand, adventurous　*MS* her　876 *MS* To>Might　*MS 1868 1872* the life　877 *MS* to
the first guardian's>up to the guardian's　878 *MS 1868 1872* employed the
same　881 *MS* More than this that our man　*1868 1872* More than this, that
our man　883 *MS* {no new paragraph}　*MS* why—　*Yale 1* why—>why;
884 *MS* why,　*Yale 1* why—>why:　*MS* self　*Yale 1* self>self—　886 *MS*
to speak the truth　889 *MS* whatever turn　890 *MS* thrusting like a
pledge to hide　892 *MS* flaglike in　*MS* of　894 *MS* know,

　871 *his sister's voice*: Fra Celestino thinks that Pompilia speaks like his sister, whose
early death was the root of his vocation to the priesthood.
　875 *adventurous*: daring, going bravely.
　890 *badge*: token, the 'kerchief' (handkerchief) of l. 893.
　892 *flirting*: waving quickly.

Only, such scarlet fiery innocence   895
As most folk would try muffle up in shade,—
—'T is strange then that this else abashless mouth
Should yet maintain, for truth's sake which is God's,
That it was not he made the first advance,
That, even ere word had passed between the two,   900
Pompilia penned him letters, passionate prayers,
If not love, then so simulating love
That he, no novice to the taste of thyme,
Turned from such over-luscious honey-clot
At end o' the flower, and would not lend his lip   905
Till...but the tale here frankly outsoars faith:
There must be falsehood somewhere. For her part,
Pompilia quietly constantly avers
She never penned a letter in her life
Nor to the Canon nor any other man,   910
Being incompetent to write and read:
Nor had she ever uttered word to him, nor he
To her till that same evening when they met,
She on her window-terrace, he beneath
I' the public street, as was their fateful chance,   915
And she adjured him in the name of God
To find out, bring to pass where, when and how
Escape with him to Rome might be contrived.
Means were found, plan laid, time fixed, she avers,
And heart assured to heart in loyalty,   920
All at an impulse! All extemporized

---

895 *MS* {no comma}   *Yale 1* Only such>Only, such   896 *MS 1868 1872*
men   899 *MS* {beginning of fo. 144}   900 *MS* Than, {a *lapsus
calami*}   *MS* word passed   903 *MS* the thyme   904 *MS* the over-luscious
905 *MS* of   906 *MS 1868 1872* Till..   907 *MS* somewhere: for   *MS*
{no comma}   908 *MS* Pompilia, quietly,   911 *MS* or read: 913 *MS*
{no comma}   915 *MS* In   *MS* street as   *Yale 1* street as>street, as
917 *MS 1868 1872* Find out and   918 *MS* ^with him^   *MS* for her.   919 *MS*
Means found, plan laid, and time   *1868 1872* Means found, plan laid and time

---

897 *abashless*: shameless: see II. 1011 n.
903 *thyme*: a sweet herb, here symbolizing courting and dalliance.
908 *avers*: affirms.

As in romance-books! Is that credible?
Well, yes: as she avers this with calm mouth
Dying, I do think "Credible!" you'd cry—
Did not the priest's voice come to break the spell.   925
They questioned him apart, as the custom is,
When first the matter made a noise at Rome,
And he, calm, constant then as she is now,
For truth's sake did assert and re-assert
Those letters called him to her and he came,   930
—Which damns the story credible otherwise.
Why should this man,—mad to devote himself,
Careless what comes of his own fame, the first,—
Be studious thus to publish and declare
Just what the lightest nature loves to hide,   935
So screening lady from the byword's laugh
"First spoke the lady, last the cavalier!"
—I say,—why should the man tell truth just now
When graceful lying meets such ready shrift?
Or is there a first moment for a priest   940
As for a woman, when invaded shame
Must have its first and last excuse to show?
Do both contrive love's entry in the mind
Shall look, i' the manner of it, a surprise,—
That after, once the flag o' the fort hauled down,   945
Effrontery may sink drawbridge, open gate,
Welcome and entertain the conqueror?

---

923 *Yale 2* mouth>mouth,   925 *MS 1868* the spell: 926 *MS* {beginning
of fo. 145}   *MS* apart as   929 *MS 1868 1872* reassert   931 *MS*
Which   932 *MS* man mad   *MS* himself,—   933 *MS* comes to own
fame the   *Yale 1* fame the>fame, the   934 *MS* proclaim   936 *MS* Save
a poor   *1868 1872* Nor screen a   937 *MS* cavalier."   938 *MS 1868 1872*
just here   939 *MS* Where   942 *MS* show,   944 *MS* in   *MS*
surprize,   *1868 1872* surprise,   945 *MS* And   *MS* of   947 *MS* victor
then?

---

933 *Careless . . . first*: careless of his reputation, which should be his first concern.
936 *byword's*: proverb's.
940-2 *Or . . . show?*: i.e. 'Is each of them pretending to have been wooed first, and
not to have started it, because a priest is supposed to be modest as a woman is supposed
to be modest? They both have shame which demands this excuse.'

Or what do you say to a touch of the devil's worst?
Can it be that the husband, he who wrote
The letter to his brother I told you of,   950
I' the name of her it meant to criminate,—
What if he wrote those letters to the priest?
Further the priest says, when it first befell,
This folly o' the letters, that he checked the flow,
Put them back lightly each with its reply.   955
Here again vexes new discrepancy:
There never reached her eye a word from him:
He did write but she could not read—could just
Burn the offence to wifehood, womanhood,
So did burn: never bade him come to her,   960
Yet when it proved he must come, let him come,
And when he did come though uncalled,—why, spoke
Prompt by an inspiration: thus it chanced.
Will you go somewhat back to understand?

When first, pursuant to his plan, there sprang,   965
Like an uncaged beast, Guido's cruelty
On soul and body of his wife, she cried
To those whom law appoints resource for such,
The secular guardian,—that's the Governor,
And the Archbishop,—that's the spiritual guide,   970
And prayed them take the claws from out her flesh.
Now, this is ever the ill consequence
Of being noble, poor and difficult,

948 *MS* Devil's   949 *MS* Husband,   950 *MS* {no comma}   951 *MS*
In   952 *MS* Priest?   953 *MS* {beginning of fo. 146}   *MS* Priest   *MS*
befell   954 *MS* of   *MS* letters, he   956 *MS* is a   957 *MS*
him,   *1868* him;   *1872* him· {a broken sort}   958 *MS 1868 1872* read—she
could   959 *MS 1868* Burn what offended wifehood,   960 *MS* And   *MS*
{no comma}   961 {not found in *MS*}   962 *MS* Yet   *MS* all-uncalled
she spoke   *1868 1872* uncalled, she spoke   963 *MS 1868 1872* was.   965 *MS*
sprung   966 *MS* {no comma}   967 *MS 1868 1872* On the weak shoulders
MS fled   969–70 *MS* The secular guardian and the spiritual guide,>The secular
guardian—that's the Governor / And the Archbishop,—that's the spiritual guide,
969 *1868 1872* guardian—that's   972 *MS* was>is   973 *MS* When you
are

Ungainly, yet too great to disregard,—
This—that born peers and friends hereditary,—   975
Though disinclined to help from their own store
The opprobrious wight, put penny in his poke
From private purse or leave the door ajar
When he goes wistful by at dinner-time,—
Yet, if his needs conduct him where they sit   980
Smugly in office, judge this, bishop that,
Dispensers of the shine and shade o' the place—
And if, friend's door shut and friend's purse undrawn,
Still potentates may find the office-seat
Do as good service at no cost—give help   985
By-the-bye, pay up traditional dues at once
Just through a feather-weight too much i' the scale,
Or finger-tip forgot at the balance-tongue,—
Why, only churls refuse, or Molinists.
Thus when, in the first roughness of surprise   990
At Guido's wolf-face whence the sheepskin fell,
The frightened couple, all bewilderment,
Rushed to the Governor,—who else rights wrong?
Told him their tale of wrong and craved redress—
Why, then the Governor woke up to the fact   995
That Guido was a friend of old, poor Count!—
So, promptly paid his tribute, promised the pair,
Wholesome chastisement should soon cure their qualms

974 *MS* disregard,   975 *MS* That your   *1868 1872* That the   *MS 1868 1872*
hereditary   976 *MS* [ ]>help   977 *MS* man,   978 *MS 1868 1872*
purse of theirs   981 *MS* {beginning of fo. 147}   *MS* Snugly   982 *MS*
of   983 *MS 1868 1872* the friend's   *MS 1868 1872* and purse   984 *MS*
The officer may find the office-hall   *1868 1872* The potentate may find the office-
hall   986 *MS* By the bye, pay just as well traditional dues   987 *MS* By a
feather weight in the scale, a finger tip   988 *MS* At the balance tongue,—why,
only churls refuse.   *1868 1872* A finger-tip   989 {not found in *MS*}   990 *MS*
Thus,   991 *MS* when   996 *MS* had claims—   997 *MS* So promptly
Yale 1 So promptly>So, promptly   *MS* tribute—   *MS* pair   998 *MS* try
cure

977 *opprobrious wight*: disgraced person.

988 *finger-tip*: a finger-tip, left as if by accident on the pointer of a pair of weighing
scales, stops the scales moving freely, and therefore gives a false reading: an image for a
cunning partiality in dealing out justice.

Next time they came, wept, prated and told lies:
So stopped all prating, sent them dumb to Rome.   1000
Well, now it was Pompilia's turn to try:
The troubles pressing on her, as I said,
Three times she rushed, maddened by misery,
To the other mighty man, sobbed out her prayer
At footstool of the Archbishop—fast the friend   1005
Of her husband also! Oh, good friends of yore!
So, the Archbishop, not to be outdone
By the Governor, break custom more than he,
Thrice bade the foolish woman stop her tongue,
Unloosed her hands from harassing his gout,   1010
Coached her and carried her to the Count again,
—His old friend should be master in his house,
Rule his wife and correct her faults at need!
Well, driven from post to pillar in this wise,
She, as a last resource, betook herself   1015
To one, should be no family-friend at least,
A simple friar o' the city; confessed to him,
Then told how fierce temptation of release
By self-dealt death was busy with her soul,
And urged that he put this in words, write plain   1020
For one who could not write, set down her prayer
That Pietro and Violante, parent-like
If somehow not her parents, should for love
Come save her, pluck from out the flame the brand
Themselves had thoughtlessly thrust in so deep   1025

---

999 *MS 1868 1872* came and prated   1000 *MS 1868 1872* Which   1001 *MS*
try   1002 *MS* say,   1004 *MS* potentate,   1005 *MS* foot of   1006 *MS*
yore—   1009 *MS* {beginning of fo. 148}   1010 *MS* feet,   1012 *MS*
{no comma}   1013 *MS* need.   1017 *MS* priest of the city,   1023 *MS*
old love's sake   1024 *MS* the brand from out the flame   1025 *MS* deep
there

1006 *of yore*: from of old.
1011 *Coached her*: set her in a coach, or carriage.
1017 *simple friar*. Pompilia's deposition mentions him briefly as 'an Augustinian
father, whom they call the Roman': OYB lxxxiv (92).
1024 *pluck ... brand*: cf. Amos 4: 11.

To send gay-coloured sparkles up and cheer
Their seat at the chimney-corner. The good friar
Promised as much at the moment; but, alack,
Night brings discretion: he was no one's friend,
Yet presently found he could not turn about   1030
Nor take a step i' the case and fail to tread
On someone's toe who either was a friend,
Or a friend's friend, or friend's friend thrice-removed,
And woe to friar by whom offences come!
So, the course being plain,—with a general sigh   1035
At matrimony the profound mistake,—
He threw reluctantly the business up,
Having his other penitents to mind.

If then, all outlets thus secured save one,
At last she took to the open, stood and stared   1040
With her wan face to see where God might wait—
And there found Caponsacchi wait as well
For the precious something at perdition's edge,
He only was predestinate to save,—
And if they recognized in a critical flash   1045
From the zenith, each the other, her need of him,
His need of . . . say, a woman to perish for,
The regular way o' the world, yet break no vow,
Do no harm save to himself,—if this were thus?

1027 *MS* priest   1028 *MS* in the moment,   1030 *MS* But   1031 *MS*
in   1033 *MS* or his   1034 *MS* to him   1035 *MS* plain,   1036 *MS*
{beginning of fo. 149}   1039 *MS* {no new paragraph}   1042 *MS* Caponsacchi, waiting   1043 *MS* {no comma}   1044 *MS* He, only,   1047 *MS*
1868 1872 of . .   *MS* for   1048 *MS* of   *MS* vow   1049 *MS* thus,

1029 *Night brings discretion*: a version of 'Night brings counsel' or 'Night is the
mother of counsel': ODEP, 566. The normal proverb has the sense of 'taking the
advice of your pillow', 'sleeping on something'. The substitution of 'discretion' for
'counsel' hints at the friar's worldliness. Cf. iv. 825 n.
1034 *woe . . . come*: cf. Matt. 18: 7. Other Half-Rome uses the biblical text ironically
to suggest the friar's worldly caution. Jesus is talking about 'offences' (sins), particularly
against his 'little ones'; the friar is thinking of insults or annoyances to the upper class.
1039 *outlets*: cf. ll. 779–81: Pompilia is again a bird harried by a ferret.
1045 *critical flash*: lightning flash, i.e. a divine illumination.

How do you say? It were improbable;   1050
So is the legend of my patron-saint.

Anyhow, whether, as Guido states the case,
Pompilia,—like a starving wretch i' the street
Who stops and rifles the first passenger
In the great right of an excessive wrong,—   1055
Did somehow call this stranger and he came,—
Or whether the strange sudden interview
Blazed as when star and star must needs go close
Till each hurts each and there is loss in heaven—
Whatever way in this strange world it was,—   1060
Pompilia and Caponsacchi met, in fine,
She at her window, he i' the street beneath,
And understood each other at first look.

All was determined and performed at once.
And on a certain April evening, late   1065
I' the month, this girl of sixteen, bride and wife
Three years and over,—she who hitherto
Had never taken twenty steps in Rome
Beyond the church, pinned to her mother's gown,
Nor, in Arezzo, knew her way through street   1070
Except what led to the Archbishop's door,—
Such an one rose up in the dark, laid hand
On what came first, clothes and a trinket or two,
Belongings of her own in the old day,—
Stole from the side o' the sleeping spouse—who knows?
Sleeping perhaps, silent for certain,—slid   1076

1052 *MS* {no new paragraph}   *MS* Anyhow—whether,—   *Yale 1* Anyhow—
>Anyhow,   *MS* case   1053 *MS* in   1060 *MS* was   1062 *MS* in
1063 *MS* {beginning of fo. 150}   1064 *MS* {no new paragraph}   1066 *MS*
In   1069 *MS* church and in her mother's hand   1071 *MS* door,   1075
MS of

1054 *rifles*: robs, plunders (especially by picking pockets).
passenger: passer-by, someone on foot.
1065 *April evening*: 22 Apr. 1697, in Browning's chronology: see 1. 585 n.
1076 *Sleeping perhaps*: Other Half-Rome hints that Guido was only pretending to
be asleep. This accords with his interpretation of the flight. He sees it as something
contrived by Guido to give himself an excuse for murder: see below l. 1211 n.

Ghost-like from great dark room to great dark room,
In through the tapestries and out again
And onward, unembarrassed as a fate,
Descended staircase, gained last door of all,   1080
Sent it wide open at first push of palm,
And there stood, first time, last and only time,
At liberty, alone in the open street,—
Unquestioned, unmolested found herself
At the city gate, by Caponsacchi's side,   1085
Hope there, joy there, life and all good again,
The carriage there, the convoy there, light there
Broadening ever into blaze at Rome
And breaking small what long miles lay between;
Up she sprang, in he followed, they were safe.   1090

The husband quotes this for incredible,
All of the story from first word to last:
Sees the priest's hand throughout upholding hers,
Traces his foot to the alcove, that night,
Whither and whence blindfold he knew the way,   1095
Proficient in all craft and stealthiness;
And cites for proof a servant, eye that watched
And ear that opened to purse secrets up,
A woman-spy,—suborned to give and take
Letters and tokens, do the work of shame   1100
The more adroitly that herself, who helped

---

*1077 *MS* *1868* *1872* to great dark room, *1888* *1889* to great dark
room   1078 *MS* arrased doors   *MS* arrase>arrassed   1079 *MS* unem-
barassed   1080 *MS* all   1081 *MS* {no comma}   1082 *MS* time
last   1085 *MS* side   1088 *MS* *1868* *1872* into a full blaze   1090 *MS*
{beginning of fo. 151}   1091 *MS* {no new paragraph}   *MS* {no com-
ma}   1093 *MS* Priest's   1094 *MS* {no commas}   1095 *Yale 2* he
knew>knew he {'tr' in left-hand margin and caret between 'he' and 'knew'}   *MS*
{no comma}   1101 *MS* {no comma}

1078 *tapestries*: arrassed doors: *MS.*
1079 *fate*: portent of doom.
1087 *convoy*: armed escort or guide, i.e. Caponsacchi.
1097 *servant*: Maria Margherita Contenti. The lawyer Lamparelli cites the legal
objections to her evidence: OYB cclii (248).

Communion thus between a tainted pair,
Had long since been a leper thick in spot,
A common trull o' the town: she witnessed all,
Helped many meetings, partings, took her wage   1105
And then told Guido the whole matter. Lies!
The woman's life confutes her word,—her word
Confutes itself: "Thus, thus and thus I lied."
"And thus, no question, still you lie," we say.

"Ay, but at last, e'en have it how you will,   1110
"Whatever the means, whatever the way, explodes
"The consummation"—the accusers shriek:
"Here is the wife avowedly found in flight,
"And the companion of her flight, a priest;
"She flies her husband, he the church his spouse: 1115
"What is this?"

                    Wife and priest alike reply
"This is the simple thing it claims to be,
"A course we took for life and honour's sake,
"Very strange, very justifiable."   1120
She says, "God put it in my head to fly,
"As when the martin migrates: autumn claps
"Her hands, cries 'Winter's coming, will be here,
" 'Off with you ere the white teeth overtake!

1102 *MS* leprous pair   1104 *MS* of   1105 *MS* The many   1108
MS herself:>itself: *MS* lied"   1109 *MS* "And very like thus still   *MS*
[?say:]>say.   *MS* {between 1109 and 1110 deleted line: Pompilia's word which
sweeps her off in s[ ]}   1110 *MS* {no new paragraph}   *MS* [ ]>e'en   1111–
12 *MS* {no quotation marks at beginnings of lines}   1111 *MS* however the way,
1112 *MS* shriek   1113 *MS* {no comma}   1114–16 *MS* {no quotation
marks at beginnings of lines}   1114 *MS* flight a priest,   1115 *MS* Church
MS spouse,   1116 *MS* {beginning of fo. 152}   *MS* {no new paragraph}
1119–20 *MS* {no quotation marks at beginnings of lines}   1119 *MS* honor's
1121 *MS* {no commas}   1122–32 *MS* {no quotation marks at beginnings of
lines}   1123 *MS* "Winter's

1104 *trull*: prostitute.

1115 *church his spouse*: symbolically a Catholic priest is 'married' to the church, since
he devotes his whole life to Christ.

1124 *white teeth*: of winter, i.e. snow and ice. Winter is like a wolf seeking prey; the
bird (Pompilia) must flee for her life.

"'Flee!' So I fled: this friend was the warm day,   1125
"The south wind and whatever favours flight;
"I took the favour, had the help, how else?
"And so we did fly rapidly all night,
"All day, all night—a longer night—again,
"And then another day, longest of days,   1130
"And all the while, whether we fled or stopped,
"I scarce know how or why, one thought filled both,
"'Fly and arrive!' So long as I found strength
"I talked with my companion, told him much,
"Knowing that he knew more, knew me, knew God
"And God's disposal of me,—but the sense   1136
"O' the blessed flight absorbed me in the main,
"And speech became mere talking through a sleep,
"Till at the end of that last longest night
"In a red daybreak, when we reached an inn   1140
"And my companion whispered 'Next stage—Rome!'
"Sudden the weak flesh fell like piled-up cards,
"All the frail fabric at a finger's touch,
"And prostrate the poor soul too, and I said
"'But though Count Guido were a furlong off,   1145
"'Just on me, I must stop and rest awhile!'
"Then something like a huge white wave o' the sea
"Broke o'er my brain and buried me in sleep
"Blessedly, till it ebbed and left me loose,
"And where was I found but on a strange bed   1150

1125 *MS* Flee!"   *MS* {no comma}   1126 *MS* wind,   *MS* flight,   *Yale 1*
flight,>flight;   1129 *MS* again   1131 *MS* stapped>stopped   1133 *MS*
"Fly and arrive!"   1134–44 *MS* {no quotation marks at beginnings of lines}
1134 *MS* much   1137 *MS* Of   *MS* {no comma}   1138 *MS* {no comma}
1141 *MS* "Next stage—Rome!"   1143 *MS* fingers   1144 *MS* {begin-
ning of fo. 153}   1145 *MS* "But   1146 *MS* Just   *MS* awhile."   1147–
8 *MS* {no quotation marks at beginnings of lines}   1147 *MS* a white wave
of   *1868 1872* a white   1149–70 *MS* {quotation marks at beginnings of lines
added later}   1149 *MS* Blessedly   *MS* {no commas}

1140 *red daybreak*: Pompilia is so exhausted that she confuses the reds of sunset and
dawn; the reference is explained at ll. 1189–1201.

"In a strange room like hell, roaring with noise,
"Ruddy with flame, and filled with men, in front
"Who but the man you call my husband? ay—
"Count Guido once more between heaven and me,
"For there my heaven stood, my salvation, yes—   1155
"That Caponsacchi all my heaven of help,
"Helpless himself, held prisoner in the hands
"Of men who looked up in my husband's face
"To take the fate thence he should signify,
"Just as the way was at Arezzo. Then,   1160
"Not for my sake but his who had helped me—
"I sprang up, reached him with one bound, and seized
"The sword o' the felon, trembling at his side,
"Fit creature of a coward, unsheathed the thing
"And would have pinned him through the poison-bag
"To the wall and left him there to palpitate,   1166
"As you serve scorpions, but men interposed—
"Disarmed me, gave his life to him again
"That he might take mine and the other lives,
"And he has done so. I submit myself!"   1170
The priest says—oh, and in the main result
The facts asseverate, he truly says,
As to the very act and deed of him,
However you mistrust the mind o' the man—
The flight was just for flight's sake, no pretext   1175
For aught except to set Pompilia free.

1151 *MS* noise   1153 *MS 1868 1872* "Whom   *MS* husband, ay   *1868 1872*
husband, ay—   1154 *MS* God>heaven   1155 *MS* yes   1156 *MS*
{no comma}   1159 *MS* The>To   *MS* {no comma}   1160 *MS* Arezzo:
then   *1868* Arezzo: then,   1163 *MS* of   *MS* {no commas}   1166 *MS*
{no comma}   1170 *MS* I appeal to God!"   1171 *MS* {beginning of fo.
154}   1172 *MS* {no comma}   *MS* says—   1173 *MS* {no comma}
1174 *MS* of   1176 *MS* except a flight to   *MS 1868* free:

1151 *like hell*: the room, red with the sun's rays and Guido's hellish presence, is
contrasted with 'my heaven', Caponsacchi (l. 1155).

1164 *creature*: servant. Here, and in 'trembling' (previous line), the sword is personified as a servant who shakes, reflecting the cowardice of Guido, his master.

1165 *poison-bag*: poison-gland of the scorpion (Guido) in l. 1167.

1172 *asseverate*: corroborate, solemnly affirm.

He says "I cite the husband's self's worst charge
"In proof of my best word for both of us.
"Be it conceded that so many times
"We took our pleasure in his palace: then,   1180
"What need to fly at all?—or flying no less,
"What need to outrage the lips sick and white
"Of a woman, and bring ruin down beside,
"By halting when Rome lay one stage beyond?"
So does he vindicate Pompilia's fame,   1185
Confirm her story in all points but one—
This; that, so fleeing and so breathing forth
Her last strength in the prayer to halt awhile,
She makes confusion of the reddening white
Which was the sunset when her strength gave way,
And the next sunrise and its whitening red   1191
Which she revived in when her husband came:
She mixes both times, morn and eve, in one,
Having lived through a blank of night 'twixt each
Though dead-asleep, unaware as a corpse,   1195
She on the bed above; her friend below
Watched in the doorway of the inn the while,
Stood i' the red o' the morn, that she mistakes,
In act to rouse and quicken the tardy crew
And hurry out the horses, have the stage   1200
Over, the last league, reach Rome and be safe:
When up came Guido.
                    Guido's tale begins—
How he and his whole household, drunk to death

1177 *MS* Husband's   1178–84 *MS* {no quotation marks at beginnings of
lines}   1178 *MS* for her and me: 1181 *MS* No   *MS* all,—
1182 *MS* No   1183 *MS* the woman,   *MS* beside   1184 *MS* was   *MS*
beyond." 1185 *MS* {no comma}   1186 *MS* one   1187 *MS* that so
fleeing, 1191 *MS* terrible and red   1192 *MS* came   1195 *MS* dead
asleep,   *MS* corpse   1196 *MS* above, while he   1197 *MS* Inn, just
where   1198 *MS* {beginning of fo. 155}   *MS* In that same red of the morn
that she describes   1199 *MS* quicken and rouse>rouse and quicken   1201 *MS*
safe,   1202 *MS* {no new paragraph}   *MS* Guido,—Guido whose tale begins

---

1198 *that she mistakes*: see l. 1140 n.

By some enchanted potion, poppied drugs   1205
Plied by the wife, lay powerless in gross sleep
And left the spoilers unimpeded way,
Could not shake off their poison and pursue,
Till noontide, then made shift to get on horse
And did pursue: which means he took his time,   1210
Pressed on no more than lingered after, step
By step, just making sure o' the fugitives,
Till at the nick of time, he saw his chance,
Seized it, came up with and surprised the pair.
How he must needs have gnawn lip and gnashed teeth,
Taking successively at tower and town,   1216
Village and roadside, still the same report
"Yes, such a pair arrived an hour ago,
"Sat in the carriage just where now you stand,
"While we got horses ready,—turned deaf ear   1220
"To all entreaty they would even alight;
"Counted the minutes and resumed their course."
Would they indeed escape, arrive at Rome,
Leave no least loop-hole to let murder through,
But foil him of his captured infamy,   1225
Prize of guilt proved and perfect? So it seemed.
Till, oh the happy chance, at last stage, Rome
But two short hours off, Castelnuovo reached,

1207 *MS* left her wickedness   1208 *MS* the poison   *MS* {no comma}
1210 *MS 1868* means,   *MS* time   1212 *MS* of   1213 *MS* chance
1214 *MS* surprized   1215 *MS* cursed and gnashed his teeth   1216 *MS*
{no comma}   1217 *MS* roadside inn still one   1219–22 *MS* {no quotation marks at beginnings of lines}   1219 *MS* Sate   *MS 1868 1872* your horse
stands,   1220 *MS* tarry, troth?>turned deaf ear   1221 *MS* [?P]>To
1223 *MS* at>escape   *MS* Rome   1224 *MS* Leaving no loop to let damnation
through,   *1868 1872* loop to let damnation   1225 *MS* So   *1868 1872*
And   *MS* {no comma}   1226 *MS* {beginning of fo. 156}   *MS 1868 1872*
seemed: ____   1228 *MS* Castelnuovo's inn

1209 *made shift*: made an effort, bestirred themselves.
1211 *Pressed . . . after*: this is 'Guido's tale' as told by Other Half-Rome. As part of
his plan of murder, Guido tracks Pompilia and Caponsacchi rather than catching up
with them. He wants them to stop and rest together unchaperoned, thus giving him
the excuse to kill them instantly as adulterers (ll. 1215–22).

The guardian angel gave reluctant place,
Satan stepped forward with alacrity,   1230
Pompilia's flesh and blood succumbed, perforce
A halt was, and her husband had his will.
Perdue he couched, counted out hour by hour
Till he should spy in the east a signal-streak—
Night had been, morrow was, triumph would be.   1235
Do you see the plan deliciously complete?
The rush upon the unsuspecting sleep,
The easy execution, the outcry
Over the deed "Take notice all the world!
"These two dead bodies, locked still in embrace,—
"The man is Caponsacchi and a priest,   1241
"The woman is my wife: they fled me late,
"Thus have I found and you behold them thus,
"And may judge me: do you approve or no?"

Success did seem not so improbable,   1245
But that already Satan's laugh was heard,
His black back turned on Guido—left i' the lurch
Or rather, baulked of suit and service now,
Left to improve on both by one deed more,
Burn up the better at no distant day,   1250
Body and soul one holocaust to hell.
Anyhow, of this natural consequence

1229 *MS* {no comma}   1232 *MS* The   *MS* the husband's hour>the husband
had   1234 *MS* see   *MS* East   *MS* signal-streak   1239 *MS*
notice,   1240–4 *MS* {no quotation marks at beginnings of lines}   1243 *MS*
found,   1245 *MS* {no new paragraph}   1247 *MS* Guido,—   *MS* in
1248 *MS* O[ ]>Or   1249 {not found in *MS*}   *1868 1872* That he
1250 *MS* That he burn up   *MS* {no comma}

1233 *Perdue he couched*: hidden he lay. Cf. 'Instans Tyrannus', 18.

1247–51 *left . . . hell*: Guido is left in the lurch by Satan, or rather he is frustrated
('baulked') of his desire to serve Satan at this point (by murdering Pompilia and
Caponsacchi) so that he may be drawn on to damn himself even more completely,
made to 'improve' on his 'suit and service' by committing a worse crime: Satan
frustrates the double murder so as to goad him later to 'one deed more', the triple
murder of Violante, Pietro, and Pompilia.

1248 *suit and service*: attendance and service (as of an inferior to his lord).

1252 *natural consequence*: i.e. expected course of events.

Did just the last link of the long chain snap:
For an eruption was o' the priest, alive
And alert, calm, resolute and formidable,   1255
Not the least look of fear in that broad brow—
One not to be disposed of by surprise,
And armed moreover—who had guessed as much?
Yes, there stood he in secular costume
Complete from head to heel, with sword at side,   1260
He seemed to know the trick of perfectly.
There was no prompt suppression of the man
As he said calmly "I have saved your wife
"From death; there was no other way but this;
"Of what do I defraud you except death?   1265
"Charge any wrong beyond, I answer it."
Guido, the valorous, had met his match,
Was forced to demand help instead of fight,
Bid the authorities o' the place lend aid
And make the best of a broken matter so.   1270
They soon obeyed the summons—I suppose,
Apprised and ready, or not far to seek—
Laid hands on Caponsacchi, found in fault,
A priest yet flagrantly accoutred thus,—
Then, to make good Count Guido's further charge,
Proceeded, prisoner made lead the way,   1276
In a crowd, upstairs to the chamber-door
Where wax-white, dead asleep, deep beyond dream,

1253 *MS* Just the last link of the long chain must snap: 1254 *MS* {beginning
of fo. 157}   *MS* For his irruption was on the Priest, alive   *1868 1872* his eruption *Yale 1* on>o'   1255 *MS* resolute, formidable,   1256 *MS* bold
brow—   1257 *MS* {no comma}   1260 *MS* side   1264–6 *MS* {no
quotation marks at beginnings of lines}   1265 *MS* save her death?   1266 *MS*
[ ]>Charge   *MS* but this,   1267 *MS* match   1268 *MS* to call instead of
fight   1269 *MS* of   1272 *MS 1868 1872* Apprized   1273 *MS* their
way>in fault   1274 *MS* In a crowd>A priest yet   *MS* thus,   1278 *MS*
dead-asleep

   1265 *except death*: except [her] death.
   1274 *accoutred*: dressed, equipped.
   1278 *wax-white*: the resonance is that Pompilia is as if dead, as if laid in her coffin by
the priest, emphasizing her chastity.

As the priest laid her, lay Pompilia yet.

And as he mounted step and step with the crowd　　　1280
How I see Guido taking heart again!
He knew his wife so well and the way of her—
How at the outbreak she would shroud her shame
In hell's heart, would it mercifully yawn—
How, failing that, her forehead to his foot,　　　1285
She would crouch silent till the great doom fell,
Leave him triumphant with the crowd to see
Guilt motionless or writhing like a worm!
No! Second misadventure, this worm turned,
I told you: would have slain him on the spot　　　1290
With his own weapon, but they seized her hands:
Leaving her tongue free, as it tolled the knell
Of Guido's hope so lively late. The past
Took quite another shape now. She who shrieked
"At least and for ever I am mine and God's,　　　1295
"Thanks to his liberating angel Death—
"Never again degraded to be yours
"The ignoble noble, the unmanly man,
"The beast below the beast in brutishness!"—
This was the froward child, "the restif lamb　　　1300

1280 *MS* {no new paragraph}　　　1281 *MS* {beginning of fo. 158}　　　1283 *MS*
How in the terror　　1284 *MS* {no comma}　　1286 *MS* lie silent　　1287 *MS*
Show his charge just with all the crowd to see!　*1868 1872* see!　　　1288 *MS*
worm.　*Yale 1* worm.>worm?　*1868 1872* worm?　　　1289 *MS* turned:
1292 *MS* free—　　　1293 *MS* To　　*MS* late: the Past　　1295 *MS* {no
comma}　　　1296–9 *MS* {no quotation marks at beginnings of lines}
1296 *MS* his>His　　　1297 *MS* your's　　　1299 *MS* brutishness!"

1283–4 *outbreak . . . yawn*: at the breaking in of the crowd, Pompilia will be so
ashamed, she will grab any cover, even if it damns her: i.e. her flustering excuses
will incriminate her.

1289 *this worm turned*: proverbial: 'Tread on a worm and it will turn': ODEP, 837.

1295–1307 *"At least . . . now!*: Pompilia screams out that she would rather kill Guido
and die herself, than suffer his brutal treatment again. (She does not even mention or
try to explain away Caponsacchi.) Her conviction and boldness destroy the version of
the past built up by Guido: see 1301–2 n.

1300 *froward*: difficult, naughty.
restif: stubborn.

"Used to be cherished in his breast," he groaned—
"Eat from his hand and drink from out his cup,
"The while his fingers pushed their loving way
"Through curl on curl of that soft coat—alas,
"And she all silverly baaed gratitude   1305
"While meditating mischief!"—and so forth.
He must invent another story now!
The ins and outs o' the rooms were searched: he found
Or showed for found the abominable prize—
Love-letters from his wife who cannot write,   1310
Love-letters in reply o' the priest—thank God!—
Who can write and confront his character
With this, and prove the false thing forged throughout:
Spitting whereat, he needs must spatter whom
But Guido's self?—that forged and falsified   1315
One letter called Pompilia's, past dispute:
Then why not these to make sure still more sure?

So was the case concluded then and there:
Guido preferred his charges in due form,
Called on the law to adjudicate, consigned   1320
The accused ones to the Prefect of the place,
(Oh mouse-birth of that mountain-like revenge!)

1302 *MS* {quotation mark at beginning of line added later and ? then erased}
1303–6 *MS* {no quotation marks at beginnings of lines}   1304 *MS* {no
comma}   1306 *MS* mischief—   1307 *MS* One   1308 *MS* {begin-
ning of fo. 159}   *MS* of the room   1311 *MS* of the paramour   *Yale 1*
paramour>priest—thank God!—   1312 *MS* so confronts>confront   *MS* the
characters   1314 *MS 1868* who   1315 *MS* self, who   *Yale 1* self,>
self?—   *Yale 2* that>he   1316 *MS* dispute—   *Yale 1* dispute—>dis-
pute: 1319 *MS* charge in all   *MS* {Between 1319 and 1320 extra line: Laid
the facts down and bade the letters speak,}   1321 *MS* prefect   *MS* {no
comma}   *1868 1872* place.   1322 *MS* mountainlike revenge)

   1301–2 *cherished . . . cup*: cf. 2 Sam. 12: 3. An instance of Other Half-Rome's wry
wit: he has Guido cast himself pathetically as Uriah the Hittite, with his one beloved
lamb, Bathsheba (Pompilia). Pompilia's vehemence then undermines this image.
   1305 *silverly*: so used by Smart and Keats, both well known to Browning.
   1312 *confront his character*: set side by side his real handwriting (with Guido's forgery).
   1322 *mouse-birth . . . revenge*: proverbial: 'The mountains have brought forth a
mouse', adapted from Horace, *Ars Poetica*, 139: 'parturient montes, nascetur ridiculus
mus': 'mountains will labour, an absurd mouse will be born': ODEP, 547.

And so to his own place betook himself
After the spring that failed,—the wildcat's way.
The captured parties were conveyed to Rome;   1325
Investigation followed here i' the court—
Soon to review the fruit of its own work,
From then to now being eight months and no more.
Guido kept out of sight and safe at home:
The Abate, brother Paolo, helped most   1330
At words when deeds were out of question, pushed
Nearest the purple, best played deputy,
So, pleaded, Guido's representative
At the court shall soon try Guido's self,—what's more,
The court that also took—I told you, Sir—   1335
That statement of the couple, how a cheat
Had been i' the birth of the babe, no child of theirs.
That was the prelude; this, the play's first act:
Whereof we wait what comes, crown, close of all.

Well, the result was something of a shade   1340
On the parties thus accused,—how otherwise?
Shade, but with shine as unmistakable.
Each had a prompt defence: Pompilia first—
"Earth was made hell to me who did no harm:
"I only could emerge one way from hell   1345
"By catching at the one hand held me, so

1323 *MS* betook him to his place again   1324 *MS* wild cat's   1325 *MS*
Rome   1326 *MS* in the Court   1327 *MS* Which now reviews   *MS* T>
Which   *MS* work—   1328 *MS* months, no   1329 *MS* home—
1330 *MS* best>most   1331 *MS* words,   *MS* question—   1332 *MS* deputy.
1333 *MS* {beginning of fo. 160}   *MS* So Guido went by   1334 *MS* To the
Court   1335 *MS* Court   *MS* sir—   1337 *MS* in   *MS* theirs—
1338 *MS* prelude: *MS* act   1339 *MS* crown—close   *Yale 2* crown, close of
all.>crowns, closes all.   1340 *MS* {no new paragraph}   *MS* {no comma}
MS shade.   1342 *MS* Shade—   1345–8 *MS* {no quotation marks at
beginnings of lines}   1345 *MS* thence   1346 *MS* held to me

1324 *spring*: leap.
1331–2 *pushed...purple*: i.e. gained access to the powerful people (who might
influence the case).

"I caught at it and thereby stepped to heaven:
"If that be wrong, do with me what you will!"
Then Caponsacchi with a grave grand sweep
O' the arm as though his soul warned baseness off—
"If as a man, then much more as a priest   1351
"I hold me bound to help weak innocence:
"If so my worldly reputation burst,
"Being the bubble it is, why, burst it may:
"Blame I can bear though not blameworthiness.   1355
"But use your sense first, see if the miscreant proved,
"The man who tortured thus the woman, thus
"Have not both laid the trap and fixed the lure
"Over the pit should bury body and soul!
"His facts are lies: his letters are the fact—   1360
"An infiltration flavoured with himself!
"As for the fancies—whether... what is it you say?
"The lady loves me, whether I love her
"In the forbidden sense of your surmise,—
"If, with the midday blaze of truth above,   1365
"The unlidded eye of God awake, aware,
"You needs must pry about and trace the birth
"Of each stray beam of light may traverse night

1347 *MS* Heaven: 1348 *MS* was wrong,   1350 *MS* Of   *MS* as if
1351 *MS* As a man, therefore>"If as a man, then   1352–75 *MS* {no quotation
marks at beginnings of lines}   1355 *MS* blameworthiness,   1356 *MS*
1868 1872 miscreant here   1358 *MS* thus laid   1359 *MS* grave   1360 *MS*
{beginning of fo. 161}   *MS* the one fact—   1361 *MS* his soul!   1362 *MS*
1868 1872 whether..   1364 *MS* surmise,   1365 *MS* midday sun   1366 *MS*
God himself ablaze   1367 *MS* track the cause   *1868 1872* track the course
★1368 *MS* Of some stray beam of light that crosses earth   *1868 1872* earth,   *1888*
night,   DC *Br U* night,>night   *1889* night

1353–4 *reputation...bubble*: cf. 'the bubble reputation': *As You Like It*, II. vii. 152.
    1361 *infiltration*: i.e. the letters, which have been smuggled into the inn. Perhaps
suggested by 'Death's black dust, being blown, / Infiltrated through every secret fold /
Of this sealed letter': *Aurora Leigh*, ii. 1157–9.
    1366 *unlidded*: without eyelids. This is the traditional association of God with the
sun, the light that sees all that is done on the earth.
    1367–74 *trace the birth...hear*: Caponsacchi stresses that objectively he and Pompilia
neither thought nor acted anything unchaste. Only God can judge the deepest movements of their hearts.

"To the night's sun that's Lucifer himself,
"Do so, at other time, in other place,   1370
"Not now nor here! Enough that first to last
"I never touched her lip nor she my hand
"Nor either of us thought a thought, much less
"Spoke a word which the Virgin might not hear.
"Be such your question, thus I answer it."   1375

Then the court had to make its mind up, spoke.
"It is a thorny question, yea, a tale
"Hard to believe, but not impossible:
"Who can be absolute for either side?
"A middle course is happily open yet.   1380
"Here has a blot surprised the social blank,—
"Whether through favour, feebleness or fault,
"No matter, leprosy has touched our robe
"And we unclean must needs be purified.
"Here is a wife makes holiday from home,   1385
"A priest caught playing truant to his church,
"In masquerade moreover: both allege
"Enough excuse to stop our lifted scourge
"Which else would heavily fall. On the other hand,
"Here is a husband, ay and man of mark,   1390
"Who comes complaining here, demands redress
"As if he were the pattern of desert—
"The while those plaguy allegations frown,
"Forbid we grant him the redress he seeks.

1369 *MS 1868 1872* and Lucifer   *MS* {no comma}   1370 *MS* place
1371 *MS* here: enough   1373–4 *MS* Nor spoke a word that the Virgin might
not hear.>Nor either of us, thought a thought, much less / Spoke a word that the Virgin
might not hear.   1375 *MS* That is   *1868 1872* "Be that   *1376 1868 1872* {new
paragraph. Paragraphing obscured in *1888* and *1889* by this line's being at the head of the
page.}   *MS* Court   *MS* spoke   1377 *MS* question: here's a tale   *1868 1872*
and a tale   1378 *MS* {no comma}   1380 *MS* yet: 1384 *MS* And we're
unclean and must   *1868 1872* "And we're unclean and must   1385 *MS* that runs
away from home,   1386 *MS* that plays the *MS* {no comma} 1388 *MS* {begin-
ning of fo. 162}   1393 *MS* Yet there   1394 *MS* our granting him the grace

1383–4 *leprosy . . . purified*: a figure derived from Lev. 13.
1387 *masquerade*: disguise.
1393 *plaguy*: troublesome (a colloquialism).

"To all men be our moderation known!   1395
"Rewarding none while compensating each,
"Hurting all round though harming nobody,
"Husband, wife, priest, scot-free not one shall 'scape,
"Yet priest, wife, husband, boast the unbroken head
"From application of our excellent oil: 1400
"So that, whatever be the fact, in fine,
"We make no miss of justice in a sort.
"First, let the husband stomach as he may,
"His wife shall neither be returned him, no—
"Nor branded, whipped and caged, but just consigned
"To a convent and the quietude she craves;   1406
"So is he rid of his domestic plague:
"What better thing can happen to a man?
"Next, let the priest retire—unshent, unshamed,
"Unpunished as for perpetrating crime,   1410
"But relegated (not imprisoned, Sirs!)
"Sent for three years to clarify his youth
"At Civita, a rest by the way to Rome:
"There let his life skim off its last of lees
"Nor keep this dubious colour. Judged the cause: 1415
"All parties may retire, content, we hope."
That's Rome's way, the traditional road of law;
Whither it leads is what remains to tell.

[—]

1397 *MS* yet>and   1398 *MS* not one shall scape scot-free—   1399 *MS*
Priest, wife, and husband,>Yet priest, wife, husband,   *MS* show unbroken heads
1400 *MS* oil.   1401 *MS* fact at last,   1402 *MS* It shall not   *1868 1872* "It
makes   1406 *MS* craves,   *1868* cravse;   1407 *MS* plague,—   1410 *MS*
{line added later}   *MS* Nor punished>Unpunished   1413 *MS* Rome,
1414 *MS* shake off   1415 *MS* cause,   1416 *MS* {beginning of fo.
163}   *MS* to their place,>may retire,   *MS* hope!"   1418 *MS* see.

1395 *To ... known*: cf. Phil. 4: 5.
1400 *excellent oil*: oil was put on wounds to soothe and heal them. Everyone will be
both 'hurt' by some aspect of the court's judgment, and yet soothed by another aspect.
1403 *stomach*: endure.
1409 *unshent*: unharmed.
1412 *clarify*: make clear and pure (used of a liquid). The image continues in 'lees'
(1414), the sediment in wine. Caponsacchi is being laid down, as wine is, to make him
pure.

The priest went to his relegation-place,
The wife to her convent, brother Paolo   1420
To the arms of brother Guido with the news
And this beside—his charge was countercharged;
The Comparini, his old brace of hates,
Were breathed and vigilant and venomous now—
Had shot a second bolt where the first stuck,   1425
And followed up the pending dowry-suit
By a procedure should release the wife
From so much of the marriage-bond as barred
Escape when Guido turned the screw too much
On his wife's flesh and blood, as husband may.   1430
No more defence, she turned and made attack,
Claimed now divorce from bed and board, in short:
Pleaded such subtle strokes of cruelty,
Such slow sure siege laid to her body and soul,
As, proved,—and proofs seemed coming thick and fast,—
Would gain both freedom and the dowry back   1436
Even should the first suit leave them in his grasp:
So urged the Comparini for the wife.
Guido had gained not one of the good things
He grasped at by his creditable plan   1440
O' the flight and following and the rest: the suit
That smouldered late was fanned to fury new,
This adjunct came to help with fiercer fire,
While he had got himself a quite new plague—
Found the world's face an universal grin   1445

1419 *MS* Priest   1420 *MS* reclusion,>convent, and   *MS* Brother   1422 *MS* countercharged—   1425 *MS* {no comma}   1428 *MS* marriage bond   1430 *MS* husbands   1431 {not found in *MS*}   1432 *MS* She claimed   1433 *MS* {no comma}   1435 *MS* As proved,—   1437 *MS* grasp.   1438 *MS* So by the Comparini urged the wife.   1440 *MS* this creditable   1441 *MS* Of   *MS* ;>:   1442 *MS* new—   1443 *MS* {beginning of fo. 164}   *MS* fire,—   1444 *MS* plague

1423 *brace*: pair: cf. l. 529 n.
1424 *Were breathed*: had recovered breath, rested; like 'brace', usually used of animals.
1425 *bolt*: 'an arrow; a dart shot from a crossbow': Johnson.
1440 *creditable*: excellent, worthy (here ironic).

At this last best of the Hundred Merry Tales
Of how a young and spritely clerk devised
To carry off a spouse that moped too much,
And cured her of the vapours in a trice:
And how the husband, playing Vulcan's part,   1450
Told by the Sun, started in hot pursuit
To catch the lovers, and came halting up,
Cast his net and then called the Gods to see
The convicts in their rosy impudence—
Whereat said Mercury "Would that I were Mars!"   1455
Oh it was rare, and naughty all the same!
Brief, the wife's courage and cunning,—the priest's show
Of chivalry and adroitness,—last not least,
The husband—how he ne'er showed teeth at all,
Whose bark had promised biting; but just sneaked   1460
Back to his kennel, tail 'twixt legs, as 't were,—
All this was hard to gulp down and digest.
So pays the devil his liegeman, brass for gold.

[—]

1446 *MS* last, best   1448 *MS* {no comma}   1451 *MS* Sun did start
1452 *MS* so came   1455 *MS* Jove said he wished that he were Mars—
1456 *MS* {no comma}   1457 *MS* Brief,—   *MS* courag>cunning,
1458 *MS* least *Yale 1* least>least,   1459 *MS* husband's>husband—   *MS*
never   *MS* all,— 1460 *MS* biting,—   *Yale 2* biting;>biting,   1461 *MS*
betwixt   *MS* 'twere—

1446 *Hundred Merry Tales*: Boccaccio's *Decameron*, containing a hundred tales supposed to be related in ten days. Guido appears as the ludicrous cuckold of medieval
stories. Cf. *Much Ado about Nothing*, II. i. 129–30: 'that I had my good wit out of the
"Hundred Merry Tales"'. It would seem that Browning assumes that Shakespeare
alludes to the *Decameron* and not, as modern scholars suggest, to a sixteenth-century
English book of jests and tales.
1447 *clerk*: cleric, scholar (traditional seducers of wives in medieval stories).
1449 *the vapours*: depression of spirits, nervous disorder.
1450–5 *Vulcan's part . . . Mars!*: cf. *Odyssey*, viii. 266–342. Guido is like the hapless
cuckold Vulcan, the fire-god, who moved slowly because of his lameness. When
informed by the sun-god of Venus's adultery with Mars, Vulcan discovered them in
bed together and imprisoned them in a subtle net. He called the other gods to see, but
there was only merriment at his expense.
1454 *impudence*: shamelessness, immodesty.
1460 *bark . . . biting*: proverbial: 'His bark is worse than his bite': ODEP, 30.
1463 *brass for gold*: proverbial: ODEP, 81.

But this was at Arezzo: here in Rome
Brave Paolo bore up against it all—   1465
Battled it out, nor wanting to himself
Nor Guido nor the House whose weight he bore
Pillar-like, by no force of arm but brain.
He knew his Rome, what wheels to set to work;
Plied influential folk, pressed to the ear   1470
Of the efficacious purple, pushed his way
To the old Pope's self,—past decency indeed,—
Praying him take the matter in his hands
Out of the regular court's incompetence.
But times are changed and nephews out of date   1475
And favouritism unfashionable: the Pope
Said "Render Cæsar what is Cæsar's due!"
As for the Comparini's counter-plea,
He met that by a counter-plea again,
Made Guido claim divorce—with help so far   1480
By the trial's issue: for, why punishment
However slight unless for guiltiness
However slender?—and a molehill serves
Much as a mountain of offence this way.
So was he gathering strength on every side   1485
And growing more and more to menace—when
All of a terrible moment came the blow
That beat down Paolo's fence, ended the play

*1464 *MS* {new paragraph. Paragraphing obscured in *1868* and *1872* by this line's being at the head of the page} *1888 1889* {no new paragraph} *MS* But that 1466 *MS* not wanting 1468 *MS 1868 1872* not by 1469 *MS* {beginning of fo. 165} *MS* work, *1868 1872* we set 1472 *MS* the Pope's 1474 *MS* incompetence— *1868* incompetence; 1475 *MS* For *MS* changed, *MS* date. 1476-7 {not found in *MS*} 1478 *MS* {no comma} *Yale 1* counter-plea>counter-plea, 1479 *MS* to that, 1480 *MS* divorce with 1481 *MS* {no comma} 1483 *MS* slender? and the slenderest *MS* slender;> slender? 1486 *MS* growing verily formidable— 1487 *MS* sudden came the crowning blow 1488 *MS* ended the man,

1466 *nor wanting to himself*: nor failing himself, nor letting himself down.
1471 *efficacious purple*: influential cardinal. Cf. 1. 1139 n.
1475 *nephews out of date*: the pope avoids nepotism: cf. 1. 319, 323 nn.
1477 *"Render . . . due*: cf. Mark 12: 17.
1488-9 *play / O' the foil*: the legal fencing-match.

O' the foil and brought mannaia on the stage.

Five months had passed now since Pompilia's flight,   1490
Months spent in peace among the Convert nuns.
This,—being, as it seemed, for Guido's sake
Solely, what pride might call imprisonment
And quote as something gained, to friends at home,—
This naturally was at Guido's charge: 1495
Grudge it he might, but penitential fare,
Prayers, preachings, who but he defrayed the cost?
So, Paolo dropped, as proxy, doit by doit
Like heart's blood, till—what's here? What notice comes?
The convent's self makes application bland   1500
That, since Pompilia's health is fast o' the wane,
She may have leave to go combine her cure
Of soul with cure of body, mend her mind
Together with her thin arms and sunk eyes
That want fresh air outside the convent-wall,   1505
Say in a friendly house,—and which so fit
As a certain villa in the Pauline way,
That happens to hold Pietro and his wife,
The natural guardians? "Oh, and shift the care
"You shift the cost, too; Pietro pays in turn,   1510
"And lightens Guido of a load! And then,
"Villa or convent, two names for one thing,
"Always the sojourn means imprisonment,

1489 *MS* Making endeavour useless: thus it fell.   *1868 1872* Mannaia   1490 *MS*
flight;   1491 *MS* Convertites: *Yale 1* nuns>nuns: *1868 1872* nuns:
1492 *MS* being as it was for   1493 *MS* imprisonment,   1494 *MS* gained to
1495 *MS* charge—   1496 *MS* fare   1497 *MS* {beginning of fo. 166}
MS preachings—   1498 *MS* So Paolo   1499 *MS* when—what's   *MS* this?
1500 *MS 1868 1872* Convent's   1501 *MS* on the wane   1502 *MS* to
carry on her cure   1505 *MS* Which   *MS* {no comma}   1506 *MS*
whose   1507 *MS* Villa   *MS* Way   1508 *MS* {no comma}   1509 *MS*
guardians..oh,   1510–14 *MS* {no quotation marks at beginnings of lines}
1511 *MS* load: and   1512 *MS* Convent,

1489 *mannaia*: cf. i. 1328 and SS 19.
1498 *doit by doit*: coin by coin; cf. l. 499 n.
1500 *bland*: smooth, fair-seeming.

"*Domus pro carcere*—nowise we relax,
"Nothing abate: how answers Paolo?"   1515
                              You,
What would you answer? All so smooth and fair,
Even Paul's astuteness sniffed no harm i' the world.
He authorized the transfer, saw it made
And, two months after, reaped the fruit of the same,
Having to sit down, rack his brain and find   1521
What phrase should serve him best to notify
Our Guido that by happy providence
A son and heir, a babe was born to him
I' the villa,—go tell sympathizing friends!   1525
Yes, such had been Pompilia's privilege:
She, when she fled, was one month gone with child,
Known to herself or unknown, either way
Availing to explain (say men of art)
The strange and passionate precipitance   1530
Of maiden startled into motherhood
Which changes body and soul by nature's law.
So when the she-dove breeds, strange yearnings come
For the unknown shelter by undreamed-of shores,
And there is born a blood-pulse in her heart   1535
To fight if needs be, though with flap of wing,
For the wool-flock or the fur-tuft, though a hawk
Contest the prize,—wherefore, she knows not yet.
Anyhow, thus to Guido came the news.

1514 *1868 1872* "Domum   MS no wise   MS {no comma}   1515 MS {no
quotation marks}   1517 MS All's   MS fair: 1518 MS in   1519 *1868*
1872 authorised   1520 MS deed,   1521 MS to find   1522 MS and notify
1523 MS To   1524 MS {beginning of fo. 167}   1525 MS In the
Villa,—   1529 MS explain,   MS art,   1531 MS the maiden   MS
motherhood,   1532 MS Who   1533 MS {no comma}   1534 MS
undreamed of   MS {no comma}   1535 MS bloodpulse   1536 MS {no
commas}   1537 MS the hawk   1538 MS though why she

1514 *Domus pro carcere*: cf. II. 1342 n.
1529 *men of art*: cf. above, l. 41.
1530 *precipitance*: headlong flight.
1537 *wool-flock*: piece of rough wool.

"I shall have quitted Rome ere you arrive   1540
"To take the one step left,"—wrote Paolo.
Then did the winch o' the winepress of all hate,
Vanity, disappointment, grudge and greed,
Take the last turn that screws out pure revenge
With a bright bubble at the brim beside—   1545
By an heir's birth he was assured at once
O' the main prize, all the money in dispute:
Pompilia's dowry might revert to her
Or stay with him as law's caprice should point,—
But now—now—what was Pietro's shall be hers,   1550
What was hers shall remain her own,—if hers,
Why then,—oh, not her husband's but—her heir's!
That heir being his too, all grew his at last
By this road or by that road, since they join.
Before, why, push he Pietro out o' the world,—   1555
The current of the money stopped, you see,
Pompilia being proved no Pietro's child:
Or let it be Pompilia's life he quenched,
Again the current of the money stopped,—
Guido debarred his rights as husband soon,   1560
So the new process threatened;—now, the chance,
Now, the resplendent minute! Clear the earth,
Cleanse the house, let the three but disappear
A child remains, depositary of all,

1540 *MS* I   *MS* left   *MS* can arrive   1541 *MS* {line added later}   *MS*
{no quotation mark at beginning of line}   *MS* open"—quoth   1542 *MS*
of   1545 *Yale 2* beside—>beside.   1547 *MS* Of   1549 *MS* might
be,—   *Yale 1* might>should   1550 *MS* now—see,—   *MS* hers
1552 *MS* {beginning of fo. 168}   *MS* husband's! but—her heir's—   1553 *MS*
Her   *MS* his,—yes,   1555 *MS* but Pietro out of 1557 *MS* no more his
child: 1558 *MS* you>was   1560 *MS* den>debarred   *MS* {no comma}
1561 *MS* oh, the chance,   1562 *MS* Oh the   1564 *MS* The

   1542 *winch*: lever (by which the screw of the winepress is turned).
   1546–69 *heir's birth . . . baptize*: the speaker follows and expands a passage in Bottini's
argument: OYB clxxxiv (189). The lawyer asks himself the question: why did Guido
postpone his vengeance from 12 Oct. 1697—when Pompilia left the convent and went
to the Comparini's home—until 2 Jan. 1698? He answers: 'Guido was waiting for her
confinement, which took place on 18 December, so that he could make safe the
succession to the property, for which he was eagerly gaping.'

That Guido may enjoy his own again,   1565
Repair all losses by a master-stroke,
Wipe out the past, all done all left undone,
Swell the good present to best evermore,
Die into new life, which let blood baptize!

So, i' the blue of a sudden sulphur-blaze,   1570
Both why there was one step to take at Rome,
And why he should not meet with Paolo there,
He saw—the ins and outs to the heart of hell—
And took the straight line thither swift and sure.
He rushed to Vittiano, found four sons o' the soil,   1575
Brutes of his breeding, with one spark i' the clod
That served for a soul, the looking up to him
Or aught called Franceschini as life, death,
Heaven, hell,—lord paramount, assembled these,
Harangued, equipped, instructed, pressed each clod
With his will's imprint; then took horse, plied spur,
And so arrived, all five of them, at Rome   1582
On Christmas-Eve, and forthwith found themselves
Installed i' the vacancy and solitude
Left them by Paolo, the considerate man   1585
Who, good as his word, had disappeared at once
As if to leave the stage free. A whole week

1565 *MS* So   *MS* shall   *MS 1868 1872* again!   1566 *MS* master-
stroke—   1567 *MS 1868 1872* and left   1568 *MS* Make>Swell   *MS*
into evermore,   1569 *MS* baptise!   1570 *MS* in   *MS* {no commas}
1571-3 *MS* {these lines originally in the order 1573, 1571, 1572 and the new order
indicated by numbers written in the left-hand margin}   1571 *MS 1868 1872* And
1573 *MS* saw the   1575 *MS* the Villa,   *MS* of the soil   1576 *MS* in
1577 *MS* To serve   1578 *MS* {beginning of fo. 169}   1580 *MS* the clod
1581 *MS* horse with them,   1583 *MS* Christmas Eve   1584 *MS* in
1585 *MS* man,   1586 *1868 1872* word, disappeared

   1570 *sulphur-blaze*: Guido's enlightenment about his plan is imaged in a flash of
hellish light, not clear illumination. Sulphur (or brimstone) is associated with the devil
and hell-fire.
   1584-5 *solitude / Left them by Paolo*: from SS 10: 'they stayed near Ponte Milvio
[about two miles north of Rome] in a villa belonging to his brother. Here Guido and
his accomplices hid, waiting for the best opportunity to carry out their plan.'

Did Guido spend in study of his part,
Then played it fearless of a failure. One,
Struck the year's clock whereof the hours are days,   1590
And off was rung o' the little wheels the chime
"Good will on earth and peace to man:" but, two,
Proceeded the same bell and, evening come,
The dreadful five felt finger-wise their way
Across the town by blind cuts and black turns   1595
To the little lone suburban villa; knocked—
"Who may be outside?" called a well-known voice.
"A friend of Caponsacchi's bringing friends
"A letter."
              That's a test, the excusers say:
Ay, and a test conclusive, I return.   1600
What? Had that name brought touch of guilt or taste
Of fear with it, aught to dash the present joy
With memory of the sorrow just at end,—
She, happy in her parents' arms at length
With the new blessing of the two weeks' babe,—   1605
How had that name's announcement moved the wife?
Or, as the other slanders circulate,
Were Caponsacchi no rare visitant
On nights and days whither safe harbour lured,

1588 *MS* {no comma}   1589 *Yale 2* One,>One—   1590 *MS* {no comma}
1591 *MS* on   1592 *MS* earth, peace>earth and peace   *MS* Two   *Yale 2*
two,>two—   1594 *MS* Five   1597 *MS* voice,   1598 *MS* bringing
you   1599 *MS* {no quotation mark at beginning of line}   *MS* excuser's
1600 *MS* reply.   1601 *MS* and taste   1603 *MS* With menace   *MS* end,
Yale 1 end,>end,—   1604 *MS* {beginning of fo. 170}   *MS* last   1605 *MS*
babe,   *Yale 1* babe,>babe,—   1606 *MS* house?   1607 *MS* circulate,—   *Yale 1* circulate,—>circulate,   1609 *MS* Of   *MS* where stealthy
harbour was,

1592 *two*: i.e. 2 January.

1594 *felt finger-wise*: i.e. felt their way with their fingers in the dark; but also the
gothic image of Guido and his four accomplices as making up the five fingers of a hand
which feels its way across the dark city.

1595 *blind cuts*: hidden short cuts.

black turns: dark corners. Cf. 'He "knew the city", as we say, of yore, / And for
short cuts and turns, was nobody knew more': Keats, 'The Cap and Bells', 206–7.

What bait had been i' the name to ope the door?   1610
The promise of a letter? Stealthy guests
Have secret watchwords, private entrances:
The man's own self might have been found inside
And all the scheme made frustrate by a word.
No: but since Guido knew, none knew so well,   1615
The man had never since returned to Rome
Nor seen the wife's face more than villa's front,
So, could not be at hand to warn or save,—
For that, he took this sure way to the end.

"Come in," bade poor Violante cheerfully,   1620
Drawing the door-bolt: that death was the first,
Stabbed through and through. Pietro, close on her heels,
Set up a cry—"Let me confess myself!
"Grant but confession!" Cold steel was the grant.
Then came Pompilia's turn.   1625
                              Then they escaped.
The noise o' the slaughter roused the neighbourhood.
They had forgotten just the one thing more
Which saves i' the circumstance, the ticket to-wit
Which puts post-horses at a traveller's use: 1630
So, all on foot, desperate through the dark
Reeled they like drunkards along open road,
Accomplished a prodigious twenty miles
Homeward, and gained Baccano very near,
Stumbled at last, deaf, dumb, blind through the feat,   1635
Into a grange and, one dead heap, slept there

1610 *MS* in   *MS* door,   1613 *MS* The man might well have been found safe
inside   1617 *MS* the villa's   1618 *MS* And could   *Yale 1* So could>So,
could   *MS* save,   1619 *MS* end—   1620 *MS* in" quoth Violante   *Yale
1* ^poor^   1621 *MS* ^the^   *MS* her   1624 *MS* {no quotation mark at
beginning of line}   1627 {not found in *MS*}   1629 *MS* in   *MS* Ticket
1632 *MS* {beginning of fo. 171}   *MS* the open   *MS* {no comma}   1634 *MS*
Arezzo-ward, reached Baccano in very deed,   *MS* R>Arezzo-ward   1635 *MS*
dumb, blind, dead through their   1636 *MS* and slept there in a heap

1629 *to-wit*: namely.
1634 *Baccano*: a village on the road north from Rome, on the route to Arezzo.

Till the pursuers hard upon their trace
Reached them and took them, red from head to heel,
And brought them to the prison where they lie.
The couple were laid i' the church two days ago,   1640
And the wife lives yet by miracle.

                            All is told.
You hardly need ask what Count Guido says,
Since something he must say. "I own the deed—"
(He cannot choose,—but—) "I declare the same   1645
"Just and inevitable,—since no way else
"Was left me, but by this of taking life,
"To save my honour which is more than life.
"I exercised a husband's rights." To which
The answer is as prompt—"There was no fault   1650
"In any one o' the three to punish thus:
"Neither i' the wife, who kept all faith to you,
"Nor in the parents, whom yourself first duped,
"Robbed and maltreated, then turned out of doors.
"You wronged and they endured wrong; yours the fault.
"Next, had endurance overpassed the mark   1656
"And turned resentment needing remedy,—
"Nay, put the absurd impossible case, for once—
"You were all blameless of the blame alleged
"And they blameworthy where you fix all blame,   1660
"Still, why this violation of the law?

1638 *MS* them red   1640 *MS* Couple   *MS* in   *MS* Church   1641 *MS*
by a miracle.   1642 *MS* {no new paragraph}   1643 *MS* to ask what
Guido   1644 *MS* avow   1645 *MS* but, he goes on to say)   1647–
9 *MS* {no quotation marks at beginnings of lines}   1647 *MS* but by this taking
life away   *MS* [ ]>by   *Yale 1* me but [ ] by this of taking life [ ]>me, but by this
of taking life,   1649 *MS* rights, no more."   1651–72 *MS* {no quotation
marks at beginnings of lines}   1651 *MS* of the Three   1652 *MS* in   *Yale 1*
in>i'   1653 *MS* you first duped, then   1654 *MS* doors,   1655 *MS*
they resented;   *Yale 1* ^they^   1656 *MS* resentment   1657 *MS* to wrong
which needed   1658 *MS* absurd and impossible   1659 *MS* blamless>
blameless   1660 *MS* {beginning of fo. 172}   *MS* all blameworthy   *MS* fix
blame,

"Yourself elected law should take its course,
"Avenge wrong, or show vengeance not your right;
"Why, only when the balance in law's hand
"Trembles against you and inclines the way   1665
"O' the other party, do you make protest,
"Renounce arbitrament, flying out of court,
"And crying 'Honour's hurt the sword must cure'?
"Aha, and so i' the middle of each suit
"Trying i' the courts,—and you had three in play   1670
"With an appeal to the Pope's self beside,—
"What, you may chop and change and right your wrongs
"Leaving the law to lag as she thinks fit?"

That were too temptingly commodious, Count!
One would have still a remedy in reserve   1675
Should reach the safest oldest sinner, you see!
One's honour forsooth? Does that take hurt alone
From the extreme outrage? I who have no wife,
Being yet sensitive in my degree
As Guido,—must discover hurt elsewhere   1680
Which, half compounded-for in days gone by,
May profitably break out now afresh,
Need cure from my own expeditious hands.

1663 MS you or   MS due;   1664 MS And only   1665 MS you,—
when it   1666 MS Of your wife and her parents,   1667 MS the arbitrament, take the opposite course,   1668 MS And cry that honour's hurt's past cure
of law.   1868 cure?'   1669 MS Ha ha,   MS in   1670 MS in the
Courts,—   1672 MS change, and right yourself   1673 MS {no quotation
marks}   MS to do   1674 MS {no new paragraph}   1676 MS see:
1679 MS as sensitive   1680 MS some hurt   1681 MS half-compounded
for   1682 MS all afresh,

1663 *or . . . right*: or show you have no right to vengeance.
1673 *lag*: fall behind.
1674 *commodious*: convenient, spacious (in a fig. sense). Other Half-Rome argues
that Guido cannot both use the process of law and, when convenient, his claim to
honour and passion.
1676 *safest oldest sinner*: i.e. one whose sin was committed very long ago (not a
hardened, inveterate sinner): Cook, 71. As appears from ll. 1684–90, Other Half-
Rome intends a teasing reference to his listener.

The lie that was, as it were, imputed me
When you objected to my contract's clause,—   1685
The theft as good as, one may say, alleged,
When you, co-heir in a will, excepted, Sir,
To my administration of effects,
—Aha, do you think law disposed of these?
My honour's touched and shall deal death around!
Count, that were too commodious, I repeat!   1691
If any law be imperative on us all,
Of all are you the enemy: out with you
From the common light and air and life of man!

1684 *MS* to me   1687 *MS* {beginning of fo. 172ᵛ}   *MS* When my coheirs
excepted in a sort   1689 *MS* the law   1690 *MS* all round!   1691 *MS*
repeat.   1692 *MS* is   *MS* {no comma}

1684–90 *The . . . around!*: this reveals Other Half-Rome's genial nature and the
situation of the monologue. He and his listener are old friends who have quarrelled
over business and legal matters in the past. Other Half-Rome argues that Guido's plea
of injured honour is a convenience; he himself could dredge the past, and see his old
quarrels as involving insults to his honour made by his listener. He is not, like Guido,
suddenly going to resort to violence and kill his listener. The talk of business matters
here suddenly evokes Other Half-Rome's workaday world, the ordinary rhythms of
which his imagination has hardly left behind: see Introduction above.

INTRODUCTION TO BOOK IV

TERTIUM QUID

AFTER the angry tones of Book II, and the pathos of Book III, Book IV lifts us into comedy. The speaker of the monologue is 'Tertium Quid' (L.), literally 'a third thing', 'a third somewhat', a phrase meaning 'Something (indefinite or left undefined) related in some way to two (definite or known) things, but distinct from both': OED[2]. The Latin phrase was a common enough tag in English; so, for example, here is an instance of its use from the Brownings' correspondence: 'One day he [Voltaire] had on his table some liquor, & the fancy entered his head to mix *that* with the coffee, & so make a tertium quid better than either'.[1] The phrase has resonances from alchemy and chemistry; so OED[2] gives: '*Tertium Quid*, (among Chymists) the Result of the Mixture of some two Things, which forms something very different from both' (1724). The speaker of this monologue is a mixture of Half-Rome and Other Half-Rome, a person who has his own unique character and viewpoint on the murder-case. Sometimes pro-Guido and sometimes anti-Guido, he is a representative of a different class of society from the previous two speakers.

The balancing act that Tertium Quid represents—first giving an argument that endorses Guido's view of things, then giving a counter-argument that supports Pompilia and Caponsacchi's—leads us, with the previous two Books still in our minds, into a final carnivalesque confusion of argument. In the face of it, we may overemphasize the farcical nature of the monologue. In Book I, where we are introduced to this monologue's setting and context, we see Tertium Quid standing in a fashionable Roman salon, amidst candlelight and girandoles, surrounded by the upper echelons of church and state (1. 910–42). He has a magnificent wig, a grand solitaire, and an imposing front of 'lace-work and brocade', a 'flow of frill' (1. 929–30). Yet this is a brief and necessarily caricatural depiction, and the character we actually hear speaking is more complicated. As in the previous two dramatic monologues, we are presented with a view of the murder-case that reflects the presuppositions of a

---

[1] Vernon Lushington to EBB, 9 Nov. 1860: 'Some Unpublished Papers of Robert and Elizabeth Barrett Browning', ed. George S. Hellman, *Harper's Monthly*, Mar. 1916, 530–9.

distinct personality, the interrelations between intellectual judgement and moral character, a mind reflected in a whole style and manner of speech. It would be a mistake to think that this can be easily summarized.

Park Honan remarks on Tertium Quid's excessive use of phonetic, verbal, and syntactical parallels by which he enacts for his audience 'the neat and discriminating balance of his mind'.[2] There is also, from the first, a hauteur in his manner, a relaxed grandeur of phrase. He speaks on or about 5 January 1698: Pompilia is still on her deathbed, but he has had time since the murders to develop what he believes is a more complicated and adequate view of things than the undiscriminating 'rabble'. Distinctions of class are important to him: he is either an aristocrat, or more likely a person living on the favour of the aristocracy, and his monologue's aim is to win for himself more social favour by giving a witty and discerning account of the rights and wrongs of the situation. In the salon, he has drawn two listeners, a Duke ('Excellency') and a Prince ('Highness'), to a window-seat by the side of the card-tables. At l. 57 they are joined briefly by a Marquis. At a nearby card-table a Cardinal listens (ll. 55, 1414, 1485); we are probably meant to conclude that this is the Cardinal who used to be Guido's patron.[3] As the monologue proceeds, the surrounding salon is kept in view with hints of the card-playing, the beautiful aristocratic women, their jewellery, their fashionable 'patches' and pomanders. This setting goes hand in hand with Tertium Quid's concern with matters of social class, his incisive knowledge of the world of his social inferiors, and his large contrast between social and intellectual refinement on the one hand, and the coarseness of 'cits', the 'mob', and 'burgesses' on the other.

Refinement is a keynote of his speech. When he uses an analogy derived from cookery he feels he should almost apologize to his listeners for introducing subject-matter from a relatively vulgar realm (541–6). It is not just that he opposes aristocratic 'old blood thrice-refined' to 'clownish coarseness' (758–9), he is alert to gradations—to the position, for example, of 'a burgess nearly an aristocrat' (344). His display of sophisticated worldliness is one that knows about the seedier side of Roman life: the kind of house where a prostitute lives (150–64), for example, and the character of a priest's ex-mistress now set up as a dealer in wigs (440–51). He has a relish for society gossip (872–97). He is sceptical of the possibilities of human goodness, and, in an anticipation of the age of Voltaire,

[2] Park Honan, *Browning's Characters: A Study in Poetic Technique* (New Haven and London, 1961), 278–9.
[3] See II. 152–7.

he thinks, privately, that religion is absurd. In this regard, we may note, for instance, his delight in a kind of glib sophistical argument: if Violante, by lying, saved Pompilia, the prostitute's child, from a life of prostitution, and so saved her from Hell, then surely Violante's lies were actually good things—'the sin has saved a soul' (255)? At one point he comments caustically that Pompilia's dying prayer for confession was 'about the single prayer / She ever put up, that was granted her' (1431–2). He thinks it an ironic cut at Providence that the good leader of the police, Patrizi, died from a fever after giving chase to the murderers, while the murderers themselves are still alive (1405–14). 'Truth' is a mirage, something believed in, perhaps, by the lower orders, but not something that should concern someone at his critical level of thought. The climax of his monologue, the 'reduction *ad absurdum*' about the use of torture (1621–31), is an epitome of the nature of his speech.

Though we can sense in Browning's depiction of Tertium Quid his love of Molière and Sheridan, and perhaps, in the acute treatment of class, his love of Balzac, we should also acknowledge the play of liberal political sympathies that grounds it. Tertium Quid's reading of the murder-case is compromised by his adherence to the hierarchy of the seventeenth-century social order. It is his commitment to the élite, how he understands his own identity in relation to power and influence, that contributes to rendering his mind impervious to the emotion and empathy that would allow him to understand events. He attunes reality to his own ends, to a kind of sceptical play of the mind. The monologue closes on a note of selfish disgust as he observes that his ingenious arguments have failed to win him any favours. What Sullivan calls his 'ostentatious impartiality'[4] is the embodiment of a worldliness which, frozen and hard in its range of sympathy, cuts him off from wider psychological and emotional views.

[4] Sullivan, 67.

IV.

TERTIUM QUID.

TRUE, Excellency—as his Highness says,
Though she's not dead yet, she's as good as stretched
Symmetrical beside the other two;
Though he's not judged yet, he's the same as judged,
So do the facts abound and superabound: 5
And nothing hinders that we lift the case
Out of the shade into the shine, allow
Qualified persons to pronounce at last,
Nay, edge in an authoritative word
Between this rabble's-brabble of dolts and fools   10
Who make up reasonless unreasoning Rome.
"Now for the Trial!" they roar: "the Trial to test
"The truth, weigh husband and weigh wife alike
"I' the scales of law, make one scale kick the beam!"
Law's a machine from which, to please the mob,   15
Truth the divinity must needs descend
And clear things at the play's fifth act—aha!
Hammer into their noddles who was who

---

1 MS {beginning of fo. 173. At the head of the page is the title '4. Tertium Quid.' in
RB's hand}   2 MS {no comma}   3 MS two,   4 MS {no commas}
5 MS superabound,   6 MS hinders now we   Yale 1 hinders now we>hinders,
now, we   1868 hinders, now, we   10 MS rabble's brabble   13–14 MS {no
quotation marks at beginnings of lines}   14 MS In   MS Law,   15 MS
the>a   17 MS aha,   21–30 MS {no quotation marks at beginnings of lines}

10 *brabble*: discordant, confused noise.

15 *machine*: the μηχανή ('machine') of the Greek theatre. At the end of some
Greek plays, when the action has become so complicated that only divine intervention
can untangle it, a god is lowered by machine, as it were from heaven, to 'clear things'.
Similar effects occur in seventeenth-century masques and plays, as in *As You Like It*.
The complexities of the murder-case may call for the descent of 'Truth the divinity' to
sort everything out, but the speaker thinks Law an incompetent machine for introducing it.

18 *noddles*: heads (colloquial).

And what was what. I tell the simpletons
"Could law be competent to such a feat   20
" 'Twere done already: what begins next week
"Is end o' the Trial, last link of a chain
"Whereof the first was forged three years ago
"When law addressed herself to set wrong right,
"And proved so slow in taking the first step   25
"That ever some new grievance,—tort, retort,
"On one or the other side,—o'ertook i' the game,
"Retarded sentence, till this deed of death
"Is thrown in, as it were, last bale to boat
"Crammed to the edge with cargo—or passengers?   30
" '*Trecentos inseris: ohe, jam satis est!*
" '*Huc appelle!*'—passengers, the word must be."
Long since, the boat was loaded to my eyes.
To hear the rabble and brabble, you'd call the case
Fused and confused past human finding out.   35
One calls the square round, t'other the round square—
And pardonably in that first surprise
O' the blood that fell and splashed the diagram:
But now we've used our eyes to the violent hue
Can't we look through the crimson and trace lines?   40

---

22 *MS* the end of a trial,   24 *MS* {no comma}   27 *MS* and   *MS* in
28 *MS* {beginning of fo. 174}   *MS* the death   30 *MS* passengers: 31 *MS*
"*Trecentos*   32 *MS* {no quotation mark at beginning of line}   *MS*
appelle!"—   *MS* be: 33 *MS* {no comma}   38 *MS* Of   *MS* diagram

26 *tort, retort*: action, counter-action. 'Retort' (a quick-witted or incisive reply) is
here a pun on the legal term 'tort' (literally 'wrong'), the breach of a duty imposed by
law whereby someone acquires a right of action for damages.

27 *o'ertook i' the game*: overtook her [Law] in the game. Law is so slow in taking her
course, that she is continually overtaken by different new grievances (the related
lawsuits), so that she never reaches the end (a definitive sentence).

31–2 *Trecentos . . . appelle*: 'You're cramming hundreds in: whoa, that's enough!
Bring her over here': Horace, *Satires*, I. v. 12–13. In Horace these are the cries of
passengers' slaves and boatmen as the passengers crowd on board the barges for the trip
across the Pomptine marshes. This self-consciously witty allusion by Tertium Quid
shows his love of 'silvery and selectest phrase': I. 933.

34 *rabble and brabble*: the mob and their confused noise; cf. l. 10 above.

39 *used*: accustomed.

It makes a man despair of history,
Eusebius and the established fact—fig's end!
Oh, give the fools their Trial, rattle away
With the leash of lawyers, two on either side—
One barks, one bites,—Masters Arcangeli   45
And Spreti,—that's the husband's ultimate hope
Against the Fisc and the other kind of Fisc,
Bound to do barking for the wife: bow—wow!
Why, Excellency, we and his Highness here
Would settle the matter as sufficiently   50
As ever will Advocate This and Fiscal That
And Judge the Other, with even—a word and a wink—
We well know who for ultimate arbiter.
Let us beware o' the basset-table—lest
We jog the elbow of Her Eminence,   55

---

43 *MS* trial,   46 *MS* Husband's   47 *MS* {no comma}   52 *MS*
even, a word in your ear,   53 *MS* Who   54 *MS* of   55 *MS* {begin-
ning of fo. 175}   *MS* His   *MS* {no comma}

---

42 *Eusebius*: (*c.* AD 264–349), the historian of early Christianity, cited here as a
synonym for 'history' and 'established fact' because of his careful documentation.

43 *rattle away*: talk rapidly and thoughtlessly. Cf. 'Vargrave thus rattled away in
order to give the good banker to understand that his affairs were in the most flourishing condition': Edward Bulwer-Lytton, *Alice* (1838), bk. vi, ch. 4. 'Rattle' also takes up
its senses of 'move fast', and 'beat up or chase vigorously', as in hunting: the lawyers are
pairs of hunting dogs yapping after the truth (the prey): OED² v.¹ 4 and 8.b.

53 *ultimate arbiter*: probably not the main judge or the pope, but someone who
influences even them, perhaps some influential society lady or mistress: hence 'a word
and a wink'.

54 *basset*: card game played between a banker and punters: 'Look upon Bassette,
you who reason boast, / And see if Reason may not there be lost!': Lady Mary Wortley
Montagu, 'Eclogues: Thursday', 86–7. A remark by Seymour Kirkup suggests that at
one point Browning may have intended gambling to play a larger part in the poem: see
Seymour Kirkup to William Rossetti, 18 Sept. 1868: 'Another book of his [Pietro
Aretino's] is a dialogue on Cards, in which some excellent stories of gamesters
are introduced. I sent some of them lately to R. Browning, who is writing a
poem relating to Arezzo in which gambling will make a great figure': *Rossetti Papers*,
367–8.

55 *Her Eminence*: the Cardinal: see Introduction above. 'Her' is a displaced allusion
to the Italian idiom whereby a title used periphrastically of its bearer takes third-person
feminine pronouns, referring not to the person but to the abstraction, Majesty,
Eminence, etc. The use of the idiom suggests Tertium Quid's self-conscious refinement and sycophancy. Landor exploits the comedy of the idiom in a similar way at the

Jostle his cards,—he'll rap you out a . . . st!
By the window-seat! And here's the Marquis too!
Indulge me but a moment: if I fail
—Favoured with such an audience, understand!—
To set things right, why, class me with the mob   60
As understander of the mind of man!

The mob,—now, that's just how the error comes!
Bethink you that you have to deal with *plebs*,
The commonalty; this is an episode
In burgess-life,—why seek to aggrandize,   65
Idealize, denaturalize the class?
People talk just as if they had to do
With a noble pair that . . . Excellency, your ear!
Stoop to me, Highness,—listen and look yourselves!

This Pietro, this Violante, live their life   70
At Rome in the easy way that's far from worst
Even for their betters,—themselves love themselves,
Spend their own oil in feeding their own lamp
That their own faces may grow bright thereby.
They get to fifty and over: how's the lamp?   75

56 *MS* a . . st!   57 *MS* window-seat: and   59 *MS* {line added later}
MS understand—   60 *MS* why class   62 *MS* now that's   63 *MS*
do   65 *MS* aggrandize   66 *MS* And idealize,>Idealize   68 *MS*
that . .   69 *MS* with me,   ★70 *MS 1868 1872* {new paragraph. Paragraphing obscured in *1888* and *1889* by this line's being at the head of the page}   *MS*
Pietro, and>This Pietro,   *MS* Violante live   74 *MS* thereby,—   *MS*
{between 74 and 75 deleted line: Means—plentiful for two, and none to spare.—

beginning of 'The Cardinal-Legate Albani and Picture-Dealers': 'scampa. Your
Eminence may dispose of me purely at Her pleasure. . . . corazza. I kiss the sacred
hem of Her purple, humbly inclining myself': *The Complete Works of Walter Savage
Landor*, ed. T. Earle Welby (16 vols., 1927–36), iii. 248.

56 *rap you out a* . . . : utter sharply or suddenly [an oath or swear-word].

65 *burgess-life*: common, middle-class life. Tertium Quid uses 'burgess' and 'commonalty' interchangeably.

68 *noble pair*: aristocratic couple. Breaking off his sentence and inviting confidential
talk, Tertium Quid perhaps hints that some such couple, present in the salon as he
speaks, may be the protagonists of a similarly illicit story.

Full to the depth o' the wick,—moneys so much;
And also with a remnant,—so much more
Of moneys,—which there's no consuming now,
But, when the wick shall moulder out some day,
Failing fresh twist of tow to use up dregs,   80
Will lie a prize for the passer-by,—to-wit
Anyone that can prove himself the heir,
Seeing, the couple are wanting in a child:
Meantime their wick swims in the safe broad bowl
O' the middle rank,—not raised a beacon's height   85
For wind to ravage, nor dropped till lamp graze ground
Like cresset, mudlarks poke now here now there,
Going their rounds to probe the ruts i' the road
Or fish the luck o' the puddle. Pietro's soul
Was satisfied when cronies smirked, "No wine   90
"Like Pietro's, and he drinks it every day!"
His wife's heart swelled her boddice, joyed its fill
When neighbours turned heads wistfully at church,
Sighed at the load of lace that came to pray.
Well, having got through fifty years of flare,   95
They burn out so, indulge so their dear selves,
That Pietro finds himself in debt at last,

---

76 *MS* of   *MS* of   *MS* monies   *Yale 1* monies>moneys   77 *MS*
And>But   78 *MS* monies,—   *Yale 1* monies,—>moneys,—   *MS* now
79 *MS* But when   80 *MS* {beginning of fo. 176}   *MS* a fresh twist to use
up the   81 *MS* to-whit   82 *MS* {no comma}   83 *MS* {no comma}
84 *MS* they both are set   85 *MS* Of   86 *MS* the wind   *MS* swung till
they   *1868 1872* swung   87 *MS* As the watchman's cresset he pokes here and
there   *1868 1872* As watchman's cresset, he pokes here and there,   88 *MS*
1868 1872 his   *MS* in   89 *MS* take   *MS* of   90 *MS* friends exclaimed
1868 1872 crony   91 *MS* {no quotation mark at beginning of line}   93 *MS*
goss>neighbours   *MS* mass   95 *MS* this way,

76 *Full . . . wick*: i.e. there is more than enough oil (money) to burn while the wick
(their life) lasts.
80 *tow*: fibre (of the wick).
87 *cresset*: small, portable iron lamp (filled with oil).
    mudlarks: street urchins. The change from *1868*'s 'watchman' makes more vivid the
opposition between high and low: the high 'beacon' of the upper class, as opposed to
the mudlarks using a lamp to scavenge in the dirt for food.

As he were any lordling of us all:
And, now that dark begins to creep on day,
Creditors grow uneasy, talk aside,   100
Take counsel, then importune all at once.
For if the good fat rosy careless man,
Who has not laid a ducat by, decease—
Let the lamp fall, no heir at hand to catch—
Why, being childless, there's a spilth i' the street   105
O' the remnant, there's a scramble for the dregs
By the stranger: so, they grant him no long day
But come in a body, clamour to be paid.

What's his resource? He asks and straight obtains
The customary largess, dole dealt out   110
To, what we call our "poor dear shame-faced ones,"
In secret once a month to spare the shame
O' the slothful and the spendthrift,—pauper-saints
The Pope puts meat i' the mouth of, ravens they,
And providence he—just what the mob admires!   115
That is, instead of putting a prompt foot
On selfish worthless human slugs whose slime
Has failed to lubricate their path in life,

99 MS And as the   1868 1872 for the   MS {no commas}   100 MS The
creditors   MS aside   101 MS once—   102 MS easy>rosy   104 {not
found in MS}   105 MS spilth at once   106 MS Of   107 MS By
strangers: MS {no comma}   108 MS {beginning of fo. 177}   109 MS
{no new paragraph}   111 {not found in MS}   113 MS Of   MS
improvident>the spendthrift,—   MS burgesses   114 MS in the mouths
of—   117 MS the selfish,   MS slug   118 MS Had   MS his

105 spilth: spillage.
110 customary largess: suggested by OYB cxli (145): 'And, after making a statement
of his property, [Pietro] received secret alms each month from the Papal Palace.'
111 "poor dear shame-faced ones": from It. poveri vergognosi, ashamed poor. There were
endowments throughout Italy for the relief of such people, some of good birth or
previous wealth, who had fallen on hard times. George Eliot, in Romola (1863), which
Browning read in the year it was published, describes the founding of a religious
society to help poveri vergognosi, which she glosses as 'paupers of good family': bk. I, ch.
v., n. 1.
114–15 ravens . . . he: Ps. 147: 9; Job 38: 41.

Why, the Pope picks the first ripe fruit that falls
And gracious puts it in the vermin's way.   120
Pietro could never save a dollar? Straight
He must be subsidized at our expense:
And for his wife—the harmless household sheep
One ought not to see harassed in her age—
Judge, by the way she bore adversity,   125
O' the patient nature you ask pity for!
How long, now, would the roughest marketman,
Handling the creatures huddled to the knife,
Harass a mutton ere she made a mouth
Or menaced biting? Yet the poor sheep here,   130
Violante, the old innocent burgess-wife,
In her first difficulty showed great teeth
Fit to crunch up and swallow a good round crime.
She meditates the tenure of the Trust,
Fidei commissum is the lawyer-phrase,   135
These funds that only want an heir to take—
Goes o'er the gamut o' the creditor's cry
By semitones from whine to snarl high up
And growl down low, one scale in sundry keys,—
Pauses with a little compunction for the face   140
Of Pietro frustrate of its ancient cheer,—
Never a bottle now for friend at need,—
Comes to a stop on her own frittered lace
And neighbourly condolences thereat,
Then makes her mind up, sees the thing to do: 145

121 {not found in *MS*}   122 *MS* expence   124 *MS* harmed   *MS* old
days—   126 *MS* Of   *MS* for: 127 *MS* should you say,   128 *MS*
in distress,   131 *MS* Pompilia, {a *lapsus calami*}   133 *MS* sin.   135
{not found in *MS*}   137 *MS* of   138 *MS* {beginning of fo. 178}
140 *MS* [ ]>for   142 {not found in *MS*}   145 *MS* And   *MS* up as
to   *MS* do—

127–30 *How...biting?*: unlike innocent sheep, who are patient even when roughly
handled and near to slaughter, Violante is quick to 'bite', i.e. tell lies and fight her fate.
135 *Fidei commissum*: a Roman legal phrase, 'entrusted to faith' (L.), referring to
property entrusted to one legatee to be transferred to another. Cf. SS 1 and nn.
143 *frittered*: broken, worn.

And so, deliberate, snaps house-book clasp,
Posts off to vespers, missal beneath arm,
Passes the proper San Lorenzo by,
Dives down a little lane to the left, is lost
In a labyrinth of dwellings best unnamed,   150
Selects a certain blind one, black at base,
Blinking at top,—the sign of we know what,—
One candle in a casement set to wink
Streetward, do service to no shrine inside,—
Mounts thither by the filthy flight of stairs,   155
Holding the cord by the wall, to the tip-top,
Gropes for the door i' the dark, ajar of course,
Raps, opens, enters in: up starts a thing
Naked as needs be—"What, you rogue, 't is you?
"Back,—how can I have taken a farthing yet?   160
"Mercy on me, poor sinner that I am!
"Here's . . . why, I took you for Madonna's self
"With all that sudden swirl of silk i' the place!
"What may your pleasure be, my bonny dame?"
Your Excellency supplies aught left obscure?   165
One of those women that abound in Rome,
Whose needs oblige them eke out one poor trade
By another vile one: her ostensible work
Was washing clothes, out in the open air

---

146 *MS* so deliberately   *MS* shuts>snaps   *1868* deliberately snaps   *MS* missal>
house-book   147 *MS* under   154 *MS* room inside,   155 *MS* {no
comma}   157 *MS* in   *MS* dark ajar   160–4 *MS* {no quotation marks at
beginnings of lines}   161 *MS* am,   162 *MS* Here's ..   163 *MS*
silk sudden in this poor place!   164 *MS* Dame?"   165 *MS* sees what's
left unsaid—   166 *MS* {beginning of fo. 179}   *MS* who   *MS* {no
comma}   167 *MS* to eke   168 *MS* whose ostensible   169 *MS*
{no comma}

---

147 *Posts*: hurries.

152 *sign of we know what*: i.e. a prostitute's sign; a candle in the window of a dark
house (not in the room).

159 *as needs be*: as she has to be (to do her work).

159–64 *"What . . . dame?*: the prostitute at first thinks that Violante is her pimp
returning early, and masks her mistake by flattery, explaining that she thought Violante
was a vision of the Madonna.

At the cistern by Citorio; her true trade—   170
Whispering to idlers, when they stopped and praised
The ankles she let liberally shine
In kneeling at the slab by the fountain-side,
That there was plenty more to criticize
At home, that eve, i' the house where candle blinked
Decorously above, and all was done   176
I' the holy fear of God and cheap beside.
Violante, now, had seen this woman wash,
Noticed and envied her propitious shape,
Tracked her home to her house-top, noted too,   180
And now was come to tempt her and propose
A bargain far more shameful than the first
Which trafficked her virginity away
For a melon and three pauls at twelve years old.
Five minutes' talk with this poor child of Eve,   185
Struck was the bargain, business at an end—
"Then, six months hence, that person whom you trust,
"Comes, fetches whatsoever babe it be;
"I keep the price and secret, you the babe,
"Paying beside for mass to make all straight: 190
"Meantime, I pouch the earnest-money-piece."

Down stairs again goes fumbling by the rope
Violante, triumphing in a flourish of fire

---

170 *MS* By>At   *MS* but was wont   *1868* but true   171 *MS* To whisper
idlers   *MS 1868* {no comma}   172 *MS 1868 1872* ancles   173 *MS* {no
comma}   174 *MS 1868 1872* criticise   175 *MS* evening where the   *MS*
{no commas}   176 *MS* {no comma}   177 *MS* In   178 *MS*
Pompilia,   179 *MS* And noticed her as of   180 *MS* it,   182 *MS*
that first   185 *MS* {no comma}   186 *MS* was at end—   187–8 *MS*
{no quotation marks at beginnings of lines}   187 *MS* cousin   *MS*
trust   188 *MS* Brings it from you to me and takes the price."   189–
91 {not found in *MS*}   192 *MS* {no new paragraph}   193 *MS* {no
comma}

170 *Citorio*: the Piazza di Montecitorio.
184 *three pauls*: a small sum; a *paolo* was a tenth of a papal *scudo*.
191 *earnest-money-piece*: coin that acts as down payment and confirmation (of the
sale of the baby). Cf. II. 192 n.

From her own brain, self-lit by such success,—
Gains church in time for the "*Magnificat*"   195
And gives forth "My reproof is taken away,
"And blessed shall mankind proclaim me now,"
So that the officiating priest turns round
To see who proffers the obstreperous praise:
Then home to Pietro, the enraptured-much   200
But puzzled-more when told the wondrous news—
How orisons and works of charity,
(Beside that pair of pinners and a coif,
Birth-day surprise last Wednesday was five weeks)
Had borne fruit in the autumn of his life,—   205
They, or the Orvieto in a double dose.
Anyhow, she must keep house next six months,
Lie on the settle, avoid the three-legged stool,
And, chiefly, not be crossed in wish or whim,
And the result was like to be an heir.   210

Accordingly, when time was come about,
He found himself the sire indeed of this
Francesca Vittoria Pompilia and the rest
O' the names whereby he sealed her his, next day.

---

196 *MS* {beginning of fo. 180}   *MS* "my   *MS* away"   197 {not found in
MS}   198 *MS* round.   199 {not found in *MS*}   200 *MS* Pietro—
the enraptured much   201 *MS* puzzled more   *MS* news   202 *MS* {no
comma}   203–4 {not found in *MS*}   205 *1868 1872* Autumn   207 *MS*
Anyhow she   208 *MS* three legged   209 *MS* will: 210 {not found
in *MS*}   211 *MS* {no new paragraph}   *MS* Accordingly when   212 *MS*
in very deed   213 *MS* Of Francesca   214 *MS* Of   *MS* they   *MS*
theirs   *MS 1868* {no comma}

196–7 "*My . . . now.* Tertium Quid imagines that Violante, in her excitement, says
the Magnificat wrongly, conflating Luke 1: 25 with the proper words from the
Magnificat, Luke 1: 48. By this she compares herself with St Elizabeth and the Virgin
Mary: the baby she has bought *in utero* is her 'saviour' in a very worldly sense.
  202 *orisons*: prayers.
  203 *pinners and a coif*: two pinned-on flaps, one on each side of a close-fitting head-
cap. Cf. Sir Walter Scott, *The Black Dwarf* (1816), ch. iii: 'the venerable old dame . . .
dressed in her coif and pinners'. The humorous suggestion is that Pietro's kindness to
Violante, as expressed in this well-appreciated birthday-present, has somehow helped
her to become pregnant.
  206 *Orvieto*: 'the lightest and most delicate of Roman wines': *Roba di Roma*, i. 306.

A crime complete in its way is here, I hope?   215
Lies to God, lies to man, every way lies
To nature and civility and the mode:
Flat robbery of the proper heirs thus foiled
O' the due succession,—and, what followed thence,
Robbery of God, through the confessor's ear   220
Debarred the most note-worthy incident
When all else done and undone twelve-month through
Was put in evidence at Easter-time.
All other peccadillos!—but this one
To the priest who comes next day to dine with us?   225
'T were inexpedient; decency forbade.

Is so far clear? You know Violante now,
Compute her capability of crime
By this authentic instance? Black hard cold
Crime like a stone you kick up with your foot   230
I' the middle of a field?

                              I thought as much.
But now, a question,—how long does it lie,
The bad and barren bit of stuff you kick,
Before encroached on and encompassed round   235
With minute moss, weed, wild-flower—made alive
By worm, and fly, and foot of the free bird?
Your Highness,—healthy minds let bygones be,

---

215 *MS* hope: 216 *MS* lies every way   217 *MS* nature, civility and the
natural law: 219 *MS* Of   220 *MS* from God,   221 *MS* Of this
note-worthy incident—reserved   222 *MS* through the year   224 *MS*
peccadillos,—   225 *MS* Priest   226 *MS* inexpedient: 227 *MS*
{beginning of fo. 181}   *MS* the couple now,   228 *MS* their   229 *MS*
Black, hard, cold   230 *MS* Even as   231 *MS* In   *MS* field.   *MS* {no
new paragraph}   234 *MS* That   235 *MS* encompassed quite   237 *MS*
{no commas}   238 *MS* be—

217 *nature . . . mode*: three degrees: ordinary, civilized, and customary behaviour. Cf.
i. 287 n.
223 *put . . . Easter-time*: Violante's 'Easter duty': as a Catholic, Violante is obliged to
make a confession of her sins at least once a year, usually in Lent.
224 *peccadillos*: small or venial sins.

Leave old crimes to grow young and virtuous-like
I' the sun and air; so time treats ugly deeds: 240
They take the natural blessing of all change.
There was the joy o' the husband silly-sooth,
The softening of the wife's old wicked heart,
Virtues to right and left, profusely paid
If so they might compensate the saved sin.   245
And then the sudden existence, dewy-dear,
O' the rose above the dungheap, the pure child
As good as new created, since withdrawn
From the horror of the pre-appointed lot
With the unknown father and the mother known   250
Too well,—some fourteen years of squalid youth,
And then libertinage, disease, the grave—
Hell in life here, hereafter life in hell:
Look at that horror and this soft repose!
Why, moralist, the sin has saved a soul!   255
Then, even the palpable grievance to the heirs—
'Faith, this was no frank setting hand to throat
And robbing a man, but... Excellency, by your leave,
How did you get that marvel of a gem,
The sapphire with the Graces grand and Greek?   260
The story is, stooping to pick a stone
From the pathway through a vineyard—no-man's-land—
To pelt a sparrow with, you chanced on this:

239 *MS* virtuouslike   240 *MS* In   *MS* air: *MS* deeds—   242 *MS* of
244 *MS* To right and left, virtues   245 *MS* the one saved sin.   247 *MS*
Of   248 *MS* if>new   *MS* created—   251 *MS* the fourteen   *MS*
wretched youth,—   252 *MS* libertinage and leprosy,   253 *MS*
Death   *MS* here,—   *MS* hell—   254 *MS* {line added later}   *MS*
Look,   *MS* repose—   256 *MS* {beginning of fo. 182}   *MS* {no comma}
257 *MS* Why,   *Yale 1* Faith,>'Faith,   258 *MS* but..   259 *MS* {no
comma}   260 *MS* god's head   262 *MS* {line added later}   *MS* vineyard not your own

242 *silly-sooth*: innocently naïve, unsuspecting. Cf. iii. 805–6 n.
245 *saved sin*: i.e. the held-back lie. The lie of Pompilia's birth has been 'saved'
(hoarded like money), not paid down as it should be in the confessional. The virtues
that have resulted almost seem to compensate for the debt.
252 *libertinage*: i.e. prostitution.

Why now, do those five clowns o' the family
O' the vinedresser digest their porridge worse   265
That not one keeps it in his goatskin pouch
To do flint's-service with the tinder-box?
Don't cheat me, don't cheat you, don't cheat a friend,
But are you so hard on who jostles just
A stranger with no natural sort of claim   270
To the havings and the holdings (here's the point)
Unless by misadventure, and defect
Of that which ought to be—nay, which there's none
Would dare so much as wish to profit by—
Since who dares put in just so many words   275
"May Pietro fail to have a child, please God!
"So shall his house and goods belong to me,
"The sooner that his heart will pine betimes"?
Well then, God doesn't please, nor heart shall pine!
Because he has a child at last, you see,   280
Or selfsame thing as though a child it were,
He thinks, whose sole concern it is to think:
If he accepts it why should you demur?

Moreover, say that certain sin there seem,
The proper process of unsinning sin   285

---

264 *MS* Why, now,   *MS* of   265 *MS* Of   *MS* supper the worse   267 *MS* flint's service   ⋆268 *MS* our friends—   *1868 1872* friend!   *1888* friend   DC Br U friend>friend,   *1889* friend,   269 {not found in *MS*}   270 *MS* But strangers,   *MS* claim at all   271 *MS* and holdings of Pietro—here's the point—   272 *MS* misadventure—the defect of that   Yale 1 misadventure—>misadventure,   273 *MS* Which ought to be—which there's no worthy man   275 *MS* dares say   276 *MS* this man   *MS* God,—   277–8 *MS* {no quotation marks at beginnings of lines}   277 *MS* me—   278 *MS* away?"   *1868 1872* betimes?"   279 *MS* Well, then, God don't please,—nor his heart shall break,   *1868 1872* do n't   *1868 1872* his heart   281 *MS* The   *MS* as if   *MS* {no comma}   282 *MS* thinks—   *MS* think—   284 *MS* {no new paragraph}   *MS* was,   285 *MS* {beginning of fo. 183}

268 *Don't . . . friend*: i.e. 'I admit you shouldn't cheat your friends'. Tertium Quid points to himself, the Duke, and the Prince ('a friend').
278 *betimes*: quickly.

Is to begin well-doing somehow else.
Pietro,—remember, with no sin at all
I' the substitution,—why, this gift of God
Flung in his lap from over Paradise wall
Steadied him in a moment, set him straight   290
On the good path he had been straying from.
Henceforward no more wilfulness and waste,
Cuppings, carousings,—these a sponge wiped out.
All sort of self-denial was easy now
For the child's sake, the chatelaine to be,   295
Who must want much and might want who knows what?
And so, the debts were paid, habits reformed,
Expense curtailed, the dowry set to grow.
As for the wife,—I said, hers the whole sin:
So, hers the exemplary penance. 'T was a text   300
Whereon folk preached and praised, the district through:
"Oh, make us happy and you make us good!
"It all comes of God giving her a child:
"Such graces follow God's best earthly gift!"

Here you put by my guard, pass to my heart   305
By the home-thrust—"There's a lie at base of all."
Why, thou exact Prince, is it a pearl or no,

---

286 *MS* else   288 *MS* In   *289 *MS* Paradise wall   *1868 1872 1888*
1889 Paradise   290 *MS* Sobered   291 *MS* In   293 *MS* carou-
sals,—   *MS* out: 295 *MS* be: 296 *MS* Heaven   knows
what.   297 *MS* so the   *Yale 1* so>so,   299 *MS* And   *MS* said: *MS*
sin,   300 *MS* Her's   *MS* penance: 'twas   301 *MS* they preached   *MS*
{no comma}   *MS* through.   303–4 *MS* {no quotation marks at beginnings
of lines}   303 *MS* God's   305 *MS* {no new paragraph}   306 *MS*
home thrust—"there's   307 *MS* exact sir,   *MS* no

293 *sponge wiped out*: drinking debts were chalked up on a board; here they are
wiped out.
295 *chatelaine*: head of a household.
296 *want . . . want*: the first 'want' means both 'lack' and 'desire', the second only
'desire'. The pun suggests Pietro's bustling concern for Pompilia's future needs.
305 *pass*: make a pass, or lunge; like 'guard' and 'home-thrust', a term from fencing.
Tertium Quid is fond of this imagery: cf. ll. 548–9, 615–18, 637–40, etc.
307 *exact*: strict.

Yon globe upon the Principessa's neck?
That great round glory of pellucid stuff,
A fish secreted round a grain of grit!   310
Do you call it worthless for the worthless core?
(She doesn't, who well knows what she changed for it.)
So, to our brace of burgesses again!
You see so far i' the story, who was right,
Who wrong, who neither, don't you? What, you don't?   315
Eh? Well, admit there's somewhat dark i' the case,
Let's on—the rest shall clear, I promise you.
Leap over a dozen years: you find, these past,
An old good easy creditable sire,
A careful housewife's beaming bustling face,   320
Both wrapped up in the love of their one child,
The strange tall pale beautiful creature grown
Lily-like out o' the cleft i' the sun-smit rock
To bow its white miraculous birth of buds
I' the way of wandering Joseph and his spouse,—   325
So painters fancy: here it was a fact.

308 *MS* neck—   309 *MS* {no comma}   310 *MS* The   *MS* grit—
312 *MS* {line added later}   *MS* (*She* don't,   *1868 1872* do n't   *1868 1872* it!)
313 *MS* {beginning of fo. 184}   *MS* So, Excellency, to our brace of burgesses.
MS {Between 313 and 314 extra line: Surely the bitterness of death was
past,}   314 *MS* in the story who   316 *MS* in the case   317 *MS* is
clear, I'll   318 *MS* find   *MS* {these past, not found}   *1868 1872* passed,
319 *MS* man,   320 *MS* beaming happy face,   321 *MS* {no comma}
323 *MS* of   *MS* in the sunsmit   325 *MS* In   *MS* spouse: 326 *MS*
fancy,—   *MS* fact—

   308 *Principessa*: princess (It.), the wife of the Prince to whom Tertium Quid is
speaking.
   312 *She . . . it*: an aside: Tertium Quid perhaps implies that the Principessa is a
beautiful woman who allowed herself to be 'bought' in marriage by the Prince's
wealth, he being otherwise disagreeable.
   319 *creditable*: worthy of credit (since his financial reformation) and respectable.
   323–6 *Lily-like . . . fancy*: the lily described here is not, as Tertium Quid implies, a
regular motif in paintings of the 'Flight into Egypt'. Browning has in mind a particular
memory: 'I used to admire a little circumstance in a picture by Mantegna in the Gallery
of the Uffizi: it represented the "Flight into Egypt": and, as Mary and Joseph were
passing by a barren wall of rock, out of a crevice therein came, as if born in full bloom,
a lily-flower,—reaching to salute them': Browning to Mrs Thomas FitzGerald, 9 June
1878: *Learned Lady*, 49. There is no 'Flight into Egypt' by Mantegna in the Uffizi or

And this their lily,—could they but transplant
And set in vase to stand by Solomon's porch
'Twixt lion and lion!—this Pompilia of theirs,
Could they see worthily married, well bestowed,   330
In house and home! And why despair of this
With Rome to choose from, save the topmost rank?
Themselves would help the choice with heart and soul,
Throw their late savings in a common heap
To go with the dowry, and be followed in time   335
By the heritage legitimately hers:
And when such paragon was found and fixed,
Why, they might chant their "*Nunc dimittis*" straight.

Indeed the prize was simply full to a fault,
Exorbitant for the suitor they should seek,   340
And social class should choose among, these cits.
Yet there's a latitude: exceptional white
Amid the general brown o' the species, lurks
A burgess nearly an aristocrat,
Legitimately in reach: look out for him!   345
What banker, merchant, has seen better days,
What second-rate painter a-pushing up,

327 *MS* oh, could   328 *MS* a vase   *MS* in Solomon's   329 *MS*
Twixt   *MS* lion! In prose, this Pompilia of theirs   330 *MS 1868* bestowed
331 *MS* home—and   332 *MS* {no comma}   *MS* rank   333 *MS*
Since they   334 *MS* Throwing their savings into   335 *1868 1872*
Should   *MS* and that to be   *1868 1872* to be   336 *MS* hers,—   337 {not
found in *MS*}   338 *MS* Dimittas"   *Yale 1* Dimittas">dimittas   339 *MS*
{no new paragraph}   *1868* fault;   340 *MS* {beginning of fo. 185}   341 *MS*
Too good for the proper class to choose among.   *1868 1872* to choose   342 *MS*
latitude,—   *Yale 1* latitude—>latitude: 343 *MS* of the burgess
soul,   344 *MS* nearly like an aristocrat—   345 *MS* him: 346 *MS*
What banker, merchant, painter a-pushing up   347 {not found in *MS*}

elsewhere. We have been unable to identify this painting; Browning is misremember-
ing in some way, or the painting has been reascribed.

   328 *Solomon's porch*: i.e. a grand house-front, synonym here for a good marriage.
   338 *Nunc dimittis*: the Latin opening of the Song of Simeon, 'Lord, now lettest
thou thy servant depart in peace' (Luke 2: 29), proverbial for a contented death. Cf. 1.
542–3.
   341 *cits*: citizens (a contemptuous shortening).

Poet a-slipping down, shall bid the best
For this young beauty with the thumping purse?
Alack, were it but one of such as these   350
So like the real thing that they pass for it,
All had gone well! Unluckily, poor souls,
It proved to be the impossible thing itself,
Truth and not sham: hence ruin to them all.

For, Guido Franceschini was the head   355
Of an old family in Arezzo, old
To that degree they could afford be poor
Better than most: the case is common too.
Out of the vast door 'scutcheoned overhead,
Creeps out a serving-man on Saturdays   360
To cater for the week,—turns up anon
I' the market, chaffering for the lamb's least leg,
Or the quarter-fowl, less entrails, claws and comb:
Then back again with prize,—a liver begged
Into the bargain, gizzard overlooked.   365
He's mincing these to give the beans a taste,
When, at your knock, he leaves the simmering soup,
Waits on the curious stranger-visitant,
Napkin in half-wiped hand, to show the rooms,
Point pictures out have hung their hundred years,   370
"Priceless," he tells you,—puts in his place at once
The man of money: yes, you're banker-king

---

350 *MS 1868* had it been   351 *MS* it might pass   *1868 1872* they
may   352 *MS* been well: but unlucky fate would have   *1868* Unluckily fate
must needs   353 *MS* It should prove to be   *MS* itself: *1868 1872*
itself;   354 *MS* The real noble and not the sham—   *1868* The truth and not
the sham: *1872* The truth not sham   355 *MS* Count Guido   *Yale 1* For>
For,   *Yale 1* Head>head   358 *MS* there.   359 *MS* {no comma}   *Yale 1*
overhead>overhead,   362 *MS* In   *MS* {no commas}   363 *MS* quarter
fowl,   ★*MS 1868 1872* comb: *1888* comb   *DC Br U* comb>comb: *1889*
comb: 364 *MS* Then back with his prize again,—a liver thrown   365 *MS*
a gizzard overlooked,—   *1868* overlooked,—   366 *MS* cooking   *MS* soup
367 *MS* {beginning of fo. 186}   *MS* mess   369 *MS* halfwiped   *MS* {no
comma}   *MS* rooms—   370 *MS* {no comma}   371 *MS* "Priceless"
he tell   *MS* your place   372 *MS* money—   *MS* banker this

---

359 *'scutcheoned*: emblazoned with a coat of arms.

Or merchant-kaiser, wallow in your wealth
While patron, the house-master, can't afford
To stop our ceiling-hole that rain so rots: 375
But he's the man of mark, and there's his shield,
And yonder's the famed Rafael, first in kind,
The painter painted for his grandfather,
And you have paid to see: "Good morning, Sir!"
Such is the law of compensation. Still   380
The poverty was getting nigh acute;
There gaped so many noble mouths to feed,
Beans must suffice unflavoured of the fowl.
The mother,—hers would be a spun-out life
I' the nature of things; the sisters had done well   385
And married men of reasonable rank:
But that sort of illumination stops,
Throws back no heat upon the parent-hearth.
The family instinct felt out for its fire
To the Church,—the Church traditionally helps   390
A second son: and such was Paolo,
Established here at Rome these thirty years,
Who played the regular game,—priest and Abate,
Made friends, owned house and land, became of use
To a personage: his course lay clear enough.   395
The youngest caught the sympathetic flame,

---

373 *MS* Merchant the other, and you roll in wealth   374 *MS* the patron, the
house master can't   375 *MS* yon ceiling-hole the rains have worn—   *1868*
rots—   377   *MS* Raffael, first in its kind,   378 *MS 1868* grandfather—
379 *MS* You have paid a paul to see: good   *1868* You have paid a paul   *★MS 1868
1872* Sir!"   *1888* Sir!   *DC Br U* Sir!>Sir!"   *1889* Sir!"   380 *MS 1868 1872*
Here   381 *MS 1868 1872* too   382 *MS* There were   383 *MS* fowl:
384 *MS* The Lady Mother,—   *MS* a long life   385 *MS* In   *MS* things:
MS well,   386 *MS* rank—   387 *MS* stops—   388 *MS* parent-
house: 390 *MS* helps.   391 *MS* The second son accordingly, Paolo,
393 *MS* Played the whole   *MS* abate,   394 *MS* {beginning of fo.
187}   395 *MS* personage,   *MS* was clear   396 *MS* {no comma}

376 *man of mark*: aristocrat; as opposed to the 'man of money', l. 372.
380 *law of compensation*: i.e. the 'man of mark' has his rank but no money, the 'man
of money' has his money but no rank.
396 *youngest*: Girolamo, Guido's youngest brother.

And, though unfledged wings kept him still i' the cage,
Yet he shot up to be a Canon, so
Clung to the higher perch and crowed in hope.
Even our Guido, eldest brother, went   400
As far i' the way o' the Church as safety seemed,
He being Head o' the House, ordained to wive,—
So, could but dally with an Order or two
And testify good-will i' the cause: he clipped
His top-hair and thus far affected Christ.   405
But main promotion must fall otherwise,
Though still from the side o' the Church: and here was he
At Rome, since first youth, worn threadbare of soul
By forty-six years' rubbing on hard life,
Getting fast tired o' the game whose word is—"Wait!"   410
When one day,—he too having his Cardinal
To serve in some ambiguous sort, as serve
To draw the coach the plumes o' the horses' heads,—
The Cardinal saw fit to dispense with him,
Ride with one plume the less; and off it dropped.   415

Guido thus left,—with a youth spent in vain
And not a penny in purse to show for it,—
Advised with Paolo, bent no doubt in chafe
The black brows somewhat formidably, growled

397 *MS* And though his clipt   *MS* still at home,   398 *MS* and so   399 *MS*
Amid the poverty held on in hope.   400 *MS* as the eldest brother, went
401 *MS* in   *MS* of   *MS* was—   402 *MS* of   *MS* wive,   403 *MS*
{no comma}   *MS* order   404 *MS* good will in the cause—he clipt   *1868*
1872 clipt   405 *MS* so far   *1868* Christ,   407 *MS* of   408 *MS* soul,
409 *MS* forty six years   410 *MS* of   411 *MS* day—   412 *MS*
sort—   413 *MS* on   *MS* head—   414 *MS* with his help,   415 *MS*
Go   *MS* less,—so off   416 *MS* {no new paragraph}   *MS* his youth
417 *MS* Without a penny,—advised with Paolo, bent   *1868 1872* it,   418 {not
found in *MS*}   419 *MS* formidably the while,—   *1868* formidably the while.

399 *higher perch*: cocks seek the highest perch to crow from.
403 *Order or two*: see 1. 263–5 n.
409 *forty-six years*: see 1. 782–4 n.
418 *chafe*: anger.

"Where is the good I came to get at Rome?   420
"Where the repayment of the servitude
"To a purple popinjay, whose feet I kiss,
"Knowing his father wiped the shoes of mine?"

"Patience," pats Paolo the recalcitrant—
"You have not had, so far, the proper luck,   425
"Nor do my gains suffice to keep us both:
"A modest competency is mine, not more.
"You are the Count however, yours the style,
"Heirdom and state,—you can't expect all good.
"Had I, now, held your hand of cards ... well, well—   430
"What's yet unplayed, I'll look at, by your leave,
"Over your shoulder,—I who made my game,
"Let's see, if I can't help to handle yours.
"Fie on you, all the Honours in your fist,
"Countship, Househeadship,—how have you misdealt!
"Why, in the first place, these will marry a man!   436
"*Notum tonsoribus!* To the Tonsor then!
"Come, clear your looks, and choose your freshest suit,
"And, after function's done with, down we go

420 *MS* was   *MS* Rome,   421–3 *MS* {no quotation marks at beginnings of lines}   421 *MS* the pay of the ten years' servitude   422 *MS* {beginning of fo. 188}   *MS* shoes I wipe,   423 *MS* blacked   *424 *MS* {no new paragraph}   *1868 1872* {new paragraph. Paragraphing obscured in *1888* and *1889* by this line's being at the head of the page}   *MS* tries Paolo with the   425–42 *MS* {no quotation marks at beginnings of lines}   425 *MS* a luck like mine, 427 *MS* I have a modest competency—not more.   428 *MS* moreover, have the style,   429 *MS* Heirship and all,—   430 *MS* cards . . well, well.   431 *MS* unplayed . .   432 *MS* I have   434 {not found in *MS*}   435 *MS* how shall we deal with these?   436 *MS* they will   *1868* they   437 *MS* Notum tonsoribus!   *MS* Tonsor's   438 *MS* looks, choose you   439 *MS* And after

422 *popinjay*: cf. III. 785 n. 'Purple' is referring to the colour of the Cardinal's robes.
424 *recalcitrant*: (noun) the refractory, the rebellious one, i.e. Guido. Paolo soothes him like a child.
428 *style*: family name.
429 *expect all good*: i.e. wealth as well.
434 *Honours*: Ace, King, Queen, and Jack (the highest-scoring cards), but punning on degrees of nobility, the 'Countship' etc. of the next line.
437 *Notum tonsoribus*: 'It's known to barbers' (L.), i.e. common knowledge. Cf. II. 115 n.

"To the woman-dealer in perukes, a wench   440
"I and some others settled in the shop
"At Place Colonna: she's an oracle. Hmm!
"'Dear, 't is my brother: brother, 't is my dear.
"'Dear, give us counsel! Whom do you suggest
"'As properest party in the quarter round   445
"'For the Count here?—he is minded to take wife,
"'And further tells me he intends to slip
"'Twenty zecchines under the bottom-scalp
"'Of his old wig when he sends it to revive
"'For the wedding: and I add a trifle too.   450
"'You know what personage I'm potent with.'"
And so plumped out Pompilia's name the first.
She told them of the household and its ways,
The easy husband and the shrewder wife
In Via Vittoria,—how the tall young girl,   455
With hair black as yon patch and eyes as big
As yon pomander to make freckles fly,
Would have so much for certain, and so much more
In likelihood,—why, it suited, slipped as smooth
As the Pope's pantoufle does on the Pope's foot.   460
"I'll to the husband!" Guido ups and cries.

---

440 *MS* woman dealer   442 *MS* In   *MS* our oracle. {Hmm! not found in
MS}   443 *MS* "Dear,   *MS* Brother: Brother,   *MS* Dear: 444–51 *MS*
{no quotation marks at beginnings of lines}   444 *MS* counsel: whom   445 *MS*
1868 1872 round,   446 *MS* here, who   *MS* {no comma at end}   447 *MS*
farther   448 *MS* into   449 *MS* sends you it   450 *MS* {beginning
of fo. 189}   *MS* wedding,   *MS* I'll   *MS* too—   *Yale 1* too—>too.
451 *MS* with."   452 *MS* first: 453 *MS* him   455 *MS* girl   456 *MS*
wig and twice as thick   457 {not found in *MS*}   459 *MS 1868 1872*
slipt   460 *MS* goes   461 *MS* "I'll go to the Husband,"   *MS* cries—

---

441 *settled in the shop*: the implication here and in the 'Dear' of ll. 443–4 is that the
peruke-maker was a shared mistress in Paolo's circle, now paid off by being set up in a
shop.

448 *zecchines*: high-value gold coins.

456 *patch*: small spot of black silk worn fashionably on the face. Tertium Quid
points to a fashionable lady in the salon wearing such a patch.

457 *pomander*: fragrant ball made of herbs; this one is designed to prevent freckles.

460 *pantoufle*: slipper; famous from the gesture of kissing the Pope's foot.

"Ay, so you'd play your last court-card, no doubt!"
Puts Paolo in with a groan—"Only, you see,
" 'T is I, this time, that supervise your lead.
"Priests play with women, maids, wives, mothers—why?
"These play with men and take them off our hands.   466
"Did I come, counsel with some cut-beard gruff
"Or rather this sleek young-old barberess?
"Go, brother, stand you rapt in the ante-room
"Of Her Efficacity my Cardinal   470
"For an hour,—he likes to have lord-suitors lounge,—
"While I betake myself to the grey mare,
"The better horse,—how wise the people's word!—
"And wait on Madam Violante."
                        Said and done.   475
He was at Via Vittoria in three skips:
Proposed at once to fill up the one want
O' the burgess-family which, wealthy enough,
And comfortable to heart's desire, yet crouched
Outside a gate to heaven,—locked, bolted, barred,   480
Whereof Count Guido had a key he kept
Under his pillow, but Pompilia's hand
Might slide behind his neck and pilfer thence.

---

462 *MS* doubt,—"   464-74 *MS* {no quotation marks at beginnings of lines}   464 *MS* have a care of the game.   465 *MS* deal   *MS* mothers,—for why?   *1868* mothers,—   466 *MS* deal   468 *MS* Or rather with this sleek young barberess?   469 *MS* anteroom   470 *MS* Of the efficacious man my Cardinal   471 *MS* Count-suitors   472 *MS* myself, as the proverb bids,>myself to the grey mare,   473 *MS* To the grey mare, thats also the better horse>That's the better horse,—who {a *lapsus calami*} wise the people's word!—   474 *MS* Madame   *MS* {no new paragraph}   475 *MS* done;   476 *MS* Was>He was   478 *MS* Of   *MS* enough   479 *MS* {beginning of fo. 190}   *MS* sate   482 *MS* pillow—and which

---

462 *court-card*: Jack, Queen, or King.

467 *cut-beard gruff*: rough (male) barber.

470 *Her Efficacity*: 'the influential one', punning on the form 'Sua Eminenza': cf. l. 55 n. and 1. 1139 n.

472-3 *grey...horse*: proverbial: 'The grey mare is the better horse', i.e. the wife rules the husband: ODEP, 338.

The key was fairy; its mere mention made
Violante feel the thing shoot one sharp ray   485
That reached the womanly heart: so—"I assent!
"Yours be Pompilia, hers and ours that key
"To all the glories of the greater life!
"There's Pietro to convince: leave that to me!"

Then was the matter broached to Pietro; then   490
Did Pietro make demand and get response
That in the Countship was a truth, but in
The counting up of the Count's cash, a lie.
He thereupon stroked grave his chin, looked great,
Declined the honour. Then the wife wiped tear,   495
Winked with the other eye turned Paolo-ward,
Whispered Pompilia, stole to church at eve,
Found Guido there and got the marriage done,
And finally begged pardon at the feet
Of her dear lord and master. Whereupon   500
Quoth Pietro—"Let us make the best of things!"
"I knew your love would license us," quoth she:
Quoth Paolo once more, "Mothers, wives and maids,
"These be the tools wherewith priests manage men."

Now, here take breath and ask,—which bird o' the brace
Decoyed the other into clapnet? Who   506

484 *MS 1868 1872* mention of it, made   485 *MS* see the same   486 *MS*
the heart of the woman: "I assent—   *1868 1872* heart o' the woman. "I
assent: 487–9 *MS* {no quotation marks at beginnings of lines}   488 *MS*
life,—   490 *MS* {no new paragraph}   493 *MS 1868* lie: 494 *MS*
stroked down   495 *MS* honor: then   *MS* wiped one   *1868* one—
496 *MS* eye, went out with Paolo,   498 *MS* {no comma}   499 *MS*
bitterly   500 *MS* master: whereupon   501 *MS* Says   502 *MS 1868*
1872 licence   503 *MS* once again "Women-maids, wives and mothers,
504 *MS* {no quotation mark at beginning of line}   *MS* we manage   505 *MS*
{beginning of fo. 191}   *MS* of   506 *MS* the clapnet?

484 *fairy*: enchanted. Perhaps a memory of the enchanted key and the terrible room
in the fairytale 'Bluebeard', for there also 'la clef étoit Fée': Charles Perrault, *Histoires
ou contes du temps passé* (1698), 52.
    505 *brace*: pair.
    506 *clapnet*: net for catching birds. It can be closed quickly with a string.

Was fool, who knave? Neither and both, perchance.
There was a bargain mentally proposed
On each side, straight and plain and fair enough;
Mind knew its own mind: but when mind must speak,   510
The bargain have expression in plain terms,
There came the blunder incident to words,
And in the clumsy process, fair turned foul.
The straight backbone-thought of the crooked speech
Were just—"I Guido truck my name and rank   515
"For so much money and youth and female charms."—
"We Pietro and Violante give our child
"And wealth to you for a rise i' the world thereby."
Such naked truth while chambered in the brain
Shocks nowise: walk it forth by way of tongue,—   520
Out on the cynical unseemliness!
Hence was the need, on either side, of a lie
To serve as decent wrappage: so, Guido gives
Money for money,—and they, bride for groom,
Having, he, not a doit, they, not a child   525
Honestly theirs, but this poor waif and stray.
According to the words, each cheated each;
But in the inexpressive barter of thoughts,
Each did give and did take the thing designed,
The rank on this side and the cash on that—   530

---

507 *MS* I say.   509 *MS* both sides,   *MS* enough: 511 *MS* {no comma}   512 *MS* There was confusion   *1868 1872* was   514 *MS* backbone of the crooked fact were just   515 *MS* "I, Guido, truck my name and social power   516 *MS* {no quotation mark at beginning of line}   *MS* money, and youth and handsomeness—"   *★1868* charms."—   *1872* {there is a gap between. and —}   *1888 1889* charms.—   517 *MS* "We,   518 *MS* {no quotation mark at beginning of line}   *MS* in   *MS* thereby—"   519 *MS* The naked thought in the chamber of the brain   520 *MS* the tongue,—   522 *MS* {no commas}   523 *MS* serve [ ]>serve as   *MS* ^decent^   *MS* and Guido   524 *MS* they, good name for name,   525 *MS* he—   527 *MS* {no comma}   *MS* each,   528 *MS* minds   529 *MS* designed—   530 *MS* money

515 *truck*: exchange.
519 *naked truth*: the image is based on the idea that nakedness does not shock in one's own room.
528 *inexpressive*: not spoken, unsaid.

Attained the object of the traffic, so.
The way of the world, the daily bargain struck
In the first market! Why sells Jack his ware?
"For the sake of serving an old customer."
Why does Jill buy it? "Simply not to break   535
"A custom, pass the old stall the first time."
Why, you know where the gist is of the exchange:
Each sees a profit, throws the fine words in.
Don't be too hard o' the pair! Had each pretence
Been simultaneously discovered, stript   540
From off the body o' the transaction, just
As when a cook (will Excellency forgive?)
Strips away those long rough superfluous legs
From either side the crayfish, leaving folk
A meal all meat henceforth, no garnishry,   545
(With your respect, Prince!)—balance had been kept,
No party blamed the other,—so, starting fair,
All subsequent fence of wrong returned by wrong
I' the matrimonial thrust and parry, at least
Had followed on equal terms. But, as it chanced,   550
One party had the advantage, saw the cheat
Of the other first and kept its own concealed:
And the luck o' the first discovery fell, beside,
To the least adroit and self-possessed o' the pair.

---

531 *MS* I say.   532 *MS* {beginning of fo. 192}   *MS* world: that's just the
533 *MS* first market—Why sells the one his ware   534 *MS* customer—"
535 *MS* the other buy it? "Not to break   536 *MS* {no quotation mark at
beginning of line}   *MS* this first   537 *MS* of the bargain is—   538 *MS*
his profit and throws   539 *MS* ha>too   *MS* on the parties.   *MS* both>
each   540 *MS* renounced,>discovered,   *MS* stripped off   *1868 1872* stripped
541 *MS* The body of the transaction like garnish of legs   542, 543 {not found in
MS}   542 *1868* cook.. will Excellency forgive?   543 *1868* long loose
superfluous   *1872* long superfluous   544 *MS* From the meat and truth of the
crayfish, on both sides   545 {not found in *MS*}   547 *MS* And neither
549 *MS* In   550 *MS* Had been   *MS* terms: but,   551 *MS* One had
552 *MS* other and   *MS* concealed.   553 *MS* of   *MS* besides,   554
MS of

---

542 *Excellency forgive*: the affected and refined Tertium Quid is apologizing to the
Duke for using an analogy from the coarse realm of cookery.

'T was foolish Pietro and his wife saw first   555
The nobleman was penniless, and screamed
"We are cheated!"

    Such unprofitable noise
Angers at all times: but when those who plague,
Do it from inside your own house and home,   560
Gnats which yourself have closed the curtain round,
Noise goes too near the brain and makes you mad.
The gnats say, Guido used the candle-flame
Unfairly,—worsened that first bad of his,
By practising all kinds of cruelty   565
To oust them and suppress the wail and whine,—
That speedily he so scared and bullied them,
Fain were they, long before five months had passed,
To beg him grant, from what was once their wealth,
Just so much as would help them back to Rome   570
Where, when they finished paying the last doit
O' the dowry, they might beg from door to door.
So say the Comparini—as if it came
Of pure resentment for this worse than bad,
That then Violante, feeling conscience prick,   575
Confessed her substitution of the child
Whence all the harm fell,—and that Pietro first
Bethought him of advantage to himself
I' the deed, as part revenge, part remedy

555 MS the foolish burgess-couple that   556 MS The man though noble
was   558 MS {no new paragraph}   MS This   559 MS times—   MS
who scream   560 MS inside of your house   561 MS Gnats you yourself   MS curtains   562 MS It   563 MS {beginning of fo. 193}   MS
say that he   MS candleflame   564 MS his   565 MS practise of all
kinds   1868 1872 practise of all kind   566 MS their wail   567 MS he
speedily so   MS {no comma}   568 MS That they were fain, before five
months were out,   1868 1872 were out,   569 MS {no commas}   MS their
all   571 MS 1868 1872 had finished   572 MS Of   573 MS and that
it was   1868 1872 were   574 MS 1868 1872 In   MS {no comma}   575 MS
That Violante, feeling first her   576 MS the substitution   *577 MS
came,—and Pietro thereupon   1868 1872 1888 came,—   DC Br U came,—
>fell,—   1889 fell,—   578 MS himself—   579 MS Not only the
revenge, but remedy   Yale 1 act,>deed,

For all miscalculation in the pact.   580

On the other hand "Not so!" Guido retorts—
"I am the wronged, solely, from first to last,
"Who gave the dignity I engaged to give,
"Which was, is, cannot but continue gain.
"My being poor was a bye-circumstance,   585
"Miscalculated piece of untowardness,
"Might end to-morrow did heaven's windows ope,
"Or uncle die and leave me his estate.
"You should have put up with the minor flaw,
"Getting the main prize of the jewel. If wealth,   590
"Not rank, had been prime object in your thoughts,
"Why not have taken the butcher's son, the boy
"O' the baker or candlestick-maker? In all the rest,
"It was yourselves broke compact and played false,
"And made a life in common impossible.   595
"Show me the stipulation of our bond
"That you should make your profit of being inside
"My house, to hustle and edge me out o' the same,
"First make a laughing-stock of mine and me,

---

580 *MS* pact,   *MS* {Between 580 and 581 extra line: And getting quit of the
bond which pressed too much.   581 *MS* {no new paragraph}   *MS*
retorts   582 *MS* last   583–626 *MS* {no quotation marks at beginnings of
lines}   583 *MS* I gave   584 *MS* That   *MS* gain: 585 *MS* bye-
circumstance—   586 *MS* An uncalculated   *MS* {no comma}   587 *MS*
Which might   *MS* should   *MS* {no comma}   588 *MS* My   589 *MS*
{beginning of fo. 194}   *MS* {no comma}   590 *MS* jewel; if   *MS* {no
comma}   591 *MS* {no commas}   592 *MS* Butcher's son, the son
593 *MS* Of the Baker and candlestick maker?   *MS* {no comma}   *Yale 1* rest>
rest,   594 *MS* 'Twas   *MS* the compact   *MS* {no comma}   *MS* {Between
594 and 595 extra line: By making the stipulated provisions null,   595 *MS* The
projected life in common impossible: 596 *MS* It was scarce part of the original
pact   598 *MS* {no commas}   *MS* of it: 599 *MS* laughing stock   *Yale
1* laughingstock>laughing-stock

592–3 *butcher's son . . . candlestick-maker*: i.e. wealthy heirs, whose fathers made
money in relatively humble trades; after the nursery rhyme 'Rub-a-dub-dub'. Cf.
Benjamin Disraeli, *Sybil* (1845), bk. 1, ch. iv: ' "Oh! I have no doubt," said Lady
Marney, "that we shall have some monster of the middle class, some tinker or tailor or
candlestick-maker, with his long purse, preaching reform and practising corruption." '

"Then round us in the ears from morn to night   600
"(Because we show wry faces at your mirth)
"That you are robbed, starved, beaten and what not!
"You fled a hell of your own lighting-up,
"Pay for your own miscalculation too:
"You thought nobility, gained at any price,   605
"Would suit and satisfy,—find the mistake,
"And now retaliate, not on yourselves, but me.
"And how? By telling me, i' the face of the world,
"I it is have been cheated all this while,
"Abominably and irreparably,—my name   610
"Given to a cur-cast mongrel, a drab's brat,
"A beggar's bye-blow,—thus depriving me
"Of what yourselves allege the whole and sole
"Aim on my part i' the marriage,—money to-wit.
"This thrust I have to parry by a guard   615
"Which leaves me open to a counter-thrust
"On the other side,—no way but there's a pass
"Clean through me. If I prove, as I hope to do,
"There's not one truth in this your odious tale
"O' the buying, selling, substituting—prove   620
"Your daughter was and is your daughter,—well,
"And her dowry hers and therefore mine,—what then?

---

601 *MS* Because we made   *MS* mirth,   602 *MS* were   *MS* not.   603 *MS*
lighting-up;—   604 *MS* miscalculation, too—   605 *MS* {no commas}
606 *MS* found your mistake,—   607 *MS* {no commas}   608 *MS* in
609 *MS* That I   *MS* who have   *MS* the while,   611 *MS* creature,   *MS*
brat   613 *MS* allege is   614 *MS* in   *MS* the money to-wit: 615 *MS*
{beginning of fo. 195}   616 *MS* counterthrust   620 *MS* Of the buying
and selling and substituting and the rest,   621 *MS* That your

600 *round us in the ears*: din into our ears. This is a favourite expression of Browning's. 'Round' actually means 'whisper' and not 'din'. Browning's misuse was perhaps
suggested by 'round' and 'roundly', in the sense of 'straightforward' and 'straightfor-
wardly', 'without hesitation or reserve', in such passages as *Hamlet*, II. ii. 139, III. i.
183, *Richard II*, II. i. 122: see Cook, 81.
611 *cur-cast*: cf. II. 637 n.
drab's: prostitute's.
612 *bye-blow*: bastard.

"Why, where's the appropriate punishment for this
"Enormous lie hatched for mere malice' sake
"To ruin me? Is that a wrong or no?   625
"And if I try revenge for remedy,
"Can I well make it strong and bitter enough?"

I anticipate however—only ask,
Which of the two here sinned most? A nice point!
Which brownness is least black,—decide who can,   630
Wager-by-battle-of-cheating! What do you say,
Highness? Suppose, your Excellency, we leave
The question at this stage, proceed to the next,
Both parties step out, fight their prize upon,
In the eye o' the world?   635
                    They brandish law 'gainst law:
The grinding of such blades, each parry of each,
Throws terrible sparks off, over and above the thrusts,
And makes more sinister the fight, to the eye,
Than the very wounds that follow. Beside the tale   640
Which the Comparini have to re-assert,
They needs must write, print, publish all abroad
The straitnesses of Guido's household life—
The petty nothings we bear privately
But break down under when fools flock to jeer.   645

623 *MS* Why what do you deserve for the hatching this   624 *MS* lie merely for malice'   626 *MS* a remedy for the same   627 *MS* {no quotation marks} 628 *MS* {no new paragraph}   *MS* all I should say is this: 629 *MS* two cheats sinned   630 *MS* you>who   631 *MS* This wager-by-battle-of-cheating!   633 *MS* next.   634 *MS* {new paragraph}   *MS* out then to fight their prize   635 *MS* of   *MS* world,—take weapons, law 'gainst law; 636 *MS* {no new paragraph}   637 *MS* each upon each,   638 *MS* thrusts—   640 *MS* happen. Besides   641 *MS* reassert,   642 *MS* {beginning of fo. 196}   644 *MS* men   645 *MS* But go mad if they come to be made known.   *1868* flock around.

631 *Wager-by-battle-of-cheating*: i.e. the decision seems arbitrary; a parody of trial by wager of battle, a descendant of the medieval trial-by-combat, a challenge by a defendant to decide his guilt or innocence by single combat, on the grounds that God would support the innocent. An apparently arbitrary practice is made to seem more so: here who cheats best, not who fights best, will win.

633 *next*: next stage (understood). There is a pun in the next line: 'stage' is both 'the next point in the argument' and 'the place where the prize-fighters (boxers) meet'.

What is it all to the facts o' the couple's case,
How helps it prove Pompilia not their child,
If Guido's mother, brother, kith and kin
Fare ill, lie hard, lack clothes, lack fire, lack food?
That's one more wrong than needs.   650
                                   On the other hand,
Guido,—whose cue is to dispute the truth
O' the tale, reject the shame it throws on him,—
He may retaliate, fight his foe in turn
And welcome, we allow. Ay, but he can't!   655
He's at home, only acts by proxy here:
Law may meet law,—but all the gibes and jeers,
The superfluity of naughtiness,
Those libels on his House,—how reach at them?
Two hateful faces, grinning all a-glow,   660
Not only make parade of spoil they filched,
But foul him from the height of a tower, you see.
Unluckily temptation is at hand—
To take revenge on a trifle overlooked,
A pet lamb they have left in reach outside,   665
Whose first bleat, when he plucks the wool away,
Will strike the grinners grave: his wife remains
Who, four months earlier, some thirteen years old,

---

646 *MS* of   *MS* {no comma}   647 *MS* Who come to   648 *MS* That
MS and himself   650 *MS* There's   *MS* should be: on   651 *MS* {no new
paragraph}   652 *MS* Guido, whose   653 *MS* Of   *MS* resist   *MS*
him,   654 *MS* plague his foes   655 *MS* allow: *MS* can't—   656 *MS*
here,   657 *MS* Law meets the law,—but the gibes and jeers, you see,   658 {not
found in *MS*}   659 *MS* The   *MS* house,—   *MS* those   660 *MS*
{line added later}   *MS* aglow,   661 {not found in *MS*}   662 *MS*
Who spit at him from the height of a tower, I ask?   663 *MS* a temptation
MS hand,   665 *MS* outside the door,   666 *MS* {no commas}   667 *MS*
and spoil their sport.   *MS* {Between 667 and 668 extra lines: His wife remains,—
plague her and he plagues them— / The little wife, the poor Pompilia thing}
668 *MS* Who four   *MS* being thirteen

---

658 *superfluity of naughtiness*: cf. Jas. 1: 21.
660 *Two hateful faces*: those of Violante and Pietro. They are imagined as grotesque,
grinning gargoyles stuck on the side of the Franceschini 'House', raining down their
satire (dirty water) on Guido.

Never a mile away from mother's house
And petted to the height of her desire,   670
Was told one morning that her fate had come,
She must be married—just as, a month before,
Her mother told her she must comb her hair
And twist her curls into one knot behind.
These fools forgot their pet lamb, fed with flowers,   675
Then 'ticed as usual by the bit of cake
Out of the bower into the butchery.
Plague her, he plagues them threefold: but how plague?
The world may have its word to say to that:
You can't do some things with impunity.   680
What remains . . . well, it is an ugly thought . . .
But that he drive herself to plague herself—
Herself disgrace herself and so disgrace
Who seek to disgrace Guido?

                              There's the clue   685
To what else seems gratuitously vile,
If, as is said, from this time forth the rack
Was tried upon Pompilia: 't was to wrench
Her limbs into exposure that brings shame.
The aim o' the cruelty being so crueller still,   690
That cruelty almost grows compassion's self
Could one attribute it to mere return
O' the parents' outrage, wrong avenging wrong.

669 MS her>the   671 MS {beginning of fo. 197}   MS time was   1868 1872
was come,   672 MS [?wd]>married   MS {no commas}   673 MS had
told   674 MS behind—   675 MS As I said, the pet lamb, fed since a year
with flowers,   676 MS led   *1868 1872 1888 cake,   DC   Br   U
cake,>cake   1889 cake   677 MS By the old garden-door into the butcher's
pen: 678 MS Ill-treat her,—he ill-treats them,—but how ill-treat?   679 MS
The world, you know, has   MS that—   681 MS 1868 1872 remains . .   MS
1868 1872 thought . .   682 MS you drive her to ill-treat   683 MS so—
disgrace them   685 MS {no new paragraph}   MS There you have   687 MS
time the extremest screw   688 MS put   689 MS the exposure   690 MS
of   MS {no comma}   691 MS That it would almost grow compassion itself
693 MS Of   MS revenging wrong—

They see in this a deeper deadlier aim,
Not to vex just a body they held dear,   695
But blacken too a soul they boasted white,
And show the world their saint in a lover's arms,
No matter how driven thither,—so they say.

On the other hand, so much is easily said,
And Guido lacks not an apologist.   700
The pair had nobody but themselves to blame,
Being selfish beasts throughout, no less, no more:
—Cared for themselves, their supposed good, nought else,
And brought about the marriage; good proved bad,
As little they cared for her its victim—nay,   705
Meant she should stay behind and take the chance,
If haply they might wriggle themselves free.
They baited their own hook to catch a fish
With this poor worm, failed o' the prize, and then
Sought how to unbait tackle, let worm float   710
Or sink, amuse the monster while they 'scaped.
Under the best stars Hymen brings above,
Had all been honesty on either side,
A common sincere effort to good end,
Still, this would prove a difficult problem, Prince!   715
—Given, a fair wife, aged thirteen years,
A husband poor, care-bitten, sorrow-sunk,

694 {not found in *MS*}   695 *MS* Not simply the trying to vex   696 *MS*
to blacken   *MS* white—   697 *MS* their saint to the world   699 *MS* {begin-
ning of fo. 198}   *MS* {paragraphing concealed by new page}   700 *MS* And
Guido's friends are ready in reply.   701 *MS* Couple   702 *MS* no more, no
less.   703 *MS* They thought of   704 *MS* In bringing   *MS* marriage,—
MS this,>which,   *MS* turning ill,   705 *MS* Just as little they thought about
the victim—her   706 *MS* She meant should stay and take the chance of the
scrape   707 *MS* happily   *MS* thence.   708 *MS* the fish   709 *MS*
worm,—   *MS* of their prize,—   710 *MS* their tackle, let the worm float or
sink.   711 {not found in *MS*}   712 *MS* circumstances they could have
hoped,   713 *MS* honest and plain   714 *MS* With a   *MS* to carry out the
plan,—   715 *MS* it>this   *MS* have proved   *MS* problem to solve   716,
717 *MS* —Given—a pure beautiful girl, and a husband poor,>—Given—a pure beautiful girl, of thirteen years/And a husband poor, harrassed with many cares,

712 *Under...above*: i.e. under the best possible circumstances for a happy marriage.

Little, long-nosed, bush-bearded, lantern-jawed,
Forty-six years old,—place the two grown one,
She, cut off sheer from every natural aid,   720
In a strange town with no familiar face—
He, in his own parade-ground or retreat
If need were, free from challenge, much less check
To an irritated, disappointed will—
How evolve happiness from such a match?   725
'T were hard to serve up a congenial dish
Out of these ill-agreeing morsels, Duke,
By the best exercise of the cook's craft,
Best interspersion of spice, salt and sweet!
But let two ghastly scullions concoct mess   730
With brimstone, pitch, vitriol and devil's-dung—
Throw in abuse o' the man, his body and soul,
Kith, kin and generation, shake all slab
At Rome, Arezzo, for the world to nose,
Then end by publishing, for fiend's arch-prank,   735
That, over and above sauce to the meat's self,

718 *MS* Little, long nosed, lantern-jawed, black bush-bearded,   719 *MS* Forty-
six-years old,—she with none of her natural helps,   *1868* full,—   720 {not
found in *MS*}   721 *MS* without a   722 *MS* He in his own place and free
from all the checks   723 {not found in *MS*}   *1868 1872* As   724 *MS*
irritable,   725 *MS* to make happiness come from   727 *MS* morsels and
meats   729 *MS* spice and salt and sweet.   730 *MS* {beginning of fo.
199}   *MS* cooks   *MS* the mess   731 *MS* devil's dung—   732 *MS*
of   733 *MS* generation, shake up the pan   734 *MS* at Arezzo, for all the
world to smell,   735 *MS* And end all by revealing your arch-feat and
cheat   736 *MS* the sauce   *MS* meat itself   *MS* {no commas}   *MS*
{Between 736 and 737 extra line: The bestiality that all recognize as enough,

718 *lantern-jawed*: with lantern-jaws: 'long thin jaws, giving a hollow appearance to
the cheek': OED^2. The description here derives from SS 23, though the lantern-jaws
are an addition.
730 *scullions*: lowest kitchen servants.
mess: food.
731 *vitriol*: sulphuric acid or a sulphate; fig. caustic or hostile criticism.
devil's-dung: asafoetida: 'a gum or resin brought from the East Indies, of a sharp taste,
and a strong offensive smell...seldom used but by farriers; yet, in the East Indies, it
makes an ingredient in their ragouts': Johnson.
733 *shake all slab*: shake up the whole slab [of sticky filth]; a memory of 'Make the
gruel thick and slab': *Macbeth*, IV. i. 32. The *MS* reading 'shake up the pan' helps with
the sense.

Why, even the meat, bedevilled thus in dish,
Was never a pheasant but a carrion-crow—
Prince, what will then the natural loathing be?
What wonder if this?—the compound plague o' the pair
Pricked Guido,—not to take the course they hoped,   741
That is, submit him to their statement's truth,
Accept its obvious promise of relief,
And thrust them out of doors the girl again
Since the girl's dowry would not enter there,   745
—Quit of the one if baulked of the other: no!
Rather did rage and hate so work in him,
Their product proved the horrible conceit
That he should plot and plan and bring to pass
His wife might, of her own free will and deed,   750
Relieve him of her presence, get her gone,
And yet leave all the dowry safe behind,
Confirmed his own henceforward past dispute,
While blotting out, as by a belch of hell,
Their triumph in her misery and death.   755

[—]

737 *MS* Why even the meat thus bedevilled in his dish,   *Yale 1* meat>
meat,   738 *MS* carrion crow!   *Yale 1* carrion crow—>carrion-crow—
739 *MS* Why, what will the natural loathing grow to then?   740 *MS* to
this, that the compound plague   742 *MS* submitting to the   *MS* truth
743 *MS* To take the obvious relief it left in his way,   744 *MS* his
doors   745 *MS* And bid them take her, dowry and all—himself   746 *MS*
Quit   *MS* other: and so   747 *MS* Consummate their triumph?—No, it
rather pricked   748 *MS* In the working of rage, hate, disappointment,
thus—   749 *MS* so contrive as bring   750 *MS* How his wife
should,   751 *MS* presence and rid his house,   754 *MS* Along
with unimaginable disgrace   755 *MS* To those who suffered by disgrace
of her's

737 *bedevilled*: a pun: 'driven frantic (as if got at by the devil)' and, in cookery,
'grilled, with the addition of hot spice'.
738 *pheasant . . . carrion-crow*: referring to Guido's nature: he is not a true, aristocratic
game-bird like the pheasant, but he preys on people, as the crow preys on carcasses.
There is also an allusion to his household's mean lifestyle, particularly the miserable,
unaristocratic food: crow, unlike pheasant, is disgusting to eat.
748 *proved*: proved to be.

You see, the man was Aretine, had touch
O' the subtle air that breeds the subtle wit;
Was noble too, of old blood thrice-refined
That shrinks from clownish coarseness in disgust:
Allow that such an one may take revenge,   760
You don't expect he'll catch up stone and fling,
Or try cross-buttock, or whirl quarter-staff?
Instead of the honest drubbing clowns bestow,
When out of temper at the dinner spoilt,
On meddling mother-in-law and tiresome wife,—   765
Substitute for the clown a nobleman,
And you have Guido, practising, 't is said,
Immitigably from the very first,
The finer vengeance: this, they say, the fact
O' the famous letter shows—the writing traced   770
At Guido's instance by the timid wife
Over the pencilled words himself writ first—
Wherein she, who could neither write nor read,
Was made unblushingly declare a tale
To the brother, the Abate then in Rome,   775
How her putative parents had impressed,

---

756 *MS* {beginning of fo. 200}   *MS* {paragraphing concealed by new page}   *MS*
an Aretine,   *MS* {had touch not found}   757 *MS* Of   *MS* wit,   758 *MS*
He was   *MS* the old refined blood   *Yale 1* the old>old   759 *MS* That has
the   761 *MS* stones and throw,   762 *MS* Nor   *MS* {no comma}   *MS*
nor   *Yale 1* Or whirl>or whirl   *MS* quarterstaff?   763 *MS* a clown bestows
764 *MS* and his dinner   765 {not found in *MS*}   766 *MS* the same spirit
in another form—   767 *MS* And you have him planning and practising, as they
say,   *Yale 1* Guido,—>Guido,   768 *MS* Unmitigatedly   *1868* Unmit-
igably   769 *MS* This   770 *MS* Of   771 *MS* On Guido's com-
pulsion   772 *MS* first   *Yale 1* first,>first—   773 *MS* And set before
her   *MS* read.   774 *MS* Wherein she was made unblushingly declare
776 *MS* {no comma}

---

757 *breeds the subtle wit*: Arezzo was the birthplace of Maecenas, Guido d'Arezzo,
Petrarch, Leonardo Bruni, Aretino, and Vasari. Pietro Aretino (1492–1556), the
Renaissance scholar and wit, might particularly suggest this comment because of the
intelligence of his satires.
759 *clownish*: rude, uncultivated.
762 *cross-buttock*: throw over the hip, in wrestling.
quarter-staff: strong, six-foot pole (a weapon).

On their departure, their enjoinment; bade
"We being safely arrived here, follow, you!
"Poison your husband, rob, set fire to all,
"And then by means o' the gallant you procure   780
"With ease, by helpful eye and ready tongue,
"Some brave youth ready to dare, do and die,
"You shall run off and merrily reach Rome
"Where we may live like flies in honey-pot:"—
Such being exact the programme of the course   785
Imputed her as carried to effect.

They also say,—to keep her straight therein,
All sort of torture was piled, pain on pain,
On either side Pompilia's path of life,
Built round about and over against by fear,   790
Circumvallated month by month, and week
By week, and day by day, and hour by hour,
Close, closer and yet closer still with pain,
No outlet from the encroaching pain save just
Where stood one saviour like a piece of heaven,   795
Hell's arms would strain round but for this blue gap.
She, they say further, first tried every chink,
Every imaginable break i' the fire,

---

777 *MS* {no comma}   *MS* enjoinment thus.   778 *MS* arrived, follow you
us,   779–84 *MS* {no quotation marks at beginnings of lines}   779 *MS* rob
and fire the house,   780 *MS* of   *MS* lover you shall procure   782 *1868*
1872 "The   *MS* brisk   *MS* dare and do   783 *MS* elope   *MS* run to
784 *MS* {beginning of fo. 201}   *MS* we'll all   *MS* a honey-pot:"   785 *MS*
the exact   786 *MS* to her   *MS* into effect:—   787 *MS* {no new para-
graph}   *MS* say that   *MS* thereto,   788 *MS* steadily increased,   789 {not
found in *MS*}   790 *MS* {no comma}   791 *MS* month and week by
week   792 *MS* And day by day, and hour by hour, close, closer   793 *MS*
And closer still with pain, fire here, fire there,   794 *MS* fire save one   795 *MS*
Whereat stood—Caponsacchi: just there,—life,   796 *MS* Heaven: hell's arms
straining round with this gap left: 797 *MS* For,   *MS* she tried   798 *MS*
in the ring,

---

791 *Circumvallated*: enclosed around (as though with trenches and fortifications).
Pompilia is under siege.

As way of escape: ran to the Commissary,
Who bade her not malign his friend her spouse;   800
Flung herself thrice at the Archbishop's feet,
Where three times the Archbishop let her lie,
Spend her whole sorrow and sob full heart forth,
And then took up the slight load from the ground
And bore it back for husband to chastise,—   805
Mildly of course,—but natural right is right.
So went she slipping ever yet catching at help,
Missing the high till come to lowest and last,
To-wit a certain friar of mean degree,
Who heard her story in confession, wept,   810
Crossed himself, showed the man within the monk.
"Then, will you save me, you the one i' the world?
"I cannot even write my woes, nor put
"My prayer for help in words a friend may read,—
"I no more own a coin than have an hour   815
"Free of observance,—I was watched to church,
"Am watched now, shall be watched back presently,—
"How buy the skill of scribe i' the market-place?
"Pray you, write down and send whatever I say
"O' the need I have my parents take me hence!"   820
The good man rubbed his eyes and could not choose—
Let her dictate her letter in such a sense

---

799 *MS* she rushed into the street,   *MS* {Between 799 and 800 extra line: Ran to the Commissary and Governor,   800 *MS* {Between 800 and 801 extra line: Tried three times what the Church could do to help,   801 *MS* at the Archbishop's feet in prayer   802 *MS* And   *MS* {no comma}   803 *MS* Tell   *MS* her full heart out   805 *MS* brought her   *MS* the husband 806 *MS* but according to his natural right.   807 *MS* ever, yet   808 *MS* Failing   *MS* she came to the   809 *MS* No more than a certain monk   *1868* No more than   810 *MS* {beginning of fo. 202}   *MS* had heard   *MS* confession and   811 *MS* priest.   812 *MS* in   813–20 *MS* {no quotation marks at beginnings of lines}   813 *MS* wrongs,   814 *MS* might   815 *MS* I do not own a coin, could I find an hour   816 *MS* to this place   818 *MS* To   *MS* a scribe in the market place.   819 *MS* Will you   820 *MS* Of   *MS* should get me hence?"

---

799 *Commissary*: Governor of Arezzo. Cf. 11. 874.
809 *certain friar*: cf. 111. 1017 n.
822–4 *Let . . . over*: i.e. during dictation, he moderated the passion of her letter.

That parents, to save breaking down a wall,
Might lift her over: she went back, heaven in heart.
Then the good man took counsel of his couch,   825
Woke and thought twice, the second thought the best:
"Here am I, foolish body that I be,
"Caught all but pushing, teaching, who but I,
"My betters their plain duty,—what, I dare
"Help a case the Archbishop would not help,   830
"Mend matters, peradventure, God loves mar?
"What hath the married life but strifes and plagues
"For proper dispensation? So a fool
"Once touched the ark,—poor Uzzah that I am!
"Oh married ones, much rather should I bid,   835
"In patience all of ye possess your souls!
"This life is brief and troubles die with it:
"Where were the prick to soar up homeward else?"
So saying, he burnt the letter he had writ,
Said *Ave* for her intention, in its place,   840
Took snuff and comfort, and had done with all.

823 *MS* her parents to save her   *MS* {no commas}   824 *MS 1868 1872*
her heart.   825 *MS* went home, took counsel of sleep,   827 *MS*
am,   828–38 *MS* {no quotation marks at beginnings of lines}   828 *MS*
pushing in,   829 *MS* their duty,—what am I daring to do?   830 *MS* Just
help   831 *MS* a matter,   *MS* has marred—   832 *MS* plagues,   *Yale 1*
plagues,>plagues   833 *MS* The natural   834 *MS* oh, Hophni   *1868*
1872 Hophni   *MS* am!"   835 *MS* Oh, married   *MS* say,   837 *MS*
{beginning of fo. 203}   838 *MS* heavenward   839 *MS* saying he
840 *MS* a prayer   *MS* intention in   841 *MS* a refection,   *MS* it all.

825 *took counsel of his couch*: adapting the proverbial 'take counsel of your pillow':
ODEP, 799. Cf. III. 1029.
826 *second . . . best*: proverbial: 'second thoughts are best': ODEP, 708.
834 *Uzzah*: i.e. presumptuous man. Uzzah touched the Ark of the Covenant, and
was struck down by God: 2 Sam. 6: 6–7. Cf. I. 195 n. Browning originally wrote
'Hophni' here (rev. *1888*), one of the sons of Eli, another instance of irreverence: I
Sam. 2: 12–17, 34. He had the mistake pointed out in a query from a reader, to whom
he replied: 'I really believe that when I try to put myself in the place of any ignorant
person who figures in a poem, I adopt his very ignorance: on no other grounds can I
account for the substitution of Hophni for Uzzah': RB to James Graham, 26 Apr.
1888: SBC 2 (Spring 1974), 62–3.
836 *In . . . souls*: cf. Luke 21: 19.
840 *Ave*: the Hail Mary.

Then the grim arms stretched yet a little more
And each touched each, all but one streak i' the midst,
Whereat stood Caponsacchi, who cried, "This way,
"Out by me! Hesitate one moment more   845
"And the fire shuts out me and shuts in you!
"Here my hand holds you life out!" Whereupon
She clasped the hand, which closed on hers and drew
Pompilia out o' the circle now complete.
Whose fault or shame but Guido's?—ask her friends.   850

But then this is the wife's—Pompilia's tale—
Eve's ... no, not Eve's, since Eve, to speak the truth,
Was hardly fallen (our candour might pronounce)
When simply saying in her own defence
"The serpent tempted me and I did eat."   855
So much of paradisal nature, Eve's!
Her daughters ever since prefer to urge
"Adam so starved me I was fain accept
"The apple any serpent pushed my way."
What an elaborate theory have we here,   860
Ingeniously nursed up, pretentiously
Brought forth, pushed forward amid trumpet-blast,
To account for the thawing of an icicle,
Show us there needed Ætna vomit flame
Ere run the crystal into dew-drops! Else,   865

---

843 *MS* And touched, all but one narrow space in the midst,   844 *MS* Wherein   *MS* Caponsacchi who cried   845–7 *MS* {no quotation marks at beginnings of lines}   845 *MS* By me! But hesitate   846 *MS* And the grim fire
shuts me out and you in   847 *MS* out life to you. Whereat   848 *MS*
touched his   *MS* hers, and   849 *MS* Her out of the circle which shut behind
her back.   850 *MS* his friends   851 *MS* is>this   *MS* woman's tale—
the wife's—   852 *MS* Eve's..   *MS* Eve's since   *MS* truth   853 *MS*
(one well nigh might pronounce)   854–6 *MS 1868* {the lines stand in the order
856 854 855}   856 *MS* nature did she show   *1868* Eve's,   858 *MS* to
bite   859 *MS* {no quotation mark at beginning of line}   860 *MS* {no
comma}   861 *MS* How ingeniously nursed up, pretentiously brought forth,
862 {not found in *MS*}   *Yale 1* trumpet-blast[ ]>trumpet-blast,   864 *MS*
{beginning of fo. 204}   *MS* Showing how   *MS* to vomit   865 *MS* To
MS 1868 chrystal   *MS* dew-drops: else,

842 *grim arms*: 'arms' of the fire circle, continuing the image of l. 796.

How, unless hell broke loose to cause the step,
How could a married lady go astray?
Bless the fools! And 't is just this way they are blessed,
And the world wags still,—because fools are sure
—Oh, not of my wife nor your daughter! No!   870
But of their own: the case is altered quite.
Look now,—last week, the lady we all love,—
Daughter o' the couple we all venerate,
Wife of the husband we all cap before,
Mother o' the babes we all breathe blessings on,—   875
Was caught in converse with a negro page.
Hell thawed that icicle, else "Why was it—
"Why?" asked and echoed the fools. "Because, you fools,—"
So did the dame's self answer, she who could,
With that fine candour only forthcoming   880
When 't is no odds whether withheld or no—
"Because my husband was the saint you say,
"And,—with that childish goodness, absurd faith,
"Stupid self-satisfaction, you so praise,—
"Saint to you, insupportable to me.   885
"Had he,—instead of calling me fine names,
"Lucretia and Susanna and so forth,

867 *MS* e'er go wrong?   868 *MS* blessed: 869 *MS* goes round,—
because good men feel sure   870 *MS* Oh, not of my wife, sister, daughter!
No!   *Yale 1* Oh,>—Oh,   872 *MS* week was the lady we all know,—
873 *MS* {line added later}   *MS* of   *MS* saintly pair   874 *MS* perfect
husband we all prize   875 *MS* of   876 *MS* Caught in the act of shame
with a Negro Page: 878 *MS* fools—   *MS* fools,—   879 *MS* could—
881 *MS* no matter   *MS* it be witheld   882 *MS* {no comma}   883–
96 *MS* {no quotation marks at beginnings of lines}   883 *MS* And with   *Yale*
1 "And,>"And,—   *MS* goodness and   *MS* {no commas}   884 *MS* And
stupid self-satisfaction,—therefore insupportable.   *Yale 1* praise,>praise,—
885 {not found in *MS*}   886 *MS* he,   *MS* names   887–9 {not found
in *MS*}

869 *the world wags*: proverbial, meaning 'the world goes on as it will'. Cf. *As You
Like It*, II. vii. 23.

876 *in converse*: in conversation (used ironically), picking up 'criminal conversation',
i.e. adultery.

887 *Lucretia and Susanna*: types of the virtuous wife. Lucretia's story is told in Livy's
history of Rome, Susanna's in the apocryphal book of Susanna (Dan. 13 in the Vulgate).

"And curtaining Correggio carefully
"Lest I be taught that Leda had two legs,—
"—But once never so little tweaked my nose   890
"For peeping through my fan at Carnival,
"Confessing thereby 'I have no easy task—
" 'I need use all my powers to hold you mine,
" 'And then,—why 't is so doubtful if they serve,
" 'That—take this, as an earnest of despair!'   895
"Why, we were quits: I had wiped the harm away,
"Thought 'The man fears me!' and foregone revenge."
We must not want all this elaborate work
To solve the problem why young Fancy-and-flesh
Slips from the dull side of a spouse in years,   900
Betakes it to the breast of Brisk-and-bold
Whose love-scrapes furnish talk for all the town!

Accordingly one word on the other side
Tips over the piled-up fabric of a tale.
Guido says—that is, always, his friends say—   905

890 *MS* But once spat never so little in my face   891 *MS* peeping out of   *MS*
carnival-time,   892 *MS* thereby—"   893 *MS* this wife,>you mine,
894 *MS* my strength will serve   895 *MS* the expression of my despair!"
896 *MS* {beginning of fo. 205}   *MS* quits—I had foregone revenge."   *1868*
quits—   897 {not found in *MS*}   898 *MS* No, we   899 *MS* flesh-
and-fancy   *1868* fancy-and-flesh   900 *MS* {no comma}   901 *MS* And
betakes itself   *MS* a brisk young man   *1868* brisk-and-bold   902 *MS*
gallantries   ★903 *1868 1872* {new paragraph. Paragraphing obscured in *1888* and
1889 by this line's being at the head of the page}   *1868* Accordingly,   *MS*
Guido's word,   *MS* side,   904 *MS* piled up   905 *MS* He   *MS* say
for him—

888 *Correggio*: the painting alluded to, by the Italian artist Correggio (1489–1534),
shows a naked Leda, legs apart, at the moment when the swan rapes her. It was
notorious: Louis duc d'Orléans had mutilated it badly in the 1720s because its eroticism
so affected him. Browning's reference to the painting in *The Inn Album* as 'Correggio's
long-lost Leda' (l. 393) is puzzling. Pettigrew suggests that it is an allusion to the
restoration by Jacob Schlesinger (1792–1855) of the head of Leda, which had been cut
out of the canvas by d'Orléans: Pettigrew and Collins, ii. 1033. From the mid-
eighteenth century the painting has been in the Gemäldegalerie, Berlin.
895 *earnest of despair*: pledge of surrender, i.e. by tweaking her nose the husband
acknowledges how attractive his wife is to other men.

It is unlikely, from the wickedness,
That any man treat any woman so.
The letter in question was her very own,
Unprompted and unaided: she could write—
As able to write as ready to sin, or free,   910
When there was danger, to deny both facts.
He bids you mark, herself from first to last
Attributes all the so-styled torture just
To jealousy,—jealousy of whom but just
This very Caponsacchi! How suits here   915
This with the other alleged motive, Prince?
Would Guido make a terror of the man
He meant should tempt the woman, as they charge?
Do you fright your hare that you may catch your hare?
Consider too, the charge was made and met   920
At the proper time and place where proofs were plain—
Heard patiently and disposed of thoroughly
By the highest powers, possessors of most light,
The Governor for the law, and the Archbishop
For the gospel: which acknowledged primacies,   925
'T is impudently pleaded, he could warp
Into a tacit partnership with crime—

*906 MS "The tale is unlikely from its excessive wickedness,   1868 1872 1888
unlikely from   DC Br U unlikely from>unlikely, from   1889 unlikely, from
907 MS should treat   MS thus."   908 MS He says—"The   MS her
own: 909 MS unaided—   910 MS write, as ready to sin, as
free   911 MS To deny both when 'twas useful so to do.   912 MS They
point to the fact—   MS Herself>herself   913 MS Attributes the so-styled
cruelty to herself   Yale 1 Attribute>Attributes all   914 MS and that, jealousy
of just   915 MS Caponsacchi: how does that suit   Yale 1 Caponsacchi: how>
Caponsacchi! How   916 MS With the alleged motive of all the
cruelty   917, 918 {not found in MS. Instead there is line: To drive her precisely
into the arms of the same?}   919 MS hunt>fright   MS because you have
caught>because you would catch   MS {in right-hand margin caret written over
[ ]}   920 MS They say moreover that the case against him   921 MS the
proofs   923 MS powers and   MS {no commas}   924 MS Governor,
for the law, if you like,   1868 1872 Governor,   925 MS {beginning of fo.
206}   MS gospel,—these two acknowledged judges in chief   926 MS It is
impudently pretended he had the power to warp   927 MS in crime—

925 *primacies*: chief persons.

He being the while, believe their own account,
Impotent, penniless and miserable!
He further asks—Duke, note the knotty point!—   930
How he,—concede him skill to play such part
And drive his wife into a gallant's arms,—
Could bring the gallant to play his part too
And stand with arms so opportunely wide?
How bring this Caponsacchi,—with whom, friends   935
And foes alike agree, throughout his life
He never interchanged a civil word
Nor lifted courteous cap to—him how bend
To such observancy of beck and call,
—To undertake this strange and perilous feat   940
For the good of Guido, using, as the lure,
Pompilia whom, himself and she avouch,
He had nor spoken with nor seen, indeed,
Beyond sight in a public theatre,
When she wrote letters (she that could not write!)   945
The importunate shamelessly-protested love
Which brought him, though reluctant, to her feet,
And forced on him the plunge which, howsoe'er
She might swim up i' the whirl, must bury him
Under abysmal black: a priest contrive   950

---

928 *MS* being, according to their own account,   929 *MS* miserable.   930 *MS* They further ask—and this is a knotty point—   931 *MS* with every power to play this part   932 *MS* arms—   *Yale 1* arms—>arms,—   933 *MS* as well   934 *MS* them open to her so opportunely?   935 *MS* get   *MS* whom,—friends, foes   936 *MS* Alike agree in assuring, in all his life   937 *MS* had interchanged   938 *MS* a courteous   *MS* him,—to answer his ends,   *1868 1872* how bend him,   939 {not found in *MS*}   940 *MS* And   941 *MS* sake of a woman whom—himself and she   942 {not found in *MS*}   943 *MS* Aver alike—he had never spoken to   *Yale 1*—He> He   944 *MS* Or seen, beyond once in a public place,   945 *MS* Before she wrote him   946 *MS* shameless letters full of   947 *MS* {no commas}   948 *MS* forced him take the step   949 *MS* The event might profit her must ruin him—   950 {not found in *MS*}

---

939 *observancy*: obsequious attention.
950 *abysmal black*: dark of the abyss (of the whirlpool). Pompilia will swim to the surface, Caponsacchi will be dragged into the depths.

No better, no amour to be hushed up,
But open flight and noon-day infamy?
Try and concoct defence for such revolt!
Take the wife's tale as true, say she was wronged,—
Pray, in what rubric of the breviary   955
Do you find it registered—the part of a priest
Is—that to right wrongs from the church he skip,
Go journeying with a woman that's a wife,
And be pursued, o'ertaken and captured . . . how?
In a lay-dress, playing the kind sentinel   960
Where the wife sleeps (says he who best should know)
And sleeping, sleepless, both have spent the night!
Could no one else be found to serve at need—
No woman—or if man, no safer sort
Than this not well-reputed turbulence?   965

Then, look into his own account o' the case!
He, being the stranger and astonished one,
Yet received protestations of her love

951 *MS* No pardonable   *1868* No mitigable   *MS* {no commas}   952 *MS*
But an open flight must brand him ever more   953 *MS* The priest, the celibate,
the castaway?   954 *MS* story   *MS* true—   *MS* wronged,   955 *MS*
{beginning of fo. 207}   956 *MS* set down as   *1868 1872* registered the
957 *MS* That to right wrongs he skip from the church bounds,   *1868 1872* That to
right wrongs he skip from the church-door,   958 *MS* Take journeyings of indefinite length alone,   *MS* {Between 958 and 959 extra line: He a young man, with a
young lovely wife,}   959 *MS* at last o'ertaken and found . .   *Yale 1* pursued
o'ertaken> pursued, o'ertaken   *1868 1872* captured . .   960 *MS* sentinel at the
lone inn-door *1868* the sentinel   961 *MS* sleeps, says   *MS* know,   962
MS sleeping or sleepless,   *MS* past the night.   *Yale 1* night?>night!   963
MS serve in this sort—   964 *MS* safer man   965 *MS* turbulent priest?
966 *MS* {no new paragraph}   *MS* of the case—   967–70 *MS*
            He says that being the stranger I have said
            He received letter after letter of love
            From the lady he neither knew nor cared about—
            Which thus beginning bred disgust in him

──────
   955 *rubric of the breviary*: instructions of the prayer-book. The breviary is the prayer-
book used on a daily basis by Catholic priests.
   957 *from the church he skip*: perhaps clearer in *1868*: 'he skip from the church-door'.
   962 *sleeping, sleepless*: Pompilia sleeping, Caponsacchi sleepless (on guard); an incri-
minating situation, whether they have slept together or not.
   965 *turbulence*: disorderly character. Perhaps a memory of 'Who will rid me of this
turbulent priest?': Henry II of Thomas Becket.

From lady neither known nor cared about:
Love, so protested, bred in him disgust   970
After the wonder,—or incredulity,
Such impudence seeming impossible.
But, soon assured such impudence might be,
When he had seen with his own eyes at last
Letters thrown down to him i' the very street   975
From behind lattice where the lady lurked,
And read their passionate summons to her side—
Why then, a thousand thoughts swarmed up and in,—
How he had seen her once, a moment's space,
Observed she was both young and beautiful,   980
Heard everywhere report she suffered much
From a jealous husband thrice her age,—in short
There flashed the propriety, expediency
Of treating, trying might they come to terms,
—At all events, granting the interview   985
Prayed for, one so adapted to assist
Decision as to whether he advance,
Stand or retire, in his benevolent mood!
Therefore the interview befell at length;
And at this one and only interview,   990
He saw the sole and single course to take—
Bade her dispose of him, head, heart and hand,
Did her behest and braved the consequence,

971 *MS* incredulity rather,   972 *MS* impossible   973 *MS* when assured
MS be—   974 *MS* When had   *MS* with own   975 *MS* in   *MS*
public street   976 *MS* the lattice   *MS* {no comma}   978 *MS* came in
his head—   979 *MS* That   *MS* once for a   980 *MS* that she was young
and beautiful—   *Yale 1* beautiful—>beautiful,   *1868* so young   981 *MS*
{beginning of fo. 208}   *MS* That men reported she was suffering much
983 *MS* He saw the propriety and   984 *MS* treating and seeing if they
might   985 *MS* an>the   986 *MS* So flatteringly prayed for,—which
might help   *1868* and so   987 *MS* should go on,   988 *MS* Or stop
short, or turn back,   *MS* course   *1868* mood.   989 *MS* So did the interview
take place, says he—   *Yale 1* length>length;   991 *MS* to his satisfaction
the   992 *MS* him and all his powers,   993 *MS* all consequence

976 *lattice*: cross-patterned window.
988 *benevolent mood*: disinterested kindness. This is ironic; Tertium Quid assumes
that Caponsacchi's only possible motive was passion.

Not for the natural end, the love of man
For woman whether love be virtue or vice,⁣   995
But, please you, altogether for pity's sake—
Pity of innocence and helplessness!
And how did he assure himself of both?
Had he been the house-inmate, visitor,
Eye-witness of the described martyrdom,⁣   1000
So, competent to pronounce its remedy
Ere rush on such extreme and desperate course—
Involving such enormity of harm,
Moreover, to the husband judged thus, doomed
And damned without a word in his defence?⁣   1005
Not he! the truth was felt by instinct here,
—Process which saves a world of trouble and time.
There's the priest's story: what do you say to it,
Trying its truth by your own instinct too,
Since that's to be the expeditious mode?⁣   1010
"And now, do hear my version," Guido cries:
"I accept argument and inference both.
"It would indeed have been miraculous
"Had such a confidency sprung to birth
"With no more fanning from acquaintanceship⁣   1015
"Than here avowed by my wife and this priest.
"Only, it did not: you must substitute

994 *MS* a man   995 *MS* For a woman whether it be right or wrong,   997 *MS*
for her misery and   998 *MS* of the facts?   999 *MS* house's inmate, a
visitor   1000 *MS* And eye-witness   1001 *MS* on the remedy   1002 *MS*
Before taking   *MS* step   *1868* course,   1003 *MS* wrong moreover to the
husband he judged   1004 {not found in *MS*}   1005 *MS* Without having
let him even say a word in his own defence!   1006 *MS* But no—he felt the
truth by instinct, he says   *1868* But no,—   *1868* here!   1007 *MS* A process   *MS* time and trouble,   *1868* time,   1008 *MS* And that's his   *1868*
And there's his   *MS* its air,   1009 *MS* {beginning of fo. 209}   *MS* Trying
it by your own instinct also, since that is to be the mode?   1010 {not found in
MS}   1011 *MS* version and be fair,"   1012–42 *MS* {no quotation marks
at beginnings of lines}   1012 *MS* Cries Guido: "Yes, friends, I agree with
you: 1014 *MS* confidence   *MS* into birth   1016 *MS* Than is avowed   *MS* her friend the priest:

1014 *confidency*: intimacy; noted as rare in OED².

"The old stale unromantic way of fault,
"The commonplace adventure, mere intrigue
"In prose form with the unpoetic tricks,   1020
"Cheatings and lies: they used the hackney chair
"Satan jaunts forth with, shabby and serviceable,
"No gilded gimcrack-novelty from below,
"To bowl you along thither, swift and sure.
"That same officious go-between, the wench   1025
"Who gave and took the letters of the two,
"Now offers self and service back to me:
"Bears testimony to visits night by night
"When all was safe, the husband far and away,—
"To many a timely slipping out at large   1030
"By light o' the morning-star, ere he should wake.
"And when the fugitives were found at last,
"Why, with them were found also, to belie
"What protest they might make of innocence,
"All documents yet wanting, if need were,   1035
"To establish guilt in them, disgrace in me—
"The chronicle o' the converse from its rise

1018 *MS* old and unromantic   *MS* crime—   1019 *MS* the intrigue
1020 *MS* the old   *Yale 1* the used>the prose   *1868* the prose   *MS* {no com-
ma}   1021 *MS* Cheating and lies,   *MS* the old hackney   1022 *MS* That
the devil plies with, the shabby old useful thing,   1023 *MS* splendid novelty
from hell   *Yale 1* jimcrack novelty>jimcrack-novelty   *1868 1872* jimcrack- novelty
        1024 *MS* ^you^   *MS* by a new swift sure strange coach.
1025 *MS* woman   1026 *MS* That   *1868 1872* "That   *MS* letters
between   1027 *MS* She offers her services now to me, you must
know: 1029 *MS* the way was safe and the husband out   1030 *MS* And
to the timely slippings out in the   *MS* morn>large   1031 *MS* of   *MS*
should be back.   1032 *MS* caught   *MS* {no comma}   1034 *MS* The
protest that they made   1035 *MS* All the documents wanting to establish
disgrace,   1036 {not found in *MS*}   1037 *MS* of the connexion

1021–3 *hackney chair...gimcrack-novelty*: a hackney chair is a box vehicle, to seat one
passenger, borne on two poles by two bearers; it is a rather simple way to travel
compared to the 'gimcrack-novelty', some impressive stage-coach. In other words, the
adultery is a very ordinary affair, not something unique or surprising.
1023 *from below*: from hell.
1025 *wench*: cf. III. 1097 n.
1037 *converse*: cf. l. 876 n.

"To culmination in this outrage: read!
"Letters from wife to priest, from priest to wife,—
"Here they are, read and say where they chime in   1040
"With the other tale, superlative purity
"O' the pair of saints! I stand or fall by these."

But then on the other side again,—how say
The pair of saints? That not one word is theirs—
No syllable o' the batch or writ or sent   1045
Or yet received by either of the two.
"Found," says the priest, "because he needed them,
"Failing all other proofs, to prove our fault:
"So, here they are, just as is natural.
"Oh yes—we had our missives, each of us!   1050
"Not these, but to the full as vile, no doubt:
"Hers as from me,—she could not read, so burnt,—
"Mine as from her,—I burnt because I read.
"Who forged and found them? *Cui profuerint!*
(I take the phrase out of your Highness' mouth)   1055
"He who would gain by her fault and my fall,

1038 *MS* {beginning of fo. 210}   *MS* To its culmination in outrageous guilt:
1039 *MS* the wife to the priest, from the priest to the wife,—   1040 *MS*
them and say where they fit in   1041 *MS* To   *MS* tale of the   1042 *MS*
On either side! I rest my case thereon."   1043 *MS* reply   1044 *MS*
That priest and wife?   1045 *MS* No letter of the batch was ever written or
sent   *Yale 1* batch writ>batch or writ   1046 *MS* Or received at all   *MS*
pair   1047 *MS* "Forged,"   *MS* you   1048–54 *MS* {no quotation marks
at beginnings of lines}   1048 *MS* your case: 1049 *MS* So here   1050 *MS*
us—   1052 *MS* She   *MS* ^as^   *MS* which she   1053 *MS* I as from
her, which   *MS* read: 1054 *MS* sent these?   *MS profuerint—"*   1055 *MS*
mouth.)

1054 *Cui profuerint*: 'Who stood to gain?' (L.); the implied answer is 'Guido'. L.
Cassius Longinus Ravilla (consul 127 BC), a fearsome judge known as the *scopulus
reorum* or rock on which defendants foundered, made a point of asking *Cui bono?*, 'To
whose advantage?' Tertium Quid deserves our commendation as a Latinist. His Highness has asked—or has been politely credited with asking—*Cui profuerunt?*, a direct
question in the indicative, which Tertium Quid repeats before replying; but since in
Latin such a repeated question takes the indirect form, he makes the verb subjunctive,
Cui profuerint?

"The trickster, schemer and pretender—he
"Whose whole career was lie entailing lie
"Sought to be sealed truth by the worst lie last!"

Guido rejoins—"Did the other end o' the tale   1060
"Match this beginning! 'T is alleged I prove
"A murderer at the end, a man of force
"Prompt, indiscriminate, effectual: good!
"Then what need all this trifling woman's-work,
"Letters and embassies and weak intrigue,   1065
"When will and power were mine to end at once
"Safely and surely? Murder had come first
"Not last with such a man, assure yourselves!
"The silent *acquetta*, stilling at command—
"A drop a day i' the wine or soup, the dose,—   1070
"The shattering beam that breaks above the bed
"And beats out brains, with nobody to blame
"Except the wormy age which eats even oak,—
"Nay, the staunch steel or trusty cord,—who cares
"I' the blind old palace, a pitfall at each step,   1075
"With none to see, much more to interpose

1057–9 *MS* {no quotation marks at beginnings of lines}   1057 *MS* ignoble
trickster,   *MS* {"—he" not found}   1058 *MS* one whole falsification of facts
1059 *MS* Which thus he eventually sought to seal   *MS* {Between 1059 and 1060
extra line: By a general slaughter and smothering up of truth.}   1060 *MS* {no
new paragraph}   *MS* "Try   *MS* of   1061–89 *MS* {no quotation marks at
beginnings of lines}   1061 *MS* See how the two ends suit: I am, you allege,
1062 *MS* end,—   *MS* force,   1063 *MS* {beginning of fo. 211}   1064 *MS*
of all   *MS* {no comma}   1065 *MS* At letters   *MS* {no comma}   1066 *MS*
the will   *MS* were in me   1067 *MS* had come first not last: 1068 {not
found in *MS*}   1069 *MS* acquetta, killing   1070 *MS* in   *MS* soup,
enough—   1071 *MS* that drops in the corridor   1072 *MS* crushes life
out,   1073 *MS* worms and age that   *MS* oak   1074 *MS* sure   *MS*
cord, who cares?   1075 *MS* In   *MS* on each hand,   1076 *MS* try to
prevent

1058 *entailing*: leading to, necessitating. In relation to the next line, the legal
meaning (OED², v.² 1.) is also present: one lie leads to another, like generations
passing on land, in the hope that the lie will eventually establish itself as truth.
  1069 *acquetta*: (It.) poison, acqua tofana; from OYB ccxiii (215), ccxvii (219).
  1073 *wormy*: worm-eaten, decayed.

"O' the two, three, creeping house-dog-servant-things
"Born mine and bred mine? Had I willed gross death,
"I had found nearer paths to thrust him prey
"Than this that goes meandering here and there   1080
"Through half the world and calls down in its course
"Notice and noise,—hate, vengeance, should it fail,
"Derision and contempt though it succeed!
"Moreover, what o' the future son and heir?
"The unborn babe about to be called mine,—   1085
"What end in heaping all this shame on him,
"Were I indifferent to my own black share?
"Would I have tried these crookednesses, say,
"Willing and able to effect the straight?"

"Ay, would you!"—one may hear the priest retort,   1090
"Being as you are, i' the stock, a man of guile,
"And ruffianism but an added graft.
"You, a born coward, try a coward's arms,
"Trick and chicane,—and only when these fail
"Does violence follow, and like fox you bite   1095
"Caught out in stealing. Also, the disgrace
"You hardly shrunk at, wholly shrivelled her:

1077 *MS* Of   *MS* two or three creeping   *1868* three creeping   1078 *MS*
mine,—had   *1868 1872* mine?—had   *MS* her death   1079 *MS* There had
been nearer ways with the wife thereto   1081 *MS* unnecessarily down
1082 {not found in *MS*}   1083 *MS* Scorn, hatred, jeers and derision, even
though it succeed!   1084 *MS* do you say to my   *MS* heir   1085 *MS*
The babe about to be born to me,—what end   1086 *MS* In piling all this useless
shame on him   1087 *MS* share.   1088 *MS* crooknesses I say   1089 *MS*
able, as you say, to manage   1090 *MS* {no new paragraph}   *MS* "Ay, would
you!" the Priest and the wife may be supposed to retort   1091 *MS* in   *MS*
guile   1092–1106 *MS*   {no   quotation   marks   at   beginnings   of
lines}   1092 *MS* {beginning of fo. 212}   *MS* the ruffianism of you   *MS*
graft: 1093 *MS* ways   *Yale 1* ways,>arms,   1094 *MS* Trick, lie,
1095 *MS* come,   *MS* the fox   1097 *MS* Which hardly hurt you wholly
shrivelled her   *Yale 1* her—>her:

1091–2 *stock . . . graft*: i.e. in the main, and by inheritance, Guido is a man of guile;
'ruffianism' (violence) is a lesser trait added to his nature. The image is from the
cultivation of trees, particularly fruit trees. A 'graft', a small shoot from one species of
tree, is cut and inserted into a 'stock', a main stem or trunk of another species. 'Stock'
also has its sense 'a family, a kindred, a line of descent': OED² sb.¹ 3.c.

"You plunged her thin white delicate hand i' the flame
"Along with your coarse horny brutish fist,
"Held them a second there, then drew out both   1100
"—Yours roughed a little, hers ruined through and through.
"Your hurt would heal forthwith at ointment's touch—
"Namely, succession to the inheritance
"Which bolder crime had lost you: let things change,
"The birth o' the boy warrant the bolder crime,   1105
"Why, murder was determined, dared and done.
"For me," the priest proceeds with his reply,
"The look o' the thing, the chances of mistake,
"All were against me,—that, I knew the first:
"But, knowing also what my duty was,   1110
"I did it: I must look to men more skilled
"In reading hearts than ever was the world."

Highness, decide! Pronounce, Her Excellency!
Or... even leave this argument in doubt,
Account it a fit matter, taken up   1115
With all its faces, manifold enough,
To ponder on—what fronts us, the next stage,
Next legal process? Guido, in pursuit,

1098 *MS* wan white   *MS* hand, as it were,   1099 *MS* horny fist in the
flame,   1101 *MS* singed a little but   *MS* through—   1102 *MS* Yours,
too,   *MS* an ointment's touch   1103 *MS* To-wit, the   1104 *MS*
the bolder way   *MS* you—tried at last   1105 *MS* Because the birth of the
boy changed things at once   *MS* {Between 1105 and 1106 extra line: Saved you
from what had been loss before—that known   1107 *MS* goes on   *MS* {no
commas}   1108–12 *MS* {no quotation marks at beginnings of lines}   1108 *MS*
of   1109 *MS* *that* I   *MS* first   1111 *MS* trust   *MS* well-skilled
1112 *MS* In the heart: and, missing their verdict, wait for God's."   *1868*
"I'the   1113 *MS* {no new paragraph}   *MS* Who shall decide? How says
your Excellency?   1114 *MS* Let's even   *MS* other stage   *MS* {no comma}
1115 *MS* Call it a fit matter, taken up with all its faces,   1116 {not found in
MS}   1117 *MS* To put upon—what we find as the next stage—   *1868* To put
upon—   1118 *MS* process,—to-wit, when   *1868* process!—

1098–1101 *You...through*: shame provides an inverted trial-by-ordeal, where,
instead of virtue being untouched, it is Guido's evil that comes off unscathed.
    1104–6 *let...done*: see III. 1546–69 n.
    1116 *faces*: aspects.

Coming up with the fugitives at the inn,
Caused both to be arrested then and there   1120
And sent to Rome for judgment on the case—
Thither, with all his armoury of proofs,
Betook himself: 't is there we'll meet him now,
Waiting the further issue.
       Here you smile   1125
"And never let him henceforth dare to plead,—
"Of all pleas and excuses in the world
"For any deed hereafter to be done,—
"His irrepressible wrath at honour's wound!
"Passion and madness irrepressible?   1130
"Why, Count and cavalier, the husband comes
"And catches foe i' the very act of shame!
"There's man to man,—nature must have her way,—
"We look he should have cleared things on the spot.
"Yes, then, indeed—even tho' it prove he erred—   1135
"Though the ambiguous first appearance, mount
"Of solid injury, melt soon to mist,
"Still,—had he slain the lover and the wife—
"Or, since she was a woman and his wife,
"Slain him, but stript her naked to the skin   1140
"Or at best left no more of an attire
"Than patch sufficient to pin paper to,

1119 MS {beginning of fo. 213}   MS in the morn at the Inn   MS {Between
1119 and 1120 extra line: And finding them as was said, contented himself   1120 MS With causing   1122 MS Whither,   MS 1868 1872
proofs   MS {Between 1122 and 1123 extra line: Witnesses and those documents
aforesaid   1123 MS He betook himself,—and where we meet him now,   1868
himself, and there   1125 MS {no new paragraph}   MS some hoot   1868
some   1126 MS plead   1127–65 MS {no quotation marks at beginnings
of lines}   1127 MS all imaginable excuses   1128 {not found in
MS}   1129 MS wound,   1130 MS The passion and the madness: "irrepressible?"   1131 MS The Count   *1888 1889 {line indented}   1132 MS
his foe in   MS 1868 shame: 1134 MS slain him   1135 MS should prove
1136 MS That   MS appearance of things   1137 MS Admitted of being
cleared up afterward,—   1138 MS Then,—   1140 MS Not slain her,
1141 MS left her   MS her chemise   1142 MS a stripe   MS a paper   MS
[?le]>to   MS {no comma}

"Some one love-letter, infamy and all,
"As passport to the Paphos fit for such,
"Safe-conduct to her natural home the stews,—   1145
"Good! One had recognized the power o' the pulse.
"But when he stands, the stock-fish,—sticks to law—
"Offers the hole in his heart, all fresh and warm,
"For scrivener's pen to poke and play about—
"Can stand, can stare, can tell his beads perhaps,   1150
"Oh, let us hear no syllable o' the rage!
"Such rage were a convenient afterthought
"For one who would have shown his teeth belike,
"Exhibited unbridled rage enough,
"Had but the priest been found, as was to hope,   1155
"In serge, not silk, with crucifix, not sword:
"Whereas the grey innocuous grub, of yore,
"Had hatched a hornet, tickle to the touch,
"The priest was metamorphosed into knight.
"And even the timid wife, whose cue was—shriek,   1160
"Bury her brow beneath his trampling foot,—

1143 *MS* {line added later}   *MS* Those letters with their infamy, to wit,—
1144 *MS* innermost shrine of shame—   1145 *MS* And so sent her to her
parents, or the stews,—   1146 *1868 1872* recognised   *MS* right of the
blood.   1147 *MS* {beginning of fo. 214}   *MS* calls in   1148 *MS* heart
all-freshly made   1149 *MS* To a   *MS* turn about—   1150 *MS* Can
wait, can breathe, and   1151 *MS* of   1152 *MS* Rage and madness
are   *MS* afterthought.   1153 *MS* The fact is, he   *MS* forthwith,   1154 *MS*
with full effect,   1155 *MS* to be hoped,   1156 *MS* In a serge corselet,
armed with a crucifix;   1157 *MS* grub that was   1158 *MS* hornet not to
be lightly touched.   1159 *MS* a knight   *MS* {Between 1159 and 1160 extra
line: Down to the sword he showed all will to use:}   1160 *MS* was to
shriek   1161 *MS* And roll her naked breasts beneath his foot,—

1144 *Paphos*: brothel; from the city of Cyprus sacred to Venus.

1147 *stock-fish*: dried cod; i.e. apathetic, ridiculous, unmasculine. Cf. *Measure for
Measure*, III. ii. 109.

1149 *scrivener*: professional penman, secretary. The image here is playing with the
proverb 'the pen is mightier than the sword': Guido has failed to use the sword, so now
he is poked and wounded (figuratively) by the legal penman who writes down the
humiliating details of the case.

1156 *serge, not silk*: i.e. in rough priestly clothes, not cavalier's silk. Cf. *Aurora Leigh*,
iv. 267–8.

1158 *tickle*: hazardous, risky.

"She too sprang at him like a pythoness:
"So, gulp down rage, passion must be postponed,
"Calm be the word! Well, our word is—we brand
"This part o' the business, howsoever the rest   1165
"Befall."
          "Nay," interpose as prompt his friends—
"This is the world's way! So you adjudge reward
"To the forbearance and legality
"Yourselves begin by inculcating—ay,   1170
"Exacting from us all with knife at throat!
"This one wrong more you add to wrong's amount,—
"You publish all, with the kind comment here,
"'Its victim was too cowardly for revenge.'"
Make it your own case,—you who stand apart!   1175
The husband wakes one morn from heavy sleep,
With a taste of poppy in his mouth,—rubs eyes,
Finds his wife flown, his strong box ransacked too,
Follows as he best can, overtakes i' the end.
You bid him use his privilege: well, it seems   1180
He's scarce cool-blooded enough for the right move—
Does not shoot when the game were sure, but stands
Bewildered at the critical minute,—since

1162 *MS* lioness   *MS* {Between 1162 and 1163 extra line: And was choked off by the guards with pains enough:}   1163 *MS* So the programme broke down; rage 1164 *MS* Calmness!—was the word. We begin by branding here   1165 *MS* of   *MS* however he deserve for the rest!"   1165-7 *Yale 1* {Paragraph break moved from between 1165 and 1166 to between 1166 and 1167}   1166 {not found in *MS*}   1167 *MS* {no new paragraph}   *MS* "Nay" interpose as prompt the friends of him—   1168 *MS* way—so   1169-73 *MS* {no quotation marks at beginnings of lines}   1169 *MS* For the very forbearance and rational calm of a man   1170 *MS* inculcating and demanding.   1171 {not found in *MS*}   1172 *MS* The   *MS* any wrong—   1173 *MS* That you publish with all this compassionate scorn,   1174 *MS* "Its   *MS* revenge."   1175 *MS* {beginning of fo. 215}   *MS* Be just and calm here— you who stand apart,—   1176 *MS* a heavy   1177 *MS* poppies   *MS* his eyes   1178 *MS* ransomed>ransacked   1179 *MS* and overtakes her thus: 1181 *MS* He's not   1182 *MS* sure to fall—   1183 *MS* Stands bewildered at the critical minute: beside,

---

1162 *pythoness*: wild prophetess, witch: cf. *Sordello*, v. 81.
1183 *critical minute*: crucial moment.

He has the first flash of the fact alone
To judge from, act with, not the steady lights   1185
Of after-knowledge,—yours who stand at ease
To try conclusions: he's in smother and smoke,
You outside, with explosion at an end:
The sulphur may be lightning or a squib—
He'll know in a minute, but till then, he doubts.   1190
Back from what you know to what he knew not!
Hear the priest's lofty "I am innocent,"
The wife's as resolute "You are guilty!" Come!
Are you not staggered?—pause, and you lose the move!
Nought left you but a low appeal to law,   1195
"Coward" tied to your tail for compliment!
Another consideration: have it your way!
Admit the worst: his courage failed the Count,
He's cowardly like the best o' the burgesses
He's grown incorporate with,—a very cur,   1200
Kick him from out your circle by all means!
Why, trundled down this reputable stair,
Still, the Church-door lies wide to take him in,
And the Court-porch also: in he sneaks to each,—
"Yes, I have lost my honour and my wife,   1205
"And, being moreover an ignoble hound,
"I dare not jeopardize my life for them!"

1184 *MS* first face   1185 *MS* To judge from and act upon, not the lights which
came   *Yale 1* from and act>from, act   1186 *MS* By   1187 *MS* the
smother   1188 *MS* We outside, and the explosion's   1189 *MS* hell-fire
or a mere squib—   1190 *MS* He will   *MS* but, till that minute,   *Yale 1* but,
till then he>but till then, he   1191 *MS* Go back   *MS* not—   1192–4 *MS*
          The priest is affirming "I am innocent"
          The wife shrieking "You it is are guilty here"
          Are you not staggered like him?,—pause,—lose the move!
1194 *MS* lost>lose   1195, 1196 {not found in *MS*}   1197 *MS* your own
way, Highness!   1198 *MS* man: 1199 *MS* burgesses he's incorporate
with,—   1200 {not found in *MS*}   1201 *MS* means   1202 *MS*
Why, trundle down these respectable stairs, as he does,   1203 *MS* church-doors
lie   *MS* in   *Yale 1* in>in,   1204 *MS* law-courts'   *Yale 1* Courts'-porch>
Court-porch   *MS* either,—   1205 *MS* {beginning of fo. 216}   *MS* wife,
and my honor thereby,   1206–7 *MS* {no quotation marks at beginnings of
lines}   1206 *MS* But, being an utterly ignoble soul,   1207   *MS* I
would not peril my life to recover these,—"

Religion and Law lean forward from their chairs,
"Well done, thou good and faithful servant!" Ay,
Not only applaud him that he scorned the world,   1210
But punish should he dare do otherwise.
If the case be clear or turbid,—you must say!

Thus, anyhow, it mounted to the stage
In the law-courts,—let's see clearly from this point!—
Where the priest tells his story true or false,   1215
And the wife her story, and the husband his,
All with result as happy as before.
The courts would nor condemn nor yet acquit
This, that or the other, in so distinct a sense
As end the strife to either's absolute loss: 1220
Pronounced, in place of something definite,
"Each of the parties, whether goat or sheep
"I' the main, has wool to show and hair to hide.
"Each has brought somehow trouble, is somehow cause
"Of pains enough,—even though no worse were proved.
"Here is a husband, cannot rule his wife   1226
"Without provoking her to scream and scratch
"And scour the fields,—causelessly, it may be:
"Here is that wife,—who makes her sex our plague,

1208 *MS* Why, Religion   *MS* chairs   1210 *MS* for doing as he has
done,   1211 *MS* But would punish him   1212 *MS* There, sirs,—if
the case is clear, or not clear,—you must say—   1213 *MS* {no new paragraph}
MS {no commas}   *Yale 1* Thus anyhow it>Thus, anyhow, it   *MS* up
to   1214 *MS* In the Law Courts,—let's go on clearly from this point, at least:
1215 *MS* Priest   *MS* or true or false,   1216 *MS* Husband   1217 *MS*
With result just as satisfactory as before.   1218 *MS* Court   *MS* neither condemn   1219 *MS* other in   *MS* way   1220 *MS* dispute to someone's
1221 *MS* No: they said, in the   *Yale 1* So said,>Pronounced,   1222 *MS*
these parties,   *MS* right or wrong   *MS* wrong,>wrong   1223–79 *MS* {no
quotation marks at beginnings of lines}   1223 *MS* In   *MS* white to show and
black to hide   1224 *MS* given   *MS* trouble and been the   1225 *MS*
scandal   *MS* be   1226 *MS* husband who cannot manage   1229 *MS*
runaway wife,—who shames her sex,

1209 "*Well . . . servant*: cf. Matt. 25: 21.
1228 *scour*: run across.

"Wedlock, our bugbear,—perhaps with cause enough:
"And here is the truant priest o' the trio, worst   1231
"Or best—each quality being conceivable.
"Let us impose a little mulct on each.
"We punish youth in state of pupilage
"Who talk at hours when youth is bound to sleep,   1235
"Whether the prattle turn upon Saint Rose
"Or Donna Olimpia of the Vatican:
"'T is talk, talked wisely or unwisely talked,
"I' the dormitory where to talk at all,
"Transgresses, and is mulct: as here we mean.   1240
"For the wife,—let her betake herself, for rest,
"After her run, to a House of Convertites—
"Keep there, as good as real imprisonment:
"Being sick and tired, she will recover so.
"For the priest, spritely strayer out of bounds,   1245
"Who made Arezzo hot to hold him,—Rome
"Profits by his withdrawal from the scene.
"Let him be relegate to Civita,

1230 *MS* Makes marriage impossible,—yet perhaps with cause enough   1231 *MS* priest, worst case of all   1232 *MS* since good ends are conceivable here too: 1233 *MS* {beginning of fo. 217}   *MS* Now, we propose a little mulct for each: 1234 *MS* pupils who talk when they should sleep,   1235 {not found in *MS*}   1236 *MS* be of Saint Rose of Lima   1237 *MS* Vatican   1238 *MS* Tis   *MS* whether unwisely or wisely   1239 *MS* In   *MS* should be no talk at all,   1240 *MS* So is punished: thus we mean to punish now.   1241 *MS* herself for   1242 *MS* Convertites   1243 *MS* And keep   *MS* imprisonment—   1244 *MS* Which, being   *MS* find easy to bear.   1245 *MS* the spritely   1246 *MS* has made   *MS* too hot   *MS* what   1247 *MS* So fit as brief   *MS* scene?   1248 *MS* relegated   *MS* {no comma}

1233 *mulct*: fine, penalty.

1236-7 *Saint Rose / Or Donna Olimpia*: i.e. saint or sinner. A seventeenth-century contrast: Rose of Lima (1568-1617) was canonized in 1671 by Pope Clement X, the first saint of the New World. The scheming, avaricious Donna Olimpia Pamfili (1594-1656), née Maidalchini, widowed sister-in-law of Pope Innocent X, exercised such influence in his reign (1644-55) that she was rumoured to be his mistress. A possible source here is T. A. Trollope's life of Pamfili in his *A Decade of Italian Women* (2 vols., 1859), ii. 346-65. Story mentions one of the jokes about her: *Roba di Roma*, i. 265.

1240 *mulct*: fined.

1248 *relegate to Civita*: see II. 1177, 1180 nn.

"Circumscribed by its bounds till matters mend:
"There he at least lies out o' the way of harm   1250
"From foes—perhaps from the too friendly fair.
"And finally for the husband, whose rash rule
"Has but itself to blame for this ado,—
"If he be vexed that, in our judgments dealt,
"He fails obtain what he accounts his right,   1255
"Let him go comforted with the thought, no less,
"That, turn each sentence howsoever he may,
"There's satisfaction to extract therefrom.
"For, does he wish his wife proved innocent?
"Well, she's not guilty, he may safely urge,   1260
"Has missed the stripes dishonest wives endure—
"This being a fatherly pat o' the cheek, no more.
"Does he wish her guilty? Were she otherwise
"Would she be locked up, set to say her prayers,
"Prevented intercourse with the outside world,   1265
"And that suspected priest in banishment,
"Whose portion is a further help i' the case?
"Oh, ay, you all of you want the other thing,
"The extreme of law, some verdict neat, complete,—
"Either, the whole o' the dowry in your poke   1270
"With full release from the false wife, to boot,

1249 *MS* a year or so,   1250 *MS* Where he will at least be out of   1251
MS perhaps temptation   *MS* fair: 1252 *MS* husband—whose unwise
1253 *MS* Has itself   *MS* causing this ado,   1254 *MS* is   *MS* these judgments of ours   *MS* {no commas}   1255 *MS* He does not obtain exactly his
full will,   1256 *MS* Yet let   1257 *MS* whichever way he will,
1258 *MS* a sort of   *MS* therefrom: 1260 *MS* criminated,   *MS* say,
1261 *MS* {beginning of fo. 218}   *MS* scourge   *MS* obtain—   1262 *MS*
on   *MS* more: 1263 *MS* proved guilty? Well, were   1265 *MS* suspected man—   1266 {not found in *MS*}   *Yale 1* banishment>banishment,
1267 *MS* in   1268 *MS* thing   1269 *MS* judgment   1270 *MS* of   *MS*
assured to you   1271 *MS* a full   *MS* detested wife,

1267 *a further help i' the case*: i.e. Caponsacchi's banishment is further evidence of
Pompilia's guilt if Guido wants to see it as such.
1269 *The extreme of law*: proverbially said to be the extreme of injustice (*summum ius
summa iniuria*): ODEP, 235.

"And heading, hanging for the priest, beside—
"Or, contrary, claim freedom for the wife,
"Repayment of each penny paid her spouse,
"Amends for the past, release for the future! Such   1275
"Is wisdom to the children of this world;
"But we've no mind, we children of the light,
"To miss the advantage of the golden mean,
"And push things to the steel point." Thus the courts.

Is it settled so far? Settled or disturbed,   1280
Console yourselves: 't is like . . . an instance, now!
You've seen the puppets, of Place Navona, play,—
Punch and his mate,—how threats pass, blows are dealt,
And a crisis comes: the crowd or clap or hiss
Accordingly as disposed for man or wife—   1285
When down the actors duck awhile perdue,

1272–9 MS   And heading or hanging for the obnoxious priest—
            Or, on the other hand, full liberty again,
            With restitution of dowry falsely obtained,
            And punishment for all cruelty in the past,
            With release from fear in the future! But we've no mind
            To forego the advantages of sobriety
            And push things to extremes thus. Judged the Case!"
1280 MS {no new paragraph}   MS Well, settled or not, 1281 MS it is like a
common case—   1868 1872 like . .   1282 MS puppet-show at Piazza Navona,
1283 MS wife,—   1284 MS cry victory   1285 MS According as they are
disposed for this side or that—   1286 MS duck, are awhile below

1276–7 wisdom . . . light: cf. Luke 16: 8.

1279 to the steel point: to extremes, to the point of the sword. There is a pun between
'steel' and 'golden' in the previous line.

1282 puppets, of Place Navona: in Browning's time there was a famous puppet
theatre, the Teatro Emiliano, in the Piazza Navona. The puppets were two to three
feet high, multi-jointed, and worked by wires from above; favourite subjects were 'the
wars of the Paladins, the heroic adventures of knights and ladies of romance, the
tragedies of the middle ages, the prodigies of the melodramatic world': Roba di Roma, i.
270. Browning's allusion is loose: he assumes the theatre was working in the 1690s, and
sets Punch and Judy in it—not necessarily a subject that would have been there—
presumably on the grounds of Punch's Italian origins.

1283 Punch and his mate: a cynical comparison characteristic of Tertium Quid:
Guido and Pompilia (or their representatives) are like the battling puppets of Punch
and his wife hitting each other over the head. The Punch story comprises several
scenes of such battles: see l. 1296 n.

1286 actors: i.e. the puppets.
perdue: out of sight.

Donning what novel rag-and-feather trim
Best suits the next adventure, new effect:
And,—by the time the mob is on the move,
With something like a judgment *pro* and *con*,—   1290
There's a whistle, up again the actors pop
In t'other tatter with fresh-tinseled staves,
To re-engage in one last worst fight more
Shall show, what you thought tragedy was farce.
Note, that the climax and the crown of things   1295
Invariably is, the devil appears himself,
Armed and accoutred, horns and hoofs and tail!
Just so, nor otherwise it proved—you'll see:
Move to the murder, never mind the rest!

Guido, at such a general duck-down,   1300
I' the breathing-space,—of wife to convent here,
Priest to his relegation, and himself
To Arezzo,—had resigned his part perforce

1287 *MS* the novel rag and feather costume   1288 *MS* In private for the next
adventure wholly new,   1289 *MS* And, by   *MS* preparing to move
away,   1290 *MS* {beginning of fo. 219}   1291 *MS* whistle and up
the actors pop again   1292 *MS* In the t'other tatter with the novel
arms   *Yale 1* fresh, tinseled>fresh-tinseled   1293 *MS* To reengage in a fight
shall eclipse the first.   1294 {not found in *MS*}   1295 *MS* climax,
last appearance of all   1296 *MS* Is invariably the Devil himself, complete 1297 *MS* Horns, hoofs and tail; nor otherwise proved it here—   1298 {not
found in *MS*}   1299 *MS* Let's move to that and never mind the rest.
1300–5 *MS* Well, Guido, at this general ducking down
          In the breathing-while,—of the wife to her convent here,
          The priest to his place of relegation, himself
          To his house at Arezzo,—had given his place perforce
          To his brother the Abate, who bustled and did his best
          To retrieve matters somewhat by managing the suits—

     1292 *tatter*: ragged clothes.
     1296 *devil*: in the traditional Punch farce, popular in the nineteenth century, Punch,
who has a mistress, kills his own child, his wife, and various other characters who get in
his way. At the close of the story he kills the doctor, then Jack Ketch (or another death
figure), and is then confronted with the devil.

To brother Abate, who bustled, did his best,
Retrieved things somewhat, managed the three suits—
Since, it should seem, there were three suits-at-law   1306
Behoved him look to, still, lest bad grow worse:
First civil suit,—the one the parents brought,
Impugning the legitimacy of his wife,
Affirming thence the nullity of her rights: 1310
This was before the Rota,—Molinès,
That's judge there, made that notable decree
Which partly leaned to Guido, as I said,—
But Pietro had appealed against the same
To the very court will judge what we judge now—   1315
Tommati and his fellows,—Suit the first.
Next civil suit,—demand on the wife's part
Of separation from the husband's bed
On plea of cruelty and risk to life—
Claims restitution of the dowry paid,   1320
Immunity from paying any more:
This second, the Vicegerent has to judge.
Third and last suit,—this time, a criminal one,—

1306 *MS* were still   1307 *MS* attend to, lest   *MS* far worse: 1308 *MS*
Civil Suit,—   *MS* that Pietro   1309 *MS* the girl   1310 *MS* And affir-
ming   *MS* dowry: 1311 *MS* its Judge, Molines,   1312 {not found in
MS}   1313 *MS* Partially decided for Guido at first, as I said,—   *MS*
P>Guido   1314 *MS* decision   1315 *MS* tribunal which will judge him
now,   1316 *MS* Whereof Tomati is Judge,—this is Suit the First.   1317 *MS*
Next Civil Suit,—a demand on Pompilia's part   1318 *MS* For   *MS* marital
1319 *MS* {beginning of fo. 220}   *MS* the cruelty and danger of   1320 *MS*
Claiming restitution also   *MS* {no comma}   1321 *MS* And immunity from
keeping the other engagements—   1322 *MS* This—before the Tribunal of the
Vice Gerent:

　　1305 *three suits*: the following description of the lawsuits relies on OYB ccviii (210):
'the first lawsuit concerned the legitimacy of the parentage of the wife, Francesca
Pompilia, and the cancellation of the dowry agreement; it was brought by Pietro in the
Tribunal of the Sacred Rota. The second was for divorce, brought by the said
Francesca Pompilia, before the Vicegerent. The third was a criminal suit [brought by
Guido] concerning the pretended adultery, which is still pending in the Tribunal of
His Excellency the Governor [Lord Venturini].'
　　1311 *Molinès*: actually Tommati. Tommati heard the first case and Molinès the
appeal; Browning reverses them. See II. 740 n.

Answer to, and protection from, both these,—
Guido's complaint of guilt against his wife   1325
In the Tribunal of the Governor,
Venturini, also judge of the present cause.
Three suits of all importance plaguing him,
Beside a little private enterprise
Of Guido's,—essay at a shorter cut.   1330
For Paolo, knowing the right way at Rome,
Had, even while superintending these three suits
I' the regular way, each at its proper court,
Ingeniously made interest with the Pope
To set such tedious regular forms aside,   1335
And, acting the supreme and ultimate judge,
Declare for the husband and against the wife.
Well, at such crisis and extreme of straits,—
The man at bay, buffeted in this wise,—
Happened the strangest accident of all.   1340
"Then," sigh friends, "the last feather broke his back,
"Made him forget all possible remedies
"Save one—he rushed to, as the sole relief
"From horror and the abominable thing."
"Or rather," laugh foes, "then did there befall   1345

1324 *MS* The answer to and protection from both of these,—   1325 *MS* own
charge of adultery   1326 *MS* {no comma}   1327 *MS* Venturini who will
judge the present cause:—   1328 *MS* {line added later}   *MS* {no comma}
1330 *MS* own,—an   *MS* cut,—   1331 *MS* proper   1332 *MS* Had
ingeniously,   *MS* the other suits   1333 *MS* In the regular way at the proper
courts of law,   1334 *MS* Made interest and appealed to the Pope himself   1335 *MS* those tedious   1336 *MS* acting as   1337 *MS* the
wife guilty and give the husband his desire.   1338 *MS* strait as this,   *1868*
1872 straits,   1339, 1340 {not found in *MS*}   1339 *1868 1872*
wise,   1341 *MS* say his   *MS* {no commas}   1342–4 *MS* {no quotation
marks at beginnings of lines}   1342 *MS* And made   1343 *MS* which
he   *MS* since his sole   1344 *MS* From the horror of the abominable
accident."   1345 *MS* say his   *MS* {no commas}   *MS* did befall   *Yale 1*
rather">rather,"

1344 *abominable thing*: i.e. the apparent proof of Pompilia's adultery furnished by her
new-born baby. Cf. Lev. 7: 21; Deut. 14: 3: Guido is like the good person rushing
away from 'impurity'.

"The luckiest of conceivable events,
"Most pregnant with impunity for him,
"Which henceforth turned the flank of all attack,
"And bade him do his wickedest and worst."
— The wife's withdrawal from the Convertites,   1350
Visit to the villa where her parents lived,
And birth there of his babe. Divergence here!
I simply take the facts, ask what they show.

First comes this thunderclap of a surprise:
Then follow all the signs and silences   1355
Premonitory of earthquake. Paolo first
Vanished, was swept off somewhere, lost to Rome:
(Wells dry up, while the sky is sunny and blue.)
Then Guido girds himself for enterprise,
Hies to Vittiano, counsels with his steward,   1360
Comes to terms with four peasants young and bold,
And starts for Rome the Holy, reaches her
At very holiest, for 't is Christmas Eve,
And makes straight for the Abate's dried-up font,
The lodge where Paolo ceased to work the pipes.   1365

1346–9 *MS* {no quotation marks at beginnings of lines}   1346 *MS* imaginable   *MS* {no comma}   1347 *MS* all good effects   1348 *MS* Which
turned   *MS* attacks on himself,   1349 *MS* Dispensed with all preservatives
and defences now."   1350 *MS* {beginning of fo. 221}   *MS* The withdrawal
from the Convent to the Villa   1351 {not found in *MS*}   1352 *MS* And
the birth of his son and heir: now, here as before,   1353 *MS* facts and ask
1354 *MS* {no new paragraph}   *MS* of complete   1355 *MS* the regular
signs   1356 *MS* earthquake: *MS* was first to vanish   1357 *MS* Was
swept off like a bird and lost to the Roman sky: 1358 *MS* Wells>(So
wells   *MS* blue:>blue:)   1359 *MS* And a fortnight ago only, when Guido
heard that news,   1360 *MS* He goes to his Villa, consults there   1361 *MS*
peasants trusty young   1362 *MS* and reaches   1363 *MS* her very   *MS*
'twas   1364 *MS* make   *MS* dried basin aforesaid,   1365 *MS* Villa
MS had ceased

1346 *conceivable*: a pun, like 'pregnant' in the next line.
1357 *swept off*: 'swept off like a bird' (*MS*) makes clear the original image. Paolo is
like a bird or animal that senses the coming earthquake.
1358 *Wells dry up*: Paolo disappears from his villa, like water vanishing from wells: a
troubling prediction of the earthquake (murder).
1365 *lodge*: Paolo's villa near Ponte Milvio, where Guido and the accomplices
stayed until 2 Jan.

And then, rest taken, observation made
And plan completed, all in a grim week,
The five proceed in a body, reach the place,
—Pietro's, at the Paolina, silent, lone,
And stupefied by the propitious snow.   1370
'T is one i' the evening: knock: a voice "Who's there?"
"Friends with a letter from the priest your friend."
At the door, straight smiles old Violante's self.
She falls,—her son-in-law stabs through and through,
Reaches through her at Pietro—"With your son   1375
"This is the way to settle suits, good sire!"
He bellows "Mercy for heaven, not for earth!
"Leave to confess and save my sinful soul,
"Then do your pleasure on the body of me!"
—"Nay, father, soul with body must take its chance!"
He presently got his portion and lay still.   1381
And last, Pompilia rushes here and there
Like a dove among the lightnings in her brake,
Falls also: Guido's, this last husband's-act.

1366 *MS* taken and preparations   *Yale 1* made,>made   1367 *MS* And the
observations completed in a week,   1368 *MS* in a body proceeded, reached
the villa,   1369 *MS* (The other, Pietro's, by Santa Paolina) the silent and
propitious,   *1868* by   1370 {not found in *MS*}   *1868* snow,—
1371 *MS* At one in the evening: knocked: *1868* At one in   1372 *MS*
Canon   1373 *MS* The door opens and there   *MS* self,   *Yale 1* door smiles>
door, straight smiles   1374 *MS* her through and through   1375 *MS* And
arrives at Pietro—"With us two, good sire!"   *MS* with>With   *1868 1872* thro'
1376 {not found in *MS*}   1377 *MS* heaven though not   1378, 1379 *MS*
{no quotation marks at beginnings of lines}   1379 *MS* have   *MS*
with   1380 *MS* {beginning of fo. 222}   *MS* "Nay,   1382 *MS* last
Pompilia—rushing   *Yale 1* last Pompilia>last, Pompilia   1383 *1868 1872*
among lightnings   *★MS* brake—   *1868 1872* brake,   *1888* brake   *DC Br U*
brake>brake,   *1889* brake,   1384 *MS* Fell also: Guido did this last husband's
act   *Yale 1* husband's act>husband's-act

1370 *stupefied*: made stupid or torpid; i.e. because of the weather the Comparini are
all inside the villa.

1371 *one i' the evening*: i.e. about 6 p.m., from 'ad un' ora circa di notte': SS 11.
Browning notes the phrase in the autograph chronologies: Appendix C.

1383 *dove . . . brake*: the blows of Guido and his accomplices are like lightning flashes
into a clump of bushes, the home of a dove. The dove (Pompilia) darts about to avoid
being killed.

He lifts her by the long dishevelled hair,   1385
Holds her away at arm's length with one hand,
While the other tries if life come from the mouth—
Looks out his whole heart's hate on the shut eyes,
Draws a deep satisfied breath, "So—dead at last!"
Throws down the burden on dead Pietro's knees,   1390
And ends all with "Let us away, my boys!"

And, as they left by one door, in at the other
Tumbled the neighbours—for the shrieks had pierced
To the mill and the grange, this cottage and that shed.
Soon followed the Public Force; pursuit began   1395
Though Guido had the start and chose the road:
So, that same night was he, with the other four,
Overtaken near Baccano,—where they sank
By the way-side, in some shelter meant for beasts,
And now lay heaped together, nuzzling swine,   1400
Each wrapped in bloody cloak, each grasping still
His unwiped weapon, sleeping all the same
The sleep o' the just,—a journey of twenty miles
Brought just and unjust to a level, you see.
The only one i' the world that suffered aught   1405
By the whole night's toil and trouble, flight and chase,

1385 *MS* lifted   *MS* the length of   1386 *MS* from him   *MS* arms
length, with   1387 *MS* tried   *MS* breath came   1388 *MS* Looked
1389 *MS* Drew   *MS* breath "She is   1390 *MS* Threw   *MS* *1868 1872*
burthen   1391 *MS* ended   *MS* be off,   1392 *MS* {no new paragraph}
MS And as   *Yale 1* And as>And, as   1395 *MS* Officers and   1396 *MS*
had gotten   *MS* chosen   1397 *MS* So that   1398 *MS* as they lay tired
out with the road   1399 *MS* At the Inn at Baccano,—they had really reached so
far,—   1400 *MS* And now were heaped in the straw, huddled like swine,   *Yale 1*
huddled>nuzzling   1401 *MS* his bloody   *MS* [?h]>each   1402 *MS* one
and all   1403 *MS* of   *MS* just man,—   *MS* thirty   1404 *MS* *1868*
Bringing   *MS* see—   1405 *MS* in   *MS* suffered by the exertion   1406
{not found in *MS*}

1395 *Public Force*: cf. II. 1022 n.
1398 *Baccano*: cf. III. 1634 n.
1400 *nuzzling swine*: i.e. they are like pigs with their noses pressing into each other.
Perhaps a memory of the Gadarene swine (Mark 5: 1–13).

Was just the officer who took them, Head
O' the Public Force,—Patrizj, zealous soul,
Who, having but duty to sustain weak flesh,
Got heated, caught a fever and so died: 1410
A warning to the over-vigilant,
—Virtue in a chafe should change her linen quick,
Lest pleurisy get start of providence.
(That's for the Cardinal, and told, I think!)

Well, they bring back the company to Rome.   1415
Says Guido, "By your leave, I fain would ask
"How you found out 't was I who did the deed?
"What put you on my trace, a foreigner,
"Supposed in Arezzo,—and assuredly safe
"Except for an oversight: who told you, pray?"   1420
"Why, naturally your wife!" Down Guido drops
O' the horse he rode,—they have to steady and stay,
At either side the brute that bore him bound,
So strange it seemed his wife should live and speak!
She had prayed—at least so people tell you now—   1425

1407 *MS* Being the Officer who took them, one Patrizj   1408 {not found in
MS}   1409 *MS* {beginning of fo. 223}   *MS* Who had nothing but his sense
of duty to sustain him   *1868 1872* having duty   1410 *MS* So got   *MS* died
forthwith,   1411 *MS* to over vigilant officers.   1412–14 {not found in
MS}   1415 *MS* {no new paragraph}   *MS* Guido and his friends to
Rome,   1416 *MS* Guido "By   *MS* know   1417 *MS* {no quotation
mark at beginning of line}   *MS* deed   *MS* {Between 1417 and 1418 extra line:
You altogether mistake,—but of that, presently!   1418–20 *MS* {no quotation
marks at beginnings of lines}   1418 *MS* gave you the notion 'twas I,   1419 *MS*
to be in   *MS* and who had been there   1420 *MS* a blunder: who was
it   *MS* pray!"—   1421 *MS* wife"!   1422 *MS* On   *MS* horse,—
they   *MS* steady him on either side,   1423 {not found in *MS*}   *1868 1872
1888* him,   *DC Br U* him,>him   *1889* him   1424 *MS* the wife should be
living yet;

1408 *Patrizj*: from SS 13: 'having been overheated and wounded with a slight
scratch he [Patrizi] died in a few days'.
1412 *chafe*: heat of mind, passion.
1414 *Cardinal*: this is the Cardinal of l. 55, playing cards at a nearby table. By his
account of the death of Patrizi, Tertium Quid intends to display a witty scepticism
about religion.

For but one thing to the Virgin for herself,
Not simply,—as did Pietro 'mid the stabs,—
Time to confess and get her own soul saved
But time to make the truth apparent, truth
For God's sake, lest men should believe a lie: 1430
Which seems to have been about the single prayer
She ever put up, that was granted her.
With this hope in her head, of telling truth,—
Being familiarized with pain, beside,—
She bore the stabbing to a certain pitch   1435
Without a useless cry, was flung for dead
On Pietro's lap, and so attained her point.
Her friends subjoin this—have I done with them?—
And cite the miracle of continued life
(She was not dead when I arrived just now)   1440
As attestation to her probity.

Does it strike your Excellency? Why, your Highness,
The self-command and even the final prayer,
Our candour must acknowledge explicable
As easily by the consciousness of guilt.   1445
So, when they add that her confession runs

1426 *MS* Virgin—not simply, as Pietro did,   1427 {not found in *MS*}   *1868
1872 1888 simply,   *DC* simply,>simply,—   *1889* simply,—   *Br U* stab{*sic*},—
>stab,   *1428 MS 1868 1872 1888* saved—   *DC Br U* saved—>saved   *1889*
saved   1429 *MS* apparent to all,   *Yale 1* apparent—truth>apparent,
truth   1430 *MS* whereof truth the   splendor is: 1431 *MS* And
it   1432 *MS* was ever   *MS* her: 1433 *MS* the truth,   *Yale 1* truth,>
truth,—   1434 *MS* Being moreover familiarized with pain,   *Yale 1* beside,
>beside,—   1435 *MS* up to   1436 *MS* so was   1437 *MS* As I say,
on her father's lap, attained her point.   1438 *MS* say all this—have I done it
justice? 1439 *MS* say the last miracle of her   *Yale 1* life—>life   1440 *MS*
{beginning of fo. 224}   *MS* (And she   *MS* at this house)   1441 *MS* Is
an   *MS* innocence.   1442 *MS* {no new paragraph}   *MS* so? Why, to be
candid, your Highness,   1443 *MS* The great self-possession and even prayer are
explainable 1444 {not found in *MS*}   1868 explainable   1445 *MS* her
guilt   *MS* {Between 1445 and 1446 extra line: And fear of the punishment infallibly
her due.}   1446 *MS* {no comma}   *MS* all her   *MS* is

1430 *lest . . . lie*: cf. 2 Thess. 2: 11.
1444 *candour*: openness of mind.

She was of wifehood one white innocence
In thought, word, act, from first of her short life
To last of it; praying, i' the face of death,
That God forgive her other sins—not this,   1450
She is charged with and must die for, that she failed
Anyway to her husband: while thereon
Comments the old Religious—"So much good,
"Patience beneath enormity of ill,
"I hear to my confusion, woe is me,   1455
"Sinner that I stand, shamed in the walk and gait
"I have practised and grown old in, by a child!"—
Guido's friends shrug the shoulder, "Just this same
"Prodigious absolute calm in the last hour
"Confirms us,—being the natural result   1460
"Of a life which proves consistent to the close.
"Having braved heaven and deceived earth throughout,
"She braves still and deceives still, gains thereby
"Two ends, she prizes beyond earth or heaven:
"First sets her lover free, imperilled sore   1465
"By the new turn things take: he answers yet
"For the part he played: they have summoned him indeed:
"The past ripped up, he may be punished still:
"What better way of saving him than this?
"Then,—thus she dies revenged to the uttermost   1470

1447 *MS* That she was absolutely innocent   1449 *MS* the end   *MS* saying, in
the   1450 *MS* "May God forgive my many sins—not this   1451 *MS* I am
MS have to   *MS* I   1452 *MS* my   *MS* failure was none."   1453 *MS*
And comments   1454–7 *MS* {no quotation marks at beginnings of lines}
1454 *MS* Patience,   *MS* wrong,   1456 *MS* am,   *MS* very walk   1457 *MS*
child!"   1458 *MS* say to it all "Just what you say,   1459–74 *MS* {no
quotation marks at beginnings of lines}   1459 *MS* Of this prodigious
1460 *MS* is the natural consequence   1461 *MS* all of a piece to the end.   *Yale*
1 end.>close.   1462 *MS* Heaven   *MS* {no comma}   1463 *MS* She will
brave and deceive even now, and gain two ends   1464 {not found in
MS}   1465 *MS* set   *MS* in imminent peril   1466 *MS* have taken, to
answer yet   1467 *MS* sent for him of course,   1468 *MS* {beginning of fo.
225}   *MS* The Past will be   *MS* yet: 1469 *MS* And what   *MS* this of
hers?   1470 *MS* thus also is she

1453 *old Religious*: Fra Celestino. His words here are developed from his affidavit:
OYB lvii (57).

"On Guido, drags him with her in the dark,
"The lower still the better, do you doubt?
"Thus, two ways, does she love her love to the end,
"And hate her hate,—death, hell is no such price
"To pay for these,—lovers and haters hold."   1475
But there's another parry for the thrust.
"Confession," cry folks—"a confession, think!
"Confession of the moribund is true!"
Which of them, my wise friends? This public one,
Or the private other we shall never know?   1480
The private may contain,—your casuists teach,—
The acknowledgment of, and the penitence for,
That other public one, so people say.
However it be,—we trench on delicate ground,
Her Eminence is peeping o'er the cards,—   1485
Can one find nothing in behalf of this
Catastrophe? Deaf folks accuse the dumb!
You criticize the drunken reel, fool's speech,
Maniacal gesture of the man,—we grant!
But who poured poison in his cup, we ask?   1490

1471 *MS* On her husband, drags him down to the grave with her.   1472 {not found in *MS*}   1473 *MS* Thus two ways does   1474 *MS* death is no such price to pay for these.   1475 {not found in *MS*}   1476 *MS* supposition, you see: 1477 *MS* "The Confession," cry people,—"A Confession is true!"   1478 {not found in *MS*}   1479 *MS* Which, my friends? The public one,—as this is—   1480 *MS* one which we may never hear of?   1481 *MS* as we have experience every day,—   1482 *MS* of and penitence for the other—   1483 {not found in *MS*}   *Yale 1* say—>say.   1484 *MS* But however that be,—for   1485 *MS* And his   *MS* his   1486 *MS* Can his friends say nothing in behalf of this last   *Yale 1* say>find   1487 *MS* Of Guido's acts? Oh, they are by no means dumb!   1488 *MS* "You   *MS* reel, mad gesture of the man,   *1868 1872* fool's-speech,   1489 {not found in *MS*}   1490 *MS* Who poured the poison into

---

1478 *moribund*: dying person.

1479 *Which of them*: the point is that Pompilia could make a confession to Fra Celestino, overheard by her deathbed attendants, and then a second, private confession in which she repented the lies of the first confession.

1485 *Her Eminence*: the Cardinal: see Introduction above and l. 55 n.

1487 *Catastrophe*: i.e. the murders, Guido's disaster.

Deaf...dumb: i.e. 'You are not listening; you are accusing a man so overcome with his wrongs that he cannot speak.'

Recall the list of his excessive wrongs,
First cheated in his wife, robbed by her kin,
Rendered anon the laughing-stock o' the world
By the story, true or false, of his wife's birth,—
The last seal publicly apposed to shame   1495
By the open flight of wife and priest,—why, Sirs,
Step out of Rome a furlong, would you know
What anotherguess tribunal than ours here,
Mere worldly Court without the help of grace,
Thinks of just that one incident o' the flight?   1500
Guido preferred the same complaint before
The court at Arezzo, bar of the Granduke,—
In virtue of it being Tuscany
Where the offence had rise and flight began,—
Self-same complaint he made in the sequel here   1505
Where the offence grew to the full, the flight
Ended: offence and flight, one fact judged twice
By two distinct tribunals,—what result?
There was a sentence passed at the same time
By Arezzo and confirmed by the Granduke,   1510
Which nothing baulks of swift and sure effect
But absence of the guilty, (flight to Rome
Frees them from Tuscan jurisdiction now)

1491 *MS* Remember   1492 *MS* of her dowry next,   1493 *MS* laughing
stock of   1495 *MS* set to his infamy   1496 *MS* his wife with a Priest,—
why, sirs,   1497 {not found in *MS*}   1498 *MS* Would you know what
another sort of Tribunal than ours   1499 *MS* A worldly one   *MS* {no
comma}   1500 *MS* of   1501 *MS* {beginning of fo. 226}   1501–7 *MS*
    Guido made the same complaint before the Court at Arezzo
    In virtue of its being there that the flight began,
    That he made before the Court at Rome, since at Rome
    It was that the flight had its end: one fact, judged twice
1508 *MS* Tribunals,—and what's the   1510 {not found in *MS*}   1511 *MS*
Which was only hindered from being carried into effect   1512 *MS* By
the   *MS* guilty,—the flight   1513 *MS* Having freed ^them^ from the Tuscan
jurisdiction of course.

    1495 *apposed to shame*: fixed to (the document of) shame.
    1498 *anotherguess*: another kind of; 'a phonetic reduction of *anothergets* for
ANOTHER-GATES': OED[2], which quotes examples from James Howell's *Epistolæ
Ho-Elianæ* (1726), a work well known to Browning.

—Condemns the wife to the opprobrious doom
Of all whom law just lets escape from death.   1515
The Stinche, House of Punishment, for life,—
That's what the wife deserves in Tuscany:
Here, she deserves—remitting with a smile
To her father's house, main object of the flight!
The thief presented with the thing he steals!   1520

At this discrepancy of judgments—mad,
The man took on himself the office, judged;
And the only argument against the use
O' the law he thus took into his own hands
Is . . . what, I ask you?—that, revenging wrong,   1525
He did not revenge sooner, kill at first
Whom he killed last! That is the final charge.
Sooner? What's soon or late i' the case?—ask we.
A wound i' the flesh no doubt wants prompt redress;
It smarts a little to-day, well in a week,   1530
Forgotten in a month; or never, or now, revenge!
But a wound to the soul? That rankles worse and worse.
Shall I comfort you, explaining—"Not this once
"But now it may be some five hundred times

1514 *MS* There,—she was condemned to the opprobrious fate   1515 *MS* the
Law   *MS* death,   1516 *MS* Condemned to the House of Punishment, the
Stinche, for life.   1517 {not found in *MS*}   1518 *MS* Here, the self-same
fact is found just to deserve—a visit   1519 *MS* the object of the very
flight,   1520 *MS* is presented   1521 *MS* {no new paragraph}   *MS* For
madness at this discrepancy of judgments   *MS* In>For   1522 *MS* office of
judge,   1524 *MS* Of   1525 *MS 1868 1872* Is . .   *MS* you? that, in taking
his revenge,   1526 *MS* take it   1527 *MS* last: that really is the   1528 *MS*
"Sooner?   *MS* late?" the friends enquire.   1529 *MS* A natural wound in the
flesh wants soon redress;   *Yale 1* doubt,>doubt   1530 *MS* less day by day,
is   1531 *MS* revenge that now or never!   1532 *MS* honor—*that* grows
worse and worse,   1533 *MS* {beginning of fo. 227}   *MS* a man by saying—
"Not once only   1534–6 *MS* {no quotation marks at beginnings of lines}

1516 *Stinche*: the prison at Florence, in Via Ghibellina.
1528–40 *Sooner . . . worse*: this argument is taken from the lawyer Arcangeli, OYB xv
(16–17): 'But when we are dealing with an offence that injures the honour, this is not
merely a momentary matter, but is protracted, and indeed with the lapse of time it
becomes greater as the injured person is more despised.'

"I called you ruffian, pandar, liar and rogue: 1535
"The injury must be less by lapse of time"?
The wrong is a wrong, one and immortal too,
And that you bore it those five hundred times,
Let it rankle unrevenged five hundred years,
Is just five hundred wrongs the more and worse!   1540
Men, plagued this fashion, get to explode this way,
If left no other.

   "But we left this man
"Many another way, and there's his fault,"
'T is answered—"He himself preferred our arm   1545
"O' the law to fight his battle with. No doubt
"We did not open him an armoury
"To pick and choose from, use, and then reject.
"He tries one weapon and fails,—he tries the next
"And next: he flourishes wit and common sense,   1550
"They fail him,—he plies logic doughtily,
"It fails him too,—thereon, discovers last
"He has been blind to the combustibles—
"That all the while he is a-glow with ire,
"Boiling with irrepressible rage, and so   1555

1535 *MS* Have I 1536 *MS* The pain must sure be less by the time that's past?" *MS* ,">?" **1868 1872 1888 1889* time?" {RB has been confused by the rule that punctuation goes within the quotation marks. In this case, however, the question mark belongs with 'Shall I comfort you, explaining', not with the text within quotation marks} 1538 *MS* he has borne 1539 *MS* Or let it go 1540 *MS* wrongs more and so much worse: 1541 *MS* tried 1542 *MS* If you leave them no other." 1543 *MS* {no new paragraph} *MS* "We left this man so many others," 1544 {not found in *MS*} 1545 *MS* It *MS* arms: 1546 {not found in *MS*} 1547–62 *MS* {no quotation marks at beginnings of lines} 1547 *MS* But we did not open to him a whole armoury of such 1548 *MS* chuse *MS* and then reject after all: 1549 *MS* piece *MS* then tries 1550 *MS* the next: *MS* tries his 1551 *MS* then he tries the regular law, 1552 *MS* That *MS* and then he 1553 *MS* That he has been overlooking another way still, 1554 *MS* has been mad *MS* {no comma} 1555 *MS* Overboiling

 1553 *combustibles*: things that burn, the 'explosives' of l. 1556; fig. the passions. The ironic image is of Guido as a cheating duellist, who, having failed with various weapons (the methods of law: wit, common sense, and logic) decides to blow up his opponents instead.

"May try explosives and discard cold steel,—
"So hires assassins, plots, plans, executes!
"Is this the honest self-forgetting rage
"We are called to pardon? Does the furious bull
"Pick out four help-mates from the grazing herd   1560
"And journey with them over hill and dale
"Till he find his enemy?"

                   What rejoinder? save
That friends accept our bull-similitude.
Bull-like,—the indiscriminate slaughter, rude   1565
And reckless aggravation of revenge,
Were all i' the way o' the brute who never once
Ceases, amid all provocation more,
To bear in mind the first tormentor, first
Giver o' the wound that goaded him to fight: 1570
And, though a dozen follow and reinforce
The aggressor, wound in front and wound in flank,
Continues undisturbedly pursuit,
And only after prostrating his prize
Turns on the pettier, makes a general prey.   1575
So Guido rushed against Violante, first

1556 *MS* use that weapon   *MS* the rest.   1557 *MS* he hires   *MS* executes—   *1868 1872* "So hire assassins, plot, plan, execute!   1558 *MS* —Is
1560 *MS* companions   1561 *MS* [ ]>them over   1562 *MS* foe?
1563 *MS* {no new paragraph}   *MS* "No," is returned to this—   1564 *MS*
{beginning of fo. 228}   1564–75 *MS*
        "He was far more like a bull than that—he acted
        Bull-like: the very indiscriminate slaughter,
        The useless aggravation of the deed,
        Were all in the way of the creature who never ceases
        To remember the first aggressor, first giver of the wound,
        And, though a dozen follow and reinforce him,
        He continues undisturbedly the pursuit,
        And only after prostrating him and ending him
        Does he turn on the others and make a general slaughter.
1576 *MS* did Guido go   *MS* {no comma}

  1557 *So . . . executes*: ironic: Guido claims 'irrepressible rage' yet he is this deliberate
in his actions.

Author of all his wrongs, *fons et origo*
Malorum—drops first, deluge since,—which done,
He finished with the rest. Do you blame a bull?

In truth you look as puzzled as ere I preached!   1580
How is that? There are difficulties perhaps
On any supposition, and either side.
Each party wants too much, claims sympathy
For its object of compassion, more than just.
Cry the wife's friends, "O the enormous crime   1585
"Caused by no provocation in the world!"
"Was not the wife a little weak?"—inquire—
"Punished extravagantly, if you please,
"But meriting a little punishment?
"One treated inconsiderately, say,   1590
"Rather than one deserving not at all
"Treatment and discipline o' the harsher sort?"
No, they must have her purity itself,
Quite angel,—and her parents angels too
Of an aged sort, immaculate, word and deed: 1595
At all events, so seeming, till the fiend,
Even Guido, by his folly, forced from them
The untoward avowal of the trick o' the birth,

1577 *MS* The author   *MS fons et origo malorum*—   1578 {not found in *MS*}   *1868 Malorum*—increasingly drunk,—which justice done,   1579 *MS* Then, increasingly drunk, finished with the rest as you know.   1580 *MS* when you began!   1581 *MS* on any supposition perhaps.   1582 {not found in *MS*}   1583 *MS* much for its object of compassion: 1584 {not found in *MS*}   1585 *MS* Say   *MS* here was this   1586–93 *MS*
    Committed without any the least provocation in the world:
    Was the wife not a little weak? punished over much if you please
    But a little deserving punishment? Treated inconsiderately
    Rather [ ]>than one requiring no treatment at all of the harsh sort?
    Oh, no—they must have her pure, purity itself—
1593 *Yale 1* No—>No,   1594 *MS* An   *MS* are angels   1595 *MS* harmless in word and deed,   *1868* deed,   1596 *MS* seeming so, till Guido's own folly   1597 {not found in *MS*}   1598 *MS* Forced from them the single untoward avowal

---

    1577–8 *fons et origo / Malorum*: fountain and origin of evils (L.).
    1578 *drops . . . since*: Violante (the fountain) first gave out drops of evil, then a flood of it.

Which otherwise were safe and secret now.
Why, here you have the awfulest of crimes   1600
For nothing! Hell broke loose on a butterfly!
A dragon born of rose-dew and the moon!
Yet here is the monster! Why he's a mere man—
Born, bred and brought up in the usual way.
His mother loves him, still his brothers stick   1605
To the good fellow of the boyish games;
The Governor of his town knows and approves,
The Archbishop of the place knows and assists:
Here he has Cardinal This to vouch for the past,
Cardinal That to trust for the future,—match   1610
And marriage were a Cardinal's making,—in short,
What if a tragedy be acted here
Impossible for malice to improve,
And innocent Guido with his innocent four
Be added, all five, to the guilty three,   1615
That we of these last days be edified
With one full taste o' the justice of the world?

The long and the short is, truth seems what I show:—
Undoubtedly no pains ought to be spared
To give the mob an inkling of our lights.   1620

1599 *MS* Of what would otherwise have been secret for ever.   *1868* Would otherwise be   1600 *MS* {beginning of fo. 229}   *MS* then the   *MS* crimes—for
nothing!   1601 {not found in *MS*}   1602 *MS* is born out of roses,
dew   1603 *MS* dragon, look at him! Why, he's   1605 *MS* him, his brothers stick to him yet,   1606 {not found in *MS*}   1608 *MS* the same   *MS*
assists,   1609 *MS* in Rome, he   *MS* this   1610 *MS* the other to be
ready to trust the future,   1611 *MS* This   *MS* was   1612 *MS* have
been acted all this while   1613 *MS* to be improved upon,   1614 *MS*
Innocent   *MS* friends   *MS* {Between 1614 and 1615 extra line: (Over-zealous
only in behalf of the innocent)   1615 *MS* victims three   1616 *MS* That
you may be edified with the justice of the world?   1617 *MS* He will in that case
have been wronged indeed.   1618 *MS* {no new paragraph}   *MS* and
short   *MS* the truth is hard to understand—   *1868 1872* truth is   1619 *MS*
And undoubtedly   *MS* spared: 1620 {not found in *MS*}

1601 *Hell . . . butterfly*: i.e. 'the Hell of Guido's murderous passion was aroused by
something as innocent as a butterfly (Pompilia)': an ironic impossibility.
    1602 *dragon . . . moon*: i.e. 'the monster of revenge (Guido) was created out of sweet,
innocent things': an ironic impossibility.

It seems unduly harsh to put the man
To the torture, as I hear the court intends,
Though readiest way of twisting out the truth;
He is noble, and he may be innocent.
On the other hand, if they exempt the man   1625
(As it is also said they hesitate
On the fair ground, presumptive guilt is weak
I' the case of nobility and privilege),—
What crime that ever was, ever will be,
Deserves the torture? Then abolish it!   1630
You see the reduction *ad absurdum*, Sirs?

Her Excellency must pronounce, in fine!
What, she prefers going and joining play?
Her Highness finds it late, intends retire?
I am of their mind: only, all this talk talked,   1635
'T was not for nothing that we talked, I hope?
Both know as much about it, now, at least,
As all Rome: no particular thanks, I beg!
(You'll see, I have not so advanced myself,
After my teaching the two idiots here!)   1640

1621 *MS* It seems hard to put the man to the torture, for instance,   1622 {not
found in *MS*}   1623 *MS* The   *MS* getting us out   *MS* truth,   1624 *MS*
and may be innocent: and yet   *1868* innocent: 1625 *MS* {no comma}   *MS*
do not put him to the torture   1626–30 *MS*
    (As it is said they hesitate to do
    On the ground that the presumptive guilt is not strong enough)
    What crime that ever was or ever will be
    Will deserve it? As well abolish it altogether.
1627 *Yale 1* the ground that>the fair ground,   1631 {not found in *MS*}
1632 *MS* {beginning of fo. 230}   *MS* Your   *MS* pronounce—I have spoken for
that: 1633 *MS* you prefer   *MS* the cardplayers?   1634 *MS* And your
MS late and intends to retire?   1635 *MS* your mind—only, after all this talk,
1868 1872 talk, talked,   1636 *MS* It   *MS* I have spoken, I hope!   1637 *MS*
Now you both   *MS* it, at least,   1639, 1640 {not found in *MS*}

    1631 reduction *ad absurdum*: *reductio ad absurdum* (L.), the proof of the falsity of an
argument by showing that its logical consequence is an absurdity.
    1632–40 *Her Excellency . . . here*: one of Browning's most brilliant endings. The Duke
and the Prince ('Excellency' and 'Highness') whom Tertium Quid has been talking to
and trying to impress drift away, revealing their indifference to the speech, and their
aristocratic arrogance. In his last cynical aside (1639–40) Tertium Quid shows his real
contempt for them.

APPENDIX A

THE OLD YELLOW BOOK

THE 'square old yellow Book', purchased by Browning for a lira that memorable June day in the Piazza San Lorenzo, and described so eloquently by him in Book I, ll. 110–140 of his poem, was for him inspiration, source, and talisman. It may therefore be appropriate to append a physical description, perhaps more detailed but certainly less eloquent than Browning's own, of the volume preserved, together with a ring formerly in the possession of the poet but not that referred to in the poem, and a contemporary likeness of the unhappy Guido Franceschini, at Balliol College, Oxford.

Robert Browning's 'Old Yellow Book': a collection of *printed* pamphlets with some *manuscript* material relating to the trial for murder of Guido Franceschini and his associates; 1698. *Latin* and *Italian*. The collection appears to have been compiled by a Florentine lawyer named Francesco Cencini to whom three letters in the collection are addressed. Towards the head of the front pastedown is a paper label bearing the monogram ⚭ written in ink. In the centre of the front pastedown is a rectangular piece of paper 125 × 108 mm on which has been crudely drawn in pencil and ink, and coloured in crayon, the arms of the Franceschini family (azure, on a triple mountain or, a palm-tree proper, to which is tied a greyhound rampant proper). The piece of paper is inscribed in ink by Browning in the top right-hand corner '(From Seymour Kirkup, Florence)'. In the bottom left-hand corner is written 'Arme Franceschini / Famiglia Aretina' and in the bottom right-hand corner 'Da un MS Priorista / Aretino esistente presso / la famiglia Albergotti / Arezzo Luglio 1868'. The flyleaf (f. i) is signed 'Robert Browning / ἐμοὶ μὲν ὦν Μοῖσα καρτερώτατον βέλος ἀλκᾷ τρέφει' (cf. 1. 40 n.). The title-page (f. ii) is inscribed in a contemporary hand 'Posizione / Di tutta La Causa Criminale / Contro / Guido Franceschini Nobile / Aretino, e suoi Sicarij stati / fatti morire in Roma il di 22. / Febb:io 1698. / Il primo con la decollazione gl'altri / quattro di Forca / Romana Homicidiorum / Disputatur an et quando Maritus / possit occidere Vxorem / Adulteram / absque incursu pœne Ord:rie'. The *printed* pamphlets consist of fourteen briefs addressed by the lawyers concerned in the case to the

Governor of Rome, officially printed and bearing the imprint of the Reverend Apostolic Chamber, two extrajudicial anonymous pamphlets, an argument in vindication of Pompilia's reputation, and an instrument of final judgment absolving her, the two latter also officially printed. The pamphlets have not been bound up in chronological order, and apparently should stand as follows (the references are to the numbering used in this description): 3, 4, 5, 7, 8, 6, 16, 10, 9, 11, 12, 17, 14, 15, 13, 18.

Paper; fos. ii+130. 247 × 183 mm. The printed pages have been cropped, but appear to have been originally foliated in brown ink: 5–14, unnumbered leaf, 15–26, unnumbered leaf, 27, 29–43, unnumbered leaf, 44–73, unnumbered leaf, 74, 75 (a blank leaf), 76–111, 125–9, 114–21, 112–13. Contemporary vellum covers, entitled on the spine in brown ink and a contemporary hand 'Romana / Homicid. / an / Maritus / possit / occidere / Vxorem / Adulteram'. 258 × 192 mm.

1. fo. 1^r, 1^v. *Manuscript* index to the volume. The order of the items as bound in the volume does not always accord with that found in the index, which is closer to the old foliation, again suggesting either that the volume was originally misbound or that it was rebound at some stage. *Italian.*

2. fos. 2^r–3^v. *Manuscript* copy of the decree of the court in Florence where Pompilia was tried and convicted of elopement and adultery. *Latin.*

3. fos. 4^r–11^v. Arcangeli's outline of Guido's defence. *Latin.*

4. fos. 12^r–19^v. Spreti's defence of Guido, with discussion of the legality of torture. *Latin.*

5. fos. 20^r–23^v. Arcangeli's defence of Guido's associates. *Latin.*

6. fos. 24^r–29^v. Summary for the prosecution. *Latin.*

7. fos. 30^r–33^v. Gambi's opening statement for the prosecution. *Latin.*

8. fos. 34^r–39^v. Bottini's amplification of the argument for the prosecution and reply to the arguments of the defence. *Latin.*

9. fos. 40^r–49^v. Summary for the defence. *Latin.*

10. fos. 50^r–61^v. Arcangeli develops the defence. *Latin.*

11. fos. 62^r–69^v. Spreti lays emphasis on the illegality of the torture of the Vigil. *Latin.*

12. fos. 70^r–76^v. Anonymous 'Notizie di fatto' on the side of the defence. *Italian.*

13. fos. 77^r–78^v. Second summary for the prosecution. *Latin.*

14. fos. 79^r–80^v. Short summing-up by Gambi for the prosecution. *Latin.*

15. fos. 81^r–96^v. Final argument of Bottini for the prosecution. *Latin.*

16. fos. 97^r–102^v. Reply of Bottini for the prosecution, especially to Spreti's defence of Guido, item 4. *Latin.*

17. fos. 103^r–112^v. Anonymous 'Risposta alle notizie di fatto', a response to item 12. *Italian.*

18. fos. 113^r–116^v. Final argument of Spreti for the defence, in reply to item 15. *Latin.*

19. fo. 117^r. Letter from Arcangeli to Francesco Cencini, 22 Feb. 1698. The wrapper for the letter (fo. 122) is bound in following item 20. *Italian.*

20. fos. 118^r–121^v. Two letters to Cencini, the first from Gasparo del Torto (fo. vii^{r-v}), the second from Carlo Antonio Ugolinucci (fo. viii^{r-v}), both 22 Feb. 1698 [the day of the executions]. The paper used for the letters has been folded to form two bifolia, one inside the other, so that the first letter is written on fo. 118^{r-v} and the second on fo. 119^{r-v}; fos. 120^{r-v} and 121^r are blank, and the address is written on 121^v. *Italian.*

21. fos. 123^r–128^v. Plea by Antonio Lamparelli 'Procurator Charitatis' on behalf of Pompilia's reputation, and against the claim to her property made by the Convent of the Convertites.

22. fos. 129^r–130^v. 'Instrumentum Sententiae Definitivae', or record of definitive decree by which Pompilia's reputation was restored and the claim of the Convertites refused.

APPENDIX B

THE SECONDARY SOURCE

BROWNING's most important source for *The Ring and the Book*, after the Old Yellow Book, was an Italian manuscript probably written in 1698, the same year as the Franceschini case, titled 'Morte dell'Uxoricida Guido Franceschini Decapitato' ('The Execution by Beheading of the Wife-Killer Guido Franceschini'). This work has come to be known as the Secondary Source (SS in this edition). The manuscript came into Browning's hands through the agency of Mrs Eric Baker, a friend of Isa Blagden's.[1] We do not know how Mrs Baker acquired the manuscript. Browning eventually gave it to Mrs Sutherland Orr, his biographer, and it was still in her possession in the 1890s; since then it has been lost. It is reprinted below from the text in the *Miscellanies of the Philobiblon Society*, vol. xii (London: Whittingham and Wilkins, 1868–9), where Browning allowed it to be published at the request of his friend Sir John Simeon. He himself corrected the proofs of the text in May 1870.

Since Browning's death, five other versions of this document have been discovered in Italy; four of them are in Italian libraries, and a fifth, purchased in Rome in 1913, is now in the Armstrong Browning Library, Baylor University, Texas. These versions show the notoriety of the Franceschini case in 1698. The other manuscripts are as follows: (1) Biblioteca Comunale, Cortona, MS 250 (333); (2) Biblioteca e Musei Oliveriani, Pesaro, MS 1188.3; (3) Vatican Library, MS Urb. lat. 1696; (4) Vatican Library, MS Urb. lat. 1692; (5) Armstrong Browning Library, Baylor University, Texas, Contemporary MSS collection, filed under the title 'Deplorabile et impio Omicidio commesso in Roma da Guido Franceschini'.[2] Beatrice Corrigan describes these manuscripts as all 'copies, more or less complete, of some original narrative', which she calls 'S':

The original version of S may be Part One of the Cortona codex [Cortona, MS 250 (333)], though this is by no means certain. It is one of the most elaborately

[1] See Introduction, p. xii.
[2] There is a full translation of this manuscript in E. H. Yarrill, 'Browning's "Roman Murder Story" as Recorded in a Hitherto Unknown Contemporary Manuscript', *Baylor Bulletin*, 42 (1939), no. 4.

composed of all these accounts, its title hand-printed like a title-page, and the story divided into chapters, each with its own heading. The Pesaro manuscript preserves much of the elaborate form of the Cortona version, and is more closely related to it than any of the others, though it omits some of the material. Two Vatican accounts are also versions of S: that in Urb. lat. 1696 is very similar, though a little shorter still; the other, much briefer, in Urb. lat. 1692 ... contains some of the mistakes (though generally scored through, as though someone had undertaken to correct them) which Professor Raymond has pointed out in the Baylor MS., an even more abbreviated form of S, with no general introduction and no division into chapters. The Secondary Source is the shortest version of all, with much material omitted, as well as the divisions and general reflections.[3]

The Secondary Source is just one small instance from the vast literature of torture and the scaffold from the seventeenth and eighteenth centuries, a literature including handwritten and printed pamphlets, broadsheets, and songs. The best introduction to this material as a whole is Michel Foucault, *Discipline and Punish* (1975), Chapter 2 'The spectacle of the scaffold'.[4] The accounts of crimes and executions 'were the sequel to the trial; or rather they pursued that mechanism by which the public execution transferred the secret, written truth of the procedure to the body, gesture and speech of the criminal.'[5] His remarks on the popular literature that accrued around famous criminals like Cartouche and Mandrin can be applied to the literature generated by the now obscure Guido Franceschini:

Perhaps we should see this literature of crime, which proliferated around a few exemplary figures, neither as a spontaneous form of 'popular expression', nor as a concerted programme of propaganda and moralization from above; it was a locus in which two investments of penal practice met—a sort of battleground around the crime, its punishment and its memory. If these accounts were allowed to be printed and circulated, it was because they were expected to have the effect of an ideological control—the printing and the distribution of these almanacs, broadsheets, etc. was in principle subject to strict control. But if these true stories of everyday history were received so avidly, if they formed part of the basic reading of the lower classes, it was because people found in them not only memories, but also precedents; the interest of 'curiosity' is also a political interest. Thus these texts may be read as two-sided discourses, in the facts that they relate, in the effects they give to these facts and in the glory they confer on those 'illustrious' criminals, and no doubt in the very words they use (one should study the use of such

---

[3] *Curious Annals*, pp. xvii f.
[4] Quoted here from the translation by Alan Sheridan (Penguin Books, Harmondsworth, 1991).
[5] Ibid. 66.

categories as 'misfortune' or 'abomination' or such epithets as 'famous' or 'lamentable' in accounts such as *The History of the Life, Great Robberies and Tricks of Guilleri and his Companions and of their Lamentable and Unhappy End).*[6]

For ease of reference, paragraph numbers have been added to the text and translation given below.

[6] Ibid. 67–8.

MORTE DELL'UXORICIDA
GUIDO FRANCESCHINI DECAPITATO

THE following pages contain a MS. contemporaneous account of the execution of the principal actor in the tragedy which has been immortalized in the poem of "The Ring and the Book."

I am enabled, by the kindness of my friend Mr. Browning, to give it a place in the Miscellanies of the Philobiblon Society.

JOHN SIMEON.

[I shall not attempt to say with what a feeling I correct proof-sheets received on the day subsequent to that which brought intelligence of the death of this great-hearted and noble-minded man, characteristically good and gracious to the very last.

R. B. *May 24th*, 1870.]

1. Dimorando da qualche tempo in Roma Guido Franceschini, Nobile di Arezzo in Toscana, ed al servizio di Personaggio eminente, si decise a prender moglie, e con dote sufficiente per vantaggio di sua Casa: laonde palesato un tal desiderio ad una perucchiera vicina a Piazza Colonna, gli fù da questa proposta la Signora Francesca Pompilia di anni 13, figlia di certo Sig^r. Pietro Comparini e Violante Peruzzi, la quale oltre la dote che le veniva promessa, aveva di più la successione di un fidecommesso tra Luoghi di Monte ed effetti per 12 mila scudi. Sentito il vantaggioso partito, che gli sembrò a proposito, non tardò a palesarlo al di lui fratello Abate Paolo, che da molti anni dimorava in Roma al servizio di un Porporato; e questi col Sig^r. Guido si portarono dalla madre della giovane, lusingandosi di riuscire più per tal via che domandandola al padre, che era un pò difficoltoso. Avendo pertanto fatto essi comparire che le loro rendite erano maggiori dell'occorrenza, riuscirono nel loro intento, comecchè fosse poi riconosciuto non ascendere tutto il suo capitale alla somma dei frutti dati in nota. Fù facile al Franceschini di guadagnare la donna che, spinta dall'ambizione di collocare la figlia in casa di persone qualificate, prestò il suo consenso, e si adoperò molto col marito per indurlo a sottoscrivere i capitoli matrimoniali.

2. Informatosi però dopo il Comparini da persona di sua conoscenza della facoltà del Franceschini, e trovata la cosa diversa da quella che gli era stata rappresentata, cambiato pensiere, non volle in conto alcuno si effettuassero gli sponsali, adducendo per pretesto la troppa tenera età della figlia, ed altre ragioni. La madre di Francesca però, non vedendo l'ora di dare la figlia al Franceschini, gliela fece occultamente sposare nel Decembre del 1693 in S. Lorenzo in Lucina.

1. HAVING DWELT in Rome for some time in the service of an eminent patron, Guido Franceschini, a nobleman from Arezzo in Tuscany, decided to take a wife, one with a dowry large enough to be of advantage to his family. He explained his intentions, therefore, to a wig-maker who lived near Piazza Colonna, and she recommended Signora Francesca Pompilia, a girl of 13 years of age, daughter of a certain Signor Pietro Comparini and of Violante Peruzzi, who, in addition to her promised dowry, had the inheritance of a *fideicommissum*[7] in government bonds,[8] and other securities worth 12,000 scudi. Hearing these details, and considering it a favourable match, Franceschini moved quickly to discuss the matter with the Abate Paolo, his brother, who had lived in Rome for many years in the service of a Cardinal; he, together with Signor Guido, approached the young girl's mother, since they flattered themselves that this was more likely to succeed than asking the father, who was supposed to be somewhat difficult. They stated their income as greater than was actually the case, and were successful, though it was later disclosed that Guido's capital fell short of the sum declared. It was easy for Franceschini to persuade the lady because she was so ambitious to establish her daughter in a family of good standing. She gave her consent, and then had much ado to convince her husband to sign the marriage contracts.

2. Comparini, however, consulted one of his acquaintance concerning Franceschini's financial position, and discovered that it was not as had

[7] 'This was a form of entail which dated back to classical times, and had in the sixteenth and seventeenth centuries become very popular in Italy as a means of enabling a prosperous member of the middle class to prevent the dissipation of his property after his death': *Curious Annals*, xix. The *fideicommissum* or trust fund was originally established by the will of Pietro Comparini's father in 1645. Browning uses the word 'usufruct' to describe the income from this trust in the poem.

[8] 'Luoghi di Monte' in the Italian. Corrigan explains that this was a term for various public loans: 'The first of these Roman public loans had been floated in 1526 by Clement VII, at the rate of 10 per cent, each bond (there were 2,000) having a value of 100 scudi. The idea was so popular that there were many other issues in the sixteenth century, with rates of interest ranging from 4 to 12 per cent. In the seventeenth century there were still more loans with a generally lower rate of interest... Most of these bonds reached maturity after a certain number of years, and for some of them the interest was not annual but cumulative': *Curious Annals*, pp. xix–xx.

3. Pervenuto all'orecchio del Comparini tale sposalizio, altamente se ne dolse con Violante: ma questa tanto seppe dire, che il Comparini non solo ne convenne, ma oltre la dote di sc: 2600, a conto di cui le ne diede 700, fece anche agli sposi la donazione di tutto il suo.

4. Dopo alcuni giorni il Franceschini stabilì di condurre la di lui sposa, e i parenti di questa, in Arezzo; e ciò seguì nello stesso Decembre 1693, e colà giunti, poterono i genitori della sposa scoprire che lo stato del loro genero era molto più meschino di quale che essi medesimi si erano figurato; il perchè, amareggiatisi, vieppiù per la penuria che d'altronde osservavano negli alimenti, e per molte altre cose—stando una mattina a mensa e sentendo negare alla figlia il fuoco da scaldarsi il letto, e vedendo usarle molte altre durezze—molto se ne turbarono, e più ancora, quando viddero inveire contro la figlia un Canonico della Casa Franceschini, parente dello sposo, che investì con la spada alla mano Francesca, a cui toccò di rifugiarsi, correndo dentro una camera ove si chiuse. Una sera poi il padre di lei ito a trovare un'amico, tornatosi a casa trovò chiusa la porta; laonde la figlia, che vegliava, fù costretta a scendere per aprirgli, non senza aver prima chiamato il marito, che però non si svegliò mai; e quindi discesa ad aprire la porta, ed uscitane per alcuni passi onde incontrare il padre, tutto ad un tratto si trovò essa chiusa fuori di casa con suo padre; per lo che convenne ad entrambi per quella notte di dormire fuori, il padre all'osteria, la figlia da una sua vicina. Perciò ognora più i Sig.ri Comparini, per tanti strapazzi, si risolvettero di ritornare a Roma: ma mancando di denaro, furono costretti a chiederne al Franceschini, che appena gli diede l'occorrente pel viaggio.

5. Partiti i vecchi Comparini, pensò il Franceschini di palliare l'accaduto, inducendo la moglie a scrivere a Roma all'Abate di lui fratello, per dimostrargli che gli stava a cuore la memoria di esso cognato: la lettera fu dettata dallo stesso marito. La inesperta giovane fece quanto volle Guido, il cui scopo era di far credere che i suoi suoceri erano i fomentatori delle dissensioni che regnavano fra gli sposi e i parenti del Franceschini.

been represented to him; so he changed his mind, and set himself against the wedding, giving as one of his reasons his daughter's tender age. Francesca's mother, however, impatient to see her daughter married to Franceschini, organized a clandestine marriage in the Church of San Lorenzo in Lucina. This was in December 1693.

3. When news of the wedding reached Comparini, he was very cross with Violante; but she was so smooth-tongued, that he not only consented to it, but even made a gift of all the rest of his property to the newly-weds, and this was in addition to the dowry of 2,600 scudi, on account of which he advanced 700.

4. Some days later Franceschini decided to move to Arezzo with his wife and her parents; this was in the same December of 1693. Once they had arrived there, the parents discovered that their son-in-law's situation was much shabbier than they themselves had supposed. They were embittered not only by this, and by the lack of food that was evident, but by other matters as well—one morning, for example, at table, they had to listen as their daughter was denied coals to warm her bed, and they saw her subjected to other humiliations. Their distress was all the greater when, on one occasion, they witnessed a Canon of the Franceschini family shouting at Francesca and rushing at her sword in hand, so that she had to flee into another room and bolt the door. One evening her father went out to visit a friend, and came back home to find the door locked against him, whereupon his daughter, who was awake, had to go down to let him in— she called to her husband but he would not wake up. When she had gone downstairs to open the door, and taken a few steps through it to greet her father, it was slammed shut. That night the two of them were forced to take refuge elsewhere, the father at an inn, the daughter at a neighbour's house. Every additional hour of such ill-usage determined the Comparini to return to Rome, but their penniless condition compelled them to beg money from Franceschini, who barely gave them enough for their journey.

5. Once the elderly Comparini were out of the way, Franceschini decided to cover up the circumstances of their departure by getting his wife to write a letter to his brother the Abate in Rome, to demonstrate her affection for her brother-in-law: the letter was dictated by her husband! The naïve girl did everything Guido wanted; his aim was to make people believe that his parents-in-law were at the root of the misunderstandings which existed between the newly-wed couple and the Franceschini family.

6. Arrivati che furono i Comparini a Roma, mal contenti com'erano della casa del loro genero, presso cui vedevano allora di avere sacrificata la figlia, non si sapevano dar pace di ciò di cui essi medesimi erano stati la causa, e più dopo che venivano molestati pel residuo della dote, non ostante che vedessero in pericolo il rimanente. Mentre erano in questo stato le cose, venne pubblicato un Giubileo. Ed in questa circostanza Violante Comparini rivelò in confessione, che la Francesca Pompilia maritata al Francheschini non era altrimenti sua figlia, ma un parto supposto, e data in luce da una povera vedova forestiera, e che essa poi si era appropriata per far sì che in sua Casa cadesse il fidecommesso, onde riparare a molti debiti di suo marito. Ciò uditosi dal confessore, questi le impose di tutto palesare la cosa al marito stesso. Ubbidì la Violante, ed il Comparini, fortemente di ciò sorpreso, rampognò aspramente la moglie; e quindi, posto il fatto in giudizio avanti Mons.ʳ Tomati, fù da questo detta nella sentenza: *Manu tenendum fore et esse Dominam Franciscam Pompiliam in quasi possessione filiationis.* Perciò fù presa dal Comparini l'appellazione al Tribunale della S. Rota, ma la lite restò indecisa. Frattanto i Franceschini vedendosi per questa circostanza delusi, mentre non potevano più avere il residuo della dote, radoppiarono le sevizie alla povera Pompilia fino a minacciarla di morte, il perchè fù dessa costretta più volte a salvarsi col fuggire in qualche altra casa, o presso l'autorità, ed anche presso il Vescovo, cui pregò perfino a salvarla col metterla in qualche monastero. Ma quel Prelato stimò più opportuno di rimetterla in casa del marito, esortandolo a non maltrattarla.

7. Vedendo però la disgraziata che le ammonizioni di quel Vescovo erano state inutili, e che vane pure ritornavano le di lei maniere per ammansare il cuore del marito e dei cognati, che la rimproveravano d'infecondità e di civetteria e di altre colpe da loro immaginate, si portò essa da un Agostiniano Romano, onde scrivesse ai Superiori ed ai genitori, onde trovassero un provvedimento; ma sebbene il Frate promettesse di compiacerlo, le di lui lettere non arrivarono mai al loro destino. Disperata perciò la misera, si determinò di portarsi ad ogni modo a Roma; e conferito il tutto al Canonico Conti, cognato di Franceschini, a cui fece il quadro il più patetico della sua situazione, questi commosso, le rispose che l'avrebbe ajutata, come fece, esibendole di farnela condurre a Roma dal Canonico Caponsacchi suo amico, mentre egli stesso non doveva nè poteva farlo. Communicata quindi tal circostanza al Caponsacchi, questi si oppose per timore d'incorrere nella indignazione del

6. The Comparini arrived in Rome in a state of indignation with their son-in-law's family. They could see that their daughter had been sacrificed for nothing, and could not reconcile themselves to this, given that it was their own fault. Moreover, they were being harassed about the residue of the dowry, even though they saw their remaining wealth under threat. When things had reached this pass, a Jubilee was announced. Violante took advantage of the occasion to go to Confession and reveal that Francesca Pompilia (Franceschini's wife) was not in fact her daughter, and that her birth had been a pretence: she was actually the child of a poor widow from outside Rome, from whom Violante had adopted her in order to ensure that the *fideicommissum* came to her family, so that she could pay off her husband's heavy debts. The priest who heard this insisted she should tell her husband everything. She did as she was told, and when Comparini heard he was flabbergasted, and was again very cross with her. He decided to bring the matter to court before Monsignor Tomati, who in his judgment said the following: 'that it should be maintained that Domina Francesca Pompilia was and should be in virtual possession of her status as daughter.' So Comparini filed an appeal to the Tribunal of the Sacred Rota, but at this point the case remained pending. The Franceschini, meanwhile, seeing themselves tricked, and disappointed of the remainder of the dowry, redoubled their cruelties on poor Pompilia, even threatening her with death. In order to save herself, she fled to other houses, to the authorities, even to the Bishop. She even begged the Bishop to send her to a nunnery in order to keep her from harm, but he thought it advisable to return her to her husband's house, urging him not to mistreat her.

7. When the unfortunate girl realized that the admonitions of the Bishop were useless, and that her attempt, by submissive behaviour, to soften the hearts of her husband and her brothers-in-law, was in vain—they were forever reproaching her with barrenness, with being a flirt, and with other crimes of their own imagining—at length, she went to see an Augustinian friar from Rome, and asked him to send a message to his superiors and to her parents, that they should find a solution. Although the friar promised to do this, his letters never reached their destination. The poor thing was desperate, and determined to get to Rome by any means. She therefore confided everything to Canon Conti, a brother-in-law of Franceschini, and painted such a pathetic picture of her situation that he was moved to say that he would aid her, offering to have her escorted to Rome by his friend, the Canon Caponsacchi—he himself could not and ought not to do it. When Caponsacchi was informed of the

Franceschini; ma sollecitato e dal Conti e dalla donna vi acconsentì: e nel Lunedì ultimo di Aprile alzatasi la donna da letto prima che albeggiasse, senza che il marito se ne avvedesse, prese alcune sue robe, gioje e denari, uscì di casa, ed alla porta della Città trovò il Caponsacchi, che l'aspettava colla vettura, dove insieme saliti s'incamminarono verso Roma.

8. Svegliatosi il Franceschini, ed accortosi della fuga della moglie, sospettando già che si sarebbe diretta a Roma, prese ad inseguirla, e nel Martedì seguente appunto la raggiunse in Castel Nuovo nell'osteria della Posta, ove era col Caponsacchi. Non si atterrì la giovane alla vista del marito, ma fattasi animo gli rimproverò anzi tutte le sevizie fattele, e per cui era essa stata costretta a quel passo. Attonito allora il Franceschini, nè sapendo come o qual ripiego prendere, pensò che fosse più opportuno ricorrere alla Giustizia; e fatti arrestare dal Governatore di quel luogo i fuggitivi, vennero entrambi condotti a Roma e posti nelle Carceri Nuove, imputandoli di adulterio, perche insieme fuggiti. Si cercò di provare l'imputazione con certe lettere amorose rinvenute, e colla deposizione del vetturale; ma l'adulterio non si riuscì di provare, laonde il Canonico fù condannato per anni tre a Civitavecchia, e la donna fù rinchiusa nel Monastero delle Scalette alla Longara.

9. Vedendo però il marito che ciò nulla avevagli giovato per avere la dote, si risolvette di ripatriare, lasciando la cura della causa nelle mani del di lui fratello Abate, che era al servizio di un Cardinale; ma per quante pratiche facesse l'Abate presso i Tribunali, onde riuscire nell'intento, non gli fù possibile; laonde anch'esso si decise a partire da Roma; ed a ciò maggiormente fù spinto dall'essere rimasta incinta la cognata Pompilia; per cui Mons.ʳ Governatore di Roma lo costrinse ad acconsentire che la medesima dovesse avere per carcere la sua casa, con la sicurtà di sc: 300 da pagarsi ad ogni richiesta del Tribunale. L'Abate però non volle prestare il consenso se prima Pietro Comparini non si obbligasse per via di pubblico istromento di darle gli alimenti. E quindi licenziatosi l'Abate dal Cardinale, e venduti i suoi mobili, libri, e fattosi rendere sc: 47 trovati a Pompilia in Castel Nuovo, si partì da Roma; dopo di che partorì Pompilia un figlio maschio, cui pose il nome di Gaetano, al qual Santo ella si era votata.

10. Oppresso però il Franceschini da moltiformi affetti, e stimolato ora dall'onore, ora dall'interesse, alla vendetta, cedendo ai suoi pravi pensieri, divisò di uccidere la moglie e i sedicenti di lei genitori; e tratti al suo

plan, he objected because he was afraid to cross Franceschini; he only agreed when Conti and the lady pleaded with him. And so, on the last Monday of April, without her husband's knowledge, the lady rose up before dawn, gathered together some of her belongings, some jewellery, and some money, and left the house. She found Caponsacchi at the city gate waiting for her with a carriage, mounted up, and set off towards Rome.

8. When Franceschini woke up, he realized that his wife had escaped, and having a suspicion that Rome was her intended destination, he set off in pursuit. And so, on the following Tuesday, at the posthouse inn in Castelnuovo, he overtook her in the company of Caponsacchi. The young woman was unabashed at the sight of her husband; her spirits roused, she blamed him for all the cruelties that had forced her to flee. Franceschini was speechless, and confused as to what course of action to take, so he thought best to turn to the authorities: the runaways were arrested by the District Governor, escorted to Rome, put in the New Prisons, and charged with adultery for eloping together. The evidence to establish the case consisted of love-letters that had turned up, and a deposition taken from the coach-driver; but the adultery was not successfully proved, and the Canon was sentenced to three years at Civitavecchia, and the lady was imprisoned at the Convent of the Scalette on the Via della Lungara.

9. As the husband could see, nothing of this had helped to get possession of the dowry, so he decided to return to his native city, leaving power of attorney in the case in the hands of his brother, the Abate, who was in the service of a Cardinal. Though his brother tried every means at his disposal to win the case in the Courts, it proved impossible, and he too determined to leave Rome. Indeed, he felt he had no choice, for, his sister-in-law Pompilia being pregnant, the Governor of Rome had constrained him to agree that she should be kept only under house-arrest, with bail of 300 scudi payable on demand to the Court. The Abate withheld his consent until Pietro Comparini had agreed formally, by deed, to take over Pompilia's maintenance. And then he got leave from his Cardinal, sold his furniture and his books, retrieved the 47 scudi discovered on Pompilia in Castelnuovo, and departed from Rome. After this, Pompilia gave birth to a son, whom she named Gaetano in honour of her favourite saint.

10. Franceschini's mind was overwhelmed with varying feelings, stirred to revenge now by thoughts of honour, now by thoughts of gain. In the end he surrendered to these dark urgings and determined to kill his

partito altri quattro scellerati, partissi d'Arezzo, e nel dì della vigilia del S. Natale giunse a Roma e si fermò a Ponte Milvio, ove era una Villa di suo fratello, e dove si nascose coi suoi seguaci finche il momento fosse giunto opportuno alla esecuzione dei suoi disegni.

11. Spiati quindi tutti i passi della famiglia Comparini, nel giorno 2. Gennaio, che era di Giovedì, ad un'ora circa di notte portatosi coi compagni a casa dei Comparini, dopo aver lasciati in guardia alla porta di strada Biagio Agostinelli e Domenico Gambasini, fece bussare all'uscio; dicendo di portare da Civitavecchia una lettera del Canonico Caponsacchi, gli venne aperto. Immediatamente lo scellerato Franceschini, spalleggiato con altri due dei suoi sicarj, si fece addosso alla Violante Comparini che avevagli aperto, ed estinta la rovesciò a terra. Pompilia, in tal frangente, spense il lume, credendo così sottrarsi ai suoi assassini, e corse alla porta vicina di un magnano, gridando ajuto; ma vedendo il Franceschini provveduto di una lanterna, andò a nascondersi sotto il letto, ma di là strappata, venne la misera condotta barbaramente a morte da 22 ferite per opera del di lei marito, che non contento di ciò la trasse ai piedi del Comparini, il quale parimente ferito da un'altro degli assassini, gridava *confessione!*

12. Sentitosi il rumore di questa orribile strage, accorse gente; ma riuscì agli empj di fuggire, lasciando però nella fretta uno il ferrajuolo, e il Franceschini il suo berretto, ciò che poi li scoprì. La sventurata Francesca Pompilia, ad onta delle ferite tante con cui venne massacrata, avendo implorato dalla SSma Vergine la grazia di potersi confessare, l'ottenne, giacchè potè sopravvivere qualche poco, e raccontare l'orribile attentato. Narrò essa che dopo il fatto, il di lei marito domandò al sicario che seco avevata trucidata, *se dessa fosse veramente morta*, il che assicurandogli, soggiunse presto *non perdiamo tempo, ma torniamo alla Vigna*, e così se ne fuggirono. Intanto chiamata la Forza, venne questa col Bargello, e fù tosto procurato un confessore, ed un chirurgo che diedesi a curare la infelice giovane.

wife and her pretended parents. He drew four villains into his confidence, left Arezzo with them, and arrived at Rome on Christmas Eve, where they stayed near Ponte Milvio[9] in a country residence[10] owned by his brother. Here he and his accomplices hid, waiting for the best opportunity to carry out his plans.

11. Having spied out all the movements of the Comparini family, on Thursday, 2 January, at the first hour of night,[11] he and his companions proceeded to the house. Biagio Agostinelli and Domenico Gambasini remained on guard at the street door, while Franceschini commanded one of the others to knock and pretend he was carrying a letter from the Canon Caponsacchi at Civitavecchia. The door was opened. Instantly the villainous Franceschini—shoulder to shoulder with two of his henchmen—leapt at Violante Comparini, who had opened the door, killed her outright, and threw her body to the ground. In desperation Pompilia snuffed out the light, hoping in this way to escape her killers, and rushed next door to the locksmith and screamed for help. She then saw that Franceschini had brought a lantern. She hid under a bed, but was dragged out and—poor unfortunate girl—murdered in the most brutal way by her own husband, with twenty-two stab wounds. Not satisfied with this, he dragged her body to her father's feet; Comparini had been attacked with equal ferocity by one of the other assassins, and was now yelling out 'Confession!'

12. Hearing the sound of the terrible slaughter, people came running. The wicked ones managed to effect an escape, though, in their haste, one assassin forgot his cloak, and Franceschini left behind his hat, articles that would later incriminate them. The ill-fated Francesca Pompilia, despite the extent of her wounds, made a successful plea for the grace of confession to the Most Holy Virgin; this was granted her, so she lived on a few days and was able to give an account of the assassination. She told how, after the deed, her husband had turned to the henchman who had helped butcher her, and said 'Is she really dead?' Assured she was, he said sharply 'Let's not waste time. Let's get back to the villa.' And so they escaped.

---

[9] A bridge across the Tiber, about $1^3/_4$ miles north of the Porto del Popolo, the north gate of Rome.

[10] The Italian has *Villa*, but in paragraphs 12 and 13 it is described as a *Vigna*, literally 'vineyard'. Many Romans owned *vigne* on the roads radiating from the city. They were often relatively simple buildings, rather than elaborate villas. Just north of the city, on the Via Flaminia, going towards Ponte Milvio, was a very popular area for such retreats.

[11] Approx. 6 p.m. Italian hours were reckoned from sunset, which in winter would have been before 5 p.m.

13. Informato dell'avvenimento Monsr. Governatore, spedì immediatamente il Capitano Patrizj per arrestare i rei. Giunta però la Forza alla Vigna, seppe che questi non vi erano più, ma che da un'ora circa se n'erano andati verso la strada. Allora il Patrizj proseguì senza posa il suo viaggio, e giunto all'osteria seppe dall'oste come il Franceschini voleva a viva forza dei cavalli, che gli furono negati, perchè senza l'ordine necessario: laonde a piedi si era con i compagni incamminato verso Baccano. Continuando allora la marcia, e prendendo le necessarie precauzioni, giunto che fù all'osteria della Merluzza, ivi trovò gli assassini, che tosto vennero arrestati, ed ai quali furono trovati ancora tinti di sangue quei coltelli di cui si erano serviti per tanto eccidio, e rinvennersi pure al Franceschini 150 scudi in moneta. Tale arresto però costò la vita al Patrizj, perchè riscaldatosi troppo, e colpito da una puntura, in pochi giorni morì.

14. Il coltello del Franceschini era alla Genovese, e triangolare, ed aveva nella costa alcuni uncini fatti in guisa che nel ferire non si sarebbe potuto estrarre dalla ferita senza lacerazione per modo da rendere la ferita incurabile.

15. Conti i rei a Ponte Milvio, furono in quell'osteria sentiti nel primo esame dai Notari e Giudici ivi espressamente mandati, e se n'ebbe in buona parte la confessione.

16. Saputasi in Roma la cattura dei delinquenti, accorse un'infinità di popolo per vederli, mentre tutti quanti legati su dei cavalli vennero tradotti a Roma. Raccontasi che il Franceschini, strada facendo, avendo domandato ad uno sbirro *come mai si era scoperto il delitto*, ed essendogli stato risposto, *che ne lo aveva palesato la moglie che avevano trovata ancora viva*, ne stupì in modo che restò quasi privo di sensi. Verso le 23 ore giunsero alle Carceri. Certo Francesco Pasquini di Città di Castello, ed Alessandro Baldeschi della Città stessa, di anni 22 entrambi, furono con Guido Franceschini gli uccisori dei Comparini; e il Gambasini ed Agostinelli furono quelli che stettero di guardia alla porta di strada.

After the murders, the Force responded to the emergency with their Officer-in-Charge, and a priest and a surgeon were summoned; the latter set to work tending the young victim's wounds.

13. Once everything that had come to pass was reported to Monsignor the Governor, he immediately dispatched Captain Patrizi to apprehend the criminals. When the Force arrived at the country residence, however, they discovered the villains had fled about an hour earlier in the direction of the highway. Without pause, Patrizi pushed on with the pursuit, and arrived at an inn, where the host informed him that Franceschini had demanded horses, but had been refused because he lacked the required documentation: at this point he and his companions had headed off on foot by the road to Baccano. Continuing their march, and taking all necessary precautions, Patrizi and his band arrived at the 'Fasting-bell' hostelry, where they found the assassins, and apprehended them forthwith. On them they found the murder-weapons stained with blood, and from Franceschini they recovered 150 scudi in coin. The arrest cost Patrizi his life: overheated and slightly wounded in the scuffle, he died a few days later.

14. Franceschini's knife was in the Genoese style, triangular, with barbed hooks on the back of the blade that made fatal any wound from which it was withdrawn.

15. The criminals were escorted to Ponte Milvio, where in the inn they were given their first interrogation by notaries and judges sent especially for the purpose. These obtained reasonably full confessions.

16. Once news of the delinquents' capture reached Rome, great crowds flocked out to see them. Meanwhile, the criminals themselves were lashed to horses and escorted into the city. It is recounted of Franceschini that, on the way in, he asked one of his guards 'How ever was the crime discovered?', and when he was told 'Your wife was still alive; she told us' he almost fainted with astonishment. The troop arrived at the prison at about the 23rd hour.[12] Francesco Pasquini from Città di Castello,[13] and Alessandro Baldeschi, also from that town, both 22 years of age, were Guido Franceschini's accomplices in the Comparini's murder; Gambasini and Agostinelli were those who acted as lookouts at the street door.

---

[12] Approx. 4 p.m.
[13] A town about 18 miles east of Arezzo.

17. Vennero frattanto esposti in S. Lorenzo in Lucina i cadaveri degli assassinati Comparini, che erano così sfigurati, e specialmente la moglie del Franceschini, dalle ferite in faccia, che non erano più riconoscibili. La infelice Francesca, dopo essersi sacramentata, perdonando ai suoi uccisori, in età di 17 anni non compiti, e dopo aver fatto il suo testamento, morì nel giorno 6, che era quello della Epifania, e potè giustificare se stessa di tutte le calunnie datele dal marito. La sorpresa del popolo in vedere detti cadaveri fù grande per l'atrocità del fatto, che faceva veramente raccapricciare, vedendo due vecchi settuagenarj ed una giovane di 17 anni così miseramente periti.

18. Progredendo intanto il Processo dei rei, si fecero molte scritture su tal proposito, rimarcandosi tutte le circostanze più gravanti concorse in si orribile massacro: ed altre ancora ne furono fatte in difesa con molta erudizione, specialmente dall'Avvocato dei Poveri, ch'era certo Mons.ʳ. Spreti, lo che influì a prolungare la sentenza, anche perchè il Baldeschi fù negativo, sebbene gli si desse la corda in cui svenne due volte. Finalmente confessò, e cosi fecero gli altri, che di più svelarono ch'essi avevano divisato uccidere a suo tempo anche lo stesso Franceschini per prendergli il denaro, giacchè non aveva loro mantenuto le promesse di pagarli, appena usciti da Roma.

19. Nel giorno 22 Febbraio si vidde nella Piazza del Popolo un gran palco con mannaja, e due gran forche, dove si avevano da giustiziare i rei. Molti palchetti furono costruiti per dar comodo ai curiosi di vedere cosi terribile giustizia, e tanto fù il popolo accorso che alcune fenestre si pagarono per fino sei scudi l'una. Alle otto ore furono intimati alla morte il Franceschini e compagni, e posti in Consorteria, ivi assistiti dal Sigʳ. Abate Panciatici e dal Cardinal Acciajuoli, non stentarono a disporsi a ben morire. Alle ore 20 giunta la Compagnia della Morte e della Misericordia alle Carceri, si fecero calare a basso i condannati, e posti su di separate carrette furono tradotti al supplizio.

20. Il primo che salì sulla carretta fù Agostinelli, il 2°. Gambasini, il 3°. Pasquini, il 4°. Baldeschi, ed il 5°. Franceschini, che mostrò più degli altri intrepidezza e sangue freddo, con meraviglia universale.

17. While these things were proceeding, the corpses of the murdered Comparini were laid out to view in the church of S. Lorenzo in Lucina, their faces so badly disfigured by wounds—especially that of Franceschini's wife—that they were unrecognizable. When she had received the sacraments, and had pardoned her murderers, and had made her own will, the unfortunate Francesca died, not having completed her seventeenth year. This was on the 6th, the Feast of the Epiphany. She had been able to answer all her husband's accusations. When the people surveyed the corpses, what appalled them, what made them shudder at the atrocity, was that the victims were two septuagenarians and a young girl of 17 years of age.

18. As the criminal proceedings went forward, a considerable number of depositions were laid before the court stressing the aggravating circumstances attending the appalling massacre; likewise, for the defence, learned arguments were advanced, especially by the Advocate for the Poor, Monsignor Spreti. His influence succeeded in lengthening the trial, as also did the 'Not Guilty' plea of Baldeschi, who maintained his innocence despite being subjected to the torture of the Cord and twice fainting. In the end he confessed like the others. They also confessed their intention to choose their moment to murder and rob Franceschini, because he had reneged on his promise to pay them as soon as they left Rome.

19. On 22 February, in Piazza del Popolo, an enormous scaffold, with a mannaia,[14] and two great gallows, were erected for the executions. Many miniature grandstands were constructed to accommodate those curious to see such fearful justice. Crowds were so pressing that the views from some windows were let for as much as six scudi. At the 8th hour,[15] the death-sentence was communicated to Franceschini and his companions, and they were placed in the Consorteria: there, with the aid of Signor Abate Panciatici and Cardinal Acciaiuoli, they prepared themselves, without difficulty, to make a good death. At the 20th hour[16] the Company of Death and Mercy arrived at the Prisons, and the condemned were escorted down and each put in a tumbril to be driven to the scaffold.

20. The first to mount up on his tumbril was Agostinelli, the second Gambasini, the third Pasquini, the fourth Baldeschi, and the fifth Franceschini. The last-named showed more courage and composure than the others, and was the wonderment of the crowd.

---

[14] A kind of guillotine.
[15] Approx. 1 a.m.
[16] Approx. 1 p.m.

21. Partirono dalle Carceri tenendo la strada del Pellegrino, del Governo, di Pasquino, Piazza Navona, la Rotonda, Piazza Colonna, ed il Corso.

22. Il primo che fù giustiziato fù l'Agostinelli, il 2°. il Gambasini, il 3°. il Pasquini, il 4°. il Baldeschi, e l'ultimo il Franceschini; il quale, salito sul palco, domandò perdono delle sue colpe, e pregò a suffragargli l'anima, soggiungendo che dicessero un *Pater, Ave,* e *Salve Regina* per lui; e fatto chiamare il confessore seco si riconciliò, ed adattato il collo sotto la mannaja, col nome di Gesù sulle labbra gli venne troncata la testa, che poscia dal carnefice fù mostrata al popolo.

23. Era il Franceschini di statura bassa, magro, pallido, col naso profilato, di capelli neri e barba folta, ed era in età di 50 anni. Vestiva lo stesso abito che portava allorche commise il delitto, cioè con giustacore di panno bigio, camiciuola nera, ferrajuolo di baracano, cappello bianco, e berrettino di cotone; talche si crede che con tali abiti si partisse d'Arezzo travestito.

24. Questa Giustizia ebbe luogo sotto il Pontificato di Innocenzo XII. nel 1698.

21. They departed from the New Prisons, and then followed the Via del Pellegrino, the Via del Governo, and the Via del Pasquino; then went through Piazza Navona, past the Rotunda, and through Piazza Colonna; and finally along the Corso.

22. The first to be executed was Agostinelli, the second Gambasini, the third Pasquini, the fourth Baldeschi, and finally Franceschini. When the last-named mounted the scaffold, he begged forgiveness for his sins, implored the crowd to pray for the repose of his soul, and asked them, in addition, that they should say an 'Our Father', a 'Hail Mary', and a 'Hail Holy Queen' for him. The priest was called. Franceschini made his confession, positioned his neck under the blade, and was beheaded with the name of Jesus on his lips. The executioner then displayed his head to the crowd.

23. Franceschini was short of stature, thin and pale, with a sharp nose, black hair and a heavy beard, about 50 years of age. He was still wearing the same clothes in which he committed the murder: a grey-cloth doublet, a dark camisole, a rough cloak of barracan,[17] a white hat, and a cotton cap—clothed presumably as he had been when he had set out from Arezzo.

24. This sentence took place in the year 1698 in the Pontificate of Innocent XII.

[17] A coarsely woven fabric of wool, silk, and goat's hair.

APPENDIX C

AUTOGRAPH CHRONOLOGIES

Two autograph chronologies survive from Browning's working papers on *The Ring and the Book*, one at the Beinecke Library, Yale, the other at the Pierpont Morgan Library, New York. They appear to be first attempts to work out correctly an overall chronology for the events of the story, though the insertions in them may have been made at later dates. The Pierpont Morgan document (MA 4436) is significantly neater in appearance and has fewer insertions than the one at Yale; it is probably a revision of the latter. We thank the authorities at both libraries for permission to publish these documents.

We know from his letters that Browning used Augustus De Morgan's *The Book of Almanacs* (1851) to make calculations on phases of the moon.[1] This small book contains 37 tables by which the almanac may be found 'for every year...from any epoch...up to A.D. 2000, with means of finding the day of any new or full moon from B.C. 2000 to A.D. 2000.' The Yale chronology provides complementary evidence of Browning's use of the *Almanacs*, and also shows how he used it to establish days of the week and feast-days of the Church. At the end of the chronology he is finding out about April 1697, the time of Caponsacchi and Pompilia's flight from Arezzo: he uses Almanac 17 to establish the dates of Lent and Easter 1697, and then Almanac 37 and the instructions on p. xiii to work out that the real full moon was 7 April and the real new moon 21 April. Above this, he uses Almanac 9 to establish the days of the week in January and February 1698: that 2 January, the day of the murders, was a Thursday; that 6 January, the day of Pompilia's death, was a Monday; that 18 February, the day of Guido's sentence, was a Tuesday; and that 22 February, the day of Guido's execution, was a Saturday. He also establishes the date of Ash Wednesday as 12 February, so as to know that the execution took place well after the end of Carnival. From the pattern of his insertions in the text (indicated below in smaller typeface enclosed in ‹ ›) it is clear that Browning first drew up the chronologies using the Old Yellow Book and the Secondary Source, and then deployed the *Almanacs*. As well as providing evidence of his care in these matters, the

---

[1] See RB to [Augustus De Morgan], 26 Mar. 1866: Johns Hopkins University; and also RB to Leonard Henry Courtney, 14 May 1881: TLS, 25 Feb. 1909, 72.

Yale chronology also helps to understand his dating of the flight from Arezzo.

It has traditionally been assumed that Browning deliberately shifted the date of the flight of Pompilia and Caponsacchi from 29 April to 23 April (St George's Day) 1697, so as to emphasize the symbolic link between Caponsacchi and St George: Caponsacchi (St George/Perseus) rescues Pompilia (the maiden/Andromeda) from the dragon (Guido).[2] This change of the date by a week, however, seems at odds with his repeated claims of fidelity to the historical sources, and also with his concern—as expressed in the letters and in the chronologies—to establish the phase of the moon on the night of the flight. The Yale chronology suggests how the change came about: it was probably a fortuitous mistake. In fact it is likely that it only came about in the context of a concern to be faithful to the historical record, as witnessed in his use of the *Almanacs* itself.

The evidence suggests the following explanation for the change. Small references in OYB establish that the flight actually took place from about 1 p.m. on 29 April 1697 until the evening of 30 April, when Caponsacchi and Pompilia halted at the inn in Castelnuovo. Here they were arrested the next morning, 1 May.[3] Browning forgot these small references, and in this instance worked from the Secondary Source, paragraph 7, where it says that the flight began early 'nel Lunedì ultimo di Aprile' ('on the last Monday of April'). We conjecture that he used the *Almanacs* to determine the dates for Mondays, and then drew a calendar box for April 1697— similar to that below for January and February 1698—and that, working quickly, he erroneously concluded that 'the last Monday of April' was the 22nd. The ink and spacing in the Yale chronology bear this out: he appears first to have written 'Flight from Arezzo, [ ], the last Monday in April, 1697', and then later added '22 April' in heavier ink. As, from the *Almanacs*, he then wrote down the dates of Good Friday and Easter Day in the same April, and worked out the phase of the moon for the night of the flight, the *Almanacs* reminded him that 23 April was St George's Day. He writes this into the chronology. At the same time, he also notices that 22 April is not, of course, the last Monday of the month. By now he has forgotten that 22 April is his calculation, and assumes that the information comes wholly from his source. He simply inserts 'really, *last but one*' over the original note. The imaginative potential of St George's Day as one of the days of the flight has already begun to take hold in his mind.

---

[2] See Hodell, 310, n. 184, and also our note on 1. 585.
[3] OYB v (5), lxxxv (93), lxxxix (96–7).

(a) MS in the Beinecke Library, Yale University

Pope Innocent XII, born—(Antonio Pignatelli)	
Pietro & Violante born about	1628
Guido born about	1648
Pompilia born 17th July,	1680
ˈDeath of Pope Alexander VIII. Acces[n]. of Pope	
Innocent XII July 12——	1691ˈ
„ married, December	1693
„ arrived at Arezzo	„
Pietro and Violante returned to Rome, four months after.	1694
ˈLetter attesting the quarrels, 12 Feb. Of the Governor,	
Aug 2. Of the Archbishop, Sept. 15.——	„ˈ
Pretended Letter to Paolo, June 14,—letter from him, 6 March	„
Deposition of Angelica as to treatment at Arezzo, June 24	„
ˈWill of Pietro executed————————	1695ˈ
ˈ(really, *last but one*)ˈ	
Flight from Arezzo, April 22[4], the last Monday in April,	1697
ˈ23. St George's day, Tuesday,ˈ	
Overtaken at Castelnuovo, Apr 24, Wednesday at Daybreak,	„
ˈMayˈ	
Deposition of Pompilia, ~~March~~ 21, as to the Letter to Paolo,	„
ˈAccording to the forged letter to Pietro she was still at	
Castelvecchio, May 3.ˈ	
„ ” May 13, Tuesday, as to Caponsacchi	„
Depositions of various persons as to treatment, June 17,	„
Sentence of Relegation against Caponsacchi, Tuesday, Sept 24	„
Domum pro Carcere[5] &c Oct. 12	„
Birth of Gaetano 18 December	„
ˈDecision of the Rota approved by the Granduca———ˈ	
Guido arrived at Rome, la Vigilia di S. Natale[6]	1697
Murder, 2 January, Giovedì, ad un'ora circa di notte[7]	1698
Pompilia died Jan: ~~4~~ ⌐"Epiphany,"—6⌐ according to Confessor	
& M.S.	„
ˈDeposition of Confessor Jan. 10	„ˈ
Guido sentenced 18 February, Tuesday. Appeal.	„

---

[4] It appears that 'April 22' has been added later in a space left in the original line.
[5] 'House arrest' (L.).
[6] 'Christmas Eve': from SS 10.
[7] 'Thursday, at about the first hour of the night' (6 p.m.): from SS 11.

'Chirografo del Papa Feb. 21. alle due di notte.[8]'

Executed, Feb. 22, sentence communicated alle 8,
    Compagnia arrived 22.[9]   "

'(dopo il pranzo)[10] Sentence of Rehabilitation, September 9.—   "'

Pope Innocent XII died July 12. Clement XI. succeeding—   1700
[page break]

'24 Tues   25 Wed ⎫
              26 Th. ⎪
              27 Fr ⎬ 1697'
              28 Sat. ⎪
              29 Su ⎪
              30 Mo. ⎭

		Almanack for 1698.			Ash W.		
Dec. 31 Tu							
Jan. 1 Wed.	8	15	22	29	5	12	19
2 Th	9	16	23	30	6	13	20
3 Fr	10	17	24	31	7	14	21
4 Sa	11	18	25	Feb 1	8	15	22
5 Su	12	19	26	2	9	16	23 &c
6 M Epiph.	13	20	27	3	10	17	
7 Tu	14	21	28	4	11	18	

Shrove T.

Easter 1697
Ash Wednesday was Feb 20
Good Friday—April 5
Easter Day, Sunday Apr. 7
Full moon—April 7
New moon: April 21
        (—22, the Flight)

---

[8] 'Chirograph of the Pope Feb. 21 [signed] at the second hour of night (7 p.m.)':
from OYB ccxxxix (238). For 'chirograph' see 1. 346 n.

[9] 'Sentence communicated [to Guido] at the 8th hour (1 a.m.), Company [of Death
and Pity] arrived at the 22nd hour (3 p.m.).' This is a slip: SS 19 says that the Company
arrived at the 20th hour (1 p.m.).

[10] 'After dinner-time' (referring to the time of the execution): from OYB ccxxxix
(238).

(b) MS in the Pierpont Morgan Library, New York

Pope Innocent born at Spinazzola in the Neap. Territory,
March 13.   1615

Pietro Comparini and Violante Peruzzi were born (about)   1628

Guido Franceschini was born (about)   1648

Pompilia was born July 17,   1680

Alexander VIII died; Antonio Pignatelli, Innocent XII,
succeeded, July 12,   1691

Pompilia was married, December,   1693

Arrived at Arezzo with her Husband and Parents,   "

Pietro and Violante returned to Rome, four months after,
April,   1694

Letter attesting the quarrels, Feb. 12 ⎫

   " of the Governor, Aug. 2 ⎬   "

   " of the Archbishop, Sept. 15 ⎭

   " (pretended) to the Abate Paolo, June 14,   "

   " from Ab. Paolo, March 6th,

Deposition of Angelica as to P's ill treatment at Arezzo,
               Rome, June 24,   "

`March 17. Conceptus est G. ?`[11]

Testament of Pietro executed,   1695

            `Apr. 21. (new moon—)`

Flight from Arezzo, Monday, Apr. 22, before daybreak,   1697

          `arrive at Castelnuo. 23, St George's Day,`

Overtaken at Castelnuovo Wednesday, Ap. 24, at daybreak,   "

Deposition of Pompilia,   "

According to a forged letter, she was still at Castelnuovo May 3,   "

Deposition of Pompilia as to Caponsacchi, Tuesday, Sept 24,   "

Domum pro carcere &c Oct. 12,   "

Birth of Gaetano, Dec. 18,   "

Decision of the Ruota at Florence, approved by the

          `Cosimo III` ⌐

        Granduca ˄ Dec. 24,"

Guido arrived in Rome, Christmas Eve, Dec. 24,

Murder, Thursday, Jan 2, Thursday, ad un'ora circa di notte,   1698

[page break]

---

[11] 'G[aetano] was conceived?' Browning has inserted this conjecture one line too
high, for it relates to 1697, not 1695.

Pompilia died Jan. 6. Epiphany, Monday,   1698
Deposition of Confessor, Jan 10,   "
Guido sentenced Tuesday, Feb. 18, (Appeal)   "
Chirograph of the Pope, Friday, Feb. 21, alle due di notte,   "
Execution   Sat. Feb 22, dopo il pranzo,   "
`Sentence communicated alle 8. Compagnia arrived alle 22,´
Sentence of rehabilitation of P.'s memory, Sepr. 9,   "
                         `September 27´
Pope Innocent died ~~July 12~~ Clement XI
succeeding,   1700.

APPENDIX D

THE RING

As a goldsmith works upon pure gold ore to make a ring, so, in Book I, the poet tells us how he works upon the 'pure crude fact' (35) of the Old Yellow Book to produce his rounded (completed and shaped) work of art, *The Ring and the Book* itself. There has been considerable scholarly discussion as to the nature of this ring, both as a metaphor for poetic creation, and as a real object, the presumed basis for the description. In the former case there is a broad critical consensus, in the latter some degree of confusion remains. The manufacture of the ring as a metaphor seems clear enough. The goldsmith's ingenious manual workings and the intricacies of his processes of manufacture—notably the use of alloy to make the gold ore workable—parallel the mental work of the poet, in particular the fusing of his imagination with the raw data of history, his effort to retrieve history's meaning and to forge from it an artistic shape. The clearest accounts of this matter are by Cundiff, Wasserman, and Sullivan, who show different interpretative emphases, but also substantive agreement.[1]

Inquiry into the ring as a real object takes its lead from the poem: the poet asks, 'Do you see this square old yellow Book, I toss / I' the air, and catch again' (I. 33–4), a vividly physical image which we know relates to a real book. It is in parallel with the equally realistic image, 'Do you see this Ring? / 'T is Rome-work, made to match / (By Castellani's imitative craft) / Etrurian circlets' (I. 1–4). Because of the parallelism, these lines are assumed to relate to a particular ring. But which ring? Here confusion has arisen among scholars and nineteenth-century jewellery experts.

In 1857–8 Isa Blagden, a close friend of the Brownings in Florence, gave them each a ring, the one to EBB engraved on its bezel AEI (Greek, 'always'), the one to Browning with the raised inscription on its bezel VIS MEA (Latin, 'my strength'). This was an important gesture of love on her

---

[1] See Paul A. Cundiff, 'The Clarity of Browning's Ring Metaphor', PMLA 63 (1948), 1276–82; George R. Wasserman, 'The Meaning of Browning's Ring-Figure', MLN 76 (1961), 420–6; Mary R. Sullivan, 'The Function of Book I in *The Ring and the Book*', VP 6 (1968), 231–41: this is substantially repeated in her *Browning's Voices in The Ring and the Book* (Toronto, University of Toronto Press, 1969).

part. The rings are alluded to in the letters,[2] and also probably (as we shall see) in a conversation that Browning had with William Allingham in 1868:[3] these allusions suggest that both rings were in the Brownings' possession by 1858, and that Browning probably considered them to have been made by the Roman firm of jewellers, Castellani. Modern jewellery experts doubt this provenance, at least in the case of the one ring that survives for direct examination, the VIS MEA ring.[4]

The AEI ring was a small, simple, gold signet ring, whose delicacy was noted by Browning: 'Can you fancy that tiny finger? Can you believe that a woman could wear such a circlet as this? It is a child's.'[5] It is now lost, stolen from the British Museum in 1971, but an impression of it can be gained from a sketch made by Pen Browning in 1894,[6] and from photographs taken at the British Museum.[7] The other ring, with VIS MEA on its bezel, is formally described in a modern catalogue: 'Cast ring (type 28), plain and beaded ribs, rounded bezel with VIS MEA (My strength), sans serif, in relief. [size] P (enlarged) 1.5 mm.'[8] This is a small, lightweight ring, about 18 mm in diameter; the band is fine, 0.75 mm at its thinnest, 3 mm at its thickest at the bezel; the hollow, rounded bezel is about 8 mm high. This ring is now owned by Balliol College Library. Browning wore the VIS MEA ring for much of the rest of his life. After EBB's death, he wore the AEI ring on his watch-chain, along with a gold pencil, and one of the first coins struck in Venice in 1848 to record the popular insurrection against Austrian rule. As Judy Rudoe notes, 'photographs taken of Browning in his later years show the watch-chain clearly, though the ring is usually hidden behind the coin.'[9] The confusions about

---

[2] EBB to Isa Blagden, [n.d.], British Library MS Add. 40730, f. 40, printed in *Dearest Isa*, 11 n. 5; EBB to Isa Blagden, 8 July 1858: *Dearest Isa*, 10–11; RB to Isa Blagden, 19 Nov. 1864: *Dearest Isa*, 198.

[3] Allingham, 195.

[4] 'Browning's [VIS MEA] ring does not bear the monogram used by the Castellani firm to identify their works and is very lightweight by comparison with known Castellani pieces, which tend to be solid and well constructed': Judy Rudoe, 'Elizabeth Barrett Browning and the Taste for Archaeological-Style Jewelry', *Philadelphia Museum of Art Bulletin*, 83 (Fall 1986), 22–32 (hereafter Rudoe). Rudoe goes further than this: 'I would now see no grounds for attributing the VIS MEA ring to Castellani': letter to the editors.

[5] Recorded by Katherine de Kay Bronson, in 'Browning in Venice', *The Cornhill Magazine*, NS 12 (1902), 152.

[6] Griffin Collections, vi. 43ʳ⁻ᵛ.

[7] Most easily seen in Rudoe, 29.

[8] Gerald Taylor, *Finger Rings from Ancient Egypt to the Present Day* (London, Lund Humphries, 1978), 90, no. 921.

[9] Rudoe, 29.

these rings that began after Browning's death in 1889 have been carefully examined by A. N. Kincaid.[10] We agree with Kincaid's account of the mistakes made in Browning scholarship, but not with his conclusion that the VIS MEA ring is necessarily the eponymous ring.

Browning's biographer, William Hall Griffin, working on the assumption that 'the Ring' must be as real as 'the Book', wrote to Pen Browning in 1894. Pen replied:

With regard to the 'ring', my impression is—(one I have always had, without having ever enquired into the matter,)—that my father had in his mind a simple and modern Castellani ring which my mother wore, and which my father had afterwards on his watch-chain. . . . I have it in Venice, but can give you the shape, and do so. The letters A. E. I. are on the flattened upper surface of the ring. It was either given to my mother by him or by an american lady, now dead, with whom she was, at that time, very intimate.[11]

Pen admits the vague nature of his impression, and Kincaid has shown how unsubstantiated his view is. (Pen seems to think that the ring was given to EBB by Sophia Eckley, and not by Isa Blagden.) The crucial point is that he has no definite recollection from his father. A few years later, Griffin consulted Mrs Sutherland Orr, and received a different answer:

I see no reason for taking the ring in Mr Browning's poem as other than imaginary. Mr Browning never to my knowledge wore such a one, nor did he need to buy it for purposes of illustration. . . . It was always his way to put real things and imaginary ones on the same planet.[12]

Griffin died without completing his biography. In the meantime Pen became convinced that he was right, and repeated his view more definitely to Charles Hodell.[13] Christopher Minchin, completing Griffin's biography, took over Pen's letter rather uncritically,[14] and Pen's view passed into the stream of Browning scholarship.[15] Until the time of Kincaid's article in 1980, the claims of the VIS MEA ring to be considered as the eponymous ring were virtually unknown. The evidence here comes from one source, Fannie Barrett Browning (née Coddington),

---

[10] 'The Ring and the Scholars', BIS 8 (1980), 151–60.
[11] Griffin Collections, vi. 43–43^{v}.
[12] Griffin Collections, vi. 66.
[13] Hodell, 337–8.
[14] Griffin and Minchin, 236.
[15] See *Handbook*, 330, for example.

Browning's daughter-in-law, and is contained in a letter she wrote to the Master of Balliol College in 1914:

> Hotel Rembrandt
> Thurloe Place
> SW
> Jany 2nd 1914

Dear Dr Davidson;

I have sent off to you today the 'Ring', of the 'Ring & The Book' fame—which I have taken from Elizabeth Barrett Browning's jewelery [*sic*] case, given me by my dear Father-in-law 6 months after our marriage—He then told me this respecting this identical ring.

I send it broken as it was when I received it.

As the original 'Book' is in the Library at Balliol College (& as you know given by my husband at his Father's desire) I want to have the satisfaction during my own lifetime of knowing the 'Ring' is there too. I am Dear Dr Davidson

> Yours very sincerely
> Fannie Barrett Browning[16]

Kincaid considers this letter as conclusive proof, though it too has weaknesses: its evidence is at second-hand and unsupported by any of Browning's friends (in particular, unsupported by Mrs Sutherland Orr), and it relates to 1888, when Browning was 75 years old, twenty years after the publication of the poem. Our annotations to the opening passage of the poem (1. 1–32) give a brief summary of our own conclusions, which we will further substantiate here. The VIS MEA ring may have played a part in generating the image, but, in the absence of clearer evidence, it is important to consider the image in a fuller biographical context. Within such a context, Fannie's letter seems less important, while Browning's image seems a focus for memory and emotion.

The opening passage of Book I hinges upon the interrelations between the famous Castellani firm of jewellers in Rome, the Tuscan town of Chiusi (about 23 miles north of Orvieto, and about 37 miles south-east of Siena), and nineteenth-century reproduction Etruscan-style jewellery. Chiusi was one of the primary sites of the ancient Etruscan civilization, with over 400 tombs on its outskirts from approximately the fifth century BC. As the standard nineteenth-century work on ancient Etruria notes, 'the discovery of tombs around Chiusi is of every-day occurrence, the neighbourhood being so full of them'.[17] The Museo Casuccini in the

---

[16] We thank Balliol College, Oxford, for permission to quote this letter.

[17] George Dennis, *The Cities and Cemeteries of Etruria*, 2 vols. (1848), ii. 374.

town was full of articles from the tombs 'more singular, quaint, and archaic in character, than those of any other part of Etruria, with the exception of Veii and Cære.'[18] Much significant ancient Etruscan jewellery had been found in the tombs. Occasionally, as Browning notes, items were uncovered after heavy rains, not usually though near the tombs, but often on a slope called Campo degli Orefici ('Jeweller's Field'); such jewellery consisted mainly of scarabaei. These 'are found much more abundantly at Chiusi than on any other Etruscan site, are very rarely the produce of her tombs, or the fruit of systematic research, but "the unlettered ploughboy wins / The casual treasure from the furrowed soil." '[19]

Nineteenth-century Etruscan-style jewellery, with which the Castellani firm was intimately associated, was a fashion of the 1850s that became more marked in the 1860s. Owing to the lectures given by the Castellani sons, and to various prestigious exhibitions at which the firm's work was displayed, the Castellani name was well known in Paris and London, as well as in Italy, by the time Browning wrote his allusion. Fortunato Castellani (1794–1865), the firm's founder, took a great interest in the excavations in the Etruscan tombs from the 1820s onwards. He founded the 'Archaeological School' of jewellery, imitating the ancient Etruscan designs, and also ancient jewellery from other periods and places. This interest passed to his sons, Alessandro Castellani (1823–83) and Augusto Castellani (1829–1914), who carried on and in various ways extended their father's work.[20]

The Brownings were well aware of the fashion for Etruscan-style jewellery. In June 1859, for example, they gave 'Etruscan gold' to Charlotte MacIntosh as a wedding present when she married EBB's brother, Octavius: 'I hope you opened the little gift for Charlotte,' EBB wrote to her sister Arabel, 'Was it pretty enough? Etruscan gold after antique patterns.'[21] We have not been able to identify this piece of jewellery, but it might well have been by Castellani. There is no reason to suppose that Browning's visit to the Castellani shop at 88 Via Poli in 1860 was his one and only visit. The shop was a recognized tourist attraction in Rome. One reading of the aside 'Craftsmen instruct me' (l. 9) would be literal, that Browning is implying that he had spoken to the Castellani or to their workers about goldsmith's techniques. His knowledge of the shop, and

[18] Dennis, *The Cities and Cemeteries of Etruria*, 338.   [19] Ibid., 375.
[20] For a full account of their careers, see Geoffrey C. Munn, *Castellani and Giuliano* (1984).
[21] 3 June 1859: Berg Collection, New York Public Library.

what he may have learnt there, is important, but so too—as we shall see—is the political affiliation of the Castellani.

The Brownings visited the Castellani shop in January 1860 to see the presentation swords made for Napoleon III and Victor Emmanuel II on the occasion of their joint victory over the Austrians in northern Italy. Fourteen thousand Romans had subscribed for the swords. The Brownings' visit was part of their political and imaginative engagement with the ongoing Risorgimento. We conjecture that either on this visit, or on a subsequent one, Browning was shown imitation Etruscan jewellery and maybe, also, part of the Castellani collection of ancient Etruscan jewellery. Given the relationship between the Castellani and Chiusi (discussed later), it may well have been Fortunato Castellani who spoke to Browning about Chiusi as a site of archaeological and cultural interest. Nathaniel Hawthorne visited the Castellani shop in April 1858, and his account in his *Notebooks* gives a sense of Fortunato Castellani's enthusiasm about Etruscan-style jewellery. His mention of 'immemorial tombs' suggests that he and Browning received similar information:

After this latter visit, Mr. Akers conducted us to the jeweller's shop of Castellani, who seems to be a great reproducer of ornaments in the old Roman and Etruscan fashion. These antique styles are very fashionable just now, and some of the specimens which he showed us were certainly very beautiful, though I doubt whether their quaintness and old-time curiosity, as patterns of gewgaws dug out of immemorial tombs, be not their greatest charm. We saw the toilette-case of an Etruscan lady—that is to say, a modern imitation of it—with her rings for summer and winter, and for every day of the week; and for thumb and fingers; her ivory comb, her bracelets, and more knicknacks than I can half remember. Splendid things of our own time, were likewise shown us; a necklace of diamonds, worth eighteen thousand scudi, together with emeralds, and opals, and great pearls. Finally, we came away, and my wife and Miss Shepard were taken up by the Misses Weston, who drove with her to visit the Villa Albani. On their way, my wife happened to raise her arm, and Miss Shepard espied a little Greek cross of gold which had attached itself to the lace of her sleeve, thus making an involuntary pilferer of my poor wife. Pray Heaven the jeweller may not discover his loss before we have time to restore the spoil! He is apparently so free and careless in displaying his precious wares—putting inestimable gems, and pins and brooches great and small, into the hands of strangers like ourselves, and leaving scores of them strewn on the top of his counter—that it would seem easy enough to pocket a diamond or two; but I suspect there must needs be a sharp eye somewhere. Before we left the shop, he requested me to honor him with my autograph, in a large book that seemed full of the names of his visitors. This is probably a measure of precaution.[22]

[22] Hawthorne, 190–1.

In the late 1850s the Castellani were building up a collection of ancient Etruscan jewellery, and by the time Browning visited the shop this collection may have been extensive. Eventually, in 1872, Alessandro Castellani sold a large quantity of this jewellery, from the period 600 to 200 BC, to the British Museum, where some of the 'Castellani Collection' is still on display: it contains, among other objects, necklaces, earrings, brooches, and finger rings, and some of the most significant pieces—including a striking gold-foil wreath and some magnificent rings—come originally from Chiusi. The British Museum's catalogue of purchase is detailed, but it does not record when the items of the collection came into Castellani ownership. We conjecture that some of the items were in the Castellani's possession by the time the Brownings visited the shop, and that they may have played a part in alerting Browning to the interest of Chiusi. Subsequent to the visit to the shop, the Brownings took a different route from Rome to Florence in June 1860, travelling by *vettura* not by the main routes via Siena or Perugia, but by what was then the comparatively little frequented route, via Orvieto and Chiusi, and then to Siena. Both Brownings were struck by the beauty of the landscape along the way, and by troop movements connected with the Risorgimento. It was, in other words, a memorable and happy time for Browning, particularly when seen from the perspective of EBB's death. On the 5 or 6 of June 1860 he admired the frescoes by Luca Signorelli in Orvieto cathedral. On the morning of 7 June he saw some of the tombs at Chiusi: 'I may say briefly that we travelled prosperously thro' a beautiful country and that I, leaving Ba to rest herself, saw wonderful things at Orvieto & Chiusi.'[23]

The Risorgimento was still an ongoing ferment at the time of the visit to Chiusi: 'We dream, talk, eat & drink Garibaldi just now', wrote EBB on 14 June 1860. By the time Browning published *The Ring and the Book* Italian unification was a more established fact. He was proud of EBB's support of the cause, and of the way her work had been recognized by Italians. It is via these concerns that he comes to his allusion to Castellani. The *Dizionario biografico degli italiani* outlines the personal and political problems of the Castellani, and how, at the time of the Brownings' visit, the family was about to be split up:

---

[23] RB to Story family, 15 June 1860: Hudson, 59. The two letters that confirm that RB saw the tombs at Chiusi are RB to Story family, 8 June 1860: Hudson, 58, and EBB to Fanny Haworth, 16 June 1860: *Letters of EBB*, ii. 394.

As he became involved in his art, Alessandro Castellani became involved in politics; he devoted himself to both causes for the rest of his life. In 1847 he followed republican and democratic ideals and joined the Progressive Popular Circle. For a short time, during the course of the Roman Republic, he was a member of the commission that chose the government representatives. After the restoration of the Pope's rule, he was arrested together with his brother Augusto (16 July 1849) and released after a few days owing to a 'generous' intervention from his father, well known for his wealth in Rome. Regardless of these events, Alessandro maintained his connections with the republicans, headed by the exiled Mazzini, organized in the Italian National Association. Alessandro headed one of the Roman cells, for which he collected the membership money. In August 1853, after the discovery of the revolutionary plot organized by some exiles together with the members of the National Association in Rome, he was arrested together with Giuseppe Petroni, Cesare Mazzoni, and others. Denunciations and betrayals enabled the police to arrest all the conspirators; Alessandro shared the others' fate only in part, because in January 1854 he began to show serious mental problems while in the prison of San Michele. It is still doubtful whether he was feigning insanity to protect himself from papal justice, or whether, as his family claimed, it was genuine. In either case, he was placed in an asylum until 1856, when he was given back into the hands of his family, under their responsibility, with the judicial case still pending. He slowly resumed his work in the family business, under supervision from the police. They became persuaded of his recovery at the end of 1859, and offered him the alternatives of proceeding to trial or going into exile. Unwillingly, Alessandro left for Paris in June 1860, where he brought a flat in Rue Talbot and opened a branch of the family business in the Champs-Élysées, so increasing the family fortune.[24]

Alessandro commissioned the swords celebrating the victories of Napoleon III and Victor Emmanuel II. The reason that the Brownings hurried to see the exhibition is that it was under censure from Pius IX, and was closed shortly after their visit. It is in this context that we can appreciate the warm welcome given them by Fortunato Castellani: 'we were received . . . most flatteringly as poets and lovers of Italy; were asked for autographs; and returned in a blaze of glory and satisfaction'.[25]

This biographical context, showing the factors that made Castellani and Chiusi vivid to Browning, is as significant as the attempt to identify one ring as the eponymous ring. The VIS MEA ring may have contributed to the image, since Browning believed it was by Castellani, but the

[24] Translated from the *Dizionario biografico degli italiani*, xxi. 591–2.
[25] *Letters of EBB*, ii. 355.

wider context—what Browning saw and learnt at the Castellani shop, what he saw and learnt at Chiusi, his own purchase of Etruscan-style jewellery—makes apparent the fuller resonance of the opening passage. Any number of rings, ancient ones or modern imitations, could have contributed to the impressions lying behind the passage, and the search to identify one ring is potentially the fallacy of a single source, in a context where (as we have shown) memory is playing an important role.

Other considerations need to be taken into account. As Mairi Calcraft-Rennie has shown, the impression in the opening passage is of some fairly magnificent ring, one with a 'lilied loveliness' and 'rondure brave', one that is the product of the goldsmith's elaborate craft. The VIS MEA and AEI rings tally poorly with this impression. The VIS MEA ring, in particular, is a plain, lightweight ring, with only tiny beading, and is not conspicuously 'Etruscan' in design. One prominent ancient Etruscan design fits the description of the passage much better: this has a chunky, oval, raised bezel, 2 to 3 cm across; intricate designs around the bezel; a cornelian at the top of the domed bezel; and a thick finger-band, approximately 5 mm in width. It is a striking and elaborate design, in a form of gold that really shines. Calcraft-Rennie goes further than this. She examines a photograph made by William Hall Griffin of a particular Etruscan ring of this design, and a note left by him which seems to indicate that he consulted Augusto Castellani in Rome in the 1890s concerning Browning and 'the Ring'. From a reading of this evidence, she conjectures that this ring—once owned by the Castellani, and now in the British Museum (Finger Ring 356)—is the eponymous ring.[26] Her evidence, though, is circumstantial, and, as she concedes, there is nothing that directly links this ring with the poem.

A second consideration is that Browning himself did not conspicuously identify one ring, excepting of course his remark to Fannie Barrett Browning. During the time of the poem's publication, a remark recorded by William Allingham suggests the extent to which he did not think of 'the Ring' as an equal object to 'the Book'. Allingham reports a conversation after lunch on 27 December 1868:

B. again shows me the original *Book*, and translates to me the letter of the lawyer, de Archangelis, written on the day of the execution, saying, among other things, 'Guido is lamented for by all respectable people.' ... Shows me proofs of 'Pom-

---

[26] Mairi Calcraft-Rennie, 'Wordcraft and the Goldsmiths: Browning and the Castellani', BSN 23 (1996), 54–66.

pilia'; also two rings of *pure* gold, very soft; Castellani of Rome makes them. He gives me Volume II. of *The Ring and the Book*.[27]

Most likely these were the AEI and VIS MEA rings, but Browning does not distinguish between them, but rather uses them to demonstrate the malleability of pure gold.

This leads to a third consideration: that the title as we now have it, which sets the ring in such prominence, was not Browning's working title, and that its elements originated with his publisher's suggestion of 'The Book and the Ring', a suggestion made as late as June 1868. Had the poem been finally titled, as Browning suggested, *The Franceschini*, the ring's status as metaphor would have been more marked, its status as an individual object a little less prominent.

As a metaphor, the ring has two elements: its process of manufacture as a parallel to the artistic making of the poem, and its finished roundness as a metaphor for the completed, achieved poem. In this second aspect, the most important source for the image is again Browning's memories of EBB, echoed in the tablet set up on the wall of Casa Guidi by the City of Florence:

QUI SCRISSE E MORI

ELISABETTA BARRET BROWNING

CHE IN CUORE DI DONNA CONCILIAVA

SCIENZA DI DOTTO E SPIRITO DI POETA

E FECE DEL SUO VERSO AUREO ANELLO

FRA ITALIA E INGHILTERRA

PONE QUESTA MEMORIA

FIRENZE GRATA

1861[28]

['Here wrote and died Elizabeth Barrett Browning, who in the heart of a woman united the learning of a scholar and the spirit of a poet and made with her verse a golden ring between Italy and England. Grateful Florence places this memorial 1861.' This inscription was composed by the poet Niccolò Tommaseo.]

Browning alludes to this commemoration plaque in the closing lines of the whole poem (XII. 872–4) where he lays the metaphorical 'ring' of his completed poem next to EBB's 'rare gold ring of verse (the poet praised) / Linking our England to his Italy!' In this fuller context, we can see that I. 1–32 is forged out of memories of Browning's life with EBB in 1860,

---

[27] Allingham, 195.
[28] There is a photograph of the tablet in *Dearest Isa*, 220.

memories connecting her passion for a united Italy with Castellani and Chiusi. In this sense it anticipates the end of Book 1, the invocation to 'Lyric Love' (1. 1391–1416).

APPENDIX E

YALE VARIANTS

Yale MS 1p / B821 / 868c is a set of sheets from vols. I, III, and IV of the second edition of *The Ring and the Book*, sent by George Smith to Browning in 1883, and revised by him, apparently over the next few years. With one exception made in ink, Browning made his corrections and revisions on the Yale sheets in pencil, in a slapdash manner quite in contrast with his usual neatness—so much so, indeed, that Philip Kelley and Betty Coley (Kelley and Coley, p. 434) doubted if they were in his hand. The letter forms, however, together with the substance of the revisions, make it clear that only Browning could have been the reviser. There are 120 corrections and revisions, spread unevenly across the nine books (Books IV, V, and VI, of course, were not concerned), Book XI having no corrections or revisions at all. Ninety-six are unique to the Yale sheets; twenty-four, of which eight, possibly nine, are to typographical errors, are shared with *1888*. In fourteen cases the revisions found in *1888* conflict with those in the Yale sheets. Seventy of the corrections and revisions concern accidentals, fifty substantives. Many of the revisions are clear improvements on the text of 1872, but with much regret we have not adopted them for our copy text. In fourteen cases they clash with revisions made by Browning in *1888*, in at least two cases revisions made to adjacent lines in *1888* make it impossible to fit them in, the coverage of the nine books is uneven, and one revision is tentative. To adopt those revisions that it is possible to adopt, but to ignore those where there is a difficulty, would have resulted in an eclectic text, and in producing this we have not felt justified. The revisions relating to Books I–III are listed below; the rest will appear in Volumes VIII and IX of our edition.

Revisions in *Yale 2* and *1888* compared

Line	In *Yale 2* only	In *Yale 2* and *1888* (★ = corrected literal)	In *1888* conflicting with *Yale 2*	Adjacent revision in *1888* precluding *Yale 2* (noted ‖)
Book I				
21	works,>works.		works:	
22	But>But,			
88		since>since.		
180		fellows', which> / fellows', —which		
183	simplicity:>simplicity.			
191	friends:>friends.			
515	Husband and wife and priest, met face to face. > Husband, wife, priest, next morn met face to face. {see 1. 515 n.}			
702		malleolable>malleable {see 1. 702 n.}		
769	{New paragraph removed. In 1888 the pagination obscures the paragraphing}			
817	"His....reared;> / "—His....reared;—			
830		digests,>digests——>digests,		=

Revisions in *Yale 2* and *1888* compared (*cont.*)

Line	In *Yale 2* only	In *Yale 2* and *1888* (* = corrected literal)	In *1888* conflicting with *Yale 2*	Adjacent revision in *1888* precluding *Yale 2* (noted ‖)
443	God?>god?			
505	counterblast,> counterblast,—			
506	din;>din!			
518		left,—>left.		
575	her>her,			
623		The stealing sombre element comes in>The sombre element comes stealing in		
764		[? wife s>wife's]*		
881	foot,—>foot.			
897	wide and>wide, and			
1313	Inasmuch as no question could be more,>Inasmuch as no more could question be,		Inasmuch as no question more could be,—	=
1315	now:>now.			

ground>ground?

It may be worthwhile to draw attention to some of the more characteristic revisions which are unique to *Yale 2*, and therefore never took their
place in the edition of 1888–9. The examples are taken from the first three
books of the poem. The earliest of these, 1. 515, is interesting because it
was made in response to a criticism from a reader, Leonard Courtney, and
is therefore important additional evidence that the revisions in *Yale 2* were
made by Browning himself. Courtney claimed that the following passage
suggested that the meeting between Guido, Pompilia, and Caponsacchi at
the inn outside Rome took place in the evening:

> Farther then I fared,
> Feeling my way on through the hot and dense,
> Romeward, until I found the wayside inn
> By Castelnuovo's few mean hut-like homes
> Huddled together on the hill-foot bleak,
> Bare, broken only by that tree or two
> Against the sudden bloody splendour poured
> Cursewise in his departure by the day
> On the low house-roof of that squalid inn
> Where they three, for the first time and the last,
> Husband and wife and priest, met face to face. (1. 505–15)

Even though Browning was referring to the time of day when he himself
was imagining the appearance of the inn, he clearly felt that the passage
should be made more explicit.

1. 702 contains a word, 'malleolable', which appears in all the witnesses, but has required a certain amount of explication, being a neolo-
gism of Browning's from *malleolus*, Latin for 'a little hammer', apparently
implying fine workmanship. On the evidence of *Yale 2* Browning would
seem to have repented of the egregious reading, and reverted to the more
usual word.

1. 885 is an example of a passage where different revisions were made in
Yale 2 and in *1889*, the latter being on the whole preferable. In l. 895, on
the other hand, the revision in *Yale 2* from 'and' to 'till' clarifies both the
sense and the chronology, while the changes in punctuation at the end of
ll. 949 and 953 strikingly increase the dramatic impact of Guido's plight.
Indeed, it is noticeable that many lines have been improved by Browning's tightening up the punctuation.

In 1. 1087 the change from 'For friend and lover' to 'Nor friend nor
lover' is a marked improvement, changing the sense as it does from
'Instead of friend and lover, leech and man of law' to 'Neither friend
nor lover are present—merely leech and man of law'.

The change of punctuation at the end of 11, ll. 505 and 506, gives more prominence to l. 506, and introduces humour and more life to the whole passage. By the same token, the comma added at the end of l. 575, by introducing a slight pause, gives more weight to the phrase that follows. On the other hand, Browning's substitution of 'foot.' for 'foot,—' at the end of l. 881 cuts a logical and syntactical sentence into two parts, and destroys the sense.

In iii. 337 the change from 'dread' to 'lack' destroys the alliteration between 'dread' and 'daughters', and overloads the alliteration with 'lured', 'larks', and 'looking-glass', while substituting a banal for an unusual noun. In both ll. 504 and 923, however, the addition of a comma at the end of the line improves the rhythm and clarifies the sense.

iii. 1339 is rendered much more dramatic by the substitution of 'what comes, crowns, closes all' for 'what comes, crown, close of all', and this heightening of effect is even more marked in ll. 1589 and 1592, where the substitution of 'One—' for 'One,' and 'two—' for 'two,' introduces a longer pause after each stroke of the bell.

APPENDIX F

COMPOSITORS

I.

1–106	Broadhead
107–217	Ker
218–342	Grace
343–452	Jarvis
453–561	Plumb
562–670	Malcolm
671–779	B. Suth[erland]
780–886	Grace
887–993	Aylward
994–1100	Ker
1101–1217	Broadhead
1218–1325	Jarvis
1326–1378	Grace
1379–end	Ker

II.

1–107	Plumb
108–214	Ker
215–321	Broadhead
322–428	Malcolm
429–536	Grace
537–645	Jarvis
646–756	Aylward
757–63	B. Sutherland
764–866	Ker
867–974	Grace
975–1082	Aylward
1083–1191	Ker
1192–1300	Plumb
1301–54	Grace
1355–1407	Aylward
1408–62	B. Suth[erland]
1463–1515	Broadhead

1516–III. 18	Malcolm

III.

19–163	Chace
164–325	Robinson
326–487	Jenkins
488–594	Barsham
595–706	Parsons
707–812	Chace
813–925	Jenkins
926–1035	Robinson
1036–1143	Chace
1144–1253	Jenkins
1254–1307	Barsham
1308–1415	Robinson
1416–42	Parsons
1443–68	Barsham
1469–1551	Chace
1552–end	Jenkins

IV.

1–226	Parsons[1]
227–339	Chace
340–449	Jenkins
450–504	Robinson
505–62	Jenkins
563–641	Yelf
642–70	Robinson
671–729	<Robinson> Chace
730–83	Robinson
784–836	Jenkins
837–95	Yelf
896–954	Chace
955–1008	Jenkins

1009–1118	Parsons	1290–1349	Jenkins
1119–74	Robinson	1350–1467	Barsham
1175–1206	Parsons	1468–1532	Robinson
1207–32	Barsham	1533–99	Jenkins
1233–89	Chace	1600–end	Chace

[1] At 108 there is a pencil mark such as usually indicates the beginning of a compositor's stint, but no name.